CONRAD GREBEL, c. 1498-1526

THE FOUNDER OF THE SWISS BRETHREN

CONRAD GREBEL

c. 1498--1526

THE FOUNDER OF THE SWISS BRETHREN
SOMETIMES CALLED ANABAPTISTS

By

Harold S. Bender

Wipf and Stock Publishers
EUGENE, OREGON

To

John Horsch
1867-1941

In Grateful Memory

Ich glaub dem Wort Gottes einfaltiklich uss Gnad, nit uss kunst.

Züch mit dem Wort und mach ein Christenliche Gemein mit hilf Christi und siner Regel

—Conrad Grebel in 1524

Wipf and Stock Publishers
199 West 8th Avenue, Suite 3
Eugene, Oregon 97401

Conrad Grebel
By Bender, Harold S.

ISBN: 1-57910-157-7
Publication date 9/22/1998
Previously published by Herald Press, 1998

TABLE OF CONTENTS

LIST OF ILLUSTRATIONS

Plates I to VIII come between pages 128 and 129.

PREFACE

The origin of this book lies in my later student days when I met the late John Horsch (1867-1941), for nearly half a century a leading American Mennonite historian and writer. From that first contact until his recent lamented death, the privilege of fellowship with this able and devout scholar was a source of constant stimulus and inspiration. John Horsch knew the early history of the Swiss Brethren, commonly called the Swiss Anabaptists, more thoroughly, perhaps, than any other modern historian. But he was still more a devoted exponent of the heritage in faith which they have left to their modern descendants. From him I learned something of the meaning of this faith and the life which it requires. Through him I was drawn into historical studies, and to him I owe a deep debt of inspiration and guidance, both in the study of Mennonite history and in the service of the Mennonite brotherhood, some of which I have tried to repay in this book.

I owe a debt to others in connection with the writing of this biography of Conrad Grebel which I here gratefully acknowledge, particularly to two good friends and co-workers through the years, Ernst Correll and Edward Yoder. It was through John Horsch in 1923 that I first met Ernst Correll, at that time a Fellow of the Bavarian Academy of Sciences (Samson Stiftung) at the University of Munich, where he was working on an authoritative sociological study and economic history of Swiss Anabaptism *(Das schweizerische Täufermennonitentum,* Tübingen, 1925), subsequent to his extended survey on *Die Ehe im Täufertum des europäischen Kontinents.* From this contact has come a long, happy, and fruitful collaboration in the field of Anabaptist-Mennonite history. Even before Dr. Correll came to the United States in September, 1924, when both of us joined the faculty of Goshen College, we had discussed the founding of a journal of Mennonite history, the preparation of a biography of Conrad Grebel as the founder of Anabaptism, and the inauguration of a series of *Studies in Anabaptist and*

Mennonite History. Our intention was to encourage much-needed inquiries into significant source material, and deeper-reaching interpretative work. The journal was established in 1927 as *The Mennonite Quarterly Review.* The biography, originally planned as the first monograph in the series of *Studies* now appears in 1950 as Number 6.

Preparatory work and preliminary publications relating to the life and letters of Conrad Grebel (see bibliography) were first undertaken by Ernst Correll and myself as a commission from the newly organized Mennonite Historical Society of Goshen College, given at its first regular meeting on November 7, 1924. The announcement of that action stated that Dr. Correll was to carry the major burden of non-theological research; and added that Edward Yoder, a young Mennonite Latin scholar and student of humanism, then a graduate student at the University of Iowa, and later a Ph.D. at the University of Pennsylvania in classical philology, was to translate Grebel's Latin letters. The book itself was planned to be modest in size and popular in character.

The first intent of the Society was that the book should be published as a quadricentennial volume in June, 1925. Work was accordingly pushed energetically during the academic year 1924-25, and Edward Yoder carried out his part of the assignment by presenting a complete translation of Grebel's Latin letters as published in the *Vadianische Briefsammlung* (*St. Galler Mitteilungen* . . . 1888-1913) and *Zwinglis Werke* VII. However, discovery of new sources, and greater intimacy with the material, led the authors to decide to concentrate on a critically annotated edition of all of Grebel's writings and to plan a more thorough biography. Since this was a task which could not conceivably be completed in the short time originally allotted, the publication date was postponed. Dr. Correll made a vital contribution by his research in Zurich, St. Gall, and Munich during the summer of 1926 and the first semester of the academic year 1926-27 while on leave of absence from Goshen College. His transfer from Goshen in 1928 made his withdrawal from participation in the actual preparation of the biography inevitable. The plan was then changed to provide that I should prepare the biography as a separate task. Dr. Yoder's untimely death in March, 1945 terminated his active participation in the editing of the letters of Grebel, but Dr. Correll, now Professor of Economic History in The American University, Washington, D.C., continues to look with me toward the completion of our original program of collaboration: a full presentation of all *Grebeliana* extant, with critical commentary and English translations of essential sections.

The manuscript of the biography was completed in the summer of 1935 when it was submitted as a doctoral dissertation in German at the University of Heidelberg, Germany. During 1936 the first third of the manuscript was printed in English translation in a series of articles in the *Mennonite Quarterly Review* (January, April and July, 1936, Vol. X) and privately reprinted in the same year under the title *Conrad Grebel: Humanist Years*. Three further chapters appeared in the *Mennonite Quarterly Review* in 1938 and 1941. However, the difficulty of financing the publication, and other factors, compelled the postponement of full publication, and also led to the decision to publish in two volumes what was originally intended as one. The first volume, the biography, is now appearing. It is essentially a translation of the German original though with substantial revisions. An attempt was made to take account of all the pertinent literature which has appeared since the date of the original composition in 1935. The publication date of the second volume, the writings, is still uncertain.

In preparation of this first volume, I am much indebted to Ernst Correll and Edward Yoder for their assistance. Dr. Yoder's thorough English translation of Grebel's Latin letters, with his valuable philological notes, have been an indispensable aid which I have constantly used. Dr. Correll's research notes have been of great value, and the stimulus and concrete suggestions which both friends have brought to me in conference and correspondence throughout the years have been most helpful.

At the University of Heidelberg in the years 1930 and 1935 I had the privilege of studying under the late Walther Koehler, Professor of Church History, who was deeply interested and thoroughly versed in Anabaptist history. I am grateful for his generous and gracious assistance in the planning and the execution of the Grebel biography. Professor Fritz Blanke, Professor Koehler's successor in the chair of church history at the University of Zurich, kindly assisted at various times. Dr. Robert Friedmann of Vienna, Austria, now of Kalamazoo, Michigan, gave generously of his time, both in Vienna and in Goshen, and has kindly read the entire manuscript. I must also express my gratitude to other scholars who were of assistance in securing source material. Among them are the late Dr. Hans Nabholz, *Staatsarchivar* at Zurich; the late Dr. Theodor Schiess, Librarian of the *Stadtbibliothek Vadiana* at St. Gall; Dr. Huber, *Staatsarchivar* at Basel; Dr. Largiader, *Staatsarchivar* at Zurich; Professor Leonhard von Muralt of the University of Zurich, and Dr. A. Corrodi-Sulzer, Zurich. Dr. Hans von Grebel of Zurich, *Staatsgerichtspräsident,* the only living descendant of Conrad Grebel who heads a family bearing the Grebel name, has also kindly assisted. One of the happy phases of the preparation of the biography was the collaboration of my wife, Elizabeth Horsch Bender, in the first composition of the German original of the biography, and also in the English translation, the form in which it is now published. She and Dr. Correll as well as Mrs. Edward Yoder have kindly read the proof sheets of the entire volume. Beulah Loucks prepared the index.

A word should perhaps be said about the choice of the term "Swiss Brethren" to name the group of which Conrad Grebel was the founder. Two other names might have been chosen, "Anabaptist," and "Mennonite." "Mennonite" would have been an anachronism and historically inexact, since Menno Simons did not become an Anabaptist until 1536. The term

"Menist," meaning follower of Menno Simons, was first used at Emden in 1544, and did not come into general use until much later. It was at first applied exclusively to the Dutch-North German group of evangelical Anabaptists, and was never officially accepted by the Swiss group. Furthermore, the group of which Conrad Grebel was the leader was in no sense connected with Menno Simons. Menno never traveled farther south than Cologne, and none of his writings were available in German until 1575. In 1555 and 1557 conferences of South German and Swiss elders at Strasburg formally disagreed with Menno's teachings in two points, the doctrine of the incarnation and the practice of the ban. It is only because the 100,000 baptized descendants of the Swiss Brethren in North America, and the 5,000 in South Germany and France, today call themselves "Mennonites," that this name might be at all considered. The name "Anabaptist" was rejected because it is commonly used in English today to describe the entire left wing of the Reformation and thus to cover a motley collection of groups of no common faith. In German the term "Täufer" is gradually coming into use to describe the peaceful, evangelical Anabaptists, but no comparable English term is available; and Ludwig Keller's proposal, "Altevangelische Taufgesinnte" (*Die Reformation und die älteren Reformparteien,* 1885) has not found acceptance, even though it has become the official name of the Swiss Mennonite Conference.

The name "Swiss Brethren" is justifiable because of the geographical connotation of "Swiss," and the use by the group itself of the name "Brethren." The Hutterian Brethren very early referred to the non-communal Anabaptists of Switzerland, South Germany, and the Rhineland, who were all of Swiss origin, as "Swiss Brethren," and may have been the originators of the designation.

The earliest discoverable use of the name "Swiss Brethren" by the group itself is that found in the *Ausbund,* the hymnbook of the Swiss and South German Mennonites. The first edition of 1564 bears the following title: *Etliche schöne Christliche*

Geseng wie sie in der Gefengkniss zu Passaw im Schloss von den Schweitzer Brüdern durch Gottes gnad geticht und gesungen worden. However, outside the group, the *Geschichtbuch der Hutterischen Brüder* uses the name "Schweizer Brüder" much earlier and uses it consistently. In this chronicle it appears first in connection with events dated in 1543, and since the chronicler wrote contemporaneously with the events described, this use would antedate that in the *Ausbund* of 1564. The 1543 *Geschichtbuch* passage states with reference to a certain Hans Klöpffer, "Er ist vorhin bei den Schweizer Brüdern ein Diener gewesen." The noted Thomas von Imbroich, martyred in 1558 at Cologne, is consistently referred to in the *Geschichtbuch* as a "Schweitzer Bruder." The first known use of the name in a public document is in a decree of the government of Württemberg, issued at Stuttgart in 1559. It is found in *Quellen zur Geschichte der Wiedertäufer, I. Band, Herzogtum Württemberg* (Edited by Gustav Bossert), Leipzig, 1930, page 194, and reads as follows: "1559. Herzogliche Verordnung Schwenckfelden und Widertaufer, auch anderer Secten halben. Item was fur ein sect und bruderschaft die Schweizer brueder genannt." The published record of the important *Franckenthal Gespräch* (Heidelberg, 1571) speaks of three major groups among the Anabaptists, "die Hutterischen," "die Mennoniter" and "Ihr." The "Ihr" are clearly "die Schweitzer Brüder," who are however not actually referred to by this name.

If I then use the name "Swiss Brethren" in this volume to refer to the original Anabaptists who arose in Zurich under Conrad Grebel's leadership in 1525, and who in 1559 were recognized by the authorities of Württemberg as a South German-Swiss group quite distinct from the other two major groups, the "Mennonites" and the "Hutterites," I am employing a name which is both historically justified and linguistically precise.

It may be thought strange that the memory of the career and significance of Conrad Grebel, indeed his very name, should have faded so completely from the pages of history as well as from the consciousness of the modern groups who owe their very existence to his early leadership. But the fact that Grebel died young, less than a year and a half after the founding of the movement, that he left no published writings, and that the severely repressive measures of the authorities in Zurich and surrounding cantons prevented the development of an effective organization of his followers, readily accounts for this. It is a simple duty for modern historians, who have recovered the original sources, to give Conrad Grebel his rightful place in the history of Anabaptism and of the Christian church.

I accordingly put this volume into the hands of those who may read it, in the hope that the revival of the memory of Grebel may not merely recover for historical scholarship some slight relics from the dead embers of the past, but that it may also stir a deeper commitment to the truest Christian living among those who live today from the heritage of faith and life which the Swiss Brethren purchased by their blood. Perhaps through this book also the message of the ancient Swiss Brethren may again be able to speak some words of healing to a Christendom and to a world which so sorely needs it.

Goshen College, December, 1949. Harold S. Bender

FOREWORD

CONRAD GREBEL, THE ACKNOWLEDGED LEADER OF THE FIRST SWISS BRETHREN

The Swiss Brethren movement, commonly called Anabaptism and later known as Mennonitism, was formally initiated on January 21, 1525, in the city of Zurich, Switzerland, or the nearby village of Zollikon. In a prayer service on that night a company of about fifteen earnest Christians, formerly devoted supporters of Ulrich Zwingli's evangelical reformation, were led by what they were convinced was a divine call to establish a brotherhood of believers under the outward sign of adult baptism as a confession of faith and a pledge to live a true Christian life.

The unique contemporary account of this historic event in the chronicles of the Hutterian Brethren[1] names Conrad Grebel with Felix Manz as the originators of the new brotherhood. In the vividly pictured story of the baptismal scene the chronicler relates that after prayer George Blaurock[2] entreated Conrad Grebel for God's sake to baptize him with the right Christian baptism, whereupon as he kneeled down, Grebel baptized him. The story further proceeds with the baptism of the remainder of the company by Blaurock and concludes with the ringing words: "And so they together dedicated themselves in the high fear of God to the name of the Lord, confirmed one another in the service of the Gospel, and began to teach and to hold the faith. Therewith was the separation from the world and its evil works begun."[3]

It is clear from this ancient eyewitness account, which goes back at least to 1534 in its present form, that the Brotherhood viewed that night in Zurich as the birthday of the movement and Conrad Grebel as its founder.

A further confirmation of this important ancient tradition of the Brethren is found in the unpublished report of the important discussion held in 1538 at Berne, Switzerland, between certain leaders of the Brethren and representative preachers of the Reformed Church. At this meeting thirty-five Brethren from the canton of Berne, together with five Brethren from other cantons, were thoroughly examined by three Reformed preachers of Berne in the presence of many other clergymen. In the course of the discussion, one of the Brethren related how he had come to join the group. He testified that he had come to a knowledge of the truth by the preaching of Conrad Grebel. One of the preachers asked the brother the question: "What church commissioned the first Anabaptist or Grebel to preach?" Thereupon the brother answered: "Grebel was the first one to teach me, and I perceived that he himself believed what he taught, and that he lived accordingly. . . Therefore I accepted him as one commissioned by God."[4] This brother, it is clear, counted Grebel as the first leader of the Brethren, "the first Anabaptist," a witness to the truth by word and by life, whose powerful testimony still stood out brightly in memory although he had been dead for twelve years.

The fact that Grebel's name soon disappeared out of the tradition of the Brethren does not speak against the validity of the earliest tradition, for this happened to all the early leaders of the Swiss Brethren, to Manz, Blaurock, Marpeck, and the others. Only Michael Sattler remained in part a living figure in the tradition, due to the fact that the account of his martyrdom was printed almost immediately after his death and was later reprinted several times.[5] The Swiss Brethren kept no chronicles as did the Hutterites,[6] hence the memory of their early leaders was not kept alive in succeeding generations.

That Conrad Grebel was recognized as the leader of the Swiss Brethren by his immediate enemies as well as by his brethren is abundantly evident from the sources. In a letter to Vadian dated January 19, 1525, shortly after the great debate with the Brethren, Zwingli says, "Conrad Grebel and a few other less important persons are holding fast to their standpoint."[7] Again on March 31, 1525 he writes to Vadian, "Grebel is with us just now, and is drawing all whom he can to his party."[8] In a letter to Oecolampad and others dated November 29, 1526, he calls Grebel the ringleader *(coryphaeus)* of the Anabaptists.[9] Felix Manz, by contrast, is not once mentioned by name in Zwingli's letters, while Blaurock is mentioned only once, and then as having been imprisoned along with Grebel.[10]

The contemporary Swiss chroniclers also reflect the common impression that Conrad Grebel was the founder and leader of the Swiss Brethren. Fridolin Sicher refers to him as "Conrad Grebel, who accomplished much in the sect."[11] Johannes Kessler calls him "the arch-Anabaptist."[12] Johann Stumpf lists Grebel as the first in his catalog of the "chief of their teachers."[13] Bernhard Wyss, strange to say, mentions the Anabaptist movement only in connection with the drowning of Felix Manz, when he speaks of "this Manz, also Blaurock and Conrad Grebel, who had died earlier, and their adherents."[14] The other Swiss chroniclers do not mention the Anabaptist leaders by name at all.[15]

Thus in the thought of his Swiss contemporaries, whether in the circle of his co-laborers and brethren, or in the circle of the leaders of the Reformation who had come into personal contact with the Anabaptist movement, or among the chroniclers who were further removed from the immediate events, Conrad Grebel stands out as the founder and leader of the Swiss Brethren, "the first Anabaptist," the originator of a powerful movement which to some appeared as the glorious revival of the true apostolic church of Jesus Christ, but to others as only a religious party, a new and heretical sect, a revolutionary body, or perhaps even the devil's handiwork.

I

THE YOUNG PATRICIAN IN ZURICH 1498-1514

The Grebel Family

Conrad Grebel, who became the founder of the despised and "accursed sect" of the Anabaptists, was born into one of the very distinguished families of the lesser landed nobility of Switzerland, and his entire youth and early manhood reflect the social background of such a family. Wealth, prestige, culture, and political power were at his disposal. For one hundred years before his birth the family had played a major role among the small number of wealthy patrician families of Zurich who directed the political, military, and economic affairs of that most wealthy and powerful of all the cities and cantons of the Swiss Confederacy, and in the person of Conrad's father Jacob it reached the height of its influence and prestige.

The origin of the Zurich family[1] can be traced to Lütold Grebel (d. 1435), who left the ancestral home in Kaiserstuhl near Aargau and became a citizen of Zurich in 1386. As far back as the records go, the Grebels possessed land at Kloten near Zurich, which was the basis for their nobility and which gave them the right to the title of "Junker" for which the prefix "von" was later substituted in conformity with modern usage.

From the earliest times the Grebels were members of the patrician guild known by the name "zur Meise," and beginning with Johannes, the only son of Lütold, every generation had one or more members of the family as guildmaster. In every generation also one or more members of the family were members of the Zurich Council. The first Grebel, Lütold, was member of the council 1420-1430 (d. 1435), his son Johannes was a member 1428-1444 (d. 1445), and others followed in their steps. It seems also to have been a tradition of the family that there should be a representative in the nunnery at Oetenbach near Zurich, the first one having been Anna, daughter of Lütold. The one daughter of Johannes Grebel did not enter the convent, but a granddaughter, Agatha, was a member in the convent until the nuns began to renounce the order in June, 1523. A daughter of Jacob died as an Oetenbach nun in 1520.

In addition to the revenue from the family estate at Kloten, the Grebels early established a good income as merchants and manufacturers. Ulrich Grebel, the grandson of Lütold, is known to have been an iron merchant,[2] while his brother Hans Grebel became a papermaker. The descendants in each case carried on the business. The wealth of the family was quite large although it suffered during the Burgundian War 1474-1477.

Politically the Grebel family was outstanding. The first Lütold had been burgomaster at Kaiserstuhl, his son Johannes was an imperial bailiff, and other members of the family later were prominent members of the Zurich Council, delegates to meetings of the Swiss Confederacy, and magistrates. The family took an equally prominent part in the military affairs of Zurich, serving in all the important wars, and participating in the notable victories of Murten, Novarra and Marignano. At the turn of the sixteenth century, Felix Grebel, a son of Hans Grebel, made a pilgrimage to the Holy Land, for which he was knighted. As Caspar Keller-Escher, author of the Grebel family history, says, no important political event of the years 1470 to 1530 took place in which a Grebel did not take part. Ulrich Grebel, grandfather of Conrad, was a close friend of the noted burgomaster Hans Waldmann, and several Grebels were close friends and supporters of Ulrich Zwingli. In 1471 Ulrich and Hans Grebel were jointly granted a new coat of arms by the Emperor Frederick III.[3] Through marriage the Grebel family was associated with many of the leading families of Zurich such as Escher, Wirz, Murer, Schweizer, Stucki, Ammann, Holzach, Fries, Keller, and Engelhard.[4]

The most influential of all the Grebels was no doubt Junker Jacob Grebel (d. 1526), only son of Ulrich Grebel, born about 1460.[5] He inherited his father's wealth and his iron business after the latter's death in 1495. With a secure position in the guild "zur Meise," where his father was guildmaster, he was elected in 1494 to the Council, and in 1512 to the Inner Council.[6] In 1486 he had temporarily surrendered his citizenship, possibly for a few years of travel or soldiering away from home, but in 1490 he was again a citizen. On March 10, 1490, he purchased from Thomas Schoub the house at Neumarkt 15,[7] which he possessed until 1517 (1518?), when he sold it to his nephew Junker Hans Wernli Schweizer. On March 19, 1492, he bought a second house *An der nüwen Gasse* from Uly Buren.[8] In which of the two houses he made his residence is not known. The date of his marriage is unknown,[9] but it is possible that the purchase of one of the two houses took place in connection with his marriage. In the year 1508 he bought a third house from Junker Anton Schenk von Landegg. This house, called *Thurm auf dem Bach,* also *Bilgerithurm,* was his residence after 1512.[9]

The oldest documentary record of Jacob Grebel's family dates from 1504. It has been preserved in the list of the purchasers of shares in the great lottery held in connection with the extraordinary *Schützenfest* (Shooting Festival) of 1504, at Zurich. Here the entire family is listed under the date of September 3, 1504 in the following form:[10]

Dorothe, Jacob Grebels von Zurich Husfrow[11]
Barbeli Jacob Grebels töchterli
Barbeli Grebel von Grüningen
Effarsino Grebel von Grüningen
Cunrat Grebel von Grüningen
Andres Grebel von Grüningen
Martli Grebel von Grüningen
Jacob Grebel, Vogt zu Grüningen

According to this list, on September 3, 1504, Jacob Grebel and his wife, Dorothea Fries, then living in Grüningen, were the parents of 5 children, the oldest of whom must have been born not less than five years before (1499), possibly as much as ten years or more before. It is hardly probable that Barbara, who was married in 1512, was less than 15 when married. The date of the marriage of her parents must therefore be put between

1492 and 1497. A sixth child, Dorothea, was born in 1509. Unfortunately there seems to be no evidence concerning the ages of the children except Dorothea, who had the unhappy experience of having her marriage annulled on June 15, 1525, when she is listed as being 16 years old.[12]

Little is known of the six children except Conrad.[13]

In the absence of direct evidence, it is impossible to identify unequivocally the time and place of Conrad Grebel's birth. As the third child of parents who married about 1492, he was probably born after 1495, and since two younger Grebel children were living in September, 1504, he was probably born before 1500. His first matriculation as a university student in Basel in October, 1514, points to the year 1498 as his approximate birth year, since it was customary for students to enter the university at about sixteen years of age. No other evidence of age has been found.

The house in which Conrad was born in Zurich must have been either the house at Neumarkt 15, which had been purchased in the year 1490 by his father, or the house *An der Nüwen Gasse,* which had been purchased in 1492.

Conrad Grebel's Family

On February 6, 1522, Conrad Grebel was married to a girl who bore the name of Barbara. Conrad himself reported the marriage to Vadian on the same day that it occurred. "I have just married Barbara, mine as I hope. I confessed it first to our friend Hans Wirz and then to Doctor Engelhard and a few others who promised to intervene with father when he returns. Mother weeps unceasingly."[14] About the first name of Grebel's wife there can be no doubt, even though the family name appears nowhere in the records and must remain unknown. In a letter of November 2, 1521, shortly before the marriage, he calls her jokingly his "Barbarity."[15] About a year and a half after Grebel's death in 1526 his widow was married to Jacob Ziegler, the exact date of the marriage being December 5, 1527. In Dürsteler's *Ehebuch* her name is entered as *Barbel Ziegler.*[16, 17]

The social status of Conrad's wife must have been somewhat below his own, for otherwise it is difficult to explain the serious opposition of his parents to the marriage, an opposition which was so stubborn that Grebel felt himself compelled to postpone the marriage for an entire year at the cost of a very serious inner conflict, and finally to enter upon it very hastily during the absence of his father. When the marriage had actually occurred, he found it necessary to secure a mediator to overcome the conflict between the father and son and to arrange a contract which would provide for the financial aspects of their relationship.[18] The mediator who was chosen was Heinrich Utinger, a prominent citizen of Zurich.

Conrad Grebel announces the birth of two of his three children in letters which have been preserved. A Joshua was born about August 11, 1523,[19] and a Rachel on January 6, 1525.[20] The third and oldest child, a son Theophil, is not named in Grebel's extant letters, but appears along with the other two in the records of the Orphans' Court in Zurich.[21] The daughter Rachel must have died in infancy, for the first court record which mentions the children in 1527 speaks of "the two children of Conrad Grebel." In 1530 the two children are mentioned by name for the first time as *Theophil* and *Josua.* In the record of the Orphans' Court for 1539 Theophil is expressedly named "the elder." In 1541 the financial accounts of the two children are combined into one and after this the name of Joshua appears alone with an account which is as large as the total of the previous two accounts. In 1547 also Joshua is listed as the possessor of the silver dish which his brother Theophil had originally inherited from the great-aunt Agathe Grebel. In 1547 also Joshua appears in the records in possession of a fourth of the income of the estate of Kloten. This means that he was the sole heir of his father Conrad's share in the estate, his father having been one of four heirs of Jacob Grebel, namely Barbara, Martha, Conrad and Dorothea.[22]

The date of the birth of Theophil is nowhere reported, neither in the letters of Conrad Grebel nor in the records of the Orphans' Court. The last will and testament of Dame Agathe

Grebel, which is dated in 1533, contains a bequest for "Theophil Grebel, Conrad Grebel her nephew's legitimate [*eelicher*] son."[23] Theophil therefore was not an illegitimate child as Dürsteler[24] and others following him have asserted. Nor was he born in 1520 as Dürsteler claims, for Grebel was in Paris until the middle of June, 1520. Since the second child Joshua was born in August, 1523, the *terminus ad quem* for the date of the birth of Theophil must be November, 1522. In a letter to Vadian dated November 21, 1522, Grebel mentions the necessity which faces him of supporting his "family."[25] He would scarcely have spoken of his "family" if he had not had any children at that time. So Theophil must have been born between February 6, and November 21, 1522, a period in which no letters of Grebel have been preserved. He must have died in 1541.

From Joshua, the only son of Conrad who survived to marry, all of the posterity of Conrad Grebel derive their descent, and through him the family has continued to exist to the present day in Zurich. Joshua was married on June 21, 1549, to Catherina Steiner.[26] They had three sons and four daughters. Of the three sons, only the one named Conrad survived to marry, but he became an important personality in Zurich and occupied the office of treasurer of the city in 1624. A grandson of this Conrad, who also bore the name of Conrad Grebel, became burgomaster of Zurich in 1669.[27] The sole head of a family who today bears the name of Grebel is Dr. Hans von Grebel, for many years President of the Supreme Court of Zurich.

Conrad's Early Education in Zurich

In the year 1499 Junker Jacob Grebel was appointed by the Zurich Council to serve for a term of six years as magistrate (*Vogt*) of the township of Grüningen, just east of the city, one of the largest territories in the canton. His appointment was renewed in 1506 for another six years, hence he served until 1512.[28] The magistrate was required to live in the territory, and the above-mentioned lottery list of 1504 proves that this was actually the case with Jacob Grebel. The official residence of the magistrate was the castle of Grüningen,[29] and in this castle the young Conrad probably spent his boyhood years up to seven or eight, after which he attended the Latin school in Zurich. Of this period in his life we know nothing, except that he must have lived the life of the patrician lad of that time, including such adventures as the visit to the *Schützenfest* of 1504.

Little more is known of Conrad's Latin school years in Zurich (probably 1506-1514) than of his boyhood in Grüningen castle. The Latin school is not mentioned in the extant sources, but attendance at it can be inferred from the fact that his matriculation at the University of Basel in October, 1514, must have required the customary minimum of six years of Latin schooling. Conrad found a good Latin school at his command in Zurich, the so-called *Carolina*[30] of the *Grossmünster* church, supposed to have been founded by Charlemagne. It was under the supervision of the canons of the *Grossmünster* and was conducted in the canon house on the northeast side of the *Chorherrnplatz*.[31] With the typical pre-university student he would have entered the school at the age of seven or eight and continued until the entrance to the university at fifteen or sixteen years.[32]

Like the other schools of its kind the *Carolina* was actually a *Latin* school.[33] Not only was Latin taught as a language, but the entire instruction was in Latin and an attempt was made to latinize the pupils completely. The three chief subjects of the curriculum were Latin grammar and literature, dialectic, and music. In dialectic the art of disputation, chiefly with theological themes, was taught. The disputation was often unedifying, but it had its value as an exercise in public speaking. In Zurich disputation was particularly popular and the papal legates often attended the sessions. "Music" was not what is understood as music today but was training in Latin liturgical forms.

The general atmosphere in the *Carolina* was not conducive to good teaching and learning. Crudeness and rudeness, fist-fights and altercations of various kinds were a regular part of the day's procedure. The pupils carried daggers, knives, and short swords, and frequently used them. Card playing was a very common custom.[34] Most of the pupils in the Latin school were in need of support and were given the opportunity to earn part of their expenses by singing in the streets and begging, although it is unlikely that the young Grebel was compelled to follow this practice.

The *Schola Carolina* was conducted quite in the old medieval, scholastic spirit. Nothing of the new humanistic spirit was to be felt in it at the time that Grebel studied there. It was only with Myconius, a humanistic school teacher and good friend of Zwingli, who came to Zurich in the year 1516, that a more progressive spirit came into the school. Unfortunately no records at all have been preserved for the period of Grebel's attendance, and it is therefore impossible to report names of either teachers or scholars of that time. From Conrad's student life later on we may imagine him to have been a typical scholar in his Latin school days, a good learner, but a lively and unrestrained *scholarius*.

II

AMONG THE SCHOLARS OF BASEL AND VIENNA 1514-1518

Study in Basel, October, 1514, *to May,* 1515

In the autumn of 1514 young Conrad Grebel came to the University of Basel for a semester of study, the winter semester 1514-1515. His name appears in the matriculation record in October, 1514, as *Conradus Grebel de thurego constan-dioc.*[1]

The University of Basel was at that time in a low estate.[2] It had lost its earlier brilliance, and only a few outstanding professors remained after Sebastian Brant and Ulrich Krafft had left in the year 1501. The enrollment had dropped so greatly that on the average not more than fifty new students were matriculated each year. In 1514, the year that Conrad Grebel came to Basel, the number of matriculants had risen to eighty-one, the highest number between 1510 and 1520.

"The most of what we read of the University in these years is strife, quarreling among the professors, and lawsuits," says Wackernagel.[3] Although the older humanism had celebrated its victory in Basel fifty years before, it had now virtually disappeared. The newer humanism was already manifesting itself in Basel but was as yet to be found chiefly outside the University. It was beginning to make its way inside in 1514 and the following years. A forerunner was Thomas Wyttenbach, who had been in Basel since 1505 and who had had among his pupils Ulrich Zwingli and Leo Jud.[4] In the year 1513 Ludwig Baer, who had just become a Doctor of Theology in Paris, joined the faculty in Basel as a teacher in theology. He was a man of good humanistic training and a friend and supporter of Erasmus, through whom he had been won for a thorough study of the Holy Scriptures.[5] But without doubt the most important of the young humanists of the University was Heinrich Loriti (1488-1563), usually called Glarean because of his home in

Glarus,[6] who had come to Basel in May, 1514, not as a professor in the University but as a private scholar. The only humanistic members of the University faculty proper were Wyttenbach and Baer, and they were not outstanding personalities.

The students of the philosophical faculty to which Grebel belonged were required to live in houses or dormitories called *bursae.*[7] Fifteen or more men lived in a *bursa* under the supervision of a proctor who was required to have a master's degree and to be approved by the University. The *bursa* was usually directly under university control, but there were a few exceptions, the most prominent of which was the *bursa* conducted by Glarean. For the young "freshmen" this arrangement had a double advantage. On the one hand it reduced expenses, and on the other it gave them the benefit of direct personal supervision, discipline, and instruction by a capable young teacher at the time when they most needed it. The young teacher also profited by being able to earn his living while continuing his "graduate" study at the university.

Conrad Grebel was a member of Glarean's *bursa,* as may be seen in a letter to Ulrich Zwingli from Vienna dated September 8, 1517, in which he praises Glarean in contrast to Vadian, calling Glarean his friend and teacher, *preceptor meus.*[8] Other members of the *bursa* were Johannes Hinwiler,[9] Valentin[10] and Peter Tschudi of Glarus, and in all probability also Johann Leopold Grebel and Conrad Moser, both of Zurich. Rudolph Collin, who came to Basel in 1516, and Melchior Macrinus, were later members of Glarean's *bursa,* but it is doubtful that they were in Basel in 1514. Johann Jakob Zurgilgen of Lucerne, who had been in Vienna in 1511-1515, came to Basel in 1515, as did also Wolfgang Capito and Johannes Oecolampad. Oswald Myconius, who had been in Basel since 1510 and who was later a close friend of Grebel, had already won his *Baccalaureus* in 1514, and had been appointed to a position as a school teacher in Basel. Possibly Grebel became acquainted with him during his study in Basel.

The subjects which Glarean taught in his *bursa* are mentioned in several interesting extant letters which his scholars wrote during this time. Tschudi mentions "perfection in Latin speaking, the Decades of Titus Livius, Aulus Gellius, introduction to Greek grammar, and Greek literature." Hinwiler mentions further "Lucanus in Pharsalis, Virgil, Ovid, and Geography (Ptolemy)." Collin says in his autobiography that his studies in Basel with Glarean included "Principles of Mathematics."[11] Wackernagel reports that Hebrew was studied in Glarean's *bursa,*[12] although this seems doubtful for it is not mentioned in the sources.

Glarean was an excellent teacher, and his pupils were enthusiastic about him. Tschudi says, "I doubt whether there are ten like him in all Switzerland." Conrad Grebel says, "He is a faithful instructor." And Collin calls him "the most faithful instructor of all." Wackernagel has painted a vivid picture of Glarean, which fully justifies his pupils' enthusiasm for him. It reads as follows: "Erasmus was delighted with the scholarship of Glarean, with his zeal, his strict morals, his vigor. He seemed to him to be the leader and standard-bearer of the Swiss humanists. Even we today must marvel at the talent of the man. Developed without a favorable background or environment, supported only by a native soundness of mind and body, Glarean proceeds in a fresh and naive way without much hesitation. The extent of his talent and strength manifests itself in an amazing richness of interests and attainments. . . . His little quarrels with the University show with what difficulty he tries to fit into the academic forms of the day. In a similar fashion Glarean stands isolated in the circle of his humanistic comrades, Glarean the impetuous, the irascible, the man of rapidly changing moods, appreciated by all, but congenial to none. Full of life, it is the vehemence and occasional rudeness of his nature with its exuberant speech full of wit and mockery but also with its egoism, which makes him an unassimilable and disquieting element in the sodality. The secondhand life of the printer and editor does not satisfy him, he must engage in personal productivity; an insatiable urge for work drives him on; an inner compulsion urges him into contact with men and life; he must have fellowship with youth. He is the born teacher and as such he fills a place for Switzerland."[13]

Under the formative influence of such a teacher Conrad Grebel began his educational career. It is to be regretted that he could enjoy the thorough instruction of this great instructor but one semester; he himself later regretted it in Vienna where he says that he found no such thorough teacher as Glarean.[14] And Rudolph Collin, who also came to Vienna after a semester in Glarean's *bursa,* was likewise bitterly disappointed. He found the instruction in poetry for instance quite childish in comparison with the instruction he had received in Switzerland.[15]

The letters of Glarean's students indicate that the house which he provided for his scholars was large and well-furnished.[16] Glarean says in a letter to Erasmus, dated September 5, 1516, that the inclusive charge for board, room, and tuition was one hundred and twenty guilders a year, and adds that at the time thirty excellent young men lived together under his roof.[17] The students were organized into a civil senate after the model of ancient Rome. Discipline in the *bursa* was very strict, for the students had to swear obedience to the master and were required to be in their rooms at eight o'clock under complete prohibition of all frivolous conduct and noise.[18]

As a pupil of Glarean and a member of his *bursa* young Grebel was reared in the spirit of humanism in Basel, for it was in Glarean's *bursa* that humanism reigned in the fullest sense in contrast to the other University *bursae.* In the University proper he received little if any humanistic stimulus, for as a beginning student he would not have been permitted to attend the lectures in theology of Professor Baer, who was the only active humanistic professor in the University; and in the philosophical lectures the superficial sophistry of the late scholastic period was still in full sway. In comparison with the sterility and pedantry of the university professors and the typical university *bursa,* the spirit of the new humanism of a Glarean, with its new subject matter and its new methods as well as its new ideals, must have stood out in sharp contrast. Here not only was subject matter taught, but emotion, taste, and judgment were also developed. How different conditions were here from those in the Latin school in Zurich where the attempt was made to latinize the young boys in the spirit of the old scholasticism and to lead them to unconditional acceptance of the traditions of the old church.

Although there are no direct sources from which to draw a picture of Grebel's development in Basel, it is possible through Wackernagel's excellent and exhaustive description of the humanist world of Basel at that time[19] to learn something of the environment in which Grebel moved during the five months of his stay there, and thus to secure an insight into the influences bearing upon him.

The Basel of 1514-1515 was not yet the great humanist center whose fame was soon to be known far and wide. The older humanists were gone. Leontorius and Petri had died in 1511, Kuno and Johannes Amerbach passed on in 1513, and Conrad Pellican had left Basel in 1508 not to return until 1516. The younger group of humanists were just beginning to come into prominence. Among these were Beatus Rhenanus, proofreader in the Froben printing house, Ludwig Baer, professor of theology at the University, Erasmus and Capito as private scholars, and Glarean as a teacher and private scholar. Rhenanus had come to Basel in 1511 as a young scholar of twenty-five with a splendid humanistic training secured at the University of Paris. Baer had come in March, 1513, with his Paris theological training. Capito had appeared in the spring of 1513 although no traces of his activity are noticeable until 1515. Erasmus himself appeared in Basel for the first time at the end of August, 1514, and remained until the middle of March, 1515, returning in July, 1515, after a brief absence, to remain till May, 1516.[20] Glarean was in Basel from May, 1514, to May, 1517.[21] Oecolampad came in 1515, Cantiuncula in 1517. Of the lesser humanists at that time in Basel the following might be mentioned: Oswald Myconius and Hieronymus Artolf, two school teachers; three proofreaders in Froben's printing house, Wilhelm Nesen, Conrad Brunner (Fonteius) and Bruno Amerbach; also Ludwig Kiel (Carinus) and several others. The great Froben had begun his activity as an independent printer in 1513; in that year also he began to print for Erasmus with his edition of the *Adagia*. Cratander was away from Basel 1513 to 1515, and did not begin his own printing establishment until 1518. Hans Holbein, then a young and inexperienced artist, may have come as early as 1514, or as late as the spring of 1515.

But it was only after Erasmus made his influence felt in Basel that the humanists there became a definite and permanent group. The *Sodalitas Basiliensis* or *Sodalitium Literarium,* that free society of humanists in which the humanist life at Basel was concentrated and stimulated, was not established until he came to be the guest of Froben in the summer of 1514. Next to Erasmus the young Rhenanus was the outstanding personality in this group. Glarean, still only twenty-six years old, was apparently somewhat independent of the *Sodalitas*[22] and hence it is quite likely that the humanist life at Basel was centered around two groups, the group of Erasmus-Rhenanus-Froben, and the group around Glarean. With Glarean were associated the young Swiss humanists like Myconius, Brunner, Carinus, Nesen, and Artolf, while the Alsatians and other foreign humanists in Basel were attracted more to Erasmus and Rhenanus. Nevertheless, there was close contact between these two groups, particularly between Glarean and Erasmus, for the two men developed a genuine friendship,[23] and the students in Glarean's *bursa* must have had the privilege of some contact with the great scholar himself.

The friendship with the great Erasmus was a decisive influence on Glarean's life. Glarean himself testifies of Erasmus' significance for him in a letter to the latter dated at Basel, September 5, 1516. "You taught me to know Christ," he says, "and not only to know him, but to imitate him, to honor him, and to love him."[24] The Christian ideals that Glarean acquired and which he attributes to the influence of Erasmus, found expression in a book of elegies which he published in December, 1516, with the express purpose of encouraging the young men of Switzerland to higher Christian virtues, especially in sex morals. He did not wish to compete with contemporary writers in indecency, but preferred to write as a follower of Paul and of Christ rather than of Catullus or Properz.[25]

Even though Erasmus was not a cordial admirer of Glarean, he was impressed by his character and abilities, and praised his qualities as a scholar and a Christian in a letter of recommendation to Bishop Poncher of Paris, dated February 14, 1517, in the following words: "With scholasticism he is familiar, but now rejects it. He once pursued the study of theology at length but was driven from it by the fruitlessness of the instruction and the incredible strife among the theologians, and began to study Christ from the sources. In addition he began to study Greek literature and is not without merit as a poet, having won the laureate's wreath from the Emperor Maximilian. He has great knowledge of history, and is remarkably able in music, cosmography, and mathematics, deserving to be called master in these fields. In respect to morals he has a good and clean character, and is devoted to piety. He is, it is true, very free to attack the sophists, and by his bellicosity has often gotten into trouble with the theologians. Nevertheless he is free from conceit and haughtiness. He likes to sing and has congenial manners."[26]

From the above witnesses to Glarean's character and Christian attitudes it is evident that he must be reckoned with the group of Christian humanists who were inspired by Erasmus and in general followed his leadership. By Glarean's own testimony he was a convinced Erasmian as early as 1516, and no doubt he was constantly growing into this spirit from the beginning of his contact with him in August, 1514. How much of this new Christian spirit of his was transmitted to the young students in his *bursa* during the winter semester of October, 1514 to March, 1515, must remain uncertain. Nevertheless even beginning students like Conrad Grebel probably heard and felt at least something of the new life and new ideas that were stirring the minds and spirits of their teachers and their humanist friends and forming a new type of Christian character and piety as a preliminary stage of the rebirth of Christianity that was soon to come upon Europe in the great Reformation of 1517 and after.

These Basel humanists of 1514-1516, as Wackernagel characterizes them, were men of strict morals and high religious concerns, vastly different from the humanists of the type of the Italians or a Mutian. They wanted to be disciples of the sciences and of Christ at the same time (*literarum Christique cultores*), in whom was to be united *eruditio* and *doctrina, recta studia* and *vera pietas,* and whose culture was above all intended to serve true religion. The desire for a religious revival was powerful among them and for this reason they strove to attain the purity of the early New Testament beginnings. The church was to drink at the Gospel sources instead of the stagnant pools from which it had dipped for centuries. Since without a knowledge of the biblical languages an original knowledge of the true Christ was not possible, they studied Greek and Hebrew; and since the early church fathers were nearer to the truth than later theologians, a printer like Bruno Amerbach gave his best energy to the publication of an edition of Jerome in order that the genuine ancient theology might revive again. And above all Erasmus found his life work in this field, for the great challenge of the time to him was the moral reform of Christendom. He took up the fight against the vices and temptations of the world and the flesh as a true "soldier of Christ." All these men felt themselves engaged in a labor that was to mean a renaissance in Christianity.[27]

How Grebel would have developed if he had remained in this more earnest and serious Christian humanistic circle of Basel can only be surmised. But he did not remain in this circle, and when he left Basel in the spring of 1515 he broke the connection with it and its influence forever, except insofar as the contact with Glarean in Paris for a short time (1518-20) represents this influence.[28] (The few months which he spent in the autumn of 1521 in Basel as a proofreader in Cratander's printing house were too brief to have any significance.[29]) He can scarcely have become an Erasmian humanist in these early months of his development at the age of sixteen even though he may have had a touch of this spirit, and it was only after five years had passed, years spent among the very different humanists of Vienna and Paris, that he once more found himself in a group where the spirit of Erasmian humanism was dominant, namely the group around Zwingli in Zurich, in 1520-22. But by that time it was Zwingli himself who was fast moving on beyond the mere humanism of a moralistic Erasmus[30] to become the reformer of German Switzerland.

Study in Vienna, September, 1515 *to June,* 1518

In the summer of 1515 Conrad Grebel left Basel to study in Vienna. A number of causes may have led to this decision. In the first place his teacher Glarean had closed his *bursa* at the end of the winter semester 1515, and had gone to Italy in the fore part of April to study at the University of Pavia on the basis of a stipend which Duke Maximilian Sforza had offered to him and other Swiss students.[31] Although, because of the Duke's failure to keep his promise, Glarean soon returned to Basel, sadly disappointed, to reopen his *bursa* and continue it for another two years, it was too late for at least four of his former pupils who had meanwhile made other plans. The students were four young men from Zurich, Conrad Grebel, his cousin Johann Leopold Grebel, Conrad Moser, and Johannes Hinwiler. Hinwiler had been in Vienna earlier for a year as a student under the patronage of Vadian,[32] and it is possible that he promoted the move. But there were also other students from Zurich in Vienna at this time, such as George Binder,[33] who had been there since 1513. Valentin Tschudi, a fellow scholar in Glarean's *bursa,* had also been in Vienna as early as 1512. Another important factor which no doubt influenced Conrad Grebel's decision to go to Vienna was the four year stipend which his father, the distinguished councillor of Zurich, had secured for him from Emperor Maximilian.[34] In addition, the reputation of the great Swiss humanist, Joachim von Watt of St. Gall (1484-1551), called Vadian, who had been a professor for several years in Vienna, must have attracted the young Swiss students. And finally Zwingli himself, at that time still a parish priest in Glarus, was encouraging as many as possible of the promising young Swiss students of that day to go to Vienna. He had, for example, sent his own brother Jacob Zwingli with Valentin Tschudi as early as 1512.[35] Huldreich Kramer went at his advice in 1517.

Whatever the cause may have been, the four young Zurichers mentioned above, all pupils of Glarean, set out in the summer of 1515 on the journey to Vienna. On July 4, 1515, three of them surrendered their citizenship in Zurich.[36] In the matriculation record at Vienna Conrad and Johannes Leopold Grebel are enrolled side by side in the "Rhine Nation" for the summer semester of 1515 and the winter semester 1516/17.[37] Both times Conrad Moser's name is also enrolled. In Vienna the young students from Zurich were taken under the wing of their compatriot, Vadian. Very likely they lived with other students in the *Brücken Bursa* which was located just across the street from the main building of the University.[38] The procurator of this *bursa* receipted Vadian on August 31, 1516, for payment in full of the accounts of all of Vadian's *discipulos* whom he had guaranteed.[39] When Collin came to Vienna in the summer of 1517 he was received in the house where the Swiss students lived and where Conrad Grebel gave him a special welcome.[40]

The group of Swiss students in Vienna under Vadian's patronage, among whom in the judgment of Vadian himself Grebel was the most outstanding, consisted primarily of young men from Zurich and eastern Switzerland. In the dedication to Conrad Grebel of his 1518 edition of the *Commentary on Pomponius Mela,* Vadian mentions "Rudolph Clivanus, George Binder of Zurich and the other youths from Switzerland who have come to Vienna to study the noble arts," and "my other pupils among whom is Andreas Eggius my faithful helper." A total of at least twenty young Swiss were in this group, of whom an inner circle of eight or nine were on most intimate terms with the master and each other. This circle with Grebel at its center included Johannes Hinwiler, George Binder, Rudolph Collin, Christoph Dick, Conrad Moser, Andreas Eck, Johannes Leopold Grebel, and Melchior von Watt.[41] In a letter dated January 29, 1519, in Paris, Grebel greets the following students in Vienna : Melchior von Watt, "my close friend"; Johannes Hinwiler, "my old friend"; Collin, "a close friend"; Binder, "dearer to me, although he did not exactly desire it"; Andreas Eck, "bound to me by love and mutual service."[42] Ulrich Lener writes to Vadian from Appenzell, February 14, 1516, mentioning a visit to the parents of Conrad Grebel, George Binder and Johannes Hinwiler.[43] On February 27, 1517, Lener writes again to Vadian and greets *"omnes discipulos tuos,* especially your brother, Johannes Hinwiler, George [Binder], and Conrad [Grebel]."[44] It is interesting to note that when Rudolph Collin wrote his autobiography in 1576, fifty years after coming to Vienna, the friendly reception which Conrad Grebel gave him upon his arrival in the summer of 1517 still stood out in his memory, for Grebel is the only one of the Vienna group whom he mentions by name.[45]

But more important for the development of Grebel than his student comrades were his teachers. Here it is Vadian who stands out above all the others as his particularly beloved teacher and patron, and still more as an intimate friend. In a letter to Zwingli from Vienna dated September 8, 1517, Grebel speaks with great respect of Vadian. "You desire to hear, I presume, the trend of my fortune or some news. Vadian I have as a teacher, a man singularly deserving of all titles of honor; by him I am loved as a brother, while he is himself loved and cherished and respected by me as a most devoted father."[46]

The fifty-seven extant letters (from July, 1518 to May, 1525) which Grebel wrote to his honored teacher, who was also his brother-in-law after July, 1519, testify in a lively and interesting fashion to the warm and intimate relations between the two.[47] In the very first letter Grebel addresses Vadian as "dearest teacher" (*preceptor charissimus*).[48] His respect for Vadian at times becomes worship. In Paris January 29, 1519, he writes to Vadian that he and Leopold are ready to fight if any one should attempt to undertake anything against the honor of Vadian.[49] A beautiful tribute to Vadian from Grebel's pen also occurs in this letter, where Grebel expresses himself as follows: "You are the only one, the one who transcends all others in sincerity, in uprightness, in fineness, in refinement, and in erudition, easily the first among all the Swiss. . . . You are, if I may say it in a few words, the oracle of our entire fatherland." Almost every letter of Grebel's contains some tribute to Vadian. This may be in part explainable as a humanistic custom, but the tributes go far beyond the customary practice. Grebel also brings to Vadian his most intimate problems and concerns.[50] Vadian is his father confessor, his counselor, his dependable personal friend, and his physician. The regard was mutual, for again and again the letters which Grebel wrote and Vadian's own statements testify that Vadian held Grebel in very high esteem, higher than any other of his pupils.[51] Vadian dedicated the first edition of his *Commentary on Pomponius Mela* (1518) to Grebel and chose him to write the introduction for the second edition of 1522. As late as 1540, after Grebel had been dead for fourteen years, Vadian still referred to him as "my Conrad Grebel of Zurich endowed with great gifts."[52]

When Grebel came to Vienna in 1515, Vadian was at the height of his career.[53] He had come to Vienna in 1501 as a seventeen-year-old student and remained there, with the exception of three years, until 1518, a total of fourteen years. At first he was a student in the philosophical faculty where he heard Celtes, Camers, and Cuspinian, and where he studied the classical disciplines as well as natural science and astronomy. In 1508 he became a professor in the same faculty. Thanks to his rich endowment of natural gifts, Vadian enjoyed rapid progress in the academic world. Beginning in 1509 he published a long series of poems, addresses, monographs, and new editions of Latin authors, the latter often with his own commentary. In 1514 he was crowned poet laureate by the Emperor Maximilian, and in 1516 he was appointed professor of rhetoric as the successor to the great Angelus Cospus. In the same year he became rector of the University for the winter semester. About this time he spent some time in the study of medicine and in 1517 won the degree of doctor of medicine in addition to his earlier doctorate of philosophy.[54] He had a particular interest in geography and was one of the chief promoters of this new study at the University, a subject which had been altogether forgotten in the Middle Ages.[55] He was one of the first to undertake travels for the study of geography. His ascent of Mt. Pilatus near Lucerne in August, 1518, said to have been the first scientific mountain ascent (Conrad Grebel accompanied him), made him a forerunner of the alpinists of modern times.[56] In the opinion of Professor Aschbach, as expressed in his history of the University of Vienna, "Joachim Vadianus was one of the most versatile, most learned, and most important humanists of his time; he was also one of the most fruitful authors, who devoted himself in his writings not only to the humanistic disciplines but also to other fields of knowledge, so that he may rightfully be called a polyhistor. He distinguished himself not only by his exceptional erudition but also by his critical judgment and his fine taste. More than this he was a splendid man, who made friends everywhere in the learned world as well as in the common walks of life by his congeniality and his willingness to render service."[57] But the great Vadian did not feel altogether at home in Vienna. In June, 1518, he suddenly left the city and the university of his great achievements, and returned to his native town of St. Gall,[58] where he soon became a leading figure as a physician and statesman. In December, 1525, he was elected burgomaster of St. Gall and as such fought the battle of the Reformation as a true friend and loyal supporter of Zwingli.

Such was the man who for three years in the decisive period of Conrad Grebel's development was his teacher, friend, and guide. Small wonder that Grebel esteemed him so highly. It may well be that Vadian was not the pedagogue that Glarean was, as Grebel openly states in his letter to Zwingli,[59] but as a man and a personality, he towered far above that restless and confused figure whom Grebel had known for five months in Basel some years before.

It is not possible to determine exactly what Grebel studied in the three years of his university career in Vienna. He himself reports very little about his studies. The only extant letter written from Vienna, the one addressed to Zwingli on September 8, 1517, contains a brief statement in which he reports that he is devoting himself to the seven liberal arts but will probably not attain the baccalaureate degree.[60] The traditional "seven liberal arts," required for the baccalaureate degree at Vienna as at all medieval universities, were grammar, rhetoric, logic, arithmetic, geometry, music, and astronomy. To these seemingly Grebel felt little attraction. "If I am not at present quiescent as regards polite letters, I shall sometime be wholly quiescent," he reported in the letter to Zwingli. Johann Leopold, he says, will probably secure the degree, and is so busy with his study of logic that he must leave the letter writing to Conrad. Later, in letters from Paris and Zurich, Grebel refers twice to his study in Vienna under Vadian. In January 29, 1519, he mentions the fact that Budé in Paris interpreted a passage in Pliny somewhat differently than Vadian had interpreted it in Vienna.[61] And on July 15, 1520, he writes from Zurich and mentions "Solinus, whom I now remember that you taught to us an age ago."[62] Without doubt Grebel studied geography with Vadian, for otherwise his warm and active participation in the two editions of Mela in 1518 and 1522 would be impossible.[63] The fact that Grebel mentions many new editions of the classics in his letter to Zwingli from Vienna indicates also that he knew the Latin classic writers quite well.[64] Greek he probably learned first in Paris.

Of teachers in Vienna in addition to Vadian, Grebel mentions only Wolfgang Hailigmaier. Twice in letters to Vadian he calls him his patron, *patronum meum*.[65] In the letter of January 29, 1519, from Paris he expresses himself in a very warm manner regarding the love, friendship, and scholarship which he had experienced in his contact with Heiligmaier and acknowledges openly his debt to him. Other good friends of Vadian at the University[66] with whom Grebel no doubt became acquainted were Rudolph Agricola the younger, professor of rhetoric and poetics 1515 to 1518; George Tannstetter (Collimitius), professor of mathematics and astronomy 1503 to 1535; Angelus Cospus, professor of Greek 1505(?)-1516; and Johann Spiesshaimer (Cuspinian), professor of philosophy 1493-1529. The last was, with Conrad Celtes and Vadian, the most noted of the Vienna humanists, famed both as a statesman and historian. He was the particular friend and coworker of Vadian. Finally Johann Camers, 1498(?) to 1531 (?), should be mentioned, a scholar who published many new editions of the Latin classics. The great Celtes, who had been the founder of humanism in Vienna, died in 1508. After his death Vadian was the outstanding humanist at the University.[67]

The humanism of Vienna was far removed from the humanism which Grebel had briefly touched in its Erasmian form in Basel. In Basel the humanists constituted a group of men who in general stood on a high moral plane and who strove with conscientious religious zeal toward the goal of a renaissance of Christianity.[68] Glarean was probably the only one in Basel who devoted himself expressly to the natural sciences and geography, and concerned himself less with religious interests. Vienna was a different place.[69] There humanism had made its entry at the end of the fifteenth century under Conrad Celtes, who came to Vienna in 1497. Although Celtes himself was German, most of the early Vienna humanists were Italians. The latter were quite different in moral character from Erasmus and Rhenanus, and the later Vienna German humanists like Collimitius. Agricola and Vadian devoted themselves chiefly to geographic and historical studies or busied themselves editing the Latin classics. Both types in Vienna, Italian and German, concerned themselves little about a renaissance of Christianity. In the main they found their satisfaction in editing and commenting upon the old Greek and Latin writers, particularly in the period from 1510 to 1520. Vadian has the record of editing about twenty such classics in eight years from 1511 to 1518.[70] Celtes had founded a "Danubian Society," a sort of humanist "sodality," which however soon disintegrated. Certainly there was nothing of the close and intimate friendship of humanists in Vienna during Grebel's residence there (1515-1518) such as characterized the *Sodalitas Basiliensis,* and in view of the secular character of the Viennese humanism, it is safe to infer that the contribution which the Vienna period made to Grebel's ethical-religious development was quite small, even though intellectually it undoubtedly did much for him.

Just as important for the development of the personality of the young Grebel as his teachers were the conditions and mode of life of the students and professors, and the general character of life in the city of Vienna. The University at that time was enjoying a golden age, with an annual enrollment of approximately 5,000 students, of whom a full half were members of the so-called "Rhine Nation," coming chiefly from South and West Germany and Switzerland. The annual number of new matriculants was between six and eight hundred, with the largest enrollment in the years 1515, 1516, 1517. After 1520 the enrollment declined so rapidly that by 1530 only a few dozen students are reported to have listened to the lectures of the professors.[71]

The city of Vienna itself was also enjoying a golden age at this time. Under Emperor Maximilian (1490-1518) it had become a great, beautiful, wealthy, luxury-loving city, characterized by "tall houses, broad courts, resplendent churches, commerce on a grand scale with all corners of the world, together with a love for display, luxury, and sensual pleasures."[72] Such was the city in which Grebel spent three impressionable years. But this lavishness of life in the city on the Danube constituted a great hindrance for the students. Enea Silvio said with justification that Vienna had many obstacles to study,[73] for he was astonished at the combativeness of the Viennese and the drunkenness and prostitution which were common everywhere. Rudolph Collin was astonished at the great amount of drunkenness among the students and citizens when he arrived in Vienna in 1517, and shocked at the "barbaric" morals of the city.[74] Excess and licentiousness increased on every hand.[75] Student brawls were frequent, and the overseers were not able to maintain discipline. It is highly improbable that the young Swiss students were an exception to the rule, and Vadian himself, as an eighteen-year-old student, had manifested an unusual tendency to brawling.[76] A letter of Johannes Hinwiler has been preserved from the year 1518 in which he requests 130 guilders from his father as payment for damages for an arm which he had cut off in a brawl.[77] Grebel had also been wounded in a fight, as he reports in a letter of July 31, 1518, to Zwingli.[78] He refers to this same experience in a letter of January 14, 1520, to Vadian from Paris[79] in which he says that his father had ordered him to forsake the bad company which had twice already almost cost him not only his money but also his life. But, says Grebel, the companions who had dragged him down in Vienna were honorable young men, although he had been so badly hurt there that his hand was half cut off. His father, says Conrad, had heard things from Vienna which were colored much worse than they really were, and for this reason had requested the son to return home. There is no justification for thinking that Grebel's life was different from that of the average student of Vienna in these years. On the contrary it is evident that he suffered both morally and spiritually from the life that he lived, and it is altogether probable that the illness from which he suffered the rest of his life was acquired in Vienna.[80]

The three student years which Grebel spent in Vienna at the age of seventeen to twenty were not only among the happiest years of his life but the most important for his personal growth. A careful study of the letters which he wrote from 1517 to 1522 together with the scattered sources found elsewhere indicates that the characteristics of his personality were fixed in its essential points during this time. He left Vienna at the age of nineteen or twenty as a cultured, gifted, attractive and congenial but temperamental young humanist with significant attainments in the study of the ancient classics and geography, and with abundant promise of becoming a leader. He looked forward to a leading position among the humanistic scholars of his homeland, a land for which he already had a strong feeling.[81] Like his revered teacher, Vadian, whom the Viennese printer Lucas Alantsee so sharply rebuked because he had left beautiful, cultured Vienna to live among "the crude unlearned peasants and cow-herds of Switzerland,"[82] Grebel was a patriotic Swiss, eager to contribute effectively to raising the level of culture in the homeland, and ready to play his part in the Swiss

Renaissance. That little of ethical concern or religious depth is evident in him at this time cannot be made a charge against him for in this he merely reflects the spirit of his Viennese teachers and the typical humanist university life of the times. The religious awakening was to come later.

III

STRESS AND STRAIN IN PARIS[1]

October, 1518 to June, 1520

Interlude in Zurich, July to September, 1518

About the middle of June, 1518, Conrad Grebel, in company with his good friend and teacher Vadian, left Vienna to return to his home in Zurich where he arrived about the middle of July.[2] A number of things indicate that the departure was rather sudden. Both men left their books behind,[3] and Grebel failed to make arrangements for the further payment of his stipend which was valid for one more year.[4] Vadian found it necessary to return to Vienna in November, 1518, to make a final settlement of his affairs which had been left in a somewhat confused state by his sudden departure.[5] There is evidence, however, that Vadian had been considering for some time a permanent change in residence from Vienna to St. Gall. In February, 1518, Ursinus was already protesting against Vadian's plan to leave Vienna.[6] Perhaps the suddenness of the actual departure was due to the plague which had just begun to ravage the city.

Why Grebel was ready to return home with Vadian at this time is not quite clear. In his letter to Zwingli a year earlier he had expressed a desire to go to Paris in order to benefit by the instruction of Glarean,[7] and his cousin, Johann Leopold Grebel, with whom he had come to Vienna in 1515, had already gone to Paris in 1517, a year earlier.[8] Another bit of interesting evidence is found in the records of the trial of Jacob Grebel, Conrad's father, in October, 1526, where he was charged with having received an illegal French pension. Jacob Grebel admitted that French legates had offered him money for his sons in the year 1516.[9] Other witnesses asserted that the father had brought Conrad home from Vienna in order to secure the French pension which was greater than the imperial stipend which Conrad had in Vienna, and that Jacob had actually received French money in 1517 and 1518. One witness went so far as to say that Conrad had mentioned his father's plans to this effect when he was a student in Vienna. However, Jacob Grebel denied that he had called Conrad home from Vienna, or that Conrad had planned to go to Paris on a scholarship of 300 crowns annually. The records of the trial simply say "the son came home and took the larger pension." The evidence suggests strongly that Jacob Grebel had secured a three-year pension of 300 crowns a year for his son from the French king as early as the year 1516 and that he had reported this to the son. However, it is not clear that Conrad had accepted this pension while he was still in Vienna or that he had already decided to go to Paris at that time. In fact there is considerable evidence to the contrary. For instance Conrad Grebel was among the young men of Zurich who made application in the summer of 1518 for one of the four pensions for study in Pisa which the pope annually awarded to Zurich.[9] He was also one of five applicants for the two scholarships to Paris awarded annually by the King of France to Zurich.[10] Furthermore Jacob Grebel testified in his trial that he had endeavored to secure an appointment for his son from the papal legate Pucci, who was legate in Switzerland from August, 1517, to June, 1521, but that his application was too late, and that Pucci had therefore offered as a substitute to give the son 30 guilders and to take him with him to Italy and to see that he would be provided for at Bologna or elsewhere.[11] Grebel himself says that he returned home from Vienna because his father had requested it as a result of reports of serious brawls in which his son had been involved.[12]

One of Grebel's first concerns after his arrival in Zurich was to establish contact with the Swiss humanists in the city and vicinity. He hoped to have three of these great men as guests in his house at the same time, Myconius, Vadian, and Zwingli.[13] Myconius had come to the *Grossmünster* School in Zurich in 1516 as a teacher and had become a good friend of the Grebel family.[14] It is possible that Conrad had already learned to know him in Basel at the time of his study there since Myconius was a teacher in Basel 1514 to 1516. At any rate the acquaintance with Myconius now rapidly ripened into an intimate friendship, so that henceforth Myconius, next to Vadian, was Grebel's best friend. Vadian actually came to Zurich on August 4, 1518, for the promised visit.[15] Zwingli, who was at that time serving as pastor at Einsiedeln, could readily have come.

Shortly after Vadian's arrival in Zurich, the three friends, Vadian, Myconius, and Conrad Grebel, together undertook a very interesting expedition to Lucerne to make the ascent of Mt. Pilatus and to visit the lake which is located high up on the mountain, and concerning which many legends circulated among the people. In Lucerne the necessary special permission of the civil authorities for the ascent was secured, and under the leadership of Johannes Xylotectus (Zimmermann), a canon at Lucerne and an old friend of Vadian and Myconius, the expedition was successfully carried out. Vadian himself briefly reports the ascent in the second edition of his commentary on *Pomponius Mela* (1522). Strange to say there is no trace of this interesting trip in any of the extant letters of the four participants.[16]

After the return from Lucerne Grebel carried out his previously announced plan to take the cure at nearby Baden, where he visited his sister Barbara, wife of Leonhart Karli, who apparently lived in the vicinity.[17] About September 20, 1518, he returned to Zurich. In the meanwhile preparations for the journey to Paris had been made, and on September 30, 1518, he took his departure.

In Paris, October, 1518 *to June,* 1520

The little group which set out on September 30 from Zurich to Paris was composed of Conrad and two other students, escorted by George Hedinger, one of his father's servants.[19] The other two young men were going as appointees of the Zurich council, each having received the award of a royal stipend which had been placed at the disposal of the Zurich council by the King of France,[20] and for which Conrad had also been an applicant. The route of the journey to Paris is not known except that it passed through Freiburg (Switzerland). On October 20, 1518, they arrived in Paris. The letters of recommendation to Glarean and to the great humanist, Budé, which Conrad had brought with him from Vadian, were promptly delivered.[21]

Grebel went to Paris, as is evident from his correspondence, with the primary purpose of enjoying the excellent instruction of his former Basel teacher, Heinrich Glarean. It is probable that he was also planning to attend lectures at the University, but Glarean was the chief attraction. Already in Vienna in September, 1517, Grebel had spoken of his desire to go to Glarean again,[22] and shortly before his departure from Zurich he wrote to Vadian specifically that he was going to Paris for Glarean's sake.[23] Accordingly he at once enrolled in Glarean's pension and joined the group of students under the latter's care there in October, 1518.[24] "Fain would I," he writes to Vadian on his arrival, "with the friendly favor of the muses and of all the poetic deities and even of Almighty God, be advanced to that elevation of learning that I might be a fellow-philosopher with you, which you say you much desire. . . . It is your preference, O teacher most dear, that I shall some time be first in my homeland. . . . Accordingly I could wish that I too might some time be reckoned among famous men. . . . But what is this you say: that one must needs take account of the illustrious arts, upon the dignity of which all eloquence depends? What these illustrious arts may be . . . please expound fully once more in a lengthy Iliad. . . . Furthermore, sweetest teacher, did you not exhort me finely, do you not again teach me very faithfully, when you bid me so to apply myself to virtue and to the noble studies while I am absent from my homeland, so that whenever I visit again my fond parents I may by all means not be devoid of good character and letters (*bonis moribus et litteris*). . . . I shall comply . . . and carefulness will never be lacking on my part, if only my talent and the muses, whose doors they proverbially say stand open, will not be lacking. . . ."[25] A few months later in July, 1519, he describes his purpose to Myconius in the following terms: "I desire this one thing only, that it may be my lot to spend what time I have left to live, in acquiring a mastery of *belles lettres.*"

The goal which Grebel set for himself was clearly that of the typical humanist scholar. He desired to achieve a mastery of the classic Latin and Greek writers, be they poets, orators, philosophers, geographers, or naturalists, so that by knowing what they had written about man and the world, he too might become skilled in the understanding of human experience and be able to interpret life effectively in his own forms of expression. Repeatedly he uses the terms *doctrina* and *eloquentia* to refer to this understanding and expression. Ultimately Grebel wanted *eloquentia,* that is the capacity to see life clearly and wisely and to express this vision attractively and with power. One of the reasons, without doubt, for the extended and rather "literary" espistles which he wrote as a young student from Paris, was his deliberate purpose to practice his "eloquentia" in the epistolary style which was so much favored by the humanist masters of rhetoric.

But the high hopes with which Grebel came to Glarean in Paris were soon rudely shattered; he did not long remain in Glarean's house. Before three months had elapsed, on January 1, 1519, he left Glarean, not to return until January 1, 1520, after an entire year had passed.[26] In April, 1520, Glarean himself left Paris for Switzerland where he remained until June, not returning to Paris until June 20, 1520, which was after Grebel had left Paris permanently.[27] Thus of the twenty months which Grebel spent in France from October 20, 1518, to June, 1520, only five months were spent with Glarean, two months at the end of 1518 and three at the beginning of 1520. Nevertheless since the time spent in Glarean's pension and the events and influences connected with his stay there were of considerable importance it will be useful to describe the conditions there.[28]

After three years in Basel (1514-1517) Glarean had finally succeeded, with the help of Peter Falk of Freiburg, and the further aid of two letters of recommendation from the Swiss Confederate Assembly,[29] in securing a pension from the King of France with an annual grant of 150 francs.[30] He thereupon removed to Paris at the end of May, 1517, taking with him many of the pupils who had lived in his *bursa* in Basel,[31] and re-establishing his *bursa* there. At the same time he did his best to secure a teaching appointment at the University. When the professor of poetry at the University of Paris, Faustus Andrelinus, died on February 25, 1518, he worked hard to secure the appointment to this vacancy, but his efforts were fruitless, the chair remained vacant.[32] He did however receive the pension of 180 francs which Andrelinus had enjoyed, without being obligated in any way to lecture publicly at the University.[33] When he heard soon after of the plan promoted by King Francis I to establish a new humanistic college at the University, he sought the appointment as rector,[34] and to this end he secured a warm recommendation from Erasmus to the King and to the King's counsellor, Bishop Poncher of Paris,[35] but this likewise in vain. The new college, called the College of Paris, was not established until 1530 and then William Budé was appointed as the first professor. Glarean was thus compelled to remain in Paris as an independent scholar with his own private *bursa* and pupils, but without any direct connection with the University.[36]

The first location of Glarean's *bursa* in Paris was a house in the *Rue St. Jacques* in the section of the city where the scholars and printers lived, a beautiful and spacious villa with a court and a garden.[37] Here he conducted his private school from May, 1517, to the end of 1518, and here Conrad Grebel lived from October to December, 1518. At the end of that year Glarean was compelled to change the location of his school because several of his pupils had given grave offense to the landlord.[38] The new location of the school is not known.

The number of pupils who came to Glarean's school in Paris was not quite so large as it had been in Basel, since there were on the average fifteen to twenty in contrast to the former thirty. Altogether, in the course of the nearly five years from May, 1517 to February, 1522 which Glarean spent in Paris, at least forty different students are known to have lived in his *bursa*, most of them as holders of the royal scholarships which King

Francis I had promised in the year 1517 to each Swiss canton. The names of nearly all of these students are known.[39]

It is difficult to say which of these students became friends of Conrad Grebel since but few of them are mentioned in his letters. Johann Leopold Grebel is mentioned five times, but apparently only because he was a relative and an earlier fellow-student in Vienna and a fellow-citizen of Zurich, not because of any great friendship.[40] On the other hand another citizen of Zurich, Johann Jakob Ammann, whom Grebel mentions twice, became a close friend. Grebel planned at one time to go with him to Italy but the plan was never carried out.[41] Valentin and Peter Tschudi, whom Grebel had known in Basel, are mentioned three times together and several times separately in Grebel's letters.[42] When the plague broke out in Paris in the summer of 1519, they with Grebel and Peter Girod of Freiburg took up residence in Melun where they lived for six months.[43] When Grebel left Glarean's pension on January 1, 1519, he moved into a house with two other students of Glarean, Johann Heinrich Frei of Zurich and Heinrich Lingk of Schaffhausen.[44] Two further students are mentioned in Grebel's letters: Jodocus Schwarzmurer of Zug, who once sent a greeting to Myconius;[45] and Johann Jacob Zurgilgen of Lucerne, who is mentioned by Grebel in a letter written from Zurich very shortly after his return from Paris.[46] Zurgilgen, who had left Paris earlier, had been living for some time in Lucerne. Of all the students in Glarean's *bursa* it is quite probable that only Ammann, Zurgilgen and the two Tschudis became close friends of Grebel and none of these except Ammann had any further significance for his life or even any further contact with him.[47]

Since Grebel was introduced to the humanistic circles of Paris through Glarean, it is of importance to know who Glarean's acquaintances and friends in Paris were. The group was not large but it included the leading humanists of the time: William Budé, a famous writer and scholar; William Kop, a native of Basel who had lived in Paris for years as the royal physician of King Louis XII and King Francis I, and who was also an outstanding humanist scholar; John Lascaris, a native of Greece and professor of Greek at the University; Faustus Andrelinus and Nicholas Beraldus, both professors at the University; and finally Faber Stapulensis, the Christian humanist, professor at the College of Cardinal Lemoine, and forerunner of the Reformation in France. To this circle Glarean had been introduced by letters of recommendation from Erasmus to Budé and Bishop Poncher of Paris.[48]

Glarean was happy to be a friend of these great men. In a letter of August 5, 1517, he wrote to Erasmus about his friendly reception by Budé, Kop, and Faber, particularly by the last named with whom he was already intimate and whom he esteemed very highly.[49] A few days later, on August 29th, he wrote much the same to his friend Zwingli, mentioning, in addition to his first three friends, Faustus Andrelinus as well.[50] In two later letters to Zwingli he again mentioned his humanist friends by name. In a letter of January 13, 1519, he called Budé his intimate friend,[51] and on March 25, 1519, he reported that he often visited the Greek, John Lascaris, in the company of his pupil, J. J. Ammann.[52]

But it is only with Faber Stapulensis among all the humanists of Paris that Glarean achieved an intimate friendship. As indicated above, this fellowship began soon after his arrival in Paris in the summer of 1517, and apparently continued until Faber left Paris at the end of 1519,[53] a period of more than two years. In the letter of August 29, 1517, to Zwingli, Glarean relates that Faber often came to his house and that the two of them spent many happy hours in song and jest, debating together and making sport of the foolish world.[54] On January 13, 1519, he wrote to Zwingli telling him that he had written to the provost and canons of Zurich requesting material for a history of the Zurich martyrs which Faber desired to write; and on May 15, 1519, he reported to Zwingli that upon the advice of Faber he had written the history himself.[55]

The contact with Budé, however, seems not to have led to such a fruitful friendship. This greatest of the French humanists of the time received Glarean into the circle of his friends on the basis of the recommendation by Erasmus, but never manifested cordiality toward him, and in fact rarely saw him.[56]

Glarean's pension or *bursa* in Paris was a faithful continuation in spirit and form of the institution which he had earlier conducted for three years in Basel. It was a Latin institute in which the primary subject of instruction was Latin language and literature. Here again as in Basel the language of conversation was Latin and the life of the school was organized as a community on the pattern of the old Roman republic. Almost every letter which Glarean wrote to Zwingli was signed S.P.Q.R.", i. e. *Senatus Populusque Romanus,* followed by a list of the *Praetors, Censors, Quaestors,* and *Aediles.*[57] A very interesting letter of December 10, 1520, has been preserved, in which Glarean described in detail for his Swiss friend, Jörg uff der Flüe, his methods of instruction as well as the life in the pension.[58] He says, for instance, "I have only such students about me as wish to learn Latin . . . a goodly proportion are also learning Greek whom I aid as best I can. . . . For such I am reading at the present time Homer in Greek and Livy in Latin. I am planning also to read several commentaries on Cicero and Caesar, in connection with which I shall not fail to work through the fundamental principles of geography and mathematics." It is true, he says, that he was giving some instruction in Greek, although he was still studying Greek himself. It is probable that Glarean did not give much time to the formal instruction of his pupils, but rather confined his contribution to their studies to the general supervision of the life of the pension and the inculcation of conversational Latin, so that the young students of necessity had to attend lectures in the philosophical faculty of the University. Glarean himself took advantage of the opportunity to attend lectures at the University and to advance his own learning. He had hoped when he came to Paris to devote himself chiefly to the study of Greek literature, but was disappointed at first to find no one of the faculty lecturing in that field.[59] Before long, however, he found such a lecturer in the person of the noted Greek, John Lascaris, with whom he studied Homer's Odyssey and the orations of Demosthenes.[60]

No record of matriculation by Conrad Grebel in the University of Paris has been found,[61] but since he, together with other pupils of Glarean, attended lectures at the University, it is important to note carefully the atmosphere of the institution at that time. It is true that there were a few humanistic professors on the faculty during the period 1517 to 1522, such as Beraldus, Lascaris and others, but they had little influence on the spirit of the University, which was still dominated by late scholasticism in its worst form. Faber Stapulensis did not teach at the University but at the College of Cardinal Lemoine. Not the least fresh breeze of humanism had penetrated into the Sorbonne with its almost suffocating atmosphere of the old dialectics. There, says Glarean, one found only scholastic sophists, "gymnosophists," and "thousands of them."[62] Shortly after his arrival in Paris in the summer of 1517 Glarean had attended a public disputation at the Sorbonne and had written his impressions of it to Erasmus.[63] He says that what he saw and heard was so bad that he had not the least desire to enter the gates of the Sorbonne again or to take part in the life and activity of that institution, for he was sick and tired of farces. He preferred to spend his time at home, "singing and studying, diverting himself with his Horace and laughing with Democritus at the world."[64]

One of the best introductions to the actual conditions at the University is a very interesting and significant letter which one of Glarean's students, Valentin Tschudi, wrote to Zwingli on June 21, 1518.[65] Tschudi's judgment about the spirit of the University of Paris and its professors is devastating. The spiritual atmosphere, he says, is absolutely poisonous, and he who comes to Paris is in danger of being destroyed spiritually as though by a wild beast or by a plague. The professors are altogether childish in their attitudes and conduct, and are at the same time filled with a terrible barbarity; they are wild beasts who have become raving and have lost their human nature. Tschudi says that he has decided to accept Zwingli's counsel and to abandon any attempt to secure a master's degree. The professors in Paris are altogether different from the professors in

Basel and Vienna; he considers them the most stupid of all men. That Tschudi has not exaggerated the conditions is proved by the fact that modern scholars endorse his description, as for example, Abel Lefranc, one of the best authorities on French humanism, who reprinted in his *Histoire du College de France* in its entirety that portion of Tschudi's letter which concerns the University.[66]

In the light of these conditions it is not surprising that Grebel profited so little from his four semesters in Paris and that he apparently did not achieve more than private linguistic studies. To get the full force of the situation let us look back a moment to the Conrad Grebel who had made such splendid progress in Vienna. It was there that he had become an enthusiastic humanist, a devotee of the liberal arts, with a great ambition to fill a worthy place in the service of his native land and city; and it was in this spirit and with this ambition that he had come to Paris. Gifted as few young men of his time, full of enthusiasm and youthful energy, somewhat presumptuous but basically charitable and generous, equipped with exceptional training, a master of Latin, well acquainted with the ancient classics, and a good student of geography, he had come to Paris in 1518 for the climax of his student years. The leading humanists of Switzerland, men like Vadian, Myconius, and Zwingli, were watching his progress with interest, and, as his good friends, shared his hopes and ambitions, sending him to Paris with their best wishes and blessings. Nor did Conrad lack fatherly counsel and advice from these friends, especially from Vadian and Myconius. He promised them to devote himself zealously and conscientiously to his studies, and to report regularly and frequently concerning his life and progress in Paris.[67] Fortunately he did write at least twelve letters from Paris to these two good friends, six to each, in which his life in the French capital and university city is mirrored. Much of interest is omitted from these epistles, but they nevertheless constitute most significant documents and afford an otherwise unattainable insight into Grebel's inner life during these two years to 1520.

Grebel arrived in Paris October 20, 1518, with letters from Vadian to Glarean and Budé, and from Myconius to Glarean, and with copies of the new book by Vadian, the commentary on *Pomponius Mela* (published in Vienna, May, 1518), which he displayed with pride to such Paris friends as Johann Jakob Zurgilgen of Lucerne.[68] He was welcomed in a most friendly way by Glarean into the *bursa* and installed as *Scipio* in the Latin community which it constituted[69]—a signal honor, for *Scipio Africanus* was a great leader of Greco-Roman culture, the best that republican Rome had, and the appointment testifies to the high regard in which Grebel's fellows and Glarean held his personality and intellectual achievements. The long letter which he wrote to Vadian shortly after his arrival, as well as the reply letters by Budé, Glarean, and Zurgilgen, to Vadian and Myconius, all of which were taken back to Switzerland by the returning travelers who had accompanied Grebel to Paris,[70] tell us that Grebel had made a good impression in his new environment and that he felt quite at home among the many old friends and acquaintances whom he had earlier learned to know in Basel and Vienna.

But soon the friendly atmosphere and good feeling with which Grebel began his life in Paris were radically changed. Unfortunate events occurred, and a very unhappy situation developed which was to cast a shadow on Grebel's entire experience in Paris and to make him increasingly unhappy. The first of the many long, frequently doleful letters, some of them real confessions, which he wrote to Vadian and Myconius, is dated January 29, 1519.[71] Quarrels with Glarean over housing conditions built up to a climax in a drunken bout by Grebel which resulted in a complete break between them which never was healed, and in which Glarean's irascible and tactless spirit was also a factor. Valentin Tschudi testified to his unfortunate disposition in a letter to Zwingli in 1517 as follows: "You know that whom he loves he loves passionately and whom he hates he hates without bounds."[72] Vadian himself expresses his judgment of Glarean thus: "He was not an unlearned man, yet a man of wanton and malicious spirit."[73] And when

Vadian later tried to persuade Grebel to be reconciled with Glarean, Grebel flatly refused on the ground that Glarean never abandoned a quarrel as long as he lived.[74] So Grebel left the house and instruction of Glarean after less than three months, taking with him Heinrich Lingk of Schaffhausen and Johann Heinrich Frei of Zurich, the latter of whom had on an earlier occasion left Glarean's *bursa*. The three students, together with a servant, rented a very good apartment with steam heat from a highly respected citizen of Paris, one of the printers of the city,[75] possibly Badius. This outcome was very painful to Glarean. He later attempted to justify himself in a letter to Myconius, insisting that he had treated Grebel in a most friendly fashion, and claiming that Grebel was alone responsible for what happened.[76] But this supposed friendliness and conciliatory attitude was never in evidence, for Glarean had even excluded him completely from his instruction.[77] Grebel apparently was not so bitter about the affair as Glarean, for in a letter to Vadian in which he reported the whole affair he remarked that even though Glarean had excluded him from his instruction, yet he would not be able to exclude him from his public lectures at the University in case he should be appointed to the chair of poetry.[78] And after a year had passed, Grebel actually returned to Glarean's pension, apparently driven to it by lack of funds, although he merely took up living quarters in the house and did not become a regular member of the student group there.[79]

This experience with Glarean made Grebel very unhappy. The good hopes with which he had come to Paris to study with Glarean had been completely destroyed. He lost interest appreciably in his study and seriously considered transferring to one of the Italian universities, to Pisa, Milan, or Bologna. His friend Johann Jakob Ammann had already formulated definite plans for study in Italy, and actually left Paris in the summer of 1519 to spend a short time in Basel and then to proceed to Milan in the autumn to continue his studies,[80] but for some reason Grebel was unable to carry out his wish, probably for lack of finances.

In addition to his difficulties with Glarean, Grebel had other troubles. His health was very unsatisfactory, and for a time he was so ill that he doubted his recovery. Another difficulty was an empty pocketbook. The two hundred guilders with which he had come to Paris had all been consumed for books, clothing, and board by January, 1520.[81] Apparently this was the only money which he received from his father in payment of the royal pension, for he often complained in his letters about his lack of funds; and in Jacob Grebel's trial in October, 1526, testimony was offered to the effect that the father had retained 600 crowns out of the money which he had received for Conrad's pension.[82] He had the further misfortune to lose a considerable sum of money in the form of a loan to a friend who died without paying it back.[83] Conrad's father accused him of having squandered his money in gambling and extravagant living, but Grebel assured his friend, Myconius, that this was not the case.[84] On the contrary he insisted that the cost of living in Paris was enormous.[85]

But the most serious difficulty which Grebel met in Paris, and which brought him into very grave conflict with his father and almost cost him the friendship of Vadian, was his embroilment in a student brawl on May 1, 1519, in which two Frenchmen were killed. Glarean's students had been involved in several brawls before, but this was the most serious of all, so serious that although Glarean referred to the affair several times in letters to Myconius, Zwingli, and Peter Falk, he endeavored to keep the details as secret as possible.[86] Among the other students involved were apparently Peter Tschudi,[87] and a certain Zophius of Glarus who had participated in a similar serious brawl the year before.[88] Glarean's report to Zurich and St. Gall concerning Grebel was of such a nature that both the father and friend Vadian severely condemned him.[89]

Conrad Grebel himself does not mention the affair openly, but indirectly discusses it at some length twice in letters to Myconius on June 9 and July 18, 1519, and briefly mentions it in a letter to Vadian of October 6, 1519.[90] According to these letters, Grebel had fallen into a misfortune so serious as to make him quite uncertain about his future. For temporary safety he had left the city, but planned to go with several of his comrades to the royal court to secure the favor of the king. According to Grebel, Paris was a veritable sink-hole of bandits and crime, where common, decent citizens were attacked in their houses and the life of everyone was in danger. A plausible explanation of the affair is that a group of Glarean's students had been attacked by bandits and that in self-defense they killed two of the bandits in the battle. Grebel mentions the bandits twice later (October 6, 1519, and January 14, 1520), when he speaks expressly of "our war against the bandits."[91]

The affair was indeed serious enough to bring Grebel and his fellow students into danger of their lives, particularly since at that time the feeling in Paris between the Swiss and the French was bad. Nevertheless, the reports which reached Jacob Grebel and Vadian were probably exaggerated, and their judgment scarcely justified. The father wrote a sharp letter to the son on September 24, 1519 (which he did not receive until January, 1520), in which he complained bitterly of the difficulties into which his son had fallen. Twice, he says, Conrad had fallen into serious danger, once in Vienna where he almost lost his hand, and now again in Paris where he almost lost his life; he was fearful lest the son should be executed by the hangman. Five days after receiving this letter Conrad wrote to Myconius that his father's fears were wholly unjustified.[92]

All the available evidence indicates that Conrad Grebel and his fellow-students who were involved in the affair were not guilty of an intentional crime, although the incident placed the whole group of Swiss students, and even the pension of Glarean itself, in serious danger.[93] Grebel himself had a clear conscience in the whole matter[94] and we learn that none of the students involved was brought to trial or suffered any punishment, since personal intervention of the students themselves as well as Glarean apparently convinced the authorities that there was no premeditated criminal intent.[95] Feeling innocent in the matter as he did, Conrad could not believe that his father and Vadian would condemn him after they received his letters of explanation. He was therefore quite shocked upon his return home to discover that the attitude of the two men toward him was still harshly negative.[96] The only known letter Vadian wrote to his brother-in-law in Paris was one in which he severely condemned him for his manner of life, and it was not until personal contact was re-established in St. Gall in the summer of 1520 that his attitude was changed.[97]

Another factor which seriously interfered with Grebel's study in Paris was the plague which ravaged Paris in the summer of 1519. Valentin Tschudi reported in a letter of January 2, 1520, after the epidemic was fairly past, that over 30,000 Parisians had lost their lives in the great plague,[98] which was raging in Switzerland at the same time.[99] Vadian spent the first six months after his marriage August, 1519, to February, 1520, in a country village to escape the plague which was raging in St. Gall,[100] and Zwingli himself was seriously stricken in Zurich.[101] In order to escape the plague in Paris, Conrad Grebel and three student friends, Valentin and Peter Tschudi and Peter Girod, fled from the city in the latter part of July, 1519, to the city of Melun, about ten miles up the Seine from Paris, where they remained until January 1, 1520.[102] Glarean with his pupils went still farther from Paris to Marnay s. Seine, where he continued his instruction in Greek.[103]

Thus, his studies interrupted, his pocketbook empty, his health undermined, his existence in Paris made unhappy by the trouble with Glarean, and his future cast under a shadow because of the attitude of his father, the temperamental young Grebel was brought to the edge of despair.[104] He had barely returned to Paris from Melun when, on the 9th of January, 1520, he received three letters which added still further to his misery, one from his father, one from Vadian, and one from Myconius, all of which criticised him severely. He had apparently lost the confidence of his parents and of Vadian altogether, although Myconius remained his faithful friend. The latter informed Conrad of the serious state of affairs in the parental household; the father could not sleep at night and was so enraged that he threatened to forbid his son the house when he came home. The father in his letter demanded that Conrad return at once to Zurich; and with the messenger who bore the letter sent twenty scutati of money to pay the expenses of the return journey. The messenger delivered the letter, but forgot the money, so Conrad would have been unable to return even if he had desired to do so. Moreover Myconius transmitted a message from Conrad's mother which advised him not to return at once but rather to wait until the plague as well as the father's wrath had moderated.

Under these trying circumstances it would not be difficult to imagine the feelings of the young student; but Conrad has made this imagination unnecessary by revealing his inner self in two long letters written on the same day (January 14, 1520), one to Myconius and one to Vadian.[105] The letter to Myconius is a sincere confession which he himself called "a discovery of my innermost being to a physician." As he considered his situation and the condition in which he found himself, Conrad's eyes were gradually being opened to himself and his conduct. For the first time in his letters he complained about the French pension and the difficulties which it created for him. Apparently the students of Glarean's *bursa* frequently discussed foreign pensions in a very patriotic spirit and condemned vigorously as traitors to the fatherland all such Swiss who sold their native land for money. Conrad explained to Myconius that he did not believe that his father had accepted forbidden money and therefore was not to be reckoned among these traitors, but he made it clear that his comrades had grave suspicions of his father's virtue. To excuse his father Conrad emphasized the fact that when the French pension was received it was he, Conrad, at that time not a citizen of Zurich, who had accepted the money, and not his father. So far as he knew the father had not taken any pension money for himself. However, although Conrad believed that his position was legally correct, he felt the moral onus of the situation; he had sold his freedom and his good name for money. Nevertheless he still hoped that this fact would not interfere with an honorable career in the service of his fatherland, and trusted that when he finally came to office he would not be handicapped by having received foreign subsidies. He insisted that he himself would much rather not have accepted the king's money the last time, and that it was really his father who had led him to do so against his preference. From Conrad's discussion it is clear that his conscience was deeply moved. He even went so far as to question seriously whether it was right for him to live in luxury with money which the King had secured from the poor French people by oppressive taxes.

The entire letter to Vadian from which the above summary has been taken bears evidence of an ethical awakening and witnesses to a certain nobility of sentiment which here appears for the first time in Grebel's extant correspondence. He begins to think seriously about death in view of the state of his health and the plague, and suddenly a remarkable sentence appears in his letter to Vadian: "I do not ask for death, but I would not fear death if it comes to me, for I am prepared to meet Christ." What did Grebel mean by this strange sentence? Had he learned something of the new Gospel of faith in Christ? Hardly. Had he suddenly adopted a certain religious mysticism? Possibly. However, the sentence is merely an isolated expression and it is impossible to derive from it alone any valid judgment about Grebel's inner development, particularly since in the very same breath Grebel said that in no case could he request the gods to lengthen his life. Only a humanist could make such an expression. Nevertheless, it is clear that through the experience of suffering in these months, Conrad Grebel had begun to feel the seriousness of life and its issues. He was learning that there was something more important in life than money, humanistic study, or pleasures, than a frivolous living without cares and without restraint; and this he was learning not from the humanists of Paris nor from books.

In this serious and somewhat melancholy frame of mind Grebel continued for the remaining few months of his stay in Paris until his return to Zurich in June, 1520. Altogether without funds and almost without friends he was compelled to go back to Glarean's *bursa* for a place to live, but he did not actively participate in the life of the place and had no obligation to Glarean.[106] Myconius was the only friend who remained faithful to him in this time of need, and two letters which Grebel addressed to him on March 7 and April 13, 1520, witness eloquently to the strength of the friendship as well as to the depth of appreciation with which Grebel cherished the friendship.[107]

As the weeks slipped by, the clouds became darker, and Grebel's melancholy was intensified. By the middle of April he felt himself nearer to shipwreck than to the harbor, a sick and weary young man who knew not what the morrow might bring. As a last desperate expedient he sent a letter to his father with Glarean, who was just then undertaking a journey to Switzerland.[108]

About this time Grebel wrote to Vadian in a tone somewhat different from that used toward Myconius, giving expression to his bitter disappointment at Vadian's treatment of him. In view of all that had happened it is not surprising to find Grebel accusing Vadian of having failed to help him. One cannot but sympathize with Grebel when he says, "you should have known me and should have recognized my need instead of condemning me."[109] The attitude of Vadian is indeed somewhat difficult to understand. To be sure he was away from home six months after his marriage in August, 1519, and again from December, 1518, to May, 1519, on a long journey through eastern Germany and in Vienna. But could he not have written more than one letter to his intimate friend during the two years that he was in Paris?[110]

The same criticism can justly be made against Conrad's father, for it is clear that he failed dismally in his parental obligations. Conrad felt this keenly. A bitter tone rings through his letter to Vadian of January 14, 1520, when he learned his father's attitude. "He does not know what I have to suffer on account of him, he who made me dependent for my support first upon the emperor and then upon the French king. If he had taught me to live within my means, to live on the basis of what one earns for himself no matter how small it is, I mean, to live after the custom of our fathers, and if he had not taught me as a young bird to spread my wings too far (as he is still doing with his second son so that my brother in the nest at home is spreading his wings only to fall a prey to the vultures), then I would not be in the place I am today. I would not have the bad reputation which I am compelled to bear publicly and privately."[111]

This expression from Conrad is no light-hearted alibi in which a son might take refuge from his own shortcomings, for one must admit in the light of all that is known about Jacob Grebel that Conrad's bitter accusation was justified. The father lived in a world in which money was too important, and he never treated his son justly in money matters. The French pension which was due to his son he took to himself, paying the son only a third, and keeping two-thirds to use in his business. When Conrad was married in 1522 Jacob, out of passion, refused to pay the usual dowry, and, although compelled by the intervention of mediators to arrange his financial obligations to Conrad through a contract, he failed to observe it.[112] Repeatedly Conrad attempted in vain to induce his father to pay the contract sums which he owed him. Ultimately the amount reached the total of approximately 1,000 guilders, and after the death of Conrad, Jacob Grebel was forced to admit before the court that he still owed a large sum to the orphaned children of his son.[113] During the years when Jacob Grebel owed his son these large amounts of money which he refused to pay, Conrad was compelled to live in constant need. Often in the years 1520 to 1525 he complained in letters to his brother-in-law[114] Vadian about his poverty.

The last letter which Grebel wrote to his father from Paris (April, 1520) apparently brought the necessary funds for the journey home, for at the beginning of July Conrad was back in Zurich, from where he wrote a letter to Myconius on July 6.[115] Since the journey from Paris to Zurich usually required about two weeks at that time, Grebel probably left Paris about the middle of June.[116]

The reunion with the parents was not so painful as Conrad had feared; the father smiled, the mother wept. Letters written to Myconius shortly after the return testify to a genuine love for his parents.[117] The reconciliation which had been prepared by Myconius stirred Grebel's gratitude, and the touching poem praising the friendship of Myconius which Grebel included in the first letter written after his return furnishes vivid evidence of the depth of feeling which infused the relationship between the two men.[118]

Grebel's student years were now ended,[119] though he still hoped for a period of study in Italy, as will be seen later. It is therefore fitting to pause to inquire at this point what the years in Paris meant for him.

Unfortunately Grebel reports very little about the nature of his studies in Paris. He says nothing at all about the instruction which he received from Glarean, and the only clear information which can be found in his letters about other lectures which he heard at the University is contained in a letter of January 29, 1519, written to Vadian shortly after his departure from Glarean's *bursa*.[120] In this letter he remarked incidentally that he was hearing the lectures of Nicholas Beraldus on Quintilian's *Institutiones Oratoriae* in which the lecturer used Valla's commentary on Quintilian. This book was the standard humanist textbook in rhetoric and indicates that Grebel was following the typical humanist major interest, that of "eloquence" in the best sense, as suggested earlier. Grebel could not have heard the lectures long, for as early as March, 1519, Beraldus left Paris to engage for some time in the service of the King of France.[121] Nevertheless he would have found with Beraldus instruction and spirit quite similar to what he had with Glarean. Beraldus was no outstanding leader, but an average humanist scholar in the middle of the stream of intellectual life of the time. Like Glarean he was a friend, at least by correspondence, of Erasmus, interested in the better things, doing his part by teaching the youth of his time the humanist heritage.

Beraldus was apparently the only regular teacher Grebel had in Paris outside of Glarean. Grebel had some direct contact with Budé for he mentions an interpretation by Budé of a passage in Pliny which was different from Vadian's interpretation in Vienna. Since Budé was not a professor at the University, this cannot refer to regular lectures by Budé but probably to some group discussion by humanist scholars in which Grebel was present. Vadian had recommended him to Budé when he first came to Paris, it will be remembered. Except for these two humanists, Beraldus and Budé, none other of the scholars of Paris are mentioned in Grebel's letters. It is possible that Grebel heard lectures by John Lascaris, the professor of Greek, for we know that Glarean and his young friend Ammann, also a close friend of Grebel, attended his lectures.[122] Valentin Tschudi, one of Grebel's close friends, was studying Latin, Greek, and Hebrew in 1517, and on January 16, 1519, he wrote to Zwingli that he was enjoying the Hebrew instruction of the famous new professor of Hebrew, Bishop Augustinus Guistiniani of Nebbio.[123] It is quite possible that Grebel also studied Hebrew with Guistiniani but there is no direct evidence to this effect. In 1523 he knew enough Hebrew to write the name of his second son, Josua, in Hebrew letters in a letter to Vadian, but so much Hebrew he could have learned from Ceporin under whom he probably received Hebrew instruction in company with Zwingli and others in 1522.[124] One might speculate whether Grebel heard Faber Stapulensis, but this is scarcely possible since Faber was not a professor at the University. Faustus Andrelinus, the professor of poetry, had died as early as February 23, 1518, nine months before Grebel arrived in Paris.

Grebel's intellectual activities are further indicated by his interest in the newest publications of the humanist press, evidenced by the purchase of new books for his friends Myconius and Vadian. In January, 1519, he sent both men a copy of the book by Petrus Pontanus, *De Helvetiorum Fuga*.[125] In June of the same year he secured for Myconius copies of *Juvenal* and *Valerius,* and promised to secure for him a copy of the new edition of *Asconius Pedianus,* a Roman grammarian and historian, as soon as it should appear.[126] He remarked in a letter to Myconius of March 7, 1520, that there were many beautiful and cheap books of all types on the market in Paris in both languages, Latin and Greek, among them publications of the Aldine Press in Venice. A beautiful edition of *Homer* in Greek was to be had just at that time at a very low price, actually less than two scutati.[127] On his return to Switzerland Grebel took with him as a present for Vadian a copy of *Asconius Pedianus*.[128]

Before the effect of Grebel's Paris experience can be properly appraised it is necessary to know the character of French humanism at this time and whether Grebel was influenced by it. On this point it may be said at the outset that the Parisian humanism of 1520 was essentially of the Erasmian type and not of the Italian.[129] The leading humanists were friends of Erasmus and worked in his spirit for a reform of French life and culture in theological, religious, and moral aspects, and for an improvement in education. Such were men like Budé,[130] Faber Stapulensis,[131] and Badius,[132] all men of solid character and earnest and praiseworthy motives. Some of the typical Italian humanists were to be found in Paris with their scandalous manner of life, such as Balbi and Faustus Andrelinus, but they were few in number and were not influential. Faber Stapulensis was one of the finest and noblest spirits of this entire period of European culture. Not only he, but the others also, like Budé and Badius, cherished the dogmas of the Christian Church and endeavored to maintain a Christian ethic. Consequently humanism in Paris did not take on an anti-religious or anti-ecclesiastical form. On the contrary, a certain half-mystical, pre-Reformation piety manifested itself in these circles. Faber, for instance, although he was shy and cautious almost to the point of fearfulness, had already taken a position against justification by works and for justification by faith in his commentary on the epistles of the apostle Paul, which he published in 1512,[133] though to be sure he did not hold Luther's position in full. As late as 1519 he still held to a superstitious worship of images and saints.[134]

But before coming to a final conclusion as to the meaning of Paris for Grebel, the question must also be asked whether any influence from Luther could have reached Grebel in his student days in Paris. On this point, there is evidence that early Luther pamphlets were circulated in Paris soon after publication, and that they reached the circle in which Glarean moved. For instance, on May 17, 1519, Peter Tschudi, a close friend of Grebel, and student in Glarean's *bursa,* wrote a friend in Basel that the writings of Luther were much read by the scholars of Paris,[135] and Luther himself had heard much the same report as early as February 14, 1519.[136] However the first mention of Luther in Glarean's correspondence occurs in a letter to Myconius dated October 15, 1520, over four months after Grebel had left the city.[137] In view of this fact, and the fact that Grebel's own correspondence shows no trace of interest in Luther, or indeed in any serious religious question, it is scarcely possible that any influence from this quarter reached Grebel in Paris.

What then did Paris mean for Grebel? First of all, by no means as much as one would naturally expect of twenty months of residence and study in the great intellectual center of western Europe. True, he met here again the spirit of Erasmian humanism which he had already learned to know in a limited way in Basel, but this contact had little vitality for him. Occasional incidental touches with men like Faber and Budé, a slight acquaintance with a new religious pamphlet or two, a few months of exposure to the spirit and instruction of Glarean's *bursa* did not reach deeply into Grebel's inner life, for his whole experience in Paris was too much one of confusion, tribulation, and disappointment. Poor health, financial distress, and six months' flight from normal routines to escape the plague, all played their part in preventing a normal development and stamping the mark of frustration on the period. Perhaps Grebel should have been able to overcome these obstacles, but he was also handicapped by inner uncertainty and weakness. Lack of a clear purpose, uncertainty as to his future career, resentment at the difficulties into which he was placed by his father, lack of self-discipline, all this and more drove Grebel into a blind corner from which he seemingly had neither the strength nor the courage to deliver himself. The frequent lamentations of the ill-fortune which dogged his steps, and his despair of finding a way out, bring this inner frustration vividly to light.

The Paris period of Grebel's life must accordingly be viewed rather as a period of storm and stress, a period which was to continue until his marriage and conversion in early 1522. What inner development there was must be found in a certain forced maturing of personality, a being brought face to face with the ultimate questions of life from which he could not escape without probing deeply into the meaning and purpose of his own existence. When, under this pressure, he did probe within, he found that his life was empty and worthless; henceforth he swung back and forth between a fatalistic resignation and an incipient apprehension of something better, an awakening to a new life. But this awakening was not to come until later after he had come back to Zurich, had listened to the preaching of Ulrich Zwingli, and heard from him both in sermon and in personal contact the message of the new Gospel of the redemption through Christ which comes by faith.

If it be suggested that Grebel got more in Paris in the way of religious influence than the above analysis would show, and that it was here in the semi-Erasmian humanistic environment of Glarean and Faber that he received the first impetus toward his later Anabaptist position, the sufficient answer is that there is not the least trace of this influence in any of the sources of this period, which are exclusively the letters written from Paris by Grebel and his friends. It would be comforting to those who hold, as a recent writer in this field[138] insists, that "Grebel's later Anabaptist views are unthinkable without the influence of Erasmian humanism, even though the Zwinglian Reformation added new and different elements," to find the beginnings of this influence in Paris. But even the above-mentioned writer agrees, after picturing in their most favorable light the religious interests and expressions of Faber and Glarean and Glarean's students, that "we can find no trace of the influence of the Erasmian ideas concerning a reform of Christendom, nor of the ideas of Faber Stapulensis, in the [Grebel] letters of the Paris period." Yet he, like others, cannot dismiss the idea that Erasmianism had a role in the genesis of Anabaptism, and hence continues to insist, in spite of the total lack of evidence, that "it is thoroughly possible that Grebel was led into these matters by the tides of influence in Paris, the discussions, the exchange of thoughts by letter, and the reading of writings, and thus prepared for later decision in regard to them." He promises a later and fuller examination of this subject. Whatever this later investigation may bring forth in this regard, one need not hesitate to say that the Paris period of Conrad Grebel's life must be cancelled out completely as a possible source of the influence of Erasmian ideas on Anabaptism, and that the genesis of Grebel's Anabaptist ideas must be sought in another and later time and place.

IV

CRISIS

Grebel in Zurich and Basel

July, 1520, *to February,* 1522

At the beginning of July, 1520,[1] as reported earlier, the unhappy young Grebel returned to the paternal roof in Zurich, weary of life, and filled with uncertainty and anxiety about the future. In the autumn of 1514 he had left that roof full of youth and enthusiasm, riding out into the world equipped with everything that the heart could desire—money, social prestige, talent, the future bright and large before him, but after six years of university study in Basel, Vienna, and Paris, he returned to his home frustrated and in conflict, a relative failure. In this mood he struggled for two years before finding the way out.

When Myconius, who was now in Lucerne, received the news that his good friend Conrad Grebel had returned home, he hastened to Zurich to complete the reconciliation between Conrad and his parents toward which he had been working for many months.[2] He wanted to help the young man whom he had learned to love and whom he had so faithfully supported during the time of trial and suffering in Paris. The visit to Zurich was not in vain for he succeeded in accomplishing a measure of reconciliation between father and son, which Conrad gratefully recognized.[3] However a certain tension remained in Conrad's relationship with his father, partly because of the serious failure of the father to deal justly with his son in the discharge of his financial obligations to him, as has been indicated earlier.[4] In consequence of this failure, the tension between the two grew gradually worse until the complete break came eighteen months later in connection with Conrad's marriage.

After his return home Grebel continued to suffer from the illness which had troubled him ever since he left Vienna.[5] In

November, 1520, he referred to his ailment,[6] and in April and July, 1521, he mentioned particularly an inflammation in the feet.[7] More than once he asked Vadian, who was practicing medicine in St. Gall, for medical aid, and in October, 1521, his parents advised him to return from Basel to take the baths at Baden.[8]

But in addition to his physical ailment Conrad also suffered mentally under the situation in which he was compelled to live after his return from Paris. The future was altogether uncertain and dark to him.[9] The weeks and the months passed by in an aimless existence without plan and without goal. His father gave him no indication of any plan for his future, and yet Conrad could do nothing without his father's consent.[10] Much of the time he had literally nothing to do. His books did not arrive from Paris until the middle of September, two months after he himself had returned.[11] For a short time he was occupied in the iron shop of his father, since Jacob Grebel was frequently absent in the service of the canton or as a delegate to the meetings of the Confederacy, and the new manager of the shop, Beatus, was not familiar with the business.[12] Conrad thought of travel. He planned to go to Lucerne to visit Myconius and Xylotectus, but something always interfered to prevent the journey.[13] Vadian invited him again and again to come to St. Gall, and finally in the latter half of October Conrad did succeed in getting away from Zurich.[14] The visit to Vadian had two purposes, one the restoration of the intimacy of the friendship of earlier days, and the other to discuss with Vadian plans for the future, in particular plans for future study. As a result of the visit it was agreed that Conrad should continue his studies. This time it was to be in Italy, for the father had succeeded in securing for the son a two year papal stipend for study at the University of Pisa,[15] granted by the papal legate, Pucci,[16] who had come to Zurich September 11, 1520. Definite plans were made, and at the beginning of November Conrad reported to Vadian that he was ready for the journey.[17]

Nevertheless the plan to spend two years in Pisa was never carried out, in spite of the fact that the thought of going to Italy had been considered for years, indeed as early as the summer of 1518 before the journey to Paris was undertaken.[18] (It will be remembered also that after the break with Glarean in Paris in January, 1519, Grebel had indicated his desire to go to Italy to study at either Pisa or Bologna.) Vadian, who had heard from Conrad that all that stood between him and the departure was a trip to Einsiedeln to make a vow,[19] actually wrote to Jacob Grebel at the beginning of January, 1521, on the assumption that Conrad had proceeded to Pisa according to plan, and was quite surprised to be informed to the contrary.[20] By the first of February, 1521, Conrad's enthusiasm for the trip had markedly declined[21] and he began to consider going to Basel instead.[22] Again the papal legate promised the stipend and even offered to pay the cost of the journey, but stipulated that the money be paid to Grebel only after he should arrive in Pisa. The legate then left Zurich for Italy, having secured the mercenaries for the army of the pope for which he had come, in full expectation that Grebel would join his company at Uri. But once again Grebel's plan changed; he did not join the legate at Uri, for he much preferred to go to Basel whither he intended to come before Easter.[23] By April 8, 1521, the unstable young man was once more in doubt whether to go to Pisa or to Basel, but about that time both his parents became so seriously ill that the journey to either place became impossible.[24] It was four months, or the beginning of August, 1521, before Grebel actually got away from Zurich, and then it was to Basel. But his stay there was short, only a brief ten weeks from the beginning of August to the end of October. And when he came back to Zurich it was with the determination to give up forever any thought of traveling to foreign lands to continue his study, for he had decided to settle permanently in Zurich.[25]

It is possible that for a time Grebel even considered studying in Wittenberg, for on December 8, 1520, he wrote to Vadian, "I had preferred to make my way to Saxony for certain sweet reasons, but something or other is in the way."[26]

What did Grebel actually do in the year that elapsed between his return from Paris in 1520 and his departure for Basel in August, 1521? Did the young humanist who had made such progress in his intellectual development in six years of university study simply stand still and mark time?[27] Grebel himself answers in the affirmative; he even thinks that he went backward.[28] Much of what he had learned, he says, was lost.[29] However Grebel did not altogether lose his interest in study and books, for in Zurich he found a group of friends who had been studying Greek zealously under the leadership of Ulrich Zwingli since the spring of 1520, and with whom he could have pleasant fellowship.[30] In the circle were the masters of the two schools of the city, several of the canons of the cathedral, a village priest by the name of Simon Stumpf of Höngg, and others. George Binder, one of the schoolmasters and an old friend of Grebel in Vienna, presided over the group. In October, 1521, two other good friends of Grebel, Valentin Tschudi and J. J. Ammann, both fellow-students in Paris, also came to Zurich and joined the circle. After his return from Basel, Grebel reports to Myconius on November 4, 1521, that he was reading Plato with Zwingli, Tschudi and Ammann.[31] Not much is known about this little circle of scholars and their Greek studies, although it seems quite clear that Zwingli was the recognized leader or teacher of the group and that the group considered itself more as a learned society than as a school. A very interesting report of the activities of the *Sodalitium* is given by Albert Burer in a letter to Beatus Rhenanus in the spring of 1520 when he attended the meetings of the group several times as the guest of Simon Stumpf.[32] He reports that the circle met several times a week and occasionally took meals together. It is quite likely that the members of the group did some original composition in Greek. Several times in letters to Vadian Grebel mentions certain Greek epigrams which he had written, and reports that the samples which he was sending to Vadian had not yet been examined by Zwingli. Later he sent other epigrams which Zwingli had corrected.[33]

Evidence found in the correspondence of Grebel with Vadian during this period indicates that Grebel's chief scholarly interest was the study of Greek language and literature, which he had begun in Paris.[34] In one letter he mentioned that he was studying Homer's *Iliad* as his chief occupation and had prepared a collection of notes in connection with his study, which he offered to Vadian for use.[35] He planned to take the book along to St. Gall as a traveling companion.[36] In another letter Grebel commiserated Vadian on the fact that he had not yet learned the Greek language, and offered to help him, urging him to undertake the study in spite of his age. In order to help Vadian to get started he sent several books for his personal study.[35]

The renewed fellowship with old friends in Zurich brought Grebel much satisfaction. His first contact with Zwingli had been in 1517 when Zwingli, then at Einsiedeln, opened correspondence with Grebel while he was a student in Vienna.[37] The contact had never been close before, but now the relation became more intimate. For instance, in a letter to Vadian in November, 1520, Grebel commented with admiration on the zeal and diligence with which Zwingli performed the duties of his office, and promised to carry out a commission which he had received from Vadian with the same zeal which he admired in Zwingli.[38] Zwingli himself apparently learned to appreciate and admire young Grebel, for he soon took him into the intimate circle of his close friends, and in August, 1522, permitted him to publish a poem as an appendix to his *Apologeticus Archeteles*. The group of intimate friends which was gradually gathering about Zwingli was composed at the end of 1521 of the following: Grebel, George Binder, J. J. Ammann, Valentin Tschudi, *Leutpriester* Heinrich Engelhart, Canon Heinrich Utinger, Konrad Luchsinger, provost Felix Frei, and the city clerk Kaspar Frei. Felix Manz joined the circle in 1522.[38a] In this circle Zwingli found several young men who had acquired a good humanistic training at various universities and whom he probably hoped to be able to depend upon as active helpers in his endeavors for the moral and religious reform of the city and canton of Zurich. Good friends and faithful supporters they were, but at this early date the common interest which bound them to Zwingli was the humanistic study of

Greek and Hebrew rather than ecclesiastical and theological reform. The reform interest was soon to come.

Through his fellowship with Zwingli, Grebel no doubt gradually came into closer contact with other humanists of Switzerland, particularly with Zwingli's friends in Basel.[39] There was Beatus Rhenanus, with whom Zwingli conducted regular correspondence from the middle of 1518 to the beginning of 1522. In the year 1519 Hedio entered into Zwingli's circle of friends; in 1520 came Capito, and in 1521, Butzer. In addition to these well-known figures Zwingli enjoyed the friendship of the noted Basel printers Froben and Amerbach, as well as other lesser figures. At the beginning of 1520 Zwingli had visited his friends in Basel, and when the great Erasmus himself came to Basel to live, Zwingli gradually developed a friendship with him. The two men had exchanged letters once in 1516, but the regular correspondence between them began in September, 1522.

As early as January 12, 1522, Grebel reported to Vadian that Zwingli desired to visit Erasmus in Basel.[40] Grebel's interest in Erasmus began in August, 1520, when Myconius sent him a copy of an unprinted epistle by Erasmus concerning Luther.[41] In the middle of July, 1521, Grebel had learned through correspondence from the Basel printer, Cratander (Grebel was acting as intermediary between Vadian and Cratander in the matter of the second edition of Vadian's *Pomponius Mela*), that Erasmus, so Froben said, was soon to come to Basel. This news Grebel quickly reported to Vadian.[42] On November 15, 1521, Erasmus actually arrived in Basel, as Grebel reported to Vadian on December 18, 1521.[43] Some weeks later, in a letter dated February 6, 1522, Grebel proposed to Vadian that they should together make a journey to Basel to visit Erasmus.[44] Since none of Grebel's letters for a period of nine months immediately following this proposal have been preserved it is therefore impossible to say whether Grebel actually met Erasmus or not. However it is possible that the plan mentioned above was carried out during the summer of 1522, for Erasmus reports in a letter to Zwingli of September 3, 1522, that he had seen Vadian.[45]

How deep the interest was which Grebel manifested in Erasmus, it is difficult to say. Naturally all the humanists of the time knew about him and honored and revered him as the great star of the world of learning. All of Grebel's humanist friends were admirers of the great scholar and leader to a greater or less degree. Glarean was a particularly close friend, but Myconius and Zwingli were not far behind in their admiration for him. Vadian had never met Erasmus personally and had little correspondence with him, but his friendly attitude is indicated by a laudatory passage in the second edition of his commentary on *Pomponius Mela* which was written in 1520 and published in January, 1522.[46] Zwingli thought so much of Erasmus that in the summer of 1522 he invited him to come to Zurich to live.[47] The invitation made little impression on Erasmus for he rejected it at once; indeed, he did not even visit Zurich although he had intended to stop there in September, 1522, on his return journey from Constance to Basel.[48]

The interest and activity in the study of Greek language and literature in which Conrad Grebel participated together with the Zurich circle of humanistic friends about Zwingli, is of significance, but it should not be unduly emphasized. His life, he says in one letter to Vadian, was a "miserable story," and if he did not soon find a solution to his problems he would drown "in the boundless depths of his tribulations."[49]

In the midst of Grebel's tribulation came the new experience of love. It was an experience which made him at one and the same time most happy and most miserable. In it he found meaning and value, but in it he found a source of increased tension with his own parents which soon became almost unbearable. Just when the affair began is not clear. In a letter to Myconius of November 4, 1521, Grebel reported that he had been "attacked by the little god 'Cupid' not a few months before,"[50] and as early as February 19, 1521, he reported to Vadian that he did not feel worthy of the deep and pure love which his beloved bestowed upon him, that in fact they loved each other so desperately that they could not long remain separate. In this letter as well as in several other letters Grebel calls his beloved his *Holokosme,* that is, his "whole world."[51]

The great difficulty into which the love affair had brought him was reported in person by Conrad to Vadian on the occasion of a visit by Vadian and his wife Martha to Zurich at the time of the serious illness of Conrad's mother in April and May, 1521. Grebel confided in Vadian the whole affair. He could not give up his beloved and yet could not marry her because of the opposition of the parents. He unfolded a plan to go to Basel and set up his home there. Vadian apparently approved the idea because he later expressed surprise that Conrad had not gone to Basel at once and wondered why his father had opposed the plan.[52] Others also gradually learned of Conrad's affair and of his plan to go to Basel. The situation became so serious that Conrad had to find sympathetic friends to whom he could go for counsel. One of the first of those to whom he turned was his aunt Agathe, a nun in Oetenbach convent, to whom he poured out his heart. She encouraged him to carry through his plan to go to Basel in spite of everything.[53] Conrad's sister Barbara, who was at that time living with her parents in Zurich during the first months of her widowhood, also came to Conrad's aid.[54]

Conrad was determined to go to Basel, but he did not have the courage to make a complete break with his parents at once. In the first place, his father was seriously ill at the end of May.[53] But even after he had recovered, Conrad was not ready to leave, for on July 14, 1521, he wrote to Vadian that he would not promise when he would go; he would announce his departure to Vadian only after it had actually taken place, so that he would be able to shout with rejoicing, "Conrad has broken through, he has broken his chains and his fetters, he is free."[54] When he finally disclosed his intentions to his parents, the father would hear nothing of it. But it was too late to turn back now for Conrad had already sent his beloved to Basel in advance,[55] and it was but a question of time until he could gather sufficient courage to make the final break. While he was struggling with the decision he could not sleep; he was under a tremendous strain; he felt that he was near death.[55] The parents were angry and flatly refused to grant permission. But Conrad had in essence made his decision months before; in accord with the motto of Ulrich Hutten, *Ieci aleam,* he had cast the die.[56] He was resolved to stop at nothing, and "prepared the horse" for the moment when he was ready to fly. Finally his father yielded and even gave Conrad forty francs to take with him. In addition to this small fund, Conrad had secured a stipend from the papal commissar, Wilhelm de Falconibus, which he concealed from his father.[57] On August 21, a month after his beloved had arrived, Grebel finally reached Basel. With rejoicing he wrote to Vadian on the occasion of his arrival, "I have reached Basel and have fulfilled my heart's desire. My beloved is with me; we get along fine together, except that now and then we have little quarrels as is the manner of lovers. The quarrel is usually short and peace comes quickly. She says that she is mine, and I am hers so absolutely that I could not be it more completely. I have not yet rented a house where we can live together but I will do so at once. As soon as this occurs, if she keeps her promise, we will be happy with a multitude of joys. But let us see how the matter will work out. At last the heart of your poor Grebel is enraptured, hence rejoice with me if you love me."[58]

Grebel remained about two months in Basel. He took lodging with Cratander, the famous printer, together with Kaspar Ursinus Velius, who had recently come to Basel to work for Cratander. The printer was delighted to have these two talented young scholars in his shop, and on September 20, in a letter written from Frankfurt a.M. where he was attending the fall book fair, he expressed his rejoicing to his friend Capito over the addition of these new talents to his business. His shop would in the future be able to do much better work, he felt sure, and would have much greater fame because of the contribution of these able scholars.[59]

Grebel's first plan had been to support his friend in a separate lodging while he himself took lodging with Cratander, but this arrangement turned out to be too expensive and had to be given up. For his own living expenses he had to pay twenty-four guilders a month, and for his friend twenty guilders, in addition to other expenses for clothing and furniture. In order to cut down expenses he considered living with his beloved in her quarters where they might have a common household.[60] But on second thought he decided against this plan because he felt certain that if his parents should hear of it they would cast him off as one who was living with a light woman and had so disgraced the family that he was no longer worthy to bear the name of Grebel. Further the father would probably hear of the papal stipend before long, and in his wrath would withdraw all financial support so that he would not have enough money for even the one household. Since Grebel returned to Zurich in October, 1521, it is highly probable that he continued to live with Cratander during his entire short stay in Basel.[61]

Little is known of Grebel's activity during the few weeks of his employment in Cratander's shop. It is probable that he read proof on the second edition of Vadian's *Pomponius Mela* which was just then in the press and was to be completed by the end of the year.[62] Ursinus was planning a complete edition of his own poems and reported to Vadian on October 1, 1521, he was happy to have secured the assistance of Conrad Grebel in preparing the book for the press.[63] It is doubtful, however, whether Grebel ever did much for Ursinus, since the book was printed by Froben in March of the following year, 1522.[64] There is no evidence that Grebel was enrolled as a student at the University at this time, as has been asserted.[65] Ursinus was matriculated at the university on August 1, 1521,[66] but Grebel's name does not appear among the matriculants.

The date of Grebel's departure from Basel is uncertain, but it was soon after Cratander's return from the Frankfort Fair, which must have been early in October. His parents urged him to come home to take the baths in the hope that they might benefit his health.[67] Conrad wrote to Myconius on November 4, 1521, that he was very glad to be at home again, and that he had resolved never again to leave Zurich for foreign climes, for he had experienced so much unhappiness in his various residences abroad that the mere mention of another trip to a foreign country was sufficient to make him shudder.[68] He wrote much the same to Vadian two days earlier, on November 2, 1521, saying that he had decided to give up foreign travel for a long time.[69]

He gave emphasis to his decision by resuming (some time in October, 1521) his Zurich citizenship which he had surrendered in July, 1515, when he left for Vienna.[70]

Grebel's stay in Basel seems to have had little significance for his future. The time was too short and his interest was too much engaged in his love affair to leave much time for other things. It is possible that he met Erasmus at this time, although it is rather doubtful since the latter was absent almost the whole month of September on a journey to Constance.[71] Cratander himself was absent almost the entire time at the Frankfort Fair. It is possible that Grebel came into contact with Beatus Rhenanus who was one of the outstanding humanists in Basel at this time.[72] Glarean did not come back to Switzerland from Paris until February or March of the next year, 1522.[73] Oecolampad, Ulrich von Hutten, and Hartmut von Kronberg did not appear in Basel until November, 1522. Capito had left Basel in April, 1520, and Hedio, his faithful disciple, had followed him in the autumn of the same year. The new ideas from Wittenberg were already taking root in Basel but it is scarcely likely that Grebel was influenced by them in the brief time of his stay in the city.

It might be of interest to inquire whether Grebel came into contact in Basel in 1521 with certain men who later were prominent in the Anabaptist movement. Only two names come into consideration in this respect, Wilhelm Reublin and Ulrich Hugwald. Balthasar Hubmaier was in Basel for a short time but did not come until July, 1522, eight months after Grebel had left.[74] Hans Denk came still later, in 1523, although he too, like Grebel, was for a time a proofreader in Cratander's shop (as Oecolampad also was).[75] Ulrich Hugwald, who was one of the little group of Anabaptists who were discovered and arrested in Basel in August, 1525,[76] had already matriculated at the University as early as 1519, and was living in Basel in the summer of 1521, engaged in writing.[77] Wilhelm Reublin of Rottenberg on the Neckar, one of the early agitators in Zurich against infant baptism (1524) and later (1527) one of the leaders of the movement in Moravia,[78] had come to Basel about July, 1521, as pastor of St. Alban's Parish Church, just shortly before Grebel arrived. He was chosen for a term of one year and according to an ancient report "began at once to preach excellently out of the Holy Scriptures of the Old and New Testament and to expound them in a Christian way,"[79] which was quite different from what had hitherto been the custom. It would be interesting to report contact between Grebel and these men during his stay in Basel, but unfortunately there is no evidence on which to base any conclusion.

It is quite probable, therefore, that Grebel returned to Zurich much the same man as he had been when he left, very little changed by his two months in Basel. He had in no way been able to help himself by the Basel expedition, for the secret love affair had still to be kept secret, and the conflict with the parents had only been increased. What would ultimately become of his love affair was totally uncertain. Marriage apparently seemed out of the question,[80] but he was firmly resolved never to give up his *Holokosme*.[81]

But suddenly the wedding occurred after all.[82] On February 6, 1522, at a time when his father had left for an eight-day business trip, the ceremony was performed, probably by Heinrich Engelhart, parish priest at the Fraumünster Church. Dorothea and Margareta Wirz, daughters of Hans Wirz, were present at the ceremony. Engelhart, Hans Wirz, and a few other friends, were commissioned by Conrad to seek a reconciliation with the father upon the latter's return home. Conrad's mother was enraged beyond measure at the sudden plunge into matrimony, and quite lost her senses thereby; she wept unceasingly. In a letter written to Vadian on the day of the wedding Grebel said that if his father would take the same attitude as his mother he would not be able to remain much longer in the city. Since little else was to be expected of the father, Conrad looked forward to being banned from the paternal home and said that he would himself have gone into voluntary exile already if he had not considered the grey hairs of his parents.

Now at last the final plunge had been taken, the Gordian knot had been cut. Conrad Grebel had made the only possible honorable decision. In so doing he won his spiritual independence and self-respect, and as a consequence his inner development approached its decisive stage.

V

GREBEL'S HUMANISM[1]

Conrad Grebel was a humanist for eight years, and these years constitute one of the most important periods of his life. They were the best years of his youth and early manhood, the formative period from sixteen to twenty-four. Of this period, the first half year was spent in Basel with Glarean, three years were spent in Vienna with Vadian, two years were the years of storm and stress in Paris spent in part under Glarean's influence, while the last two years, except for two months in Basel, were spent in Zurich and brought Grebel into vital association with Zwingli. But in all these years, whether in Basel, Vienna, Paris, or Zurich, Grebel was constantly among humanists, and his development in these significant years took place under the star of the declining renaissance. It is therefore of importance to understand the significance of this humanistic influence in the molding of his personality and his thinking.

The successive portions of Grebel's humanistic period were not of equal importance for his inner development. The most important periods were the second and the fourth, the three years in Vienna and the two years at the close under Zwingli's influence. The first period in Basel was of less significance because it was too short and Grebel was too young. What Grebel received in Basel from Glarean was primarily a thorough discipline in the Latin language, for Glarean was without doubt the best teacher among the humanists of Switzerland, if not among all the German humanists, and in addition one of the best Latin poets of his time.

The twenty months which Grebel spent in Paris were likewise of slight importance for his profounder development so far as humanism was concerned. His life there was much too disturbed by frequent changes in residence and in teachers to permit a consistent and steady influence to operate upon him. With Glarean he lived not more than five months, possibly not more than two, and the lectures of Nicholas Beraldus he could not have heard longer than four months. Faber Stapulensis he probably never heard, or if at all, for not more than a few months, for after the autumn of 1519 Faber was no longer in Paris. Budé could not have been an influence in his life, for his contacts with him were certainly few; Budé was not a professor at the university and spent most of his time at his country place at Marly. Perhaps the most important thing that Grebel secured in Paris was a knowledge of the Greek language and literature. Beraldus was an excellent Greek teacher and without doubt the enthusiasm for the Greek language and literature which Grebel manifested in Zurich after his return from Paris was due to this contact. But in his profounder development Grebel stood still; a really vital influence of French humanism upon him was inhibited by the circumstances of his life.

In the early years in Vienna, 1515-1518, on the contrary, Grebel lived a happy, carefree, productive life. For three long years he was able to study without interruption and to devote himself to the humanistic arts; these years were therefore most fruitful in his intellectual development. Among the influences which determined the course of Grebel's development in Vienna Vadian was certainly the chief contributing factor. Grebel himself testifies to this. After he had returned to Zurich from Paris at the conclusion of his student years, as he looked back over his life, he wrote at one time to Vadian: "I confess that I owe more to you than to any other man, and I bring you the greatest appreciation and thanks that it is possible for me to bring."[2] Vadian was Grebel's hero; to Grebel Vienna meant Vadian. Of all the possible other figures of the humanist world in Vienna whom Grebel might have remembered, only Wolfgang Hailigmaier's name is mentioned in his later correspondence, and he was not one of the great men of Vienna.

It is evident then that of the numerous figures of the men of learning and scholarship among the humanists of Basel, Vienna, and Paris, Vadian was the only one who exerted a dominant influence upon the development of the young Grebel. Among the others of Grebel's acquaintance, only Glarean was significant and his influence was more on the formal side of learning than on inner growth. Zwingli occupies a peculiar place in Grebel's development, since his influence was effective only at the end of Grebel's period of growth and then primarily effective in the field of religion. With the greatest personalities of northern humanism Grebel scarcely came into contact. Men like Erasmus, Budé, Faber Stapulensis, Beatus Rhenanus, moved on the horizon of his life; they were not in the inner circle of his friends. Even the writings of these great humanists seemed to have had little place in Grebel's development, at least in so far as the evidence of the meager sources permits a conclusion. Erasmus alone appears in the list of humanist writers whom he read, and the writings referred to by Grebel are not the great productions of that noted scholar but rather some of the shorter pamphlets of minor significance, a few ephemeral polemic booklets. It is of course possible that Grebel read Erasmus extensively, but no evidence of such influence has been preserved in the extant sources. Grebel did develop a warm and intimate friendship with one of the Swiss humanists, namely with Oswald Myconius. But his relations with Myconius were exclusively epistolary except for the two brief months in the summer of 1518 when he had the privilege of personal fellowship with him in Zurich. When Myconius returned to Zurich in 1524 after a number of years' absence in Lucerne, the possibility of an intimate friendship between the two men had been destroyed by the growing conflict between Grebel and Zwingli. In any case Myconius was but a minor figure at this time.

Since Grebel's teachers and friends were chiefly Vadian, Zwingli, Myconius, and Glarean, it is clear that the humanism which molded Grebel's thinking was primarily a Swiss humanism. This is significant in view of the fact that recent scholarship has learned to distinguish various phases of humanism. Men like Burdach, Walser, and Kaegi, have demonstrated that it is no longer possible to view humanism as a unified movement, but rather as a general cultural trend containing differentiated points of view. The distinction between Italian and northern humanism was of course drawn long ago, but until recent years the view that northern humanism was a spiritual unity has prevailed. Now it is clear that no such unity ever existed, not even among the more limited group of German humanists. When humanism first came across the Alps, to Basel, to Vienna, and to Paris, the influence of Italian thought and philosophy was very strong. But very soon, particularly in Basel and Paris, the movement developed its own original pattern with a different content and spirit from that found among the Italians. In Basel and Paris there was little of the ethical and religious indifferentism and libertinistic materialism of cis-alpine humanism. The paganizing tendencies of the Italians did not flourish among the Swiss at all, and very little among the French in the early years.

But it can be shown that the more sane and pious trans-alpine or northern humanism was also not a unified movement. In spite of the fact that Erasmus was the dominant personality in the north not all German and French humanists can be classed as Erasmian even though they almost worshipped him as the great father of the new learning. The chief interest of Erasmus was the moral, religious, and ecclesiastical reform of the existing Christian society, a reform in which the new learning, the *bonae literae,* constituted the chief force in producing a more peaceful, sane, and Christian way of living. According to Erasmus this meant primarily the study of the ancient classics and church fathers, with the Bible in the original Greek and Hebrew languages as the supreme source. Kaegi has characterized this Erasmian conception of a new Christianity effectively as follows: "In contrast to the scholastic religion of the theologians, Erasmus saw in Christianity an undogmatic, simple, practical morality, which had found its fullest and most perfect expression in the early Christian Church of apostolic times with its spiritual unity based upon mutual love. . . . Through the 'renaissance' of this Christianity he hoped for peace between nations as well as the exorcism of all dogmatic strife within the church."[3] Paul Wernle calls this Erasmian Christianity a "simple, practical, lay-Christianity."[4]

But much as they honored Erasmus for his learning and his

leadership, by no means all the German and French humanists were active participants in this great Erasmian program for the construction of a new Christian world, for Erasmus was one of those rare free spirits with a cosmopolitan, international outlook, who lived in the rarefied atmosphere of intellectual and moralistic theory without a practical and personal commitment to any particular state, nation, people, society, or church. He was under the constraint of no loyalty or patriotism, and he shared no local cultural obligations. In contrast to his attitude, many of the northern humanists were not cosmopolitan or internationally minded, but were rather concretely attached to homeland and homepeople. Many likewise felt no inner urge to occupy themselves with religious questions or to give themselves to religious interests. In these respects they were therefore not Erasmians. "Non-Erasmian" humanists were Vadian and the earlier Glarean, the teachers of Conrad Grebel. Of this type in the earlier days were also Grebel's friend Myconius and his greater friend Zwingli, and even a man of the type of Budé. And such a humanist was Conrad Grebel himself.

In general this type of humanist was interested primarily in historical, geographical, and philological study, and only incidentally in moral and religious matters. Vadian and Glarean for instance were both deeply interested in geography and poetry. Glarean had more of the Erasmian spirit than Vadian, but even in his case very little of the Erasmian interest in ecclesiastical and religious affairs is evident. Vadian manifested no interest at all in such affairs while he was in Vienna; he was a thorough scholar, a polyhistor, a humanist, but in no sense an Erasmian, although like the other humanists of the day he honored Erasmus afar off. He did not know Greek at all. Even Budé, as Walser has so well said, manifested practically nothing of the "commonly accepted marks of humanism and the renaissance. Aesthetic appreciation and interpretation of classic antiquity is scarcely noticeable in his thinking; political cosmopolitism, aristocratic pride of learning as over against the common man, religious indifferentism . . . all are equally foreign to him."[5] Budé's chief interest lay in the use of the historico-critical method, and in practical matters such as ancient coinage. One of his great ambitions was to demonstrate to the world as a patriotic Frenchman that French learning was capable of competing with the learning of the Italian humanists. His chief writings dealt with ancient Roman law and coinage. Similarly Vadian's chief work was a commentary on the geographical treatise of Pomponius Mela, an ancient Roman geographer. And Glarean's chief literary productions were philological text books and musical treatises. None of these men ever wrote anything remotely approaching *The Praise of Folly* or *The Handbook of the Christian Soldier.* The French patriotism of Budé was matched and exceeded by the Swiss patriotism of Vadian and Glarean. When such men were away from home in foreign lands they thought of themselves as exiled Swiss scholars temporarily living abroad, not at all as international cosmopolites. One of their chief aims was the development of young Swiss scholars, even though they taught them far from home in Vienna and Paris, scholars who would prepare for a greater and more glorious future for the fatherland in the field of learning. A patriotic Swiss of this type was Conrad Grebel.

In order to complete the characterization of the humanism which Grebel assimilated, the character and personality of the men who were his close associates must be briefly indicated. With the possible exception of Glarean, they were all men of solid character, moral earnestness, clean living, and strong personality. Indeed men like Vadian, Zwingli, and Myconius may well be characterized as men of high moral character. In them was nothing of the typical loose-living Italian humanism. They were worthy tutors of the Swiss youth of their time.

Conrad Grebel, as we know him from the letters of his humanist years, and as we see him revealed in the judgment of his teachers, comrades, and friends, bears the stamp of these men and the type of humanism which they represent. Repeatedly he is characterized by such men as Vadian, Myconius, Clivanus, Ammann, Ursinus, Hinwiler and Zwingli as a youth of exceptional intellectual talent and upright, congenial character. Only Glarean's voice fails to fit into this chorus of favorable judgment, but it is clear that his attitude was colored by the personal conflict between the two men. When Grebel entered a new circle of friends he was at once recognized as an outstanding character, as was the case in Vienna with Vadian and in Zurich with Zwingli. If in spite of this favorable judgment of his talents and personality, Grebel was not able to fulfil the promise of his early years, the cause for the failure is to be sought rather in a personality weakness than in a moral or intellectual deficiency. His failure was one of self-discipline; he never learned to hold himself to a systematic plan of procedure in his studies; nevertheless a dissolute and depraved life he did not live (although he was by no means a saint), in spite of the representations to this effect by most of the church historians of the nineteenth century who have attempted to characterize him. On the rare occasions on which he spoke of moral transgressions in his confidential letters to Vadian and Myconius, he did so with a sense of reluctance and personal guilt. He always retained a healthy ethical feeling, as is indicated in his reaction toward the question of foreign pensions during his stay in Paris.

Finally, in religious attitudes Grebel also reflects the neutral humanist type of Vadian and Glarean. He is far removed from the paganism of the Italian humanists, although his letters frequently carry classical and mythological expressions. He often speaks of "gods and goddesses" (twenty-six times), of "fate" (sixteen times), of the "Dirae" and "Fatae" (eight times), but these expressions are quite manifestly used in a purely formal sense or as symbols, not in any way as a vital expression of his inner life. Grebel's religion was quite certainly of the traditional sort, but it was a religion for him. In the later letters of his humanist years he changed some of his expressions in referring to deity; for instance, he substituted the name *deus optimus maximus* for the formula *dei et deae* which had been the common term for deity in his earlier letters. This is particularly the case after he had come under Zwingli's influence. There are other evidences of his religious thinking. Twice he mentions prayer and indicates that he believes in the efficacy of prayer. He speaks of a divine power as a power which comes to the aid of human beings in time of need, as for instance in times of sickness and tribulation. Since the cast of his mind in the latter years became somewhat somber and melancholy because he suffered considerably under his afflictions, he frequently refers to death. (Men of Grebel's time were naturally compelled to think about death because of the frequently recurring plagues.) In death Grebel sees a release from tribulation. He indicates a belief that in the future world men will be rewarded by a merciful God in accord with their earthly deeds. In this connection it is very interesting to notice the consolation with which he comforts his brother-in-law Vadian on the occasion of the death of his brother Melchior, in which he finally produces a sort of *Weltanschauungspredigt.* Vadian is to bear the blow "philosophically" for we humans can not change anything anyway; the brother would have had to die sometime; he was born to die; he died young and unspoiled; he has gone to that place where all human beings must ultimately go; Vadian's loss is not eternal; it was best according to the decree of God that it should be so; "see that you conduct yourself as a Christian." This "philosophy" was written in December, 1521, shortly before Grebel's conversion, so the attitude which it presents may not be characteristic of his humanistic thinking alone. Once Grebel refers superficially to the possibility of entering monastic life as a way of escape from his troubles.

However in spite of the evidence just presented above that Grebel had a traditional religious attitude toward life, it must be said that he actually mentions religious matters very seldom in his letters. Religion certainly played no vital part in his thought. The Erasmian concerns never appear to have entered his mind. On the other hand what Grebel did not say about religion is perhaps just as important as what he did say. In his letters there is no trace of the rationalistic skepticism and cynicism which was so characteristic of the southern humanists with their mocking and scoffing at the traditional religion of the people.

Grebel's return to Zurich in July, 1520, marked the beginning of a new epoch in his life, for in Zurich Ulrich Zwingli had set in motion spiritual forces that were to make of him a new person. The return to Zurich was thus more than a homecoming of a student from foreign sojourn; it was an entrance into an altogether different sphere of living. In Zurich in the person of Ulrich Zwingli Grebel found for the first time a man who merited full recognition as a scholar and a humanist, and who at the same time held a positive Christian position. Thus in Zwingli two streams of influence were united for Grebel, classical antiquity and biblical Christianity. In this narrower sense of Christian humanism Zwingli was in reality an Erasmian, not bound to Erasmus solely by common scholarly interests, but by friendship as one who esteemed him as the leader of a Christian renaissance, the promoter of reform in the church, and co-laborer in the Gospel. If Grebel was ever influenced at all by Erasmian humanism it was through the channel of Ulrich Zwingli in his contact with him after July, 1520. But when Grebel came into contact with him Zwingli was already so far beyond Erasmus in his thinking that he soon broke with him, although it is worth while remembering in this connection that as late as 1521 Zwingli had invited Erasmus to settle permanently in Zurich.

Just how much of Erasmus Grebel may have received through Zwingli is difficult if not impossible to say, for much of the Erasmian spirit was in the air everywhere, and it is very difficult to infer a direct influence from Erasmus through Zwingli on Grebel for any particular point. Grebel's interest in the writings of the church fathers, which is indicated in several letters to Vadian in the latter part of 1521, may possibly be attributed to this source. Possibly also the pacifism of Erasmus may have influenced Grebel in a round-about way through the temporary pacifism of Zwingli and his group. However, this is more than dubious as will be pointed out later in the discussion of Grebel's theology, for there is after all a wide gap between the absolute denunciation of the taking of life and the use of force which Grebel advocated in the year 1524, and the more or less humanitarian and eclectic opposition to war which Erasmus manifested even though with a religious coloring. Erasmus did not reject all war, in spite of his strong words against the war system. He defended defensive war.

Perhaps the most important question in considering the alleged influence of an Erasmian type of humanism upon Conrad Grebel, is the question whether the Erasmian conception of Christianity as primarily an ethical culture based upon simple, universal religious ideas, was taken over by Grebel and through him by early Anabaptism. The issue has sometimes been stated in terms of a religion of the Sermon on the Mount over against a religion of dogmatic theology. Certain superficial likenesses between Grebel's emphasis on genuine conversion and holy living in practical application to the life of the individual and society (an emphasis characteristic of Anabaptism as a whole), and Erasmian moralistic Christianity, have led some to the erroneous conclusion that Conrad Grebel and his friends were Erasmians. If this similarity indicates a fundamental agreement, if it means that Grebel had derived some of his basic ideas from Erasmus, it must have come primarily through the mediation of Ulrich Zwingli. But if this were true, then Zwingli himself would have had to be an Erasmian at this time (which has not been demonstrated), and one would find it difficult to explain how Zwingli shed his Erasmianism, while Grebel, who was under his influence at the time, retained it. But there are other good reasons for rejecting the thesis of Erasmian influence upon Grebel. It will be made clear in the chapter on Grebel's theology that Grebel's conception of Christianity was not that which Erasmus held, namely an undogmatic, simple, practical, religious morality based upon ethical preaching, the reading of the Bible and the church fathers, and the elevation of the general level of culture by the work of the scholars. It is not even correct to say that Grebel's religion was primarily the religion of the Sermon on the Mount. A free, individualistic, mystical, religious moralism of undogmatic type may have characterized Hans Denk, but it was foreign to Conrad Grebel. At the center of Grebel's thinking stood the Word of God with its absolute authority, and the Spirit of God with its divine power to transform the life of the believer; and as a second central thought, the holy body of believers, the church of Christ, made possible by the individual's experience, bound to the Word of God, and commissioned to proclaim the Gospel in the world as a "suffering church" (*Leidensgemeinde*). How different such a Christianity was from the moralism of Erasmus! Could this have been a humanistic religion, derived out of Grebel's humanistic period, or was it perhaps rather a deepening and purifying of the religion of Ulrich Zwingli as Grebel had learned to know it in the years 1520 to 1523, a faith which was won in the earnest struggle for a sound religion during the controversy with Zwingli 1523-1525. Perhaps what Grebel received from Zwingli, the humanist, and from the whole body of Erasmian humanism, was more than anything else that conception of the source of true religion which pointed him away from the traditional church and society of his day, away from all human thinking, to the true source in the Bible, the Word of God.

VI

ZWINGLI'S CONVERT, 1522-1523[1]

The year 1522 marked an epoch for Conrad Grebel which was to lead to a transformation of his entire life. On the surface, at first, there was nothing to show this. After their marriage in February he and his wife lived with his parents in the family home, at least until the end of 1523.[2] The tension between the older people and the young couple was rather serious, but it could not be avoided, for the young husband had no money or regular work, and the parents' opposition to the marriage was intense. Conrad's mother was irreconcilable. "Against me she is godless and against my wife she rages," Conrad had to write to Vadian as late as the end of 1522.[3] In November, 1522, the first child was born, a son named Theophil; and in August of the following year the second child came, also a son, Josua.[4] The family lived in considerable poverty. Again and again Conrad complained about the unbearable situation. He had to make debts, which oppressed him like a tyrant.[5] "May Plutus damn me if I have an obol," he wrote half humorously at the end of 1522.[6] In August, 1523, he wrote that he was altogether dependent upon strangers, for his father had quite abandoned him. He was attempting to secure a small income by taking on some pupils in Greek.[7] His father had not carried out the financial agreement entered into at the time of the marriage, and the considerable sum which he owed his son was never paid. The mother was still less inclined to help.[8] Conrad's health on the other hand seems to have improved somewhat in contrast to earlier times, although he still had to take to his bed occasionally.[9]

The outward circumstances, as described above, remained much the same as before, poverty, poor health, conflict in the family, no secure position in life—but now it is an altogether different man who faces the outward circumstances of life. Now, instead of pouring out a doleful and despairing complaint in his letters, Conrad speaks of trust in God and of a desire to learn wisdom and patience. He stands as a man and manfully bears his burdens. No longer is life for him a dark road, it is a battleground. Courageously and hopefully he goes about the round of his daily life. How is this new attitude toward life to be explained?

The answer is that a change has come about in the inner life of Conrad Grebel; it may well be called a conversion. An entirely new tone rings in the letters which reappear in June, 1523, after a nine months' silence. The new tone is that of a believing Christian. Gone is the humanist of former days whose speech was full of gods and goddesses, who delighted in the ancient Greek and Latin writers and filled his letters with quotations from them. *Fortuna,* dame fortune, is also gone. It is true that a few remnants of the old character may still be found in his letters, but not for long. And in place of the old humanistic exuberance of style we find moderation, simplicity, and objectivity. The letters, no longer the lengthy epistles that they once were, but now short and to the point, express the spirit of the Bible. In every letter quotations or expressions from the Scriptures are to be found, which can be accounted for only on the basis of regular and diligent Bible study. The fact that these quotations are not for the most part directly cited, but rather consist of a "biblical mode of speaking," proves still further that the writer has not only taken on the outer form of the Scriptures but has made its spiritual content his own inner possession. Grebel's thinking becomes biblical. His children receive Christian or biblical names, "Theophil" and "Josua," and when the relatives indicate their displeasure at such names, Conrad feels that their criticism is a sign of a "worldly attitude." The greeting at the close of the letters is now "in Christ," and is frequently associated with a promise to pray for his friends and with a request for their prayers.[10]

Furthermore the subjects dealt with are now quite different from the themes of the earlier letters. The names of Zwingli, Luther, Melanchthon, and Jakob Strauss, together with their writings, now appear. The ethical and religious questions of the day demand a stand and Conrad Grebel is ready to take his stand. He discusses the tithes question, the incredible attitude of the enemies of the Gospel in St. Gall, the matter of the nuns in Zurich, the steadfastness of the pastors in St. Gall, the spirit in which a pastor is to perform his duty. He has an open eye for religious conditions in the lives of his friends and neighbors as well as in his own life. His mother must experience a change in life through the new birth, else he despairs of her salvation.[11] He prays that his faith may be strengthened and that he may be able to bear his suffering patiently.[12] He suffers inwardly as he hears of the instability of Pastor Burgauer in St. Gall,[13] and he rejoices to hear of the courage of Assistant Pastor Juflius of the same city, for whom he prays that God may give him the freedom and the grace of Paul.[14]

The new spirit burning in Grebel's soul constrains him to a full dedication of his strength and personality to active service. He is ready to fight for the Gospel against the enemies of God and His cause. Although he realizes that he himself is not yet ready for immediate participation in the conflict, he does not understand why others do not launch out in the attack. He has a new standard by which to judge men and their deeds, namely, the holy, inspired Word of God.[15] The writings he reads are now analyzed as to whether they are evangelical and Christian, and men are to be judged according to whether their dealings will stand the test of the righteousness of the Gospel. This righteousness for instance is to be demanded of the Zurich council.[16] Lorenz Hochrütiner dare not be condemned, for he has not acted contrary to the Scriptures.[17] Those who do not live according to the Gospel are to be considered as "the world." And because Christ is the head of His church, Christians who do not deal with their fellow men in love according to the spirit of Christ are not to be admitted to the table of the Lord.[18]

In addition to all this Conrad Grebel has found a new source of joy which he may have in the midst of external tribulation: it is joy in the success and progress of the Gospel. Great is his gratitude for the rediscovery of the lost truth. He rejoices at each victory of the Word of God over the enemies and powers of darkness. Under the leadership of God the old light of truth is again shining forth with all the glory of the Gospel and is lighting up in brilliance the entire world. The word of the Gospel has won a glorious victory over the corrupt and superstitious church of the bishops; and thus it shall ever be.[19]

Without a deep religious renewal such a transformation in the life of Conrad Grebel is wholly inexplicable. The external circumstances of his life continued to be most unfavorable. No stimulus to such a change came from his family or from his friends. He must have experienced a genuine transformation through faith in Christ. By the grace of God he was redeemed and made free from his own inner conflicts, from his old selfish and suffering life. He had found the salvation which he sought for his mother; "by the spirit of God he was born again, he had become a new creature, he had put on Christ."[20] From henceforth his life was dedicated to a new master, to Christ the head of the church[21] whom he now desired to serve as a faithful and devoted follower. He desires that Christians should pray for him that by the grace of God he may receive "the office of minister."[22] That these manifestations of the new spirit were not idle words but a solid foundation, is amply demonstrated by the record of the four remaining years of Grebel's life. His devotion to his convictions led him through much tribulation to the place where he had to sacrifice house and home, family, profession, name, indeed everything for the sake of the cause to which he had dedicated himself. As early as October, 1524, he had the bitter experience of finding that not one of his entire family and relatives understood him or supported him, but he accustomed himself to opposition and learned to find even in tribulation the blessing of Christ.[23]

The key to the explanation of the change in Grebel is easy to find. The source of his renewal was not in the past, not in his earlier humanistic training, for the forces which brought the renewal came out of the present. Grebel had heard the Word of God in the preaching of Zwingli; he had found it in Bible study with Zwingli and his friends in the intimate circle in

Zurich; and he must also have found it in the quiet of his own soul as he read the Bible for himself. Not only was it Conrad Grebel who experienced such a change, but others also, such as the learned and respected canon Heinrich Engelhart, who through Zwingli "was changed from a doctor of Roman law to a poor scholar of Christ."[24] A similar experience may have come to Heinrich Utinger, Clivanus, Binder, Ammann and the whole *Sodalitium.* The time of Grebel's rebirth was probably the spring of 1522, for up to the time of his marriage on February 6, there was no trace of a change, while already on the 7th of July, 1522, Grebel publicly appeared in the role of a zealous defender of the Gospel.[25]

The foundation for the Reformation in Zurich had been laid in the hearts of the people by the clear and effective Gospel preaching to which Ulrich Zwingli had devoted himself with increasing zeal from the time of his coming to Zurich in January, 1519. Experiences of conversion such as Conrad Grebel and Heinrich Engelhart had, were only examples of what must have been the case with many others. At the very outset of his work in Zurich Zwingli had undertaken to preach only the pure Word of God beginning with the New Testament. According to his own testimony, from January, 1519, to April, 1522, he had expounded the Gospel of Matthew, the Acts of the Apostles, the Epistles to Timothy and the Galatians, and the two Epistles of Peter.[26] By August, 1522, he had added the letter to the Hebrews, "in order that the work of Christ might be better understood to His glory."[27] The months following brought "the excellent epistle to the Romans and almost all the epistles of Paul," and by August, 1523, the Gospel of Luke had been included.[28] Grebel must have heard this preaching and these expositions. In the few letters which have been preserved out of this period beginning with the letter dated November 1, 1522, quotations or echoes of the following New Testament books appear: I and II Timothy, I Peter, I and II Corinthians, Romans, and possibly the Gospel of John. In the latter half of 1523 quotations from Matthew, Luke, I Corinthians, Proverbs, and Isaiah appear. Grebel's expressions are strongly colored with Pauline thoughts, new ideas about faith, about the grace and peace of God, about Christ the head of the church, about the calling and service of a preacher,[29] and about the moral life of the Christian who has become a new creature. Accordingly the source of Grebel's evangelical thinking is very likely to be found first of all in the teaching and preaching of Ulrich Zwingli from the pulpit and through personal contact. In what form Grebel read the Bible at this time cannot be said with certainty. Possibly he used the Paraphrases of the books of the New Testament by Erasmus or the German translation of the same by Leo Jud which appeared in the years 1521, 1522, and 1523.[30]

But Grebel's thinking gradually took him beyond his own inner experience into the application of the Gospel to the life of the church in his day. In this also he was following Zwingli, for early in his ministry in Zurich Zwingli began to add to the simple preaching of the Gospel a free criticism of the abuses which had grown up in the old church. He gradually developed a vigorous polemic against the moral corruption among the nuns and priests, and against the superstitious and unspiritual ceremonies of the church. He began to advocate as a fundamental principle the teaching that only such doctrines and ordinances should be maintained in the church as were according to Holy Scripture, and that all others which failed to measure up to this scriptural standard should be abandoned.

This new teaching and program which Zwingli advocated won the quick support of Conrad Grebel as well as of Zwingli's other associates. Indeed he soon became one of the most zealous of Zwingli's supporters, and received public recognition from Zwingli as such by the fact that Zwingli permitted him to add a short poem as an appendix to his booklet *Archeteles,* which was published August 23, 1522. In this poem Grebel appeared before the public as a staunch co-worker of Zwingli in the cause of the Gospel. Zwingli's high opinion of Grebel is also indicated in a letter to Myconius dated August 26, 1522, in which he heartily invited Myconius to come to Zurich, for in Zurich he would find himself in the midst of good friends: "You will be with Utinger, Engelhart, and Rey, the congenial older men; with Erasmus, Zwingli and

Grossman, who are by no means to be despised; and with Grebel, Ammann and Binder, the most excellent and learned younger fellows."[31]

Outside of Zurich, Zwingli's friends were becoming increasingly aware of the importance of this promising young scholar for the cause of the Reformation. For instance, Melchior Macrinus wrote from Solothurn on the fifteenth of October, 1522, to Zwingli that he had heard that Grebel had developed into an exceptional promoter of the Gospel, a fact which gave Macrinus great joy, for such gifted and learned young men could render the Gospel and the world a great service; furthermore there were in Zurich, thanks to Zwingli's work, more true Christians than anywhere else in Switzerland.[32] In two other letters to Zwingli dated January 25, and March 6, 1523, Macrinus closes with greetings to "Grebel and the church of Christ," no other name being mentioned.[33] Johann Zwick of Riedlingen also remembers Grebel in his letter to Zwingli of November 27, 1522,[34] and Berchthold Haller of Bern greets only Grebel and Leo Jud in his letter of May 9, 1523, to Zwingli.[35]

The intimate fellowship between Zwingli and Grebel during this time is proved from various sources. Zwingli testified to it three years later, after the fellowship had been broken, in a letter of March 31, 1525, to Vadian in which he complained of Grebel's attacks against him and accused him of ingratitude, since Grebel "had received so much from him." Grebel himself had the highest opinion of Zwingli at this time. He calls him "a man of the highest integrity" (*vir incorruptissimus*),[36] and in July, 1523, he characterizes a book of Zwingli as "a most Christian book" (*liber perchristianum*).[37] Grebel was often the channel through which contacts between Vadian and Zwingli were made. On two occasions Vadian inquired of Grebel concerning Zwingli's purposes in regard to writing several books. To one of these inquiries Grebel replied that Zwingli had no intention at all of writing about the Mass, and Grebel should know, because Zwingli was living so near to him that he had only to stretch out his hand to touch him.[38] On another occasion, when the question of the appointment of a certain Schappeler as pastor in Winterthur was up, Grebel had confidential information about the matter and was asked by Zwingli to write to Vadian about it because Zwingli was too busy to do so. "We," says Grebel, meaning Zwingli, himself, and his father, "are performing our duty in the matter diligently."[39] Again on July 14, 1523, Grebel was the agent for Vadian in carrying through a plan to get three hundred copies of a newly published book by Zwingli sent to the fall fair at Nürnberg.[40] Several times in 1522 and 1523 Grebel sent the most recent writings of Zwingli to Vadian,[41] and once, at the end of 1522, he expressed his regret to Vadian that Zwingli was so overwhelmed with work and problems in Zurich that he did not have the time to prepare a written confutation of the enemies of the Gospel in St. Gall.[42] Grebel also procured copies of Zwingli's writings in 1523 for Pastor Benedikt Burgauer in St. Gall.[43]

The close relationship between Grebel and Zwingli was maintained until the second Zurich disputation between the Zwinglians and the Catholics in October, 1523. Grebel was happy to work at Zwingli's side, and recognized him as a true and faithful shepherd and leader of the church of Christ. In this period the views of the two men must have coincided in all essential respects. Positive evidence of this is available on two points. In the matter of tithes, one of the burning issues of the day, Grebel indicated agreement with Zwingli.[44] The other point is still more significant. Lorenz Hochrütiner of St. Gall had been condemned in Zurich in the fall of 1523 for assisting in a bit of iconoclasm. Both Grebel and Zwingli undertook to come to Hochrütiner's aid. Each wrote a letter on almost the same day, viz., November 11 and 12, 1523, in which they protested against the decision of the court, indicated their desire to help, and requested Vadian to receive Hochrütiner as a true Christian and to give him all the support that he needed.[45]

It will be of interest to discover what other activities Grebel engaged in during the time of his support of Zwingli, and to see whether possibly during this early period there were any connections between him and his later co-workers in the Anabaptist movement. Unfortunately there is extremely little material available on Grebel's public activity from February, 1522 to October, 1523. His own letters contain practically nothing of this sort. His interest in the Schappeler matter has already been reported. Another matter mentioned in his letters, is his interest in the affairs of the convent at Oetenbach where his father's sister, Agathe Grebel, was a nun. He knew about the decision of the city council regarding the release of the nuns, and about the appointment of Leo Jud as vicar of the convent, although of course he did not participate personally in either case.[46]

One rather interesting affair in which Grebel was involved is reported in the records of the Zurich council, as well as in the chronicle of Bernhard Wyss. It was not very important as such, but it is significant because of the attitude expressed by Grebel in it. On July 7, 1522, Conrad Grebel, Claus Hottinger, Heinrich Aberli, and Bartlime Pur, were summoned before the council and were "forbidden to speak anymore against the monks in the pulpits, and were required to cease disputing and speaking about these things."[47] The brief and somewhat ambiguous record in the archives does not tell the full story. According to testimony before the court in regard to the affair, there must have been considerable disturbance in connection with the trial. This is confirmed by Wyss. A witness reported that one of the councilmen, a certain Schlininger, had complained about the obstreperous attitude of the accused, and expressed the opinion "that the devil was sitting in the council chambers." Immediately Grebel is reported to have answered, "The devil is not only sitting in the council chambers, but he is sitting on the bench where the councilmen sit, for one of the councillors has said that one might as well preach the Gospel to a dung heap; and if the councillors stand in the way of the progress of the Gospel, they will themselves be destroyed." The witness who was reporting the above conversation added, "The councillors remained silent after this attack, and permitted the accused to go, for they had no desire to discuss the matter further."[48]

The significance of this affair is not quite clear. It is hardly possible that the four accused had been speaking against the monks from the pulpits, for they were laymen. Most likely they had been active in the growing agitation against the monks, following the leadership of Zwingli, and had been called to account by conservative elements in the city council. But when the case was brought before the council, the lords did not know what to do, for as Grebel cleverly suggested, there was a division of opinion in the council itself, and so the accused were dismissed without punishment. Without a doubt the incident proves that Grebel was among the most zealous of the lay supporters of Ulrich Zwingli, and that he, a young patrician, was not afraid to participate in public demonstrations with the common man and take the consequences involved, even to the point of challenging the city council. Already in this affair he demonstrated his ability to lead in a popular movement.

It is not known whether Grebel participated in further active demonstrations by the aggressively evangelical elements in the population who gathered around such men as Heinrich Aberli, Claus and Jakob Hottinger, Bartlime Pur and others. The archives of the city, as well as the accounts written by the various chroniclers of the time, are altogether silent about Grebel's activities except for the above affair in July, 1522. Several other interesting incidents are reported at which one might expect to find Grebel as a participant, but in no case does Grebel's name appear in the list of those involved. For instance at the end of May, 1522, a dinner was given at the large house called *Lindenhof,* which involved some of the aggressive elements, but Grebel's name does not appear among the list of participants.[49] The same is the case at the dinner which was held in Christoph Froschauer's house in April, 1522, at which there was an open breach of the Lenten fast by such prominent persons as Zwingli, Leo Jud, Utinger, and Binder.[50] Again, in the spring of 1523, a popular movement set in against some of the practices and ceremonies of the church which finally concentrated in opposition to "images" in the church and involved some iconoclasm. When, in September, 1523, Hochrütiner, Hans Oggenfuss and Klaus Hottinger participated in breaking off the crucifix at Stadelhofen, Grebel (as well as Zwingli) defended the act (as mentioned earlier), but made it quite clear that he himself was not involved, and that he would not have thought of taking part in such activities. From the very beginning of his participation in the Reformation Grebel took no part in acts of violence. His service was not to consist of precipitous and ill-considered attacks against men and things, but in an incisive proclamation of the Word of God and a demand for an unconditional obedience to the Gospel.

This attitude of Grebel is still further and more clearly indicated in the tithes issue which came to the fore in Zurich in 1522 and 1523. In a letter of July 13, 1523, he spoke sharply about the attitude of the Zurich city council on the question of tithes. He called the city fathers "Turks and tyrants," said they were acting as "the world," and suggested that they should properly be called "the destroying fathers."[51] But he never proposed that the citizens of Zurich should withhold payment of taxes and tithes, and he did not participate in the revolutionary movement of 1523 among the common people to refuse the payment of taxes and tithes. His attitude on the question of tithes was exactly that of Zwingli, who as early as the summer of 1522 had flatly declared that tithes were not consistent with divine righteousness, and that the whole institution of tithes smacked of tyranny.[52] It is essential to emphasize the unrevolutionary character of Grebel's attitude at this point in order to prepare for a just evaluation of Grebel's attitude later, after the break with Zwingli.

It is not clear to what extent Grebel established connections at this early time (1522-1523) with his later co-workers in the Anabaptist movement. Since he felt himself to be a thoroughgoing follower of Zwingli, there was no occasion for him to participate in the formation of a separatist party of any sort. Although, as was related above, Grebel was active with men like Aberli, Pur, and Hottinger in some of the agitation against the monks, yet there is no evidence that he established a permanent or organized connection with them. Andreas Castelberger, who had been in Zurich since 1516 as a bookseller and conducted Bible classes as early as May, 1522, for certain small groups, seems to have been operating on an independent basis.[53] There is no evidence of any connection between him and Grebel in 1522-23. Simon Stumpf, parish pastor at Höngg since 1520, a member of the inner circle of Zwingli's friends to which Grebel also belonged. But he does not seem to have been prominent in any public agitation until the autumn of 1523, although he did preach in September, 1522, against tithes.[54] Wilhelm Reublin did not appear in Zurich until November 1, 1522, when he was summoned before the court because of violation of the regulation concerning fasting. He had been expelled from Basel in the summer of 1522 and had received an appointment as pastor in Wytikon near Zurich sometime in the autumn of that year.[55] Ludwig Hätzer, who was not a citizen of Zurich but is supposed to have been a chaplain at Wädenswil about this time, published a tract against images in the summer of 1523.[56] Nothing is known of contact between Grebel and the two non-Zurichers Reublin and Hätzer, but there is even less reason to assume any significant relationship with them than with Castelberger and Stumpf. As for Felix Manz, all that is known of him at this time is that he had left Zurich for Paris in 1520 with a royal scholarship and probably did not return before 1522 when he is reported to have been zealous in the study of Hebrew with Zwingli.[57]

It is therefore clear from the evidence at hand that there was no "radical party" in Zurich in 1522 and 1523 as has often been asserted, and that Grebel was certainly not the leader of any such party. There were a considerable number of zealous supporters of Zwingli who had been stirred by the power of his preaching and who had a zeal for the Gospel which constrained them to active participation in every way possible in the movement of reform. The common, unlearned man of this type turned either to personal Bible study with the help of "teachers" like Castelberger, or tended to expression in the form of criticism of the monks and of the ceremonies and images. The more learned and cultivated men among Zwingli's supporters, pastors like Stumpf, Reublin and Hätzer or young humanist scholars like Grebel and Manz, were at first little interested in the activities of the other type of people. They devoted themselves to the higher studies, or to discussing with Zwingli ways and means by which the reform movement might be promoted, and no doubt frequently urged him to more active steps. There is no evidence whatsoever that any substantial differences existed in teaching or in general reform program between Zwingli and these men who were later to become Anabaptists. Zwingli himself had not yet formulated thoroughly his own program; he was still feeling his way step by step.

Gradually, however, the reform movement gained momentum as the religious ferment among the people increased. By the summer of 1523 there was a widespread demand for the inauguration of practical measures of reform which would do away with the "abominations" of the papal church. No doubt Zwingli welcomed this development, and yet it forced him, as a leader of the religious life of the city, together with the civil authorities who had the legal responsibility, to come to a decision as to what should finally be done, and whether the time had come to actually inaugurate reform. The first Zurich disputation of January, 1523, and the accompanying decision of the council had opened the way for the Gospel in Zurich. But that was not enough, for it provided only in a general way for evangelical preaching. In order to prepare for the definite reform of church life through the abolition of images and the Mass, Zwingli and the city council appointed a second disputation to be held October 26-29, 1523. But when this second disputation likewise produced no positive decision to inaugurate reform, many in Zurich were disappointed. Among the dissatisfied appeared most of those who later participated with Conrad Grebel in the Anabaptist movement, but certainly this was not due to any previous organized connection or to any concerted agreement among them.

The failure to take action was perhaps more keenly felt by Conrad Grebel than by anyone else in Zurich. His dissatisfaction with the delay was to be the beginning of a gradual change in his attitude toward Zwingli and Zwingli's program. From close co-operation with Zwingli he was to move more and more in the direction of opposition, until finally when the transition had been completely made he was to become in January, 1525, the leader of the Swiss Brethren.

VII

THE SEARCH FOR THE TRUE CHURCH[1]

1523—1524

The Transition Period

November, 1523, to January, 1525

The leaders of the Reformation in Zurich sought to revive the "pure Gospel." For Zwingli and the evangelicals the Word of God as found in the Scriptures of the Old and New Testaments was the foundation truth which contained this Gospel, and the apostolic church was the first and true embodiment of it. In the spirit of the Gospel and according to the example of the apostles the church of Christ was now to be re-established, with the individual evangelical Christian enjoying his spiritual privileges to the full. The sermons which Zwingli preached in Zurich had created a powerful demand for evangelical "truth," and the people at first could not get enough of it. In a short time a large part, possibly even the majority, of the population of Zurich fell under the influence of the new movement,[2] and, in their own opinion, became "evangelical." That is, they desired to accept the new teaching and to reform the worship and ceremonies of the church as well as the life of society in general after the pattern of the Gospel. For the mass this reformation meant to be obedient to God in all things according to the new knowledge of the Scriptures, especially of the New Testament; and the population as a whole accordingly was set in motion toward this goal. As early as the year 1521 Zwingli felt certain that the victory of the evangelical cause was guaranteed, and in the year 1523 he confidently expected nothing less than a constantly increasing spread of the Gospel among the people.[3]

When Zwingli and the people considered themselves to be "evangelical," they thought in general of the "Gospel" as a more or less clear and fixed entity to be found in the Scripture, out of which it would be possible to secure the guidance necessary to meet the needs of the church. As a matter of fact, however, no one had systematically thought through the "Gospel" and outlined a clear program which was accepted by all. The concept "Gospel," as current among the people, covered a multitude of diverse religious and ethical notions, some of which had arisen out of Zwingli's preaching, some of which were derived out of the constantly growing number of popular religious tracts, and some of which were the result of personal study of the Bible. The thirst for a greater knowledge of the Gospel was so great, and there were so many who either could not read or could not readily interpret, that many of the common people gathered around "readers" to whom they listened for exposition of the Scripture. This led to a popular movement in Switzerland for the organization of so-called "Bible schools," such as the previously mentioned "school" conducted by Andreas Castelberger in Zurich, as well as groups such as those which gathered around Johannes Kessler in St. Gall. It is to be assumed that leading men like Zwingli welcomed such popular groups for Bible study, for this was exactly what all of them, from Erasmus on down, had advocated, namely that the common man should drink at the fountain of life. However there is reason to believe that at times the religious leaders were not altogether well-disposed to such activities, being fearful of possible complications among the people. In these groups expression could be given to the social needs and the economic desires of the common man, and to his hope to be freed from the burdens which lay heavy upon him, such as tithes and rent, as well as to his conviction that he ought to have a share in determining the course of the Reformation. Again, such groups would naturally stimulate the development of popular leaders who would derive out of their own convictions and out of the enthusiastic support of the common people in the groups in which they were functioning as readers or leaders a sense of commission as servants of the Gospel and co-laborers in the Reformation.

The longer Zwingli, the recognized leader of the church, postponed a concrete program of reform, the greater grew the danger that the whole evangelical movement would suffer because of the development of parties or factions, each promoting its own program of reform. Another great danger was that individuals, stirred to a deep enthusiasm for the Gospel, would ultimately undertake direct action to eliminate "unevangelical" conditions, such as the papal "abominations" of the Mass and images, and the economic and social injustices of the time. It became increasingly necessary therefore that the leader of the Reformation movement in Zurich should march ahead of his followers and lead them step by step in the removal of the old abuses, and in the constructive work necessary in establishing the new Gospel church.

Because of the delay in the inauguration of Zwingli's reform program some of the above-mentioned possibilities actually began to appear in Zurich in the year 1522, although only in isolated form. In the year 1523 more of the same things happened. For four years Zwingli had been preaching against the unscriptural abuses of Catholicism; he had been preaching that the Mass was an abomination against God, that tithes and usury were not consistent with divine righteousness, and similar doctrines. But nothing happened; everything remained as it was. Many began to demand some concrete evidence of the change; they desired deeds as well as words, feeling it to be an intolerable burden to their consciences to participate in ceremonies such as the Mass which had been condemned again and again from the pulpit as sinful and devilish.[4] This was the case not only in Zurich but wherever the Gospel had actually made its way into the hearts of the people. In Wittenberg, for instance, Carlstadt felt the pressure so strongly that in the year 1521 he began to abolish many of the rites and ceremonies of the Catholic Church and to substitute for them a new evangelical system of ordinances and regulations.[5] Luther on the other hand felt that the time was not ripe for such measures and promptly cancelled the changes which Carlstadt had introduced in his absence at the Wartburg.

In the year 1523 it appeared that Zwingli finally was ready to begin with practical reform, but unfortunately the local situation in Zurich was such that he could not proceed without the consent of the civil authorities, since they had assumed full civil and ecclesiastical authority over the church after the nullification of the episcopal authority of the bishop of Constance in 1522. Zwingli was convinced that he should proceed in full co-operation with the city council, and not undertake anything against their wishes or without a specific ordinance which would make the changes permanently valid; but this meant that he was not planning to set up a new type of autonomous church free from all connection with the civil state, to take the place of the existing Catholic church-state system. It is possible that he contemplated doing so for a time, or at least that he had assumed all along that the city council would willingly follow his leadership whenever he was ready for practical measures, particularly since they had seemed to adopt the evangelical program in principle by various decisions of the council in the years 1520 to 1523; but when, in the disputation of October 26, 1523, it became clear that in spite of Zwingli's own willingness to proceed, the council preferred to postpone action, Zwingli was faced with the necessity of making a fundamental decision. Either he would endeavor to proceed without the consent and support of the council, or he would subordinate his practical program to the wishes of the majority and wait for official action. His final decision was in favor of the second course. It is quite probable that he was not fully aware of the significance of his decision. What he actually did, however, was to subordinate the work of reform, and therewith the life of the church, to the authority and power of the civil state, and in effect to adopt the principle of the state church. To be sure, Zwingli conceived the civil authority of Zurich to be a Christian authority, one composed of members of the church and ordained by God as a *Corpus Regens,* but the idea that Zwingli's church was to be organically related to a *Christian* state does not change the fact that Zwingli's church was in essence a state church.[6] Neither is this basic fact altered by the intention of the city council to place themselves "under the Gospel" in all their actions affecting the church. The essential issue was, who was to decide how the Gospel was to be interpreted and applied; was it to be the officials of the civil state, or the officials of the church.

It can be demonstrated that Zwingli did not have this conception of the church, and of the relation of state and church, at the beginning of his work as a reformer. At that time, when the new movement was still in its infancy and was still under the power of the Catholic civil authority because the majority of the populace was Catholic and only the minority evangelical, Zwingli thought of the church as a suffering church which would have to suffer persecution in the world and be established again with blood as it had been in the time of the first apostles. He gave expression to this view in a very important letter to Myconius, dated July 24, 1520, which is characteristic for his position at that time. The occasion for the letter, to be sure, was the personal persecution which Myconius had to suffer in Lucerne for the sake of his evangelical faith, but the fundamental principles are the same and have equal validity for the Christian church at large. Zwingli said for example: "Christ said to the apostles, 'in the world you will have tribulation'; and at another time, 'you will be hated by all men for my name's sake,' and 'the hour will come when those who kill you will think that they are doing a service to God.' So there will always be people who will persecute us Christians because Christ is in us, even though they likewise may boast of coming in the name of Christ. Such, however, as obey the law of men rather than the law of God, manifestly lack the marks of Christ, if they place His commandments lower than their own. . . . Is this not the fire which will make the work of each man manifest and bring it to the day, whether he is fighting for the honor of the world or for the honor of Christ? . . . Admonish such, that the fiercer the battle becomes, the more cruel the persecution becomes, the less right they have to surrender the battle in cowardice. For I desire to tell you openly that I believe that just as the church was born in blood, so it can only be renewed by blood, not otherwise. . . . Never will the world accept Christ, and even the promise of rewards by Christ is accompanied by the promise of persecution. He sent out His own like sheep among wolves."[7]

In January, 1523, Zwingli still believed that "the worldly lords," that is the city council of Zurich, should not have the right to decide finally about spiritual things. He expressed this view in so many words during the first disputation of January, 1523, in reply to a question by Faber which was as follows: "How would it be if I should propose that my lords of Zurich should act as judges? Would you accept the same and let them decide?" Answer by master Ulrich Zwingli: "In worldly things and actions I know well that on account of resistance judges are necessary, and I would be very glad to accept my lords of Zurich as judges. But in matters concerning divine wisdom and truth I would accept no one as witness and judge except the living Scriptures and the spirit of God which speaks out of the Scriptures."[8]

When Zwingli, in October, 1523, in contrast to his bold assertion of the previous January, agreed to let the extent and speed of the Reformation in Zurich be decided by the civil authorities, he was compelled to accept a compromise solution of the whole reform question and to recommend this compromise to the people for acceptance. The process of compromise was begun in the matter of tithes, when the city council decided on June 22, 1523, that the tithes must remain in spite of the popular demand that they be abolished.[9] In this question Zwingli appears to have changed his mind and to have abandoned his earlier position so that he probably was in agreement with the action. The second and major step in the process of compromise occurred at the time of the second disputation in October, 1523, when Zwingli recommended that the decision in the matter of abolition of the mass and images be referred to the city council.

The process of compromise and postponement upon which Zwingli now embarked resulted in a considerable change in the attitude of the more aggressive part of the evangelical population toward him. Whereas earlier the members of this group had frequently indicated their determination to co-operate with Zwingli in his program, even though at times this co-operation was expressed in some extreme attitudes and actions, they now began to manifest unrest and disquiet over the outlook. The fear arose that possibly after all the Reformation might fall short of full obedience to the Gospel.

However it is easy to arrive at a false picture of the situation. Two errors must be avoided. In the first place one should not equate the zealous and enthusiastic, though sometimes premature, attack upon existing abuses in the earlier years, which arose out of sound evangelical convictions and which was intended as support of Zwingli's work, with the criticism and opposition against Zwingli which set in in the year 1523. These two attitudes are to be kept quite distinct, even though they were adopted in succession by the same people. Zwingli himself recognized the distinction. For example, he did not condemn but rather condoned the iconoclastic action of Jacob Hottinger and Lorenz Hochrütiner in tearing down the crucifix at Stadelhofen.[10] It is not permissible therefore to draw a straight line from the agitators of 1522 to the Anabaptists of 1525 and label all the deeds and expressions of that time which were not as moderate as those of Zwingli himself as part and parcel of an opposition program and as the beginning of a counter action. Genuine opposition to Zwingli did not set in until after the second disputation of October, 1523.

In the second place it is not permissible to speak of a "radical party" in these early years, as has very frequently been done, and as Emil Egli for example has done in his introduction to the commentary on Zwingli's book, *Von Göttlicher und menschlicher Gerechtigkeit,* and in his introductions to the commentaries on several other writings of Zwingli of this same year.[11] Since this has been said in the previous chapter it will be sufficient to point out here that in the years 1522 and 1523 there was in Zurich no continuing group which was responsible for a succession of "radical" acts and attitudes, but rather a number of individual persons and small circles of friends who participated in occasional expressions. Certainly there was no definite group of opponents to Zwingli before the summer of 1524.

It is particularly misleading to speak of a party in connection with Conrad Grebel before 1524. Grebel was later the leader of the Anabaptists, and if one thinks of a party before 1524 one would naturally be inclined to place Grebel at the head of such a "radical" or "strict" party. A careful examination of the sources however makes it plain that until 1524 Grebel stood more or less alone in his attitudes. There is no evidence, for instance, that he took part in the "school" which Andreas Castelberger conducted; nor was he a member of the Zollikon group. There is no evidence that he joined Simon Stumpf and Wilhelm Reublin in their protests in the summer of 1523. The temptation to picture a more or less stable group of opponents to Zwingli in 1523 in which Grebel, Manz, Stumpf, Castelberger, Reublin, Hochrütiner, Aberli and the Hottinger brothers worked together, must be rejected, for there is no support for such a view in the sources.

Certainly Conrad Grebel, in the summer and autumn of 1523, was not the leader of a radical opposition against Zwingli. Until the second disputation in October he was a faithful and devoted follower of Zwingli. And in no sense was he a "revolutionary," either at that time or later, as he himself asserted vigorously to the city council in his petition of December, 1524.[12] It was only as the consequence of the later developments that he was finally forced, against his own preference, out of a position of friendship and support, to one of opposition to Zwingli.[12a] This transition can be clearly traced on the basis of available sources. It is understandable, justifiable, and inevitable on the basis of his fundamental convictions.

The first expression of definite opposition by Grebel occurs in a letter to Vadian written in December, 1523. "The Gospel is in a very poor way with us here (if you will believe a suspected character, Grebel, rather than a liar, Zwingli), and this evil condition began at the time when you, by the wise decision of the council, served as the president of the disputation. At that time (God sees and hears) the Word was overthrown, trodden under foot, and enslaved by its most learned heralds. . . . Here is an axiom: who thinks, believes, or says that Zwingli is performing his duties as a shepherd, he thinks, believes, and says ungodly things."[13] This bitter judgment against Zwingli expresses vividly the great disappointment which Grebel had experienced in the man whom he had followed so devotedly hitherto. What brought the young man who had stood wholeheartedly by Zwingli's side and had rejoiced but a year earlier in the victory of the Gospel in Zurich under Zwingli's leadership, to the conviction in December, 1523, that the Gospel was now in grave danger? Grebel boldly asserts that the shepherds in Zurich had denied the Word of God and had not been faithful to it, and that this unfaithfulness to the Word had come to light for the first time at the time of the October disputation; what had happened since that time had only confirmed the seriousness of the breach. Let us examine the record of this disputation to see what actually occurred to convince Grebel that he could no longer follow Zwingli.[14]

The disputation had been arranged to bring about a clarification in the matter of Mass and images. Zwingli expected this clarification to take the form of a decision by the city council that he and Leo Jud, who had been commissioned by the council to expound the Scripture as it applied to the two matters at issue, had proved that the Mass and images were "unevangelical" and should be abolished, for he says, "The authorities dare not order anything else than that which the holy and unchangeable Scripture of God teaches. If they fail to do so, and adopt some other course, which I do not expect, I would none the less severely preach against them with the Word of God."[15] Conrad Grebel and many others expected Zwingli to keep his word.

The disputation lasted three days, from October 26 to 28, 1523. According to the record, when the subject of images was discussed on the first day, Conrad Grebel spoke only once to protest against the secret retention of images. He said, "If images are not to be allowed among Christians, they should not be allowed in secret, for that would be a *dispensatio divini verbi.*"[16] The matter which he discussed was not important and no one disagreed with him, but it involved a principle which was important, namely faithfulness to the Word of God.

At the end of the second day, after it had been said repeatedly that the Mass was an abomination against God, and it nevertheless appeared that the meeting was to be closed without a definite decision, Grebel took the floor again to request that definite steps be taken and to propose that the priests should be instructed to cease conducting the Mass, for if this should not be done the whole assembly would have been in vain. Grebel also insisted that other abuses of the Mass should be discussed before the discussion on this subject should be closed as had been suggested by the burgomaster when he announced that the assembly would proceed to an examination of the question of purgatory.[17] Grebel's demand gave occasion to a most important discussion. Zwingli replied rather briefly to Grebel's proposal with the statement, "My lords will decide whatever regulations are to be adopted in the future in regard to the Mass." But this reply by Zwingli was altogether inadequate for those who wanted deeds and not only words. It appeared to some that Zwingli meant to leave the question entirely open, and to permit the city council to decide whether the Mass was after all scriptural or not. This astonishing statement by Zwingli stirred Simon Stumpf to make the reply which Grebel would also certainly have made: "Master Ulrich, you do not have the right to place the decision on this matter in the hands of my lords, for the decision has already been made, the Spirit of God decides." Stumpf closed his remarks with the courageous and open declaration: "If my lords adopt and decide on some other course that would be against the decision of God, I will ask Christ for His spirit, and I will preach and act against it."[18] Zwingli replied to Stumpf that the council was not to decide whether the Mass was scriptural or not, but only what procedure should be used in doing away with the Mass.

The record of the disputation does not state whether the discussion on this point was continued further. One thing is clear, Zwingli's answer was really an evasion. He did in reality do the very thing that he had protested to Stumpf and Grebel he would not do; he left the entire matter in the hands of the city council. He apparently had the confidence that the council would decide rightly, and that it was only a question of practical measures; but from the point of view of his opponents he had in principle submitted to a worldly jurisdiction a matter which they believed was subject only to the decision of the church and its ministers.[19] As a matter of fact it was almost two years (Easter, 1525) before the council finally abolished the Mass after earnest admonition by Zwingli.

A new situation was created by Zwingli's decision, for it is evident that Grebel believed that Zwingli had put the state in a position of dominance in the life of the church.[20] The Scripture was not to have its rightful and supreme place. Rather, human reason and human caution, together with the power of the civil magistrates, were to settle a question of doctrine and life for the church. The spiritual leadership of the church had assembled to decide a question in the light of the teaching of the Scripture, but their united decision could not make itself effective because the government of the church lay in the hands of another group of men who exercised direct civil and military power. Grebel had seen the issue and had put the challenge to Zwingli publicly and irrevocably. It was a major issue of policy for the Reformation. The two men made opposite decisions and from here their ways separated. In fact it is from the decision on this point that two major roads branch off in church history. One road led by way of Zwingli into the state church, while the other road led by way of Grebel and the Swiss Brethren into the free church. The issue is clearer today than it was in 1523, but even then Zwingli was deeply disturbed by the situation in which his decision placed him. He felt the danger of permitting the church to depend too closely upon the civil authority, but he consoled himself with the thought that in Zurich at least the city council constituted a Christian authority, even perhaps determining in his heart that if at some point along the way this Christian state would not follow scriptural principles he would break with it. Conrad Grebel and his friends could not share the confidence of Zwingli; for them such an attitude meant the surrender of a principle.

The decision of Conrad Grebel to refuse to accept the jurisdiction of the Zurich council over the Zurich church is one of the high moments of history, for however obscure it was, it marked the beginning of the modern "free church" movement. It was an historical action which, in effect, demanded the separation of church and state, though certainly without conscious awareness of its far-reaching implications. By it Grebel and the Swiss Brethren who gathered around him in the ensuing years planted the seed out of which has come, through the influence of the Anabaptists in Holland and England, the modern Protestant commitment of freedom of conscience, freedom of religion, voluntary church membership, and separation of church and state.

It may be worth while in passing to refute the charge of "spiritism" which has frequently been made against Simon Stumpf and his associates on the basis of the statement made by Stumpf in the October disputation as quoted above.[21] It is said that when Simon Stumpf demanded that the decision should be made "by the Spirit of God" he was proclaiming the principle of charismatic personal revelation as over against dependence on the written Word of God, and thus setting the "spirit" over against the Scripture. The charge is then frequently expanded into an accusation that the Anabaptists claimed the direct inspiration of the Spirit of God by an inner light to give them authority for their teaching and their decisions. Whatever impression of this sort Stumpf's language may make upon the modern critic, it is clear that it did not make such an impression upon Zwingli. Zwingli accepted Stumpf's principle; it is clear that *he* understood what Stumpf meant to say. In his answer he replaced Stumpf's phrase the "Spirit of God" with the phrase the "Word of God." Furthermore Stumpf did not say, "the decision *will* be made by the Spirit of God," but "the decision *has* already been made." What is meant is perfectly clear, namely, that the Spirit of God in the Scripture had already decided the question. If Stumpf is to be charged with spiritism on the basis of such a statement, then Zwingli must also be charged with the same heresy, for he often used similar expressions, as for instance in his concluding speech at the end of the meeting, where he said: "I admonish you most earnestly that you let God's will rule in those things that the Spirit of God teaches and commands."[22]

Grebel's further contribution to the disputation is of little importance. The chief question had been decided, even though it had been decided wrongly. Nevertheless it is of interest to notice that Grebel participated further in the discussion of the third day, which concerned among other things some of the abuses of the Mass.[23] Since this question had been placed on the order of business for the day at Grebel's personal request, it was natural that he should be given the first opportunity to speak. He excused himself however, when called, saying he was not a good speaker and had not prepared adequately in the matter at hand and therefore requested others to open the discussion. Balthasar Hubmaier then first took the floor. When Grebel spoke soon after, he referred to several minor abuses in connection with the Lord's Supper, namely, the use of unleavened bread, the addition of water to wine, the practice which the priests in general followed of inserting the bread into the mouth of the participant, the tradition of permitting the celebration only in the forenoon and after a fast, the custom of celebrating the Mass only on those days when the service was paid for, and the custom of permitting the priests to serve themselves. All of these are admittedly minor points, but Grebel's entire criticism is after all significant, because it was motivated by the spirit of complete obedience to the Scripture. In spite of a tendency to legalism it was on the whole nevertheless a wholesome attitude, for what he was demanding was that in the reformation of the forms of worship, and indeed in the whole work of the Reformation, all human tradition should be set aside and the Scripture alone should be used as a standard. Grebel's attitude is noteworthy as indicative of the remarkable progress which had been made up to this time by the typical "evangelical layman" in his thinking. He had come far enough to desire a complete break with Catholic tradition, and was willing to substitute for the authority of the past the immediate authority of Scripture.

It has been suggested above that the fundamentally opposite decisions made by Grebel and Zwingli on the major question at issue in the October disputation constituted a break between them. It is perhaps too much to speak of what happened as a break, for no doubt neither man was wholly aware of the ultimate consequences of his decision. There is evidence that the old intimate relations between the two were not immediately broken off and that Grebel still hoped to win Zwingli for his point of view. Actually neither Zwingli nor Grebel had yet fixed his reform program. It would therefore be better to speak of a tension between them than of an immediate crisis. Unfortunately, the period between the letters of December 15, 1523 and September 3, 1524, is almost a complete blank so far as Grebel's correspondence is concerned. The two letters which he wrote during this time were only brief notes dealing exclusively with personal and family matters. We learn that his health was tolerable and that his poverty was well-nigh intolerable, for his debts had risen to sixty guilders and were a heavy burden upon him;[24] but of Grebel's relation to the burning issues of the day we learn nothing. The first letter which resumes the discussion of important matters was dated September 3, 1524. The seven letters which follow in the period until January 4, 1525, contain unusually important information regarding Grebel's inner development, and concerning the small group of associates which was gradually gathering around him.

From the later letters and several other sources it is possible, however, in spite of the hiatus in the correspondence, to reconstruct to a large extent Grebel's development in these eight months. According to the letter of September 3, Grebel had written to Vadian earlier indicating that he was finally ready to step out boldly into the open.[25] When Vadian in his reply inquired as to the causes of this boldness, Grebel answered in a highly significant sentence: "I have waited and they have not spoken, they stand there and do not reply." The sentence is an exact quotation from the speech of Elihu in Job 32:16. In plain words it meant that Grebel had challenged Zwingli to a decision; he had laid a program before him, and Zwingli had refused to accept it. In the letter from which the above extract was quoted, Grebel compared the situation in which he found himself with the situation of ancient Israel when the leaders turned away from trust in God to trust in men and even in the enemies of God, as pictured in Isaiah 30:1, 3 and Ezekiel 34:18, 19. In this connection Grebel applies to Zurich the prophecy of Daniel, in Daniel 9:27, "The abomination of desolation will be in the temple, and the desolation will continue until destruction and unto the end." In these statements the sharp condemnation expressed in the letter of December 15, 1523, reappears, only now it is no longer applied primarily to a person but to the general situation. Grebel has apparently given up all hope that the situation in Zurich will change for the better. Here at last the break is complete. The letters of September 3 to Vadian, and of September 5, to Thomas Müntzer, show clearly that Grebel had actually turned away from Zwingli and Zurich in the hope of finding adequate evangelical leadership elsewhere.[26]

Grebel does not report in his letters the nature of the program which he had submitted to Zwingli and which Zwingli had rejected, but fortunately Zwingli has done so at four different places, once in his testimony before the court in the great trial of the Anabaptist brethren in Zurich in November, 1525,[27] and three times in the various accounts of the origin of the Anabaptist movement which he inserted into his writings against the Anabaptists.[28]

According to Zwingli's statements, Simon Stumpf, Conrad Grebel, and Felix Manz at different times individually submitted to him and Leo Jud a plan of reform. In general the proposals of the three men were in agreement. They asked Zwingli as the leader of the reform to abandon entirely the previous organization and constitution of the church and to set up a church of believers "according to evangelical truth and the Word of God." In this new church divine righteousness was to reign, tithes and usury were to disappear, and "all things must be in common."[29] Ministers of the Gospel were no longer to live from tithes and benefices, but were to be supported by the voluntary gifts of the church.[30] Within the church sin and vice were to be dealt with in serious earnest, and a real sanctification was to be promoted. Such members of the church as should fall into sin were to be disciplined by the church, and if they did not change their life were to be excluded from fellowship. This new church of the people should then set up a truly Christian civil authority in place of the existing city council which was worldly in character.[31]

The demand of the Brethren that a serious attempt be made to put the Gospel into practice meant a complete breach with the Catholic Church and with the idea of a state church in general as it existed up to that time, but it meant by no means a "separatist church," or a "sect and a party." Grebel, Manz and Stumpf wanted to have only one united church, not a little church outside of the big church, for they believed that the majority of the people would accept their program.[32] They planned no "alley meetings," no "gatherings by night," for they certainly hoped to take possession of the *Grossmünster,* the *Fraumünster,* and all the churches, else they would not have formally laid their program before the official head of the Zurich church, chief pastor Ulrich Zwingli, for adoption. Unfortunately, when Zwingli reported these proposals more than two years later, he was no longer capable of presenting the program correctly in the light of its original setting and in accordance with the spirit in which it was originally given. In the two years that had elapsed since then, due to the actions of Zwingli himself, the Brethren had been compelled to hold "alley meetings" and "gatherings in the dark," in order to have any meetings at all. And because of the pressure of the civil authorities, only a small group of courageous spirits had dared to follow the leaders of the new movement against the mandates of the government. This little group did seem at that time, two years after its origin, to be merely "a new sect." And since they required an earnest and consistent Christianity with a real change in life, they were compelled to separate from the large body of nominal Christians who continued largely in the old careless ways; or rather they were in reality expelled by the great church. Since their original program for a Christian civil authority was rejected, and the existing city council continued to maintain the unchristian tithes and usury, how else could they view that council than as an unchristian civil authority, and the church which had entered into an unholy alliance with it as "unevangelical" and unchristian. After all this had happened, Zwingli looked back over the intervening two years to the time when the group, which now seemed to be a separatist sect, had laid its proposals before him, and was naturally inclined to read back into the original program a plan by the little group to erect "its own special church," and to "reject the civil authorities." But by doing so Zwingli perpetrated a grave injustice against the new movement and stamped it with a character which it had not originally intended to have.

Zwingli's most severe charge against the Brethren, a charge which he repeatedly made, was this, that by their arrogant separatism and self-sufficiency they had brought division and confusion into church, that they considered themselves better than others in their self-righteousness and pharisaism, and that this was the basis on which they had withdrawn from the general church and the general society. But this charge of Zwingli was not historical truth. It was a slander which arose out of the bitterness of Zwingli's passionate fight against the Brethren. In fact, according to Zwingli's own testimony in the great trial of November, 1525, the original proposals had not seemed so bad at all, for when they were submitted he and Leo Jud had received the Brethren "in a friendly manner," and had rejected their proposals in a thoroughly kind and friendly spirit.[33]

In view of what has just been said, the time when the program of the Brethren was laid before Zwingli must have been when Grebel still had some hope that Zwingli would accept such a program. This was before September 3, 1524, which may be taken as the *terminus ad quem*. The *terminus a quo* is more difficult to determine. Zwingli does not say exactly when the proposals were first made, he simply says "formerly." But since Simon Stumpf made similar proposals to those made by Grebel this must have occurred before Stumpf's expulsion from Zurich which took place on December 23, 1523.[34] It is altogether possible that the first proposals were made in the summer of 1523, since Simon Stumpf apparently stood out in Zwingli's memory as the first one to advocate the new program.

It is not stated that Grebel and Stumpf co-operated in the production and promotion of the new proposals, nor that they jointly visited Zwingli. Nor is this asserted of Grebel and Manz. According to Zwingli's report, it was a matter of a number of conversations between him and the individual friends.[35] Zwingli reported the proposals as one final plan, because he wished to summarize the whole development in a few words. It is probable that the proposals developed into a definite program in the course of a number of successive discussions, and that the form in which Zwingli reported the program in his testimony before the court is the form in which he and Leo Jud finally rejected it.

As for Grebel, the following picture will probably approximate the actual course of history. In the summer of 1523 he was still heart and soul for Zwingli, although he was somewhat more insistent upon a change in the matter of tithes and usury than Zwingli was willing to endorse. In the October disputation he saw for the first time that he and Zwingli were not fully agreed in the procedure of actual reform. As a consequence of that discovery, he began earnest discussions with Zwingli in order to secure a clarification of the situation. As he debated with Zwingli, his own thoughts probably took form in a more definite program which he supported with increasing insistence. He endeavored to win Zwingli for this program, but made increasingly less progress toward his goal. When it finally dawned upon him that Zwingli was definitely turned in a different direction he wrote the bitterly disappointed letter of December 15, 1523, to Vadian, which has been described above. But although this letter expressed his private opinion of Zwingli, he still continued in his endeavor to influence Zwingli, in the hope that he, Jud, Grossmann and others might change their views. As the weeks and the months went by and his best endeavors remained fruitless, as "he waited and they answered not," he saw that there was nothing more to do in Zurich. His cause was lost. At that point he turned his eyes elsewhere in the hope of finding men who had more understanding for the program of the Scripture and with whom he could co-operate for the establishment of the kingdom of God as he understood it. The story of his attempt to establish connections with such leaders will be related below.

Meanwhile another development was taking place in Zurich. Others who were dissatisfied sought fellowship together and joined Grebel in his program. They gathered in the homes of friends like Felix Manz, where they read the Scripture, discussed evangelical doctrine and practice, and strengthened themselves under Grebel's leadership for the time when conditions in Zurich should be ripe for definite public action. The names of most of the group are known from the signatures to the letter of September 5, 1524: Conrad Grebel, Felix Manz, Andreas Castelberger, Hans Oggenfuss, Bartlime Pur, Heinrich Aberli, Johannes Brötli, Hans Huiuf, and several unnamed others—less than twenty in number.[36]

The group developed a strong feeling of solidarity in the face of the coming struggle which was strengthened by the persecution which began in the summer of 1524 when the preachers of Zurich publicly denounced them from the pulpits as "rascals" and as "satans in angels' clothing."[37] They held their meetings at night in the street called *Neustadt* in the house of Felix Manz's mother, where Manz occasionally expounded the Hebrew Old Testament, and where Grebel probably may have taught from the Greek New Testament.[38] Castelberger also contributed to the instruction.

In this development various diverse elements were welded together. The popular circle which had listened to Castelberger's Bible expositions earlier, and the Zollikon group around Jacob Hottinger, apparently both furnished some of the personnel of the new group. Added to them was the assistant pastor Johannes Brötli of Zollikon, and from the circle of immediate friends of Ulrich Zwingli, the two young patricians Conrad Grebel and Felix Manz. It was a remarkable group—two scholars who had been at the universities of Vienna and Paris, a pastor, a bookseller, two bakers, a goldsmith, and a stone mason.[39]

(Manz's father, until his death in 1518, had been the chief canon of the cathedral church *Grossmünster*). In the group it is clear that Conrad Grebel was from the beginning recognized as the leader.[40]

Upon the suggestion of Grebel, the group of Brethren in Zurich attempted to establish contact with Carlstadt, Luther and Müntzer in the summer of 1524. Through the writings of these men Grebel had learned something about them and their views. Carlstadt was the first with whom correspondence was started, and since his reply was received by September third Grebel's letter to him must have been written in July.[41] It was followed by a second letter to Carlstadt written by Grebel, and a few days later by a third letter to the same man written by Andreas Castelberger.[42] In the same brief period letters were sent by Grebel to Müntzer and Luther.[43] Just at this time a letter was also received from the brother of Hans Huiuf in Halle.[44] Unfortunately all of these letters have been lost.

Grebel was also gathering material for two small pamphlets which he planned to publish.[45] In such a time of great activity it is no wonder that Grebel refused an invitation from Vadian to come to St. Gall, saying that he could not spare the time from his "cares, labors, studies, and undertakings,"[56] and stating that he would come to St. Gall only if he could accomplish something worth while by his visits, something more than eating and drinking and good conversation. His free time he owed to his wife and to his pupils with whom he was reading the Gospel of Matthew in Greek.

Six weeks later, on October 8, 1524, Grebel had still more important news to report to Vadian. A messenger had come from Carlstadt with a letter and eight unprinted booklets.[47] His name was Dr. Gerhard Westerburg and he had already been six days in Zurich. On the other hand Grebel had to report in the same letter that the opposition in Zurich was growing. Among his own relatives and friends there was scarcely one who remained friendly to him; all had become his enemies.[48] Zwingli himself, in spite of Grebel's personal intervention, continued to denounce him as a satanic hypocrite whose opposition was based on jealousy.[49] In addition to all Grebel's other troubles, his creditors were a constant annoyance to him. But through his difficulties he wanted to learn patience from Christ his Master.[50]

Grebel's extraordinary activity in promotion of his program in the summer of 1524 is a vivid testimony to the strength of his faith and the depth of his conviction. He was throwing everything into the struggle sensing that sometime he would have to make the ultimate sacrifice, but he did not know that the storm was so soon to break.

It is a tribute to the breadth of Grebel's vision that in these circumstances he turned his gaze outward from Zurich and thought of achieving a closer co-operation among those who desired a thoroughgoing reform in the church, as is indicated by the letters mentioned above. By so doing he demonstrated that he was not a small man, thinking only of "alley meetings," but rather one who knew something of the currents of life and thought of the time, and who, although only a young layman, sought with all his strength to relate his movement to these currents and to strengthen it by external alliances.

Grebel's attempt to set up a contact with Carlstadt was logical and right, for of all the figures of the time Carlstadt stood nearest to Grebel and his associates. Carlstadt had attempted and in part had accomplished in Wittenberg what Grebel wanted to do in Zurich. Because of the simplicity of the program Carlstadt felt attracted to the Zurich group as soon as he heard of them, and sent to them his friend and brother-in-law, Dr. Gerhard Westerburg, with the commission to prepare them for his own personal visit.

Carlstadt must have arrived in Zurich in the latter part of October, 1524, to investigate the situation, possibly with the hope of locating there permanently. For some reason or other however, he stayed only a few days and then went on to Basel.[51] Almost nothing is known about his stay in Zurich, and still less about his reason for not permanently attaching himself to the group around Grebel. Perhaps he saw that the group was weak and that it would soon be subjected to the same persecution by Zwingli as he himself had suffered in Saxony. Perhaps he saw that Zwingli had so much power that it would be wholly impossible for the little group to maintain itself against him, and that he himself would probably shortly be expelled from the city as a foreigner. Or perhaps he could not find the necessary basis of agreement with Grebel. At any rate Carlstadt disappeared out of the field of vision of the Brethren. No further communication is known to have passed between them. It is interesting to note that Zwingli felt that the Grebel group prevented Carlstadt from visiting him during his stay in Zurich.[51a]

The second stranger with whom Grebel established a contact was Thomas Müntzer. He had learned of him for the first time shortly before September 3, 1524, through five small pamphlets, two of which had just been published, namely, the *Protestation oder empietung Tome Munzer von Stolberg am Hartzs seelwarters zu Alstedt seine leren betreffende unnd tzum anfang von dem rechten Christen glawben, unnd der Tawfe,* (1524) and the *Von dem getichten Glawben auff nechst Protestation ausgegangen Tome Munzers seelwarters zu Alsted* (1524).[52] The three liturgical pamplets which Müntzer had published earlier and which Grebel also read at this time, made little impression upon him,[53] but the two above-named pamphlets pleased the Brethren so much that they felt themselves powerfully attracted to the author. His writings were for them a strengthening in spirit and a fortification of their faith.[54] As a result, although unknown to Müntzer personally and without any request on his part, they took the initiative in establishing relations, hoping that he would not be offended thereby.[55] Their own statements make clear that the attitude of the Brethren toward Müntzer was based upon the reading of the five pamphlets mentioned above and on nothing else.

The ink was scarcely dry on the last page of the first letter to Müntzer when one of the Brethren, the goldsmith Hans Huiuf, who was a native of Halle a. d. Saale in Saxony and therefore a "Landsmann" of Müntzer,[56] received a letter from his brother who was still living in Saxony, and who had sent with the letter a booklet by Luther. The letter brought some disquieting news about Müntzer's attitude toward the princes, for it reported that Müntzer was advocating war against them.[57] This Müntzer of whom Huiuf's brother wrote was a different man from the one whom the Brethren had come to know in the pamphlets, and they reacted immediately by writing an appendix to the first letter. A grave and disquieting doubt arose in their hearts. Was it possible that this new-found hero of the Gospel might also turn out to be a false prophet like all the others? Was it possible that he was not standing on the rock of Scripture but rather on the sandy foundation of his own human opinions? The new doubt about Müntzer cast its shadow also upon the other heroes of the Gospel whom they had mentioned in their letter to Müntzer, namely Carlstadt, Jacob Strauss and Michael Stiefel. Were they also unreliable? "If you and Carlstadt, Jacob Strauss and Michael should not be wholly sound (as I and my brethren however hope that you are)," writes Grebel, "then would the world truly be in a calamitous condition."[58]

But the letter did not reach Müntzer, for it is to be found today in the original autograph of Grebel in the city library of St. Gall. Grebel had not retained a copy, as he expressly says in the letter, giving as reasons the fact that it was too long, and that the letter carrier was in haste to leave. The latter apparently failed to find Müntzer because he had already left "Alstett" to go into hiding, so he brought the letter back again to its author, for Grebel wrote that "the messenger is to return to us again."[59] Vadian may have found the Müntzer letter among the papers of his brother-in-law after the latter's death in 1526, and through him it finally reached the city library of St. Gall.

The only attempt therefore which Grebel made to establish contact with Müntzer was a failure. Since Hans Huiuf, as will be shown later, never saw Müntzer personally, and since his brother wrote also only that which he had heard, no contact was ever established between the Zurich group and Müntzer.

However about fifty years later, in the year 1572, Heinrich Bullinger of Zurich asserted in his *Reformationsgeschichte* that Grebel and Manz and the Zurich Brethren did have direct contact with Müntzer, and professed to know that this contact was made in the autumn of 1524. He says expressly: "I have related earlier in this history how Müntzer came up into these parts, and there came to him Grebel, Manz, and other restless spirits and drew their Anabaptism out of Müntzer. This doctrine they also began to promote and teach in Zurich."[60] At another place he says: "Müntzer was at Griessen and thereabouts . . . and from Zurich there came down to Müntzer Conrad Grebel, Felix Manz and other restless heads, who later on created a great disturbance in Zurich and who succeeded in publicly promoting Anabaptism together with other seditious teachings."[61] Later authors have followed Bullinger, sometimes adding to his statements, until Emil Egli finally ventured to say in his *Züricher Wiedertäufer,* "Where these teachings came from cannot be definitely proved; but the most plausible explanation is that the widely circulated writings of the head of the German Anabaptists, Thomas Müntzer, were also much read in Zurich; for when later, after September, 1524, Müntzer himself appeared in the neighborhood of Waldshut and spent eight weeks in Griessen, certain restless spirits in Zurich made frequent visits to him there, namely Conrad Grebel and Felix Manz."[62]

In his book on the history of the Anabaptists, *Der Widertäufferen Ursprung* of 1560, Bullinger gives more details on Müntzer's stay in Griessen. "He came down from Nürnberg into the Oberland and on the same journey passed through Basel and came into the Klettgau as far as Griessen where he stayed for several weeks and visited the neighboring villages as well as the county of Stühlingen. . . . Then after he had been eight weeks in the neighborhood of Griessen . . . he returned again to Thüringen."[63] Bullinger does not say, however, in this connection that Grebel and his friends visited Müntzer personally. He only says that they read his writings. "There were in Zurich in the city a number of self-important though otherwise not unlearned men, who had read diligently the books and writings of Müntzer (who was at that time still alive and had not been killed, and as herein reported had been at Griessen and was therefore well known to several) and praised them above the writings of Martin Luther and Ulrich Zwingli."[64]

Only Bullinger reports the visit of Grebel and the Brethren to Müntzer. Müntzer himself says nothing about it, though he does report the brief visit in Basel and the following stay in the Klettgau and the Hegau, in his so-called "confession" of May 16, 1525. He fails to give a definite indication of the time of his journey to South Germany, merely saying "he had not stirred up the revolt in that region, but they had already revolted."[65] It is possible however from other sources to date the movement of Müntzer during his trip south with reasonable accuracy.[66] After his expulsion from Mülhausen in Saxony on September 28, 1524, he went with Heinrich Pfeiffer to Nürnberg. From that city he was also expelled not earlier than October 29, 1524. The journey from there to Basel must have occupied at least five to seven days, and since the visit in Basel was short he probably arrived in the Klettgau on the return journey after the tenth of November. In the first days of January of the next year, 1525, Müntzer was back again in Mülhausen.[67] If the time necessary for the return journey is subtracted, it is clear that Müntzer's stay in the Klettgau and the Hegau could scarcely have been longer than six weeks at the most, not eight weeks, and must have fallen in the second half of November and December. In December Grebel wrote two letters to Vadian, dated the 11th and the 25th, and received one letter from him dated December 28. In the latter part of November and December Grebel and his friends were involved in the discussions with the Zurich pastors, and Grebel submitted his petition of protest and defense to the city council.[68] Carlstadt's visit to Zurich came in the last days of October. In the midst of all this activity there is not the slightest trace in any of the sources of a contact between Grebel and Müntzer, to say nothing of the "frequent visits" which Egli imagined. It seems quite impossible that Grebel should have even heard of Müntzer's presence in the South or that he should have ventured into the area of the peasants' revolt in the region of Griessen. As for Felix Manz, he spent some time in Basel at the end of October and the beginning of November and was busy distributing the newly printed booklets of Carlstadt for a time after this.[69]

As was said above, there is no evidence whatever, except for Bullinger's assertion, that any of the Zurich Brethren had any personal contact with Müntzer. None of the chroniclers of the time have a word to say about it. Not even Zwingli, who said all the discreditable things possible about the Anabaptists in the *Elenchus,* mentions anything about Müntzer, and he would certainly have been delighted to point out a connection between the Anabaptists and the notorious leader of the Peasants' War. Even Bullinger himself says not a word about a personal contact between Grebel and Müntzer in his two books against the Anabaptists written in 1530 and 1560. It is only in his last book, the *Reformationsgeschichte,* which he wrote in the year 1572, fifty years after the supposed events had happened, that he ventured such an assertion. Certainly he would have reported such a serious charge in his earlier books if he had known about it. Did he discover some hitherto unknown source between 1560 and 1572 which gave him new light on the relations between the Zurich Anabaptists and Müntzer, or did he perhaps owe this new discovery to the fantasy of his old age?

The gradual evolution of Bullinger's theory of the origin of the Zurich Anabaptist movement from Thomas Müntzer can be distinctly traced in the three books which he wrote in the period of more than forty years from 1530 to 1572. In his first book of 1530, *Von dem Unverschampten fräfel . . . der Widertöuffern*, the Anabaptists are pictured as only a new sect, a revival of ancient heresies. "Their Anabaptism is not from God but is only a new sect against Christian unity and is a renewal of the heresies of Novatian, Auxentius, and Pelagius."[70] But of Müntzer and the origin of Anabaptism in Saxony not a word is said. When the second book against the Anabaptists, *Der Widertäufferen Ursprung,* was written thirty years later, after Bullinger had the responsibility of leadership in the Zurich church and after sufficient time had elapsed to permit first hand knowledge of the beginnings of the Anabaptist movement in Zurich to fade and make possible the rise of legends, the author was able to report a new theory of the origin of the hated Anabaptist doctrine; namely, that it had arisen in a far-away, foreign land. He says: "About the year of Christ 1521 and 1522 certain restless spirits down there in the Saale River valley in Saxony (among whom a chief leader was Nicholas Storch) arose . . . and from the same crowd Thomas Müntzer arose who also had among his disciples Pfeiffer, Melchior Rinck, and many others."[71] So, as Bullinger reports later again, the great evil of Anabaptism "began down there in Saxony," and the honor of Zwingli and the good name of the Zwinglian Reformation was saved. Fortunately for Bullinger's thesis Müntzer made a trip to South Germany and stopped for a time near the Swiss border. This made it much easier to establish a connection between Saxony and the Anabaptists of Zurich. But in 1560 Bullinger did not venture as yet to suggest such a direct connection. He says only that the spirits in Zurich naturally knew of Müntzer's stay in the South, but insists that they derived their teachings from his writings. It was not until twelve years later that Bullinger dared to make the flat assertion that the Zurich Anabaptists went down to Griessen and drew their ideas from Müntzer in person. And now he even knows the names of those who made the journey, for it was "Conrad Grebel, Felix Manz, and other restless heads."

The explanation of Bullinger's thesis has already been hinted at, but let another state it in precise, well-chosen words. In his excellent monograph, *Das Zwinglibild und die Züricherischen Reformationschroniken* (1929), Jacob Berchtold has proved that Bullinger's history is written with a bias. "Bullinger's fundamental attitude is this: what is good had its origin in his own land, Switzerland, what is bad originated in some foreign territory whence it came into Zurich, as for instance Anabaptism and also the peasants' revolt."[72] Bullinger's bias may have been pious, but this does not change the fact that what he actually did was to falsify the history of the origin of the Anabaptist movement. So long as no material is presented from original sources to prove a personal contact between Grebel and Müntzer, the hoary theory of such a contact must be relegated to the limbo of fiction.

But this does not altogether dispose of the question as to whether Müntzer had anything to do with the origin of Anabaptism, for the possibility of literary influence still remains. Since Bullinger is disqualified, the only source of evidence for such influence is the important letter of Grebel to Müntzer of September 5, 1524, mentioned above. This source is sufficient to decide the question once and for all in the negative. The discussion above has shown that the letter was in essence a criticism of Müntzer's position in the light of certain of his writings which the Brethren had secured after their break with Zwingli and after their own position had been settled. The only addition to Grebel's program after September, 1524, was the introduction of adult baptism. This could not have been due to Müntzer's influence, for, although it may have been ultimately implied in Müntzer's theory, in practice he never advocated adult baptism and never mentioned it in his writings. In fact as late as 1523 Müntzer composed a German liturgy for the baptism of infants.[73] On the question of baptism, the Zurich Brethren and Müntzer went in opposite directions. For Grebel, baptism had increasing significance, and proper baptism was emphasized as a part of the obedience which was required of the church. Müntzer on the other hand developed more and more in the direction of a mystical spirituality in which outward forms such as baptism had no place or meaning. A similar and more radical divergence of views on war and violence can be observed between Grebel and Müntzer, as will be pointed out in more detail later.

Those who insist on a close relationship between Grebel and Müntzer point to a few isolated expressions in the letter, in which Grebel praises Müntzer as a "true and faithful herald of the Gospel," and as "his faithful and dear fellow brother in Christ." They say, did Grebel not tell Müntzer: "You and Carlstadt are esteemed by us as the purest heralds and preachers of the purest divine Word?"[74] These statements were all made by Grebel, to be sure, but further light may be cast upon their significance when it is remembered that Grebel named in one breath Thomas Müntzer, Carlstadt, Jacob Strauss, and Michael Stiefel, as the men upon whom his hope for the future of the Gospel rested. The combination in one group of these four men of rather heterogeneous types was certainly not historically justified but it helps to make clear the motives that Grebel had in praising Müntzer and in accepting him as a brother. Grebel did not know the four men personally at all. He knew them only through their writings or by their reputation. But one common characteristic he saw in all, namely, the will to be consistent in the application of the Word of God to the reform of the church, and of the four Müntzer was the most resolute on this point.

The best understanding of the relationship to Müntzer would be somewhat as follows: When the persecuted Brethren in Zurich who had been cast off by their "unfaithful shepherds," looked out of the darkness of their circumstances into the world and saw there other men such as Carlstadt and Müntzer, who had also been cast off by their leader Luther and had yet not lost heart, they likewise took new courage and hastened without much consideration or careful examination to make friends with them. Their reaction to their discovery of these men was primarily an emotional reaction, and one that is easily understood psychologically in the light of their situation at that time. It is in this sense that we must read the words of Grebel: "We have been wonderfully strengthened and rejoice to find one who is of the same Christian understanding with us and who dares to point out to the evangelical preachers their shortcomings, how that they practice a false forbearance in all the chief articles of faith and act according to their own opinions . . . setting themselves above God and against God."[75] It is in this spirit that Grebel writes at the close of his letter: "Consider us as your brethren and accept this writing as a testimony of our great joy and hope toward you through God, and admonish, comfort, and strengthen us, as you well can."[76] The favorable judgment concerning the new-found brother, Müntzer, was therefore not a theological judgment about his teaching (this they criticized freely), but an emotional judgment about the personality of the man and his general attitude in the hard and bitter conflict of the time. It must be emphatically asserted that the Zurich Brethren attested Müntzer's "common Christian understanding *with us,*" and not the opposite. They endorsed Müntzer because he shared *their* views, not because they shared his.

Although this rather hasty endorsement of Müntzer was not quite justified in view of the substantial differences between them, the situation is not so bad as it seems to us today, for we think of Müntzer as the fanatical prophet and war-lord of the Peasants' War, whereas Grebel knew only the Müntzer of early 1524 as expressed in his pamphlets of that time. The new understanding of Müntzer which has developed in the last years, thanks to Holl and Böhmer and particularly to Lohmann's study, *Zur Geistesgeschichte Thomas Müntzers,* has made it clear that before July, 1524, Müntzer was not nearly so bad as he has been painted. Until that time he was a Christian preacher, first evangelical, then spiritualistic, but not a revolutionary leader. His advocacy of the use of violence did not begin until the second half of 1524, and the advance signs of this new attitude which Grebel observed in September, 1524, were expressly rejected by the group in Zurich. The two chief pamphlets of Müntzer which Grebel read with such satisfaction actually contained very little, apart from a few exaggerations, which would be considered as definitely unevangelical or open to criticism by the modern reader.

From the above it is clear that in the summer of 1524, when Grebel first heard of Müntzer, the two men were standing on independent platforms of fundamentally different character, although Grebel did not yet clearly see this. In any case the attempt by Grebel to establish a contact was unsuccessful. It has also been made clear that a derivation of the teaching or position of Grebel from the writings of Müntzer is impossible. The statement by Correll, "The derivation of Anabaptism from the circle of Thomas Müntzer and the Zwickau prophets is eliminated," deserves full acceptance at least in so far as it concerns the Swiss Brethren, until positive source material has been adduced in support of the contrary.[78]

Just as interesting as the attempted contact with Müntzer, if not more so, is Grebel's attempted contact with Luther, which was made in the form of a letter addressed to him in September, 1524. What led Grebel to write is unknown. Possibly it was the reading of Carlstadt's writings dealing with Luther,[79] possibly merely the general information which he had about him. His intention to write was announced for the first time on September 3, 1524, to Vadian. He says that he had found courage to write through the Word of God in which he trusted.[80] This statement by Grebel must mean that he felt himself justified in admonishing Luther to a different course of action because he felt himself to be more faithful to the Scripture. Grebel certainly did not lack courage at this time, nor the will to creative activity. Unfortunately the letter to Luther has been lost. Even the copy which Grebel retained with the intention of ultimately sending it to Müntzer has also been lost. Luther actually received the letter, for Erhard Hegenwalt reported from Wittenberg in a letter of January 1, 1525, to Grebel that he had inquired of Luther whether he intended to answer the letter, to which Luther gave a negative reply saying that he did not know what he should write, but sent greetings through Hegenwalt so that the group in Zurich should not think that he was "ill-disposed" toward them. Hegenwalt states that he himself had not seen the letter.[81]

Fortunately Grebel reports in the Müntzer epistle something of the content of the letter to Luther. "I, C. Grebel, desired to write to Luther in the name of all of us to admonish him to desist from his forbearance which he is practicing without the support of Scripture, and which he is promoting in the world and in which others are following him. . . . So I wrote in my name and in the name of the other brethren to Luther and admonished him to desist from the false forbearance of the weak, which weak ones they themselves are. . . . We admonished him as well as our leaders here also. If God does not forbid we want to point out their shortcomings and will not fear what may happen to us on account of it."[82] Grebel's letter was therefore an admonition to Luther to follow the Scripture consistently and to apply it as the standard for the reform of the church without paying any attention to opponents. Grebel dealt with the same problem in Luther's case as he dealt with in Zurich in connection with Zwingli's program. The "not unfavorable" attitude of Luther toward Grebel and his friends, as reported by Hegenwalt, would permit the assumption that Grebel presented effectively somewhat the same arguments which he presented in Zurich in contending for the Scripture as the sole authority in the reformation of the church and of Christian life, before which all human opinions should be unhesitatingly surrendered. Grebel possibly said to Luther what he said to Müntzer: "Exercise discipline according to the Word, and establish a Christian church with the help of Christ and His rule[83] . . . be admonished to preach fearlessly the Word of God alone, establish divine customs alone, accept alone what may be found in clear Scripture, and reject, hate, and curse all proposals, words, customs, and opinions of all men, including your own."[84]

There is no evidence that Grebel attempted to establish a personal contact with Jacob Strauss and Michael Stiefel, the "good evangelical preachers" whom he named together with Müntzer and Carlstadt as the hope for the future.[85] His contact with them was only through their writings.[86] Since the question of their influence upon Grebel's thinking is discussed at length in a later chapter it will not be necessary to examine the question further here.

One other outside contact established by Grebel was that with Erhard Hegenwalt, a student in Wittenberg 1524 to 1526.[87] The sole evidence of this is the letter which Hegenwalt wrote to Grebel under the date of January 1, 1525. The correspondence was more extensive than this one letter, for Hegenwalt mentions two letters by Grebel, and an answer by himself. Grebel may have met Hegenwalt in January, 1523, when the latter attended the disputation in Zurich and edited the minutes which were published soon after.[88] Hegenwalt refers to the fact that when he was in Zurich he had prevented Grebel from writing a sharp letter "against the doctor and the preachers in St. Gall."[89] What Hegenwalt refers to is rather uncertain. It is possible that he was in Zurich as late as the summer or winter of 1523, or even the spring of 1524, and that he had persuaded Grebel to refrain from an attack on Vadian and the preachers of St. Gall at that time.

In order to evaluate Hegenwalt's letter properly it is necessary to outline the background of the situation which it assumes. After Hegenwalt's departure from Zurich for Wittenberg, Grebel had written to him in the name of the Zurich group. To this letter Hegenwalt replied with an admonition to the somewhat heated letter-writer to manifest more meekness and modesty, and criticized the attitude of the group in Zurich on a number of points. To this letter the Grebel group replied with a lengthy epistle in which they refuted the criticism with a twelve-point statement, and proceeded to attack Hegenwalt's position. In addition Grebel expressed himself in a thirteenth point on infant baptism, calling it "a foolish blasphemy." The Grebel group demanded an immediate reply so that the letter carrier might bring it to Zurich with him. Hegenwalt endeavored to meet their desire. He pointed out that he had unfortunately devoted so much time and space (more than half of the letter) to the first of the thirteen points, and the messenger was in such haste to leave, that he had time to reply to but six points. Only the first point was answered at length. It is clear from Hegenwalt's statements that the second letter from Zurich to Wittenberg must have been written about the middle of December, 1524, and that the first letter may have been written as early as September, 1524, about the same time that the above letters were written to Müntzer, Carlstadt and Luther. It is not impossible that the letter to Luther and the first letter to Hegenwalt were sent by the same messenger.

Hegenwalt's letter, which was addressed to "Conrad Grebel and his other fellow brethren in Christ at Zurich," gives a partial summary of the contents of the last letter from Zurich to him. Six of the thirteen points which were discussed in the Zurich letter are named by Hegenwalt: (1) How may one know that the spirit of a Christian is of God? (2) The "call," that is, the call to the preaching of the Word of God. (3) Is there to be freedom, according to the Word of God, in outward things, for example in the form of ceremonies? (4) The significance and the practice of the Lord's Supper. (5) Hegenwalt's method of proof is not based upon Scripture passages; he has faith, but it is not according to the Word. (6) Infant baptism.

It is clear from Hegenwalt's letter that he reckons the Grebel group with Carlstadt, for four times he refers them to a new booklet which Luther was writing against Carlstadt and which was soon to be published. He says in fact, at the close, that they will probably find in this booklet Luther's answer to their own letter,[90] meaning thereby primarily an answer to arguments relating to the Lord's Supper. "Martin will tear Carlstadt's arguments to pieces and will show how the devil has broken in and is fighting against the spirit by taking for himself the expression *Hoc est corpus meum.*" This identification of the Grebel group as "Carlstadtian" is noteworthy. It must be based primarily upon a similarity in the teaching of the two men on the Lord's Supper. It is possible that the last letter by Grebel to Hegenwalt reflected the influence of the Carlstadt pamphlets which were printed in Basel at the end of October, 1524, and which were so diligently read and circulated by Grebel's friends. It is also probable that Grebel's letters to Hegenwalt indicated a friendly attitude toward Carlstadt.

The final case of contact with the outside world concerns the person of Dr. Gerhard Westerburg,[91] who had come from Wittenberg to Zurich as Carlstadt's messenger before October 8, 1524. During the period (October 8-14, 1524) of his stay in Zurich, Grebel seems to have read a little booklet by

Westerburg entitled *Of the Sleep of the Soul* (*de Sopore Animarum*).[92] There is no evidence of any influence of this booklet on Grebel's thought nor of any further significance of Westerburg's visit, but it may be of interest to note here that Zwingli in his *Elenchus* attacked certain teachings by the Anabaptists regarding the "sleep of the soul."[93] Hulshof reports that Calvin attacked the Anabaptists on a similar point.[93a]

Dr. Westerburg proceeded from Zurich to Basel to arrange for the printing of several tracts by Carlstadt, accompanied by Felix Manz, and followed shortly after by Carlstadt himself. Evidence brought out in a trial of the printers connected with the printing of the booklets indicates that the Brethren in Zurich, having read the manuscripts of the booklets in advance (Grebel, at least did so), desired to have the booklets printed for distribution in Zurich. Four of them, dealing chiefly with the sacrament of the Lord's Supper, were printed in editions of 1,000 each (the fourth only 800) and delivered to Felix Manz after Westerburg and Carlstadt had left Basel, who brought them to Zurich for sale. The fifth, on infant baptism, which no doubt the Brethren were most anxious to have, was rejected by the printer and never published. According to Zwingli, the Brethren were very active in the sale of the booklets; "they filled town and country with them." Some of the Brethren continued to cherish the books, for in March, 1525, Johannes Brötli wrote from Hallau to the Brethren in Zollikon, "Send me Carlstadt's booklets."[94]

The various attempts which Grebel made to establish contact with like-minded evangelical leaders outside of Zurich have now been surveyed. Only with Carlstadt was there any definite outcome in the form of an actual personal contact. But even with him, no less than with the others, Grebel experienced nothing but disappointment. The hopeful and enthusiastic program which he had begun in the summer of 1524 had come to a fruitless end. Müntzer had not replied; even Grebel's original letter which he had written with such zest had never been delivered. Carlstadt had written him twice, had even visited him, but that was the end. Luther had not answered. Even

Hegenwalt, although friendly, did not agree with him. The weeks and months had gone by and now he stood at the end of the year 1524 with only empty hands as the result of all the labor which he had undertaken. Back again where he was before the letter writing began, alone with the small circle of Brethren in Zurich, cast off by Zwingli, condemned as a devil in angels' clothing, he faced fateful decisions. The pleasant interlude of the letter writing was now past; no hope had come from men; God alone could help for the future.

In the meantime the situation in Zurich had become more critical for the group gathered around Grebel. Since the spring of 1524 the question of infant baptism had gradually come to the fore, not only as a theoretical but also as a practical question. It seems to have arisen first in the villages of Wytikon and Zollikon, rather than in the city of Zurich itself. Under the influence of the preaching of Wilhelm Reublin, at least two fathers in the village of Wytikon had refused to have their children baptized. One of these children was born in February and another in March, 1524. In Zollikon likewise three fathers had withheld their children from baptism, with the knowledge and support of the pastor Johannes Brötli. They did this on the basis of the Word of God, for they said that "according to the Word of God children should not be baptized, but should wait until they come to their years and should be able to testify to their own faith."[95] By August 11, 1524, the question had come before the city council with the result that Reublin was put to prison, where he was to be given a hearing on his teaching by the three pastors of the city and other representatives of the city council. Parents who refused to baptize their children were to be punished with a fine of one mark in silver.[96] The records of Zurich give no further report on the question of infant baptism until January, 1525, but since on January 18, 1525, there were still unbaptized children in Zurich, and since the question was appointed to be publicly debated on January 17, it is evident that the mandate of the council was not obeyed by all.[97]

This practical opposition to infant baptism did not arise in the circle around Grebel. Grebel had heard as early as July, 1523, through pastor Benedict Burgauer of St. Gall that in St. Gall there were people who taught that children should not be baptized because they had no faith of their own.[98] Yet there is no evidence that Grebel shared such views at that time, for there is no reason to doubt that his own second child, born in August, 1523, was baptized. Zwingli's testimony concerning the formal proposals of the Brethren, as related earlier, failed to mention the question of baptism. There is likewise no trace of any interest in baptism in Grebel's correspondence before September 5, 1524. However in the letter to Müntzer of that date Grebel's position on the question of baptism is manifestly so thoroughly established that he must have given attention to the question some time previous to that date. Nevertheless it should be emphasized that it was Wilhelm Reublin and not Conrad Grebel who inaugurated the practical opposition against infant baptism in Zurich.

It is possible that Grebel's attitude on infant baptism was influenced by Reublin, but it is not necessary to postulate such a direct influence to account for Grebel's position. Early in the period of the Reformation questions were raised concerning infant baptism in many places, and in South Germany interest in the question was widespread. Emphasis upon faith was bound to raise the question of baptism sooner or later, for it was apparent that no child could have faith "until it be come to its years." Even Zwingli realized this, admitting in his *Taufbüchlein* (1524) that "outward ceremonies could not strengthen faith in infants, for they cannot believe."[99] There was a sort of inevitability about the development of the opposition to infant baptism, for when the theory of *ex opere operatum* in regard to the functioning of the sacraments was rejected, consistently thinking evangelical minds would find the ground cut from under the practice of baptism upon infants. Where the Protestant church retained infant baptism it therefore was done upon the basis of some sort of compromise. Even such leading reformers as Melanchthon at first taught that baptism was merely an external symbol and was not necessary for salvation.[100] Very early some practically minded persons applied this theory and in practice demanded the abandonment of infant baptism, for instance, the Zwickau prophets in the year 1521, as well as Carlstadt. Luther on the contrary, who had continued to believe, though somewhat inconsistently, in the *regeneratio baptismi,* always held fast to infant baptism.

In Southwest Germany and in Switzerland the reformers were long undecided as to what should be done in the matter of infant baptism. Here the situation was different from that in Wittenberg, for the reformers of the Southwest in general adopted the theory of the symbolic character of baptism and the Lord's Supper, which naturally made it difficult to continue the old practice of infant baptism. As early as 1521 Zwingli had preached "that the little children who are not baptized will not be damned," certainly a teaching which must eventually undermine infant baptism.[101] In May, 1523, he had discussed the question of infant baptism with Balthazar Hubmaier and both had agreed, according to Hubmaier's testimony, that children should not be baptized until they had been instructed in the faith.[102] To be sure, the decision seems to have been a theoretical one, since neither Hubmaier[103] nor Zwingli proceeded to put his new convictions into practice by the abolition of the ancient ceremony. Zwingli himself, in May, 1525, openly admitted that he had earlier abandoned infant baptism because of a conviction that it would be better to baptize children after they had obtained a good age.[104] And Conrad Grebel insisted in December, 1524, that he could not understand Zwingli's defense of infant baptism, for he did not know anything else but that he and Zwingli (as well as Jud and Grossmann) earlier had the same position on this question.[105] Three witnesses asserted that Zwingli had openly preached against infant baptism from the pulpit; they were Hubmaier, Hans Hottinger and an unnamed person.[106] Both Conrad Grebel and Felix Manz insisted that they had been convinced on the question of infant baptism by Zwingli himself.[107] And Usteri says that in the year 1524 Zwingli had come to think of baptism more and more as an act of confession or pledge.[108]

Oecolampad in Basel was considering abandoning infant baptism at the end of 1524, but was convinced to the contrary by Zwingli.[109] As early as August 24, 1524, Gerhard Roussel in Meaux, France, had received news that there were in Basel persons who desired to postpone the baptism of children *"ad annos discretionis,"* and Erasmus himself wrote from Basel in that summer, "Already there are many opponents of infant baptism."[110] In Strasburg in the summer of 1524 infant baptism was made optional.[111] Vadian himself hesitated on the question. He endeavored to comfort Grebel with the prospect that this question would be settled in the course of time as all the other questions had been settled.[112] Thus in 1524 the friends of Zwingli in Basel, Strasburg, and St. Gall were waiting to see what he would do in the question of baptism; they themselves had no definite conviction in the matter and would have been ready to abandon the practice.

It is evident therefore that whatever opposition there was against infant baptism in Zurich in the year 1524 was not specifically a Zurich phenomenon, nor was it anything particularly "anti-Zwinglian" or "anabaptistic." This is probably the explanation for the light penalty which the city council imposed for failure to have children baptized, as well as for its moderation in the early stages of the prosecution of the matter.

To the demand of the Zurich council that unbaptized children now be baptized, the parents involved replied that they would stand by the Word of God and would agree to baptizing their children only after they had been convinced on the matter by teaching from the Scripture.[113] The council accepted the request as reasonable, and ordered that all those who rejected infant baptism as unchristian and refused to have their children baptized, should discuss the matter with the three pastors in the presence of four representatives of the council. Both sides were to present their views on the basis of Scripture. It is not quite clear, but it seems, according to Grebel's account of the matter in his letter of December 15, 1524, to Vadian, that only one head of a family was to be examined at one time. One such discussion had taken place before the 15th of December, but the outcome was not as hoped by the city council, for the father was unconvinced. Grebel reports that the council decided "that they should meet again, as had been done before."

From other sources we learn that the preachers of Zurich had discussions with opponents of infant baptism on two Tuesdays. Zwingli reports this three times, first in a letter of December 15, 1524, to Franz Lambert, then in his *Taufbüchlein,* which was published in May, 1525, and finally in his important book of August, 1527, against the Anabaptists, the *Elenchus.*[114] In his reports he mentions only one participant by name, Ludwig Hätzer, who is said to have taken part in both discussions. Since Hätzer was absent from Zurich until the early part of October, 1524, the Tuesday discussions must have been held in the two months between the middle of October and the last Tuesday before December 15, or December 13, 1524. According to Zwingli's report, a number of Brethren who were opponents of infant baptism took part in the meetings. If this is true, then the discussion between the one father and the pastors which was reported by Grebel in his letter of December 15th, could not have been one of the Tuesday meetings. A further ground for rejecting the identification of these two meetings is Zwingli's report that the city council decided on account of the "danger" to suspend further meetings, although it had originally been the intention to hold a series of them, whereas in Grebel's report the council decided to provide for another meeting similar to the one which had been held. Possibly the two Tuesday meetings were held in November with the undesirable results referred to, after which it was decided to substitute for the more general discussions of the Tuesday meeting type, private meetings with individual fathers who had failed to have their children baptized.

The Tuesday meetings were clearly unfruitful, and led only to a deepening of the chasm between the two sides. Zwingli

PLATE I

The Center of Zurich in 1576—The Limmat River in the Foreground and Zwingli's Grossmünster Church in the Center. Taken from Jonas Murer's *Stadtplan* of 1576 as reproduced in *Bilder aus der schweizerischen Reformationsgeschichte* (Basel, 1917).

PLATE II

The Town and Castle of Grüningen about 1550. Conrad Grebel was imprisoned here in October, 1525. From a drawing in *Codex Monacensis* (Germ. 895 folio 138v) in the Bavarian State Library, Munich, Germany.

Plate III

The Grebel Family Coat of Arms of 1471.
From C. Keller-Escher, *Die Familie Grebel*
(Frauenfeld, 1884).

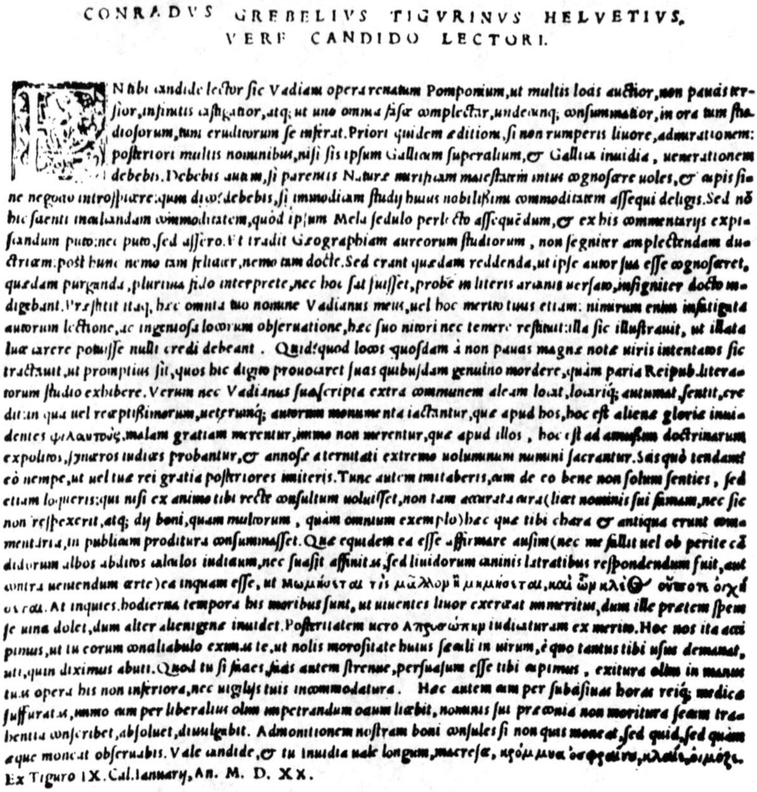

CONRADVS GREBELIVS TIGVRINVS HELVETIVS, VERE CANDIDO LECTORI.

EN tibi candide lector sic Vadiani opera renatum Pomponium, ut multis locis auctior, non paucis terſior, infinitis caſtigatior, atq; ut uno omnia ſaſce complectar, undecunq; conſummatior, in ora tum ſtudioſorum, tum eruditorum ſe inſerat. Priori quidem editioni, ſi non rumperis liuore, admirationem: poſteriori multis nominibus, niſi ſis ipſum Gallicum ſuperalium, & Gallica inuidia, uenerationem debebis. Debebis autem, ſi parentis Naturæ mirificam maieſtatem intus cognoſcere uoles, & cupis ſine negocio introſpicere: quum dico debebis, ſi immodicam ſtudij huius nobiliſſimi commoditatem aſſequi deligis. Sed nõ hic ſuenti inculcandam commoditatem, quòd ipſum Mela ſedulo perlecto aſſequẽdum, & ex his commentarijs expiſcandum puto: nec puto, ſed aſſero. Et tradit Geographiam aureorum ſtudiorum, non ſegniter amplectendam doctricem: poſt hunc nemo tam feliciter, nemo tam docte. Sed erant quædam reddenda, ut ipſe autor ſua eſſe cognoſceret, quædam purganda, plurima fido interprete, nec hoc ſat fuiſſet, probè in literis arcanis uerſato, inſigniter docto indigebant. Præſtitit itaq; hæc omnia tuo nomine Vadianus meus, uel hoc merito tuus etiam: nimirum enim infatigata autorum lectione, ac ingenioſa locorum obſeruatione, hæc ſuo nitori nec temere reſtituit: illa ſic illuſtrauit, ut illata luce carere potuiſſe nulli credi debeant. Quid quod locos quoſdam à non paucis magnæ notæ uiris intentatos ſic tractauit, ut promptius ſit, quos hic digito prouocaret ſuas quibuſdam genuino mordere, quàm paria Reipub. literatorum ſtudio exhibere. Verum nec Vadianus ſua ſcripta extra communem aleam locat, locariq; autumat, ſentit, credit: in qua uel receptiſſimorum, ueterumq; autorum monumenta iactantur, quæ apud hos, hoc eſt alienæ gloriæ inuidentes φιλαυτοὺς, malam gratiam merentur, immo non merentur, quæ apud illos, hoc eſt ad amuſſim doctrinarum expolitos, ſynceros iudices probantur, & annoſæ æternitati extremo uoluminum numini ſacrantur. Scis quò tendam? eò nempe, ut uel tuæ rei gratia poſteriores imiteris. Tunc autem imitaberis, cum de eo bene non ſolum ſenties, ſed etiam loqueris: qui niſi ex animo tibi recte conſultum uoluiſſet, non tam accurata cura (licet nominis ſui famam, nec ſic non reſpexerit, atq; dij boni, quam multorum, quàm omnium exemplo) hæc quæ tibi chara & antiqua erunt commentaria, in publicum proditura conſummaſſet. Quæ equidem ea eſſe affirmare auſim (nec me fallit uel ob peritè cãdidorum albos abditos calculos iudicum, nec ſuaſit affinitas, ſed liuidorum caninis latratibus reſpondendum fuit, aut contra ueniendum arte) ea inquam eſſe, ut μωμήσεταί τις μᾶλλον ἢ μιμήσεται, καὶ ὥρ κλί[illegible] οὕτω τι ὀχ[illegible]σεται. At inquies, hodierna tempora his moribus ſunt, ut uiuentes liuor exercitat immeritus, dum ille præter ſpem ſe uinci dolet, dum alter alienigenæ inuidet. Poſteritatem uero ἀπροσωπόληπτον iudicaturam ex merito. Hoc nos ita accipimus, ut in eorum conciliabulo eximas te, ut nolis moroſitate huius ſæculi in uirum, è quo tantus tibi uſus demanat, uti, quin diximus abuti. Quod tu ſi facies, facies autem ſtrenue, perſuaſum eſſe tibi cupimus, exitura olim in manus tuas opera his non inferiora, nec uigilijs tuis incommodatura. Hæc autem cum per ſubſicinas horas reiq; medicæ ſuffuratas, immo cum per liberalius olim impetrandum ocium licebit, nominis ſui præconia non moritura ſecum trahentia conſcribet, abſoluet, diuulgabit. Admonitionem noſtram boni conſules ſi non quis moneat, ſed quid, ſed quàm æque moneat obſeruabis. Vale candide, & tu inuidia uale longum, macreſce, κρόμμυα ὀσφραίνου, κλαίου, οἰμώζε.

Ex Tiguro IX. Cal. Ianuarij, An. M. D. XX.

PLATE IV-A.

Conrad Grebel's Preface to Vadian's 1522 Edition of *Pomponius Mela.* Reduced facsimile from the copy in the Goshen College Library.

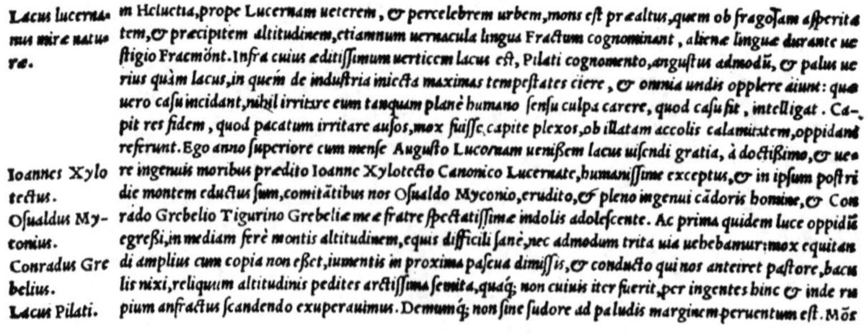

Lacus lucernanus miræ naturæ. — in Heluetia, prope Lucernam ueterem, & percelebrem urbem, mons eſt prealtus, quem ob fragoſam aſperita
tem, & præcipitem altitudinem, etiamnum uernacula lingua Fractum cognominant, alienæ linguæ durante ue
ſtigio Fracmõnt. Infra cuius æditiſſimum uerticem lacus eſt, Pilati cognomento, anguſtus admodũ, & palus ue
rius quàm lacus, in quem de induſtria iniecta maximas tempeſtates ciere, & omnia undis opplere aiunt: quæ
uero caſu incidant, nihil irritare eum tanquam planè humano ſenſu culpa carere, quod caſu fit, intelligat. Ca-
pit res fidem, quod pacatum irritare auſos, mox fuiſſe capite plexos, ob illatam accolis calamitatem, oppidani
referunt. Ego anno ſuperiore cum menſe Auguſto Lucernam uenißem lacus uiſendi gratia, à doctißimo, & ue
Ioannes Xylotectus. — re ingenuis moribus prædito Ioanne Xylotecto Canonico Lucernate, humaniſſime exceptus, & in ipſum poſtri
die montem eductus ſum, comitãtibus nos Oſualdo Myconio, erudito, & pleno ingenui cãdoris homine, & Con
Oſualdus Myconius. — rado Grebelio Tigurino Grebeliæ meæ fratre ſpectatiſſimæ indolis adoleſcente. Ac prima quidem luce oppidũ
egreßi, in mediam ferè montis altitudinem, equis difficili ſanè, nec admodum trita uia uehebamur: mox equitan
Conradus Grebelius. — di amplius cum copia non eßet, iumentis in proxima paſcua dimiſſis, & conducto qui nos anteiret paſtore, bacu
lis nixi, reliquum altitudinis pedites arctiſſima ſemita, quaq; non cuiuis iter fuerit, per ingentes hinc & inde ru
Lacus Pilati. — pium anfractus ſcandendo exuperauimus. Demumq; non ſine ſudore ad paludis marginem peruentum eſt. Mõs

PLATE IV-B.

The Account of the Ascent of Mt. Pilatus as given in the 1522 Edition of *Pomponius Mela.* From the copy in the Goshen College Library.

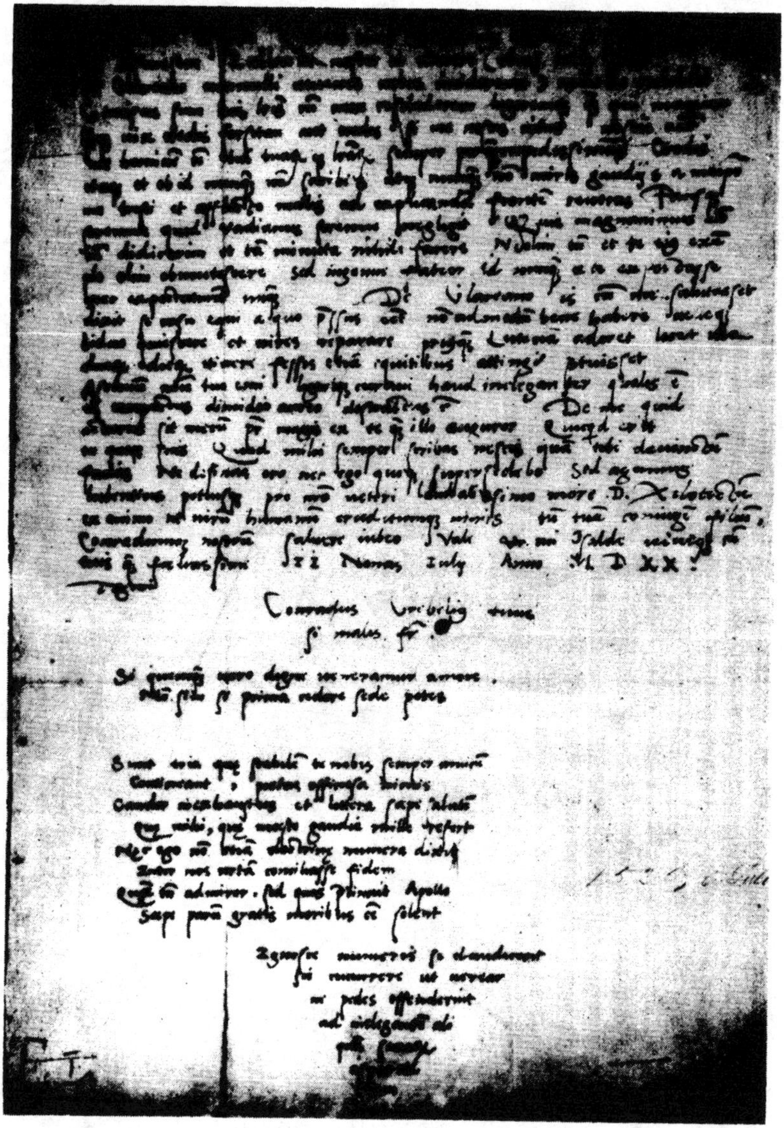

PLATE V

The Letter of Grebel to Myconius of July, 1520. From the original in the Staatsarchiv Zurich (E I.1 Nr. 34), Switzerland. Reduced facsimile.

r iubare ut in una fide unum fiat & eum qui unus eſt per-
tuo poſſideat, Amen. Valete Ex Tiguro. 23. die Augu
Anno. M.D XXII.

Rumpant ilia Epiſcopi uniuerſi
Qui ſunt nomine, re lupi uoraces,
Quod iam rurſus in orbe ueritatis
Lux Euãgelicę uetus refulget,
Atq; hoc, intrepidis trilinguibusq;
Miſſis Luciferis, deo magiſtro.
Imò (uerus enim Propheta dicam)
Quod horum imperium, tyrannidemq;,
Quod claues, Canones librum Simonis,
Parricidia conſcientiarum,
Quod iſta agmina mercium ſacratum,
Bullas, fulmina, Δεισιδαιμονίαν,
Verbum Euangelicum arduis triumphis
Ducit, perpetuóq; uicta ducet,
Qui ſunt nomine, re lupi uoraces
Rumpant ilia Epiſcopi uniuerſi.

Conradus Grebelius in gratiam
reducis Euangelij.

PLATE VI

Grebel's Poem of 1522 appended to Zwingli's *Apologeticus Archeteles*. From the copy in the Goshen College Library.

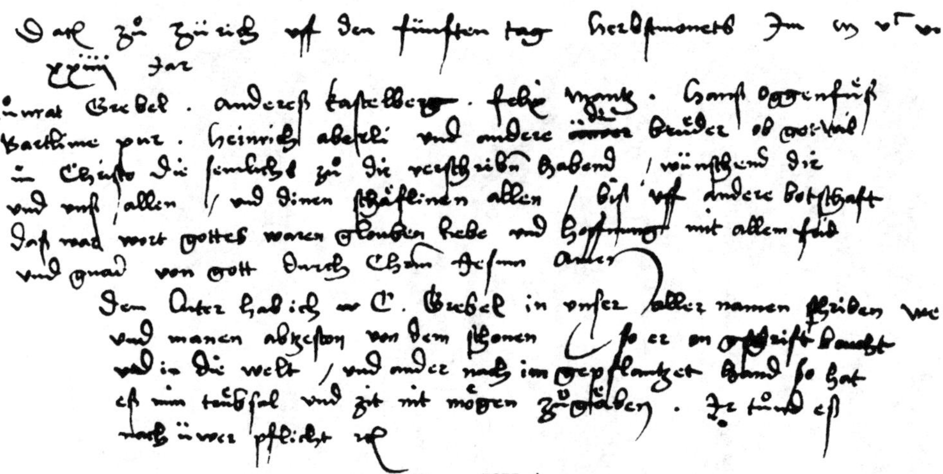

PLATE VII-A.

The Conclusion of the Letter of Grebel to Müntzer, September, 1524. From the original in the Stadtbibliothek St. Gallen, Switzerland. Reduced facsimile.

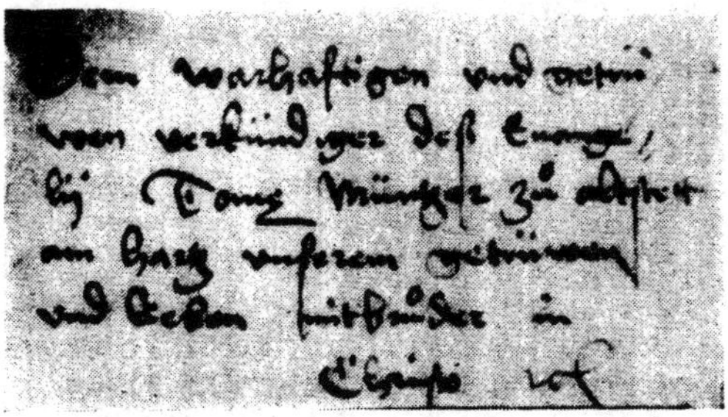

PLATE VII-B.

The Address on the Outside of the Letter to Müntzer. From the original in the Stadtbibliothek St. Gallen. Reduced facsimile.

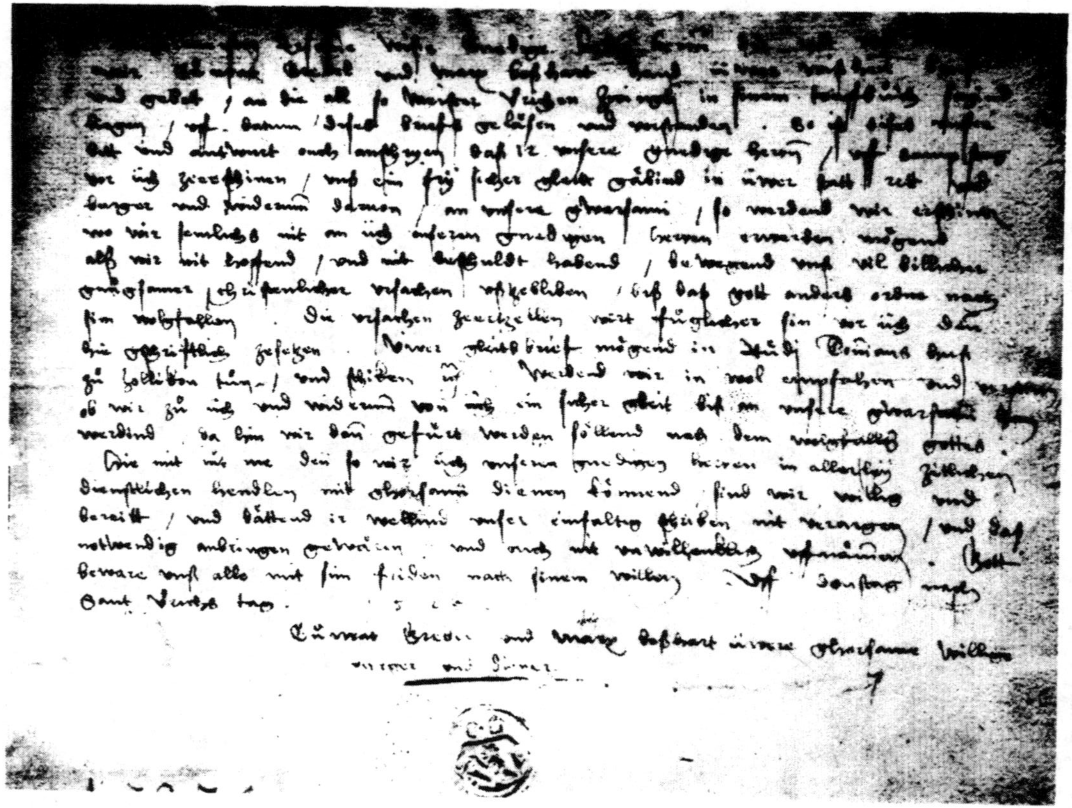

PLATE VIII

The Request for Safe Conduct by Conrad Grebel and Marx Bosshart Addressed to the Zollikon Town Council July, 1525. From the original in the Staatsarchiv Zurich (EI. 7). Reduced facsimile.

even says that the abuse of the preachers by the opponents of infant baptism was so bad that the council suspended further discussions on account of the outbreak of anger and hatred. Nevertheless, comments Zwingli, "the most of them promised to keep quiet, even if they would not promise to surrender their views."[115] At any rate in Zwingli's opinion the preachers who were defending infant baptism were victorious.

Conrad Grebel's opinion of the two meetings was somewhat different, at least according to his report in his "protest and defense" to the city council.[116] Grebel and Zwingli agree that the two sides were to present their views on the basis of Scripture, but Grebel insists that this did not happen: "They (the other side) presented their views, but not grounded in Scripture." He protests further against Zwingli, "We had no chance to speak, and there was no chance for the Scripture to be heard; for when one of us wanted to say the truth in the matter they overwhelmed us and choked the speech in our throats, demanding Scripture, whereas they themselves should have brought forth Scripture and truth." Grebel himself testified that he had experienced such treatment from Zwingli more than once. He says, "For he often earlier had overwhelmed me with much speaking so that I was unable to reply or come to an answer on account of his long speeches." For this reason Grebel preferred to have no further oral discussions in the matter of baptism; he desired to conduct the debate in the future on a written basis. Hence he submitted a written defense of his point of view to the council and requested that the council should require Zwingli to give a written defense of infant baptism on the basis of the Scripture. He gives two further reasons for preferring a written discussion. (1) "Speaking does not become me, and I have no ability . . . also am not able to dispute"; and (2) "much strife and controversy will be avoided thereby." Grebel is prepared to give an answer to every man, "may he be who he will, who should desire to prove out of the Scripture that newborn children should be baptized."

The above petition of Grebel, called by Egli and Köhler "Protestation und Schutzschrift," or "Petition of Protest and

Defense," is one of the most important products of Grebel's pen. It must have been composed about the beginning of December, for he refers in it to a booklet which Zwingli was in the process of preparing, entitled *Wer Ursach gebe zu Aufruhr* which was composed between the seventh and the twenty-eighth of December, 1524. Although Grebel does not mention the writing by name, the identification is unquestionable. Grebel's petition is not long but it is rich in content, and impressive in style. After a rejection of the charge of "revolution," which was now being brought against Grebel and the Brethren by Zwingli, the document consists almost exclusively of a rather thorough proof that infant baptism is not scriptural. Cast in a direct and vigorous form, it gives effective expression to Grebel's convictions. It is a most significant document, for here for the first time Conrad Grebel, the son of one of the leading members of the Zurich city council, appears in an "official" or at least a representative capacity on behalf of the little group of friends and brethren which had gradually grown in the course of the last months into a staunchly homogeneous body. He hoped by his appeal to forestall action by the council against them.

Grebel's denial of the charge of sedition, which has been mentioned above, highlights the danger in which the Brethren now found themselves. The situation was now entering upon a new phase. For the first time political considerations entered what had been a purely religious affair. As time went on this aspect of the situation was to increase in prominence, as the state sought legal grounds for persecution. It was becoming evident that the Brethren were to be attacked not only as proponents of heretical religious views but as a seditious party inimical to the welfare of the state.[117] Zwingli declared that they were stirring up unrest and disturbing the peace and public safety. Grebel was well aware of these charges, for in his letter to Vadian of December 15, 1524, he twice mentions such a charge: "He, Zwingli, is writing about sedition; will probably hit us. You will see that something will come of it."

This accusation of sedition was altogether incomprehensible to Grebel. He assured the council that he had never taken part in revolutionary activities, and that he had never made any speeches which could have given occasion for anything of the sort. "Never took part in sedition and never talked or spoke in any way anything which would lead to it, as all those with whom I have ever had anything to do will testify of me. Hence such a charge is unjust to me."[118] Grebel felt at once that such a charge was most dangerous for the Brethren, and for this reason protested so vigorously against it. In itself the charge is also evidence that Zwingli found the struggle against the Brethren increasingly difficult. When arguments which he used to try to convince the Brethren that infant baptism was justified had been unsuccessful because they were not "according to the Scripture," he changed the charge to sedition as a more effective means of attack, by a process of rationalization. Such a charge could only mean that Zwingli feared an undermining of the authority of the state through the fact that the Brethren were successfully defying an order of the council by refusing to accept infant baptism. Zwingli of course in addition feared, and rightly so, interference with his program of reform.

Through this latest intensification of the conflict the situation of the Brethren became much more difficult. Hitherto there had been no interference with holding their meetings in peace and spreading their teaching. But now the hour was evidently drawing near when interference from the civil authorities was to be expected. Grebel said on December 15: "I do not believe that persecution will fail to come . . . by their fruits ye shall know them, by persecution and the sword."[119]

In these circumstances, as the clouds of persecution were obviously gathering, Grebel's strong faith and trust in God finds clear expression, particularly in the above mentioned letter of December 15, 1524, to Vadian. The letter is a noble expression of true Christian piety. "May God give grace. I hope to God that He will grant the medicine of patience thereto, if it is not to be otherwise." Then he thinks of the Gospel and of the truth of God: "May God prosper His truth and righteousness and bring to naught all persons. They are (that is we all are) deceitful; the best are hypocrites, amen. May God grant us His mercy, that you may know how to deal wisely with divine things, and we, that we may stand together with you by the truth, standing fast and praying that God may send forth laborers into His great harvest. And may peace, faith and salvation be established and obtained." He says that his attitude toward the Scripture is based upon faith and not merely upon an intellectual acceptance. "I believe in the word of God simply, out of faith, and not out of skill [learning]; by skill you have much better knowledge, yes a thousand times better. For this reason I have spoken and still speak. Therefore may God grant us His perfect mercy, that we may perform it, and that you may accept the word without pretense and do accordingly."

It is in this frame of mind that Grebel faces the dark and anxious future, "praying God for the furtherance of His will and of our piety, or rather much more of my own; may God increase this through Christ Jesus, amen. . . Greet all. . . . May they also pray for us in these dangerous times." It is a genuine and simple Christian who speaks through these sincere and moving words, no fanatic and no enthusiast, and no self-righteous hypocrite.

The question of baptism had now become the chief issue, and it was on infant baptism that the conflict centered. It is true that in the letter of December 15, 1524, Grebel still mentioned "tithes and usury," but two weeks later Vadian had the correct understanding of the situation when he wrote in his letter of December 28 to Grebel: "The battle is almost altogether about baptism."[120] The concentration on baptism was certainly not intentional on the part of the Brethren, contrary to Zwingli's assertion in his *Taufbüchlein,* whose theory of the history of the conflict is interesting but is only an artificial construction. "Now when this happened (that their program was not accepted) they brought forth the matter of infant baptism. We were all much surprised that they were so heated in the matter; but finally saw that it was for the reason that, if infant baptism should be overthrown, then it would be fitting to introduce adult rebaptism, and with this rebaptism they would be able to establish their church."[121] Zwingli saw clearly indeed, that if infant baptism is surrendered, the way has been cleared to a believers' church, of which adult baptism is the necessary symbol. But it is scarcely plausible that Grebel and the Brethren had already thought through the consequences of their actions, or that they were systematically planning to introduce adult baptism. On the contrary, up to this time there is not the least trace of a thought of adult baptism in Grebel's letters or in any of the sources. Ludwig Hätzer, who had taken part in the Tuesday discussions, admitted that he was a staunch opponent of infant baptism, but insists (1526) that he had never wanted to have rebaptism: "In the matter of rebaptism, I never advocated it, and was always opposed to it."[122] Rebaptism was not yet a part of the program of Grebel and his group.

The intensity of the struggle over infant baptism was incomprehensible to an outsider like Vadian. For this reason he attempted in his letter of December 28, 1524, to restrain his impetuous brother-in-law from the battle.[123] One should only not be so intense about it, he thought, more modest and restrained, as becomes a mere layman. Zwingli and Leo Jud were after all the proper and authorized persons to regulate such matters and they had already accomplished a splendid work. Grebel should remember that it was not possible to do away with all the traditional abuses at one blow without having consideration for historical development. The proper practice of baptism "will with the time without doubt be regulated according to the Word of Truth as other things have been regulated." The main thing just now was to maintain the peace. From Vadian's argument it can be seen that he counted infant baptism as one of the traditional abuses which would have to be abolished in time. However it is clear that Vadian had little hope of restraining his brother-in-law, for he says: "But if you intend to be thorough in the matter, I cannot hold you back." And Conrad Grebel intended "to be thorough in the matter."

The decision in the matter of infant baptism was drawing near. On January 14, 1525, Grebel reported to Vadian: "They have appointed a disputation for next Tuesday in the presence of both councils, and ordered that those who are for or against infant baptism should meet. It will be announced tomorrow."[124] The Grebel group was staunch and assured, not at all afraid. Grebel reported that Jakob Hottinger had publicly challenged Caspar Grossman in the course of the latter's sermon in defense of infant baptism on the previous Thursday. Hottinger had been moderate and the authorities had thus far done nothing about it. Conrad himself had no intention of having his newborn daughter Rachel baptized, although she was now eight days old, and according to the mandate of the city council should have been baptized without delay. He even preferred not to use the word "baptism" in referring to the ceremony, saying rather, "the child has not yet been baptized and watered in the Romish water bath."[125]

The city council of Zurich intended that the disputation of January 17, 1525, should be the final and definitive discussion of baptism. They therefore appointed a formal public disputation in the style of those which had been held in 1523, to which they invited foreign guests. The report was current that Dr. Balthasar Hubmaier of Waldshut would be invited to attend, but Grebel doubted it very much, for he knew that in the question of baptism Hubmaier did not agree with Zwingli.[126] This statement of Grebel about Hubmaier is very interesting. Up to this time Hubmaier had not publicly indicated his attitude on the question of baptism. Not until January 16, 1525, did he make known to Oecolampad his opposition and inform him of his recently written booklet on baptism, which Oecolampad would soon see in print.[127] If Grebel at this time already knew about Hubmaier's intention of writing against Zwingli's views on infant baptism, as he states, he must have learned about Hubmaier's views and plans some time before this. It is possible that he acquired this knowledge at the time of the latter's brief visit to Zurich in October, 1524, when Hubmaier probably learned about the growing conflict in Zurich over the question of infant baptism.[128]

Another foreigner appeared about this time in Zurich and came in contact with Grebel and the Brethren. It was George Cajacob, also called Blaurock, a former cleric from Chur. He had come to Zurich in December with his wife to inquire of Zwingli about the new evangelical teaching. Since what Zwingli had to tell him was not satisfactory, as soon as he heard about Grebel and Manz he went to them in the hope of finding better instruction. In this he was not disappointed, and in consequence decided to join the Brethren.[129] His ability and his strong personality soon made him a leader in the group, so that before long men began to speak of "the three shepherds, Grebel, Manz and Blaurock."

VIII

TRIUMPH UNDER PERSECUTION, 1525-26[1]

The outcome of the disputation of January 17, 1525, and the two subsequent strict mandates of the council dated January 18 and January 21 compelled Grebel and the Brethren associated with him to come to a decision.[2] Zwingli and the council had definitely decided to retain infant baptism and had interdicted the meetings of the Brethren. Grebel and Manz were to desist from their "disputing and agitating," that is, they were to discontinue the whole movement. Families which continued to refuse to baptize their children were to be given eight days for consideration, after which those who persisted in a final refusal were to be expelled from the canton with wife and child and goods. Conrad Grebel himself was among the fathers who had refused to baptize their children; he must decide now what course to take. The Brethren who were not citizens of Zurich, Wilhelm Reublin, pastor at Wytikon; Hans Brötli, assistant pastor at Zollikon; Andreas Castelberger, bookseller of Zurich; and Ludwig Hätzer, who had joined the Brethren in the autumn of 1524, were ordered to leave the canton within eight days. The tone of the two mandates indicates that the council considered the matter closed. They therefore announced in advance that they would not permit any further disputations, and suggested that if the young gentlemen desired any further information they should report their wishes to the burgomaster or to the three assistant burgomasters.

Grebel and his friends had no thought of yielding to the demands of the city council, for they could not surrender their deepest convictions at command; but it was not clear to them what particular course they should follow. That they made it perfectly clear to Zwingli however that they would stand fast is evident from the fact that Zwingli wrote to Vadian on January 19, 1525, reporting that "Conrad Grebel persists in his stand, together with a few other less important persons."

In these dark days several of the Brethren, probably on the night of January 21, 1525,[3] gathered in the house of Felix Manz in Zurich to take counsel. It was a historic meeting, for it was here that the desire for baptism upon confession of faith first manifested itself in the spontaneous request by George Blaurock that Conrad Grebel, as the acknowledged leader of the group, should baptize him.[4] Grebel consented to this wish, by immediate action. Blaurock then proceeded to baptize the other Brethren who were present. Grebel apparently left the baptizing to Blaurock because he himself at this time laid no particular stress upon the outward sign.

This event is related in a moving account in the Hutterian *Geschicht-Buch.*[5] "And it came to pass as they were together anxiety came upon them, yea, pressed upon their hearts. Thereupon they began to bend their knees before Almighty God in heaven and to call upon Him as the one who knows the heart; and they prayed that He would grant them to do His divine will, and that He would reveal His mercy unto them. Flesh and blood or human wisdom had not brought them to this point, because they well knew what they would have to suffer on account of it. After the prayer George of the House of Jakob [Cajacob-Blaurock] arose and entreated Conrad Grebel for God's sake to baptize him with the right Christian baptism upon the confession of his faith. And as he kneeled down with this request and desire, Conrad baptized him, since at that time there was no ordained minister to perform such work. After this had taken place, the others likewise desired of George that he should baptize them, which also he did upon their request. And so they together dedicated themselves in the high fear of God to the name of the Lord, confirmed one another in the service of the Gospel, and began to teach and to hold the faith. Therewith was the separation from the world and its evil works begun."

In the following days the Brethren did not hesitate to carry on the program to which they had dedicated themselves in that solemn hour. Grebel and Manz went from house to house in Zurich and Zollikon, meeting with the Brethren, admonishing them regarding the new life which they were to live. Usually the service began with the reading of a passage from the New Testament and ended with baptism of such as desired it, and with a general participation in the Lord's Supper. Baptisms took place at any time and at any place, in the morning or in the evening, in the house or at the stream. The water was the symbol of the washing of repentance and the putting off of sin, the outward sign of the decisive entrance into a new and holy life. He who received it was henceforth no longer the master of his own life but a servant of Jesus Christ, ready to do His will at whatever cost. No worldly power henceforth was to be sovereign over him if it conflicted with the plain teaching of the Word of God. The Lord's Supper was a symbol of the union among the brotherhood and signified the common faith in the redemption through the death and "rose-red blood" of the son of God,[6a] and obligated those who partook of it to live a Christ-like life, to love God with all their heart and their neighbor likewise. The ceremony was made as simple as possible. The one who was conducting the service simply broke or cut a loaf of bread and pronounced over it the words of consecration, whereupon whoever desired was permitted to take a portion of the bread; the same procedure was followed in connection with the wine. The most active among the Brethren, both in preaching and in performing the ordinances, was George Blaurock.

As for Grebel, however, very little in detail is known of his activities during these first days. He performed the first baptism, as reported above, and probably conducted the first celebration of the Lord's Supper among the Brethren.[7] According to one witness who was called before the court on the sixth of February, Grebel and Manz had been seen in Zollikon together daily, morning and evening, going about from house to house, holding meetings at which people from the Balgerist and other communities gathered together.[8] Blaurock, as the abler speaker and more aggressive personality, soon surpassed Grebel in some respects. Whereas Blaurock baptized many, the names of those whom Grebel baptized are few, at least so far as they have been preserved. On February 18, 1525, Gabriel Giger of St. Gall reported that "the spirit of God came upon him and he hastened to Zurich to the house of Felix Manz where Conrad baptized him."[9] It is known that Grebel baptized Wolfgang Ulimann near Schaffhausen in February, 1525.[10] And on March 7, 1526, a certain Anna Manz testified before the court in Zurich that Conrad Grebel had baptized her.[11]

Grebel soon disappeared from Zurich, probably before the first of February, 1525. The two months from then until the end of March were spent in Schaffhausen. He apparently hoped to win the preachers of Schaffhausen, since those of Zurich had rejected his proposals. Johannes Kessler reports in his *Sabbata* that Grebel was the first of the Brethren to attempt to carry the movement out of Zurich into other regions, particularly "among the learned preachers."[12]

Grebel's first attempt with the "learned preachers" was with Dr. Sebastian Hofmeister, the chief pastor of Schaffhausen, and Dr. Sebastian Meyer of the same city. Johannes Brötli and Wilhelm Reublin, who had been expelled from Zurich before January 29, found Grebel already in Schaffhausen when they reached there on their flight from Zurich, which was certainly before February 5, and possibly before January 29, 1525. All three Brethren were guests of "the two doctors" one evening.[13] On the next day Brötli and Reublin went to Hallau, about seven miles farther west, where Brötli established a church. Reublin went on about twelve miles farther to Waldshut, where he was the guest of Dr. Balthasar Hubmaier for a short time.[14]

The Brethren must have had some success in Schaffhausen, for Brötli states that when he was there he had a definite impression that "Doctor Sebastian agrees with us in the matter of baptism."[15] The evident inclination of Hofmeister to view the new movement favorably is testified to at other places as well. In the year 1526, for instance, Balthasar Hubmaier states that Hofmeister had written to him in 1525 as follows: "We did not hesitate to publicly testify to the council of the city of Schaffhausen that our brother Zwingli was off the track and was not walking according to the truth of the Gospel when he began to insist that the children should be baptized. Verily, they could not compel me to have my children baptized." Hubmaier insists that he possessed the above statement in Hofmeister's own handwriting.[16] And in Zurich a report was circulated as early as February 8, 1525, that Schaffhausen was about to arrange a disputation on the question of infant baptism, a report which the Schaffhausen council repudiated in a letter to Zurich dated February 10.[17] It is altogether possible that the report of the proposed disputation reached Zurich through Conrad Grebel and his father Jacob Grebel, who was the member of the Zurich Council. Finally, on August 15, 1525, Hofmeister was expelled from Schaffhausen, in part because "he had preached and proclaimed from the pulpit that the sacrament of the Mass, the baptism of young children, and the confessional are works of the devil."[18] Grebel's influence on Hofmeister was undoubtedly more effective than Hofmeister himself was willing to admit at the time of the great Anabaptist trial in Zurich in the following November (1525). Hofmeister's assertion at the trial that Grebel, when he was in Schaffhausen, had declared that the civil authority should be done away with, and that he had also charged Zwingli with adultery, was vigorously denied by Grebel.[19]

The exact length of Grebel's stay in Schaffhausen cannot be determined, but it must have extended to the latter part of March, 1525, for just before the death of the young French nobleman Anemund de Coct, which occurred about March 20, he was still there.[20] During this time he endeavored to win others besides Hofmeister, particularly De Coct and Erasmus Ritter. He refers to Erasmus Ritter in a letter of May, 1525, addressed to Andreas Castelberger, in which he reports that he had given a collection of Bible quotations against infant baptism to a certain Erasmus in Schaffhausen, as he had been urged to do by the departed De Coct. He states further that he believed that Ritter had sent this document to Zwingli, for Grebel had heard that Zwingli intended to refute Grebel's interpretation of the aforesaid Scripture passages which he had collected in Schaffhausen.[21] In addition to De Coct and Ritter it is possible that Grebel also conferred with Martin Lingg, who was expelled from Zurich as an Anabaptist a few months later, on November 18, 1525.[22] There is no further evidence as to the fruit of Grebel's work in Schaffhausen although it is possible that Beatrix von Fulach, who later became an Anabaptist, and her brother Hans von Waldkirch,[23] who later sheltered Anabaptists, were influenced by him. Somewhere near Schaffhausen in February Grebel baptized Wolfgang Ulimann of St. Gall in the Rhine river.[24]

The relations of Grebel to the young French nobleman Anemund de Coct are worthy of careful notice, for Grebel was convinced that he had won De Coct in Schaffhausen for his cause. In the letter of May, 1525, to Castelberger, Grebel speaks of "the false brotherhood of the departed De Coct." Anemund de Coct, "Chevalier de Rhode et seigneur du Chastelard en Dauphine," had become a zealous Lutheran as early as 1523, and through his study at Wittenberg had won the friendship of Luther and Spalatin. On his return journey from Wittenberg to France he stopped in Zurich, where he spent two months from the end of November, 1523, to the end of January, 1524.[25] At the end of December, 1524, he seems to have been in Zurich again, for Pierre de Sebiville, a friend of De Coct, addressed a letter to him at Zurich from Grenoble on December 28, 1524.[26] On December 17, 1524, De Coct was still in Basel, according to a letter he addressed to Farel under this date.[27] At that time he was interested in such questions as baptism and the Lord's Supper, as is testified by Pierre Toussain in a letter addressed to William Farel December 17, 1524.[28] De Coct's stay in Zurich could not have been long, and could not have been very public, for Myconius complained in a letter to him written before February 20, 1525, that he had not seen him on the occasion of his visit in Zurich.[29] By January 25, 1525, De Coct was in Wehr, for on that date he wrote to his friend Farel in Montbeliard requesting him to send some money with a messenger to Zurich to repay a small debt which he owed to Conrad Grebel.[30] The messenger who brought the letter from De Coct also brought news to Farel about the Anabaptists in Zurich. It seems that De Coct had adopted a son named Nicholas when he was in Zurich, for Myconius wrote to him in his letter of February, 1525, saying that Grebel would report to him everything that was necessary about the boy and his welfare.[31] It is clear therefore that De Coct spent at least a few days with Grebel in Zurich at the turn of the year 1524-1525, and developed a friendship with him at that time, which included a common interest in the Anabaptist movement. Hofmeister indeed states that Grebel and De Coct came to him in Schaffhausen together, "and discussed infant baptism with him a great deal and attempted to lead him to accept the new view."[32] Hofmeister reports further that De Coct went back to Zurich to secure further information about Zwingli, and that upon his return he reported his impressions of Zwingli to Grebel, and was angry because Grebel had not told him the truth about Zwingli. Whereupon Grebel had replied, "he had known that if he went to Zwingli the latter would put his poison into him also." About that time, possibly even on the return journey from Zurich, De Coct became ill and died at Hofmeister's home on March 20, 1525.[33]

The visit of Felix Manz with Hofmeister in Schaffhausen, which the latter reported in his testimony at the trial in Zurich, must have taken place after March 20, for before that date Manz was still in prison in Zurich, and on March 20 he took part in a disputation with Zwingli.[34]

After Grebel's attempt to win Hofmeister failed he returned to Zurich. Near the end of March, 1525, he spent several days in the city, for on March 31 Zwingli reported that Grebel had resumed his activity for the movement in Zurich. On that date he wrote to Vadian as follows: "Grebel is with us and is drawing all that he can to his party by slandering and libeling our office so much that even though we were as bad as he makes us out to be, it would be highly improper for him to be so ungrateful to us after all that he has received from me. Take care that you are not misled by his propaganda; for he has the habit of keeping silent about what I present, while he fills your ears with his own stuff."[35]

Grebel did not stay long in Zurich but went almost immediately to St. Gall. Perhaps he hoped to win Vadian. More probably however he hastened to St. Gall to come to the aid of the Brethren there who were having considerable success. Lorenz Hochrütiner, Grebel's friend and brother in the faith, who had been expelled from Zurich in 1523, had begun to agitate against infant baptism very early in connection with Johannes Kessler's Bible classes in St. Gall. Still earlier, even as early as July, 1523, some opposition to infant baptism had made itself manifest in the city.[36] Later Gabriel Giger, whom Grebel himself had baptized in Zurich, carried the movement directly from Zurich to St. Gall. However the chief leader of the movement was Wolfgang Ulimann, whom Grebel had baptized in February near Schaffhausen,[37] and it was possibly at his request that Grebel hastened to St. Gall to play his part in the developing events there.

Under Ulimann's leadership the movement in St. Gall was growing rapidly.[38] Ulimann, a former monk and scholar, was a member of a patrician family, his father being guildmaster of the influential weaver guild. He was a friend of Johannes Kessler in St. Gall, and when the latter discontinued his Bible classes at the request of the city council, Ulimann had taken up the work. The attendance at Ulimann's "sermons" was extraordinary.[39]

In the midst of this activity, about March 25, 1525, Grebel arrived in St. Gall and stayed there for two weeks.[40] Grebel's preaching had powerful effect; hundreds of people thronged into the hall of the weaver guild to hear him. Finally many of them demanded to be baptized, and on Palm Sunday, April 9, 1525, a great crowd streamed out of the city to the banks of the River Sitter to be baptized by Grebel. The chronicler Fridolin Sicher reports that the highway was filled with people as on a procession day.[41] It must have been one of the great moments in Grebel's life. In Zurich the movement was being effectively suppressed; in Schaffhausen he had been able to accomplish very little; but in St. Gall he was gathering a rich harvest. However Grebel felt that he should return to Zurich, and left affairs in St. Gall in the hands of Eberli Bolt of Lachen of the Canton of Appenzell, who continued Grebel's work with still greater success. Great crowds thronged to Bolt's preaching and were baptized by him. It seemed that the city council of St. Gall was not inclined to undertake suppressive measures against the Anabaptists as was the case in Zurich. Finally, however, the council did request Bolt in a friendly manner to leave the city, which he did about April 21. Soon after, on May 29, 1525, Bolt was burned at the stake at Schwyz, and thus became the first martyr of the Swiss Brethren. It is not clear whether Bolt was executed because of his Anabaptist views or simply because he was an evangelical preacher in a Catholic canton. Bullinger praises his steadfastness; perhaps he would have spoken differently about him had he known that Bolt was an Anabaptist preacher and colleague of Conrad Grebel.[42]

After the departure of Bolt, Ulimann resumed the leadership in St. Gall. By this time the movement had become a powerful, popular movement, stronger than the so-called "evangelical" or "Zwinglian" movement in the same place. It is reported that no less than five hundred persons had been baptized as members of the brotherhood in and around the city.[43] This was alarming, so at the end of April the council finally decided to suppress the movement. Scarcely knowing how to begin, the council first adopted the plan of a written exchange of views by the two sides. On May 12 they requested the Brethren to submit a written defense within two weeks. A similar written statement in the form of a defense against the doctrine of the Brethren was required of the evangelical pastors, Burgauer and Wetter,[44] both of whom, by the way, were friends of Grebel as late as 1523. However both sides failed to produce the desired documents, although the Brethren wrote to Grebel in Zurich requesting him to supply a "writing." Meanwhile Vadian himself undertook to write a defense against the Brethren.

On June 5 the two parties met in the council room, where Vadian read his "book." When the Brethren stated they had in their possession a letter from Grebel addressed to the burgomaster and council, the council required it to be read, and upon hearing it, ordered that two delegates take it to Zurich to secure advice. The next day the Brethren read their own defense, possibly also written by Grebel.[45] At the conclusion of the meeting it was decided that both documents, the one submitted by Vadian and the one submitted by the Brethren, should be carefully preserved. Unfortunately these instructions were not carried out, for neither of the documents seems to be in existence today. The meeting had very little influence upon the situation in St. Gall for the council now undertook an energetic campaign against the Brethren, and the leaders were banished from the canton. Probably because of this loss, the movement rapidly declined until within a short time what had once been a very promising Anabaptist movement in St. Gall practically disappeared.

Apparently Vadian was the decisive influence in the decision of the council to suppress the movement, although for a time he had been uncertain about his attitude. This uncertainty had led Zwingli to warn him against the influence of Grebel, as reported above in the letter of March 31,[46] and had led Zwingli also to dedicate to St. Gall his first literary attack against the Anabaptists, called the *Taufbüchlein*. In great haste Zwingli had sent a shipment of the books to St. Gall on May 28, the day after the printing was completed, with a letter to accompany it.[47] Conrad Grebel also knew that the decision lay in Vadian's hands. For this reason he too sought with all the strength at his command to win Vadian, or at least to influence him to remain neutral. The letter which he wrote to him on May 30, 1525, the last letter of Grebel's which has been preserved, was a strong appeal to Vadian's conscience. In it he reminded Vadian that he had really approved the teaching of the Brethren, as Grebel probably had learned during his stay in St. Gall in March. He warned him against the shedding of innocent blood and appealed to him to separate himself from the bloody Zwinglian party, particularly in view of the coming judgment of God. He entreated Vadian not to let himself be moved by fear of persecution or by the thought that he might lose money and position, but rather to obey the divine truth in trust alone in God.[48] But Grebel's last despairing appeal was in vain. The one Swiss city in which the Anabaptists for a time enjoyed genuine freedom finally went the way of all Switzerland in persecuting them.

On the return journey from St. Gall about Easter time, April 16, 1525, Grebel stopped for a short time in Oberwinterthur. While there he was the guest of Arbogast Finsterbach, a brother-in-law of his good friend Marx Bosshard. Finsterbach was much interested in Grebel's new teaching, and when he asked what one had to do to be baptized, Grebel answered, "One must first give up fornication, gambling, drinking, and usury."[49] Finsterbach and several friends from Oberwinterthur were again in touch with the Brethren later in August, 1525, in Zollikon, but apparently did not definitely join the movement.

Shortly after Easter, 1525, Grebel was back again in Zurich.[50] Because of the tense situation he lived in retirement as much as possible until the beginning of June, trying to keep his presence secret, although he maintained contact with the Brethren in Zollikon and with his other friends such as Manz and Castelberger. The Brethren came to him at his house, and he went out to them in Zollikon. A very important letter to Andreas Castelberger written in the latter part of May gives some insight into the conditions under which Grebel lived at this time.[51] "I believe it is known that I am in my house, that I receive the Brethren here. However I do not go out, in order to protect my asylum here against a possible imprisonment by Zwingli, who according to the Apocalypse, will himself go into captivity. . . . Do not worry because of my presence here. . . . You did not say whether Adrian Grebel has paid you although I doubt not that the matter is still hanging fire. Please report in any case so that I can send out letters with less fear, and attempt to secure a settlement of this matter." Grebel goes on to say that he wanted to leave Zurich but was afraid of being discovered and so had attempted to leave by night secretly together with Felix Manz. However, since his wife had threatened to betray Manz he gave up the attempt, for he says, "In case I should be banished later and my wife should betray

Felix it would be impossible for me to go secretly to the Brethren in Zollikon, since guardsmen would certainly be placed to watch for me."

Further evidence that Grebel expected persecution at the hands of Zwingli is found in his letter to Vadian of May 30, 1525, in which he says that he and the Brethren are ready to testify to their faith by death, a death which Zwingli and others are already preparing for them.[52]

During this time Grebel suffered greatly in health, the old ailment in his feet having come back to trouble him so much that he could scarcely walk. He was also in desperate need of funds, and in order to secure enough to support himself decided to sell his books. For this purpose he prepared a catalog of his books and sent it to Andreas Castelberger with the request that he find a buyer for the entire library, perhaps the Abbott of Kappel. Since Castelberger was ill at the time, Grebel proposed that Jakob Hottinger should show the catalog to interested buyers.

Soon after this, probably early in June, Grebel left Zurich again, this time to go to Waldshut to Hubmaier. He took with him as a traveling companion Jakob Hottinger of Zollikon. An undated letter by Hottinger addressed to the city council of Zurich and laid before them on June 29, 1525, states that he had accompanied Grebel at the latter's request on the trip to Waldshut, because Grebel had received an invitation from Dr. Hubmaier and had constrained him to go along by using the words of Jesus on the Mount, "If a man asks you to go with him one mile go with him twain."[53] Hubmaier himself testified of Grebel's visit to him on the occasion of his trial before the court in Zurich on April 11, 1526, saying, "Conrad Grebel and Jakob Hottinger came to me and we discussed baptism together."[54] It would be interesting to speculate on the significance of this visit. Hubmaier was later baptized at Easter time, April 16, 1525, by Wilhelm Reublin, together with most of his congregation. Perhaps Grebel thought that Hubmaier was to be one of the leaders. Was he disappointed possibly to find in Hubmaier some views with which he could not agree and which prevented a fuller fellowship and co-operation? Nothing further appears in the records about the relationship between Hubmaier and Grebel, but perhaps it was merely a case of lack of opportunity for contact.

Upon his return from Waldshut Grebel sought new territory for conquest. This time it was the extensive township of Grüningen lying east of Zurich, but still under the sovereignty of the city. There his father had been magistrate for twelve years (1499 to 1512) and there Conrad had spent his own boyhood days. The soil in Grüningen was well prepared for the spread of the Anabaptist movement.[55] For a long time there had been tension between the population and the city of Zurich. The peasants of Grüningen, who had formerly been independent, desired to retain the largest degree of political and economic autonomy and resisted the growing centralization of the township's affairs under the central authority of the canton. As a result of the tension a strong radical opposition against the paying of the tithes had developed in the spring of 1525. Many of the local parish pastors supported the movement and demanded a complete abolition of the tithes. Matters reached the point that in April, 1525, a mob of peasants plundered the Rüti monastery. The influence of the new evangelical teaching of the Reformation led the peasants to include in their program, besides the economic points, religious demands such as the right of the local communities to choose their own pastors. But the city council of Zurich rejected all demands of the peasants whether economic, political, or ecclesiastical. As a consequence of this rejection the spirit in the township was very bitter, for the disappointed populace felt that they were being forcibly deprived of their rights on every count.

This was the situation into which Grebel and his friends came with their message of a free church composed of believers, in which "divine right" and righteousness was to prevail.[56] It is no wonder that the Anabaptist movement in Grüningen rapidly developed into a strong popular movement.

Grebel devoted his entire time from the end of June, 1525, until his arrest on October 8 to the movement in Grüningen, a total of almost four months. This period was one of the most successful in his career as a leader of the Brethren, and it was the only time when he was able to work for any extended period continuously in one territory. He was alone in the field, except for some of the lesser Brethren, for at this time Manz and Blaurock were devoting themselves to the work in Chur and Appenzell.[56a] On the whole it may be said that the Zurich Anabaptist movement had its greatest success in Grüningen.

The first documentary proof of Grebel's presence in Grüningen is a report of his preaching at several villages in the township on Sunday, July 2, 1525.[57] On this day he preached to large crowds at Hinwil and Bäretswyl. He had planned to preach at Gossau on the following Sunday, July 9, but was not able to carry out his intention. He also planned to preach at Dürnten on the next Sunday, July 16,[58] although it is not known whether he did so or not. Quite likely Grebel's activity in Grüningen began before July 2. This may be inferred from the fact that the pastor at Hinwil introduced baptismal records in order to combat the Anabaptists and made the first registry on July 3.[59] During the first days and weeks of his activity in Grüningen Grebel was assisted by Marx Bosshart of Zollikon, one of the first members of the brotherhood in Zurich.[60]

As early as the first week in July, Grebel and Bosshart were summoned to Zurich for trial on the charge of slander against Zwingli's *Taufbüchlein*. Bosshart was charged with having said, "Zwingli has written plain lies."[61] In reply to the summons Grebel and Bosshart addressed a petition to the city council on July 6, 1526, requesting a letter of safe conduct to attend the trial,[62] which they directed to be sent to the house of Rudi Thomann in Zollikon. The council rejected the request and demanded a second time that the accused present themselves in Zurich. Grebel again refused, but Bosshart, Fridli Schumacher, and Hans Oggenfuss, yielded and appeared in Zurich.[63] Grebel's caution was justified, for Bosshart and the others were thrown into prison, from which Bosshart himself was not released until August 2, 1525. Bosshart was forced to pay a fine of one mark in silver and to post a bond of one hundred pounds. He was also compelled to promise to desist from preaching and baptizing.[64]

The next evidence of Grebel's activity places him at Hirslanden on August 1, where he is reported to have read a passage from Scripture in the house of Felix Lehmann.[65]

Grebel's tactics in Grüningen were well adapted to the situation. In addition to his appeal to the common people through his preaching, he endeavored to win the local pastors. Fortunately a report has been preserved of a conversation with one of the preachers which gives some insight into Grebel's method of preaching.[66] At Hinwil he discussed the question of baptism with the pastor, Hans Brennwald. Upon Grebel's admonition to baptize children only "when they came to reason," Brennwald merely replied, "My lords have issued a writing on the question of baptism, and I intend to be obedient to my lords." Such an evasion was quite incomprehensible to Grebel who was a zealous believer in unrestricted obedience to the Scriptures and to divine truth regardless of what the civil authorities might have to say. He therefore urged Brennwald "to follow the right," and not the "lying teaching" of the priests. But Brennwald was immovable.

The contact between Grebel and Brennwald throws a clear light upon the relations between the Anabaptist movement and the peasants' unrest in Grüningen, as von Muralt has correctly said.[67] It proves that Grebel did not feel himself called to deal with political interests. Brennwald had been a leader of the peasant movement in the spring of 1525, and yet Grebel did not discuss with him the economic and political demands of the peasants, but rather the question of baptism and of the authority of the Scripture.

The same document which reports the visit of Grebel to Brennwald also gives the testimony of five witnesses about statements which they had heard Grebel make. The witnesses all agreed that Grebel had complained that the authorities in Zurich had not dealt with him justly. He had demanded his rights according to imperial law (since Zurich was still an imperial city and therefore under the jurisdiction of certain of the imperial courts, Grebel could have appealed to the supreme court of the empire), to cantonal law, to divine law, and "to several other kinds of law," which he could not name; but in no case was his appeal heard. Marx Bosshart reports the same in regard to Grebel's complaint on the occasion of his trial on August 9.[68] This reference to his failure to secure justice was very good tactics for Grebel in Grüningen just at this time, for the people of Grüningen likewise felt themselves deprived of their lawful rights by Zurich.

The witnesses mentioned above testified further that Grebel had discussed the matter of baptism and also his relation to Zwingli. They reported that Grebel had said that "Zwingli had brought him into the matter and had told him much that he was no longer willing to stand by, but now repudiated." One witness reported that Grebel had said "he would not ask for anything more, if they should put him into the tower, than that he should be in a place where he could see, and that they should give him pen and ink, so that even if they would not give him a chance to speak they would nevertheless listen to his writing." Another witness testified that Grebel had said, "if they would permit his writing to be printed, then he would be ready to dispute with Master Ulrich Zwingli, and if Master Ulrich would win out, he, Conrad, would be willing to be burned, whereas if he, Conrad would win out, he would not demand that Zwingli should be burned." Since two of the witnesses were from Ettenhausen on Greifensee it is possible that Grebel had preached at this place also.

Grebel had better success with another preacher, Ulrich Zingg of Dürnten, than he had with Brennwald. Zingg, together with two friends from Dürnten, had attended Grebel's meetings on July 2 at Hinwil and Bäretswyl, and had eagerly listened to Grebel's sermon.[69] Zingg had said, "I like it, and it is God's truth," and endorsed Grebel's arguments against infant baptism. Already on the way to the meeting he had told his companions, "I know what Grebel will say; he will say that he finds nowhere in Scripture that infant baptism should be; neither do I." After the service was past he confirmed his prophecy. However, in spite of his endorsement of Grebel's teaching, and in spite of the fact that he openly told several witnesses that infant baptism was not to be found in the Scriptures, Zingg apparently did not have the courage to do away with infant baptism in his own parish. Grebel and Bosshart promised the people from Dürnten that they would hold a meeting there in two weeks, "if the people there would turn away from sin and from drinking and carousing."

According to the same witnesses Grebel also had a conversation with Pastor Benedikt Landenberger at the time of the meeting at Bäretswyl on July 2, but no details are reported.

Nothing further is known about Grebel's activity in Grüningen until the exciting meeting at Hinwil on October 8, 1525. Magistrate Berger's reports however, as well as the later record of the trial of the arrested leaders, show that the movement constantly grew.[70] Brethren from outside the canton came to Grüningen to assist in the work; several came from St. Gall and from Chur. Two who came from Waldshut, namely, Ulrich Teck and Jakob Gross, were arrested after a period of preaching and baptizing, and were expelled from Grüningen territory on September 20, 1525.[71] Grebel must certainly have come in touch with them.

As the summer wore on, George Blaurock and Felix Manz returned from Chur and Appenzell, and joined Grebel in Grüningen. The three leaders were increasingly successful, winning more and more support among the people. It was time that the authorities do something if they were to stop the movement. So on a Sunday when all three were to be in Hinwil, Oct. 8, 1525, Magistrate Berger, who had heard about the plans, hastily rode over from Grüningen castle to put a stop to things.[72] Blaurock had preached from the pulpit of the village church before Berger arrived. When the crowd saw that the magistrate intended to interfere, they made it clear that they were on the side of the Brethren, and in spite of the order of the magistrate proceeded to hold a public assembly in an open field. To the great astonishment of the magistrate, Blaurock began to sing, and Grebel and Manz made preparations to speak, in spite of the prohibition. It was a most interesting situation, for here the nonresistant Anabaptists were visibly disobedient to the civil authorities with the full support of a great crowd of people which could easily have been turned into a mob, yet there was no evidence of any intention to use force or to create a revolutionary disturbance. Berger finally succeeded in arresting Grebel and Blaurock after he had secured help from a neighboring village. Manz escaped but was arrested later, on October 31, after having successfully hidden himself for three weeks.[73] All three of the leaders were incarcerated in the castle at Grüningen. It is quite possible that Ulrich Teck of Waldshut, Martin Lingg of Schaffhausen, and Michael Sattler of Stauffen in Breisgau, all of whom were sentenced with the others at the conclusion of the trial in November, were also at Hinwil and were arrested at the same time. The report of the arrest of Grebel in Grüningen on October 8 had reached Zwingli's ears in Zurich already on October 11.[74]

The day at Hinwil was truly a "remarkable day for all," as Berger reported to the city council at Zurich. For the authorities it meant the danger of a popular uprising on behalf of the Anabaptists such as they had not experienced before and never met after. For the leaders of the Brethren, especially for Grebel, Manz, and Blaurock, it was a heartening and powerful demonstration of the strength and popular character of their movement. The people received them with gladness in a spontaneous enthusiastic response, demanding a radical renewal of religious and social life. But the promising future was abruptly broken off by the arrest and imprisonment of the leaders. Only the strongest spirits were able to resist the pressure brought to bear upon them, and the further history of the Anabaptist movement became chiefly a record of martyrdom. From Grüningen it might have gone on to a great conquest.

Before we follow Grebel to trial and then to prison for six months, let us raise the question as to what he actually wanted to accomplish in Grüningen. On the basis of all the available sources, including the testimony of numerous witnesses who heard him speak, it is clear that Grebel delivered a purely religious message. He preached about "the right Christian baptism" and about the sanctifying of the life of Christians. In Grüningen, in spite of the restless peasants, he said practically nothing about the social and economic questions which were uppermost in the minds of his hearers, nothing about tithes and taxes. His program demanded a scriptural church and a scriptural way of life for the individual Christian. He did not devote his strength to the service of social agitation or revolution in any way, although he had the very best opportunity to do so in Grüningen. In the light of this clear evidence it is strange that most of the historians who have written about Grebel and the beginning of Anabaptism in Zurich and Grüningen assert the contrary, and insist on connecting Grebel in some way with the peasants' revolt. Emil Egli even leaves the question open "as to how far Grebel himself was the instigator of the peasants' revolt."[75] The very form of such a question is false, and quite clearly flows from a bias. As long as no positive proof for social-revolutionary activity on the part of Grebel and his co-workers has been presented from the sources, such a question can not justly be asked.

Let us briefly consider Egli's attempt to create a strong suspicion "that Grebel was connected as an instigator with the popular assembly in Töss." Egli's only real evidence is the visit that Grebel made at the home of Arbogast Finsterbach in Winterthur about Easter time, 1525, which has been referred to earlier. But the discussion held in Finsterbach's house, at least so far as the documentary record shows, concerned itself wholly with the matter of baptism and the requirements for it, altogether different matters than would have been involved in a meeting of leaders preparing for the assembly at Töss. To transform this friendly meeting into a plot for a social revolution, as Egli does, is quite a feat. Grebel could hardly have known about the peasants' meeting in the first place, and on the other hand, if he had really "attempted to exploit the social ferment in Töss as well as in Grüningen," as Egli charges, he would certainly have attended the assembly itself on June 4, 1525, rather than the preparatory meeting. But there is no evidence that he attended that meeting. When he wrote to Vadian from Zurich on May 30, 1525, he was thinking of altogether different problems. Even von Muralt, who is usually quite cautious, is unable to present any positive proof for his feeling that "some sort of a connection exists between Grebel and the big meeting of the peasants at Töss."[76] But his judgment on the whole problem of the relation of the Anabaptist movement to the peasants' revolt is sound when he says, "In my opinion the Anabaptists were not responsible for the peasants' revolt."[77]

At the suggestion of Magistrate Berger the city council of Zurich ordained a new disputation on the matter of baptism to be held on November 6, 1525.[78] Berger evidently felt that it would be wise to seek to quiet the rather excited population of his district by showing them the greatest possible consideration. Hence the purpose of the disputation was certainly primarily to let the people of Grüningen know that no hasty action was contemplated. The only reports about the disputation are those contained in the Zurich council mandate of November 30, 1525,[79] and a few lines by Bullinger.[80] Four presidents were chosen, among them Dr. Sebastian Hofmeister, formerly of Schaffhausen, but now of Zurich, and Dr. Joachim von Watt (Vadian) from St. Gall, the brother-in-law of Grebel. According to Bullinger, Anabaptist Brethren from outside of the canton were also present, although Balthasar Hubmaier of Waldshut, who had been expected, did not appear. The chief participants in the discussion were Grebel and Manz on one side, and Zwingli, Jud and Grossman on the other side. For three days the discussion continued, but in the end everything remained as before, and the affair actually had very little significance. Ten days later, on November 18, 1525, Grebel, Manz, and Blaurock were sentenced "because of their Anabaptism and their unbecoming conduct to lie in the tower on a diet of bread and water, and no one was to be permitted to visit them except the guards." There they were to lie "as long as God should please and as seems good to my Lords."[81] The foreign Brethren, Ulrick Teck of Waldshut, Martin Lingg of Schaffhausen, and Michael Sattler of Stauffen in Breisgau, were banished from the canton. It is worth noting in passing that the only reference to any connection between Grebel and the noble Michael Sattler, who played such an important role in the early Anabaptist movement in Strassburg and South Germany, is found in this mandate.

The teaching which Grebel gave in Grüningen is very likely reflected in the so-called *Grüninger Eingabe* of June, 1527, which is a petition and defense by the Anabaptist Brethren to the council of Zurich. According to the description of this document which von Muralt gives,[82] the concerns of the Grüningen Anabaptists were exclusively religious. Their chief concern above everything else was the attainment of a personal righteousness by a voluntary following of Christ. "Let every one notice that baptism belongs to those believers who devote themselves to the Son of God and separate themselves from evil." The believers, who bear the fruit of the spirit, which is "love, peace, kindness, good will, trust, meekness, humility, patience, righteousness, and truth," and "who walk therein, they are the church of Christ and the body of Christ and the Christian church. Now we hope and are assured that we are in the true church. And now they want to force us out of the Christian church into a foreign church." This simple statement demonstrates clearly, says von Muralt in his evaluation of the document and of the position of the Grüningen Anabaptists, that the goal of the Anabaptists is "the communion of the saints."[83] The conclusion is exceptionally fine: "Now let every one well understand our complaint that they call the baptism of Christ a rebaptism without proof from the Holy Scripture. But now we hope . . . that the baptism which we practice is the baptism of Christ, and that infant baptism is a rebaptism." May we not believe that the spirit as well as the content of this interesting and important document produced by the Grüningen Anabaptists in 1527 represents the spirit and the teaching of Conrad Grebel, their departed founder and leader, who was the first to preach this Gospel among them?

The sentence of November 18, 1525, imposed on Grebel, Manz, Blaurock and others arrested at Hinwil and elsewhere in Grüningen, was preceded by a thorough examination of the accused Brethren. For the first time all three leaders were together on trial, and for the first time the city council of Zurich seriously endeavored to carry through a proper trial with legal witnesses, with the hope of exposing the roots of the general movement. The chief defendants were Grebel, Manz, Blaurock, and Margareta Hottinger. The chief witnesses against them were Ulrich Zwingli and Sebastian Hofmeister. The record of the trial is first-class evidence about the faith of the Brethren and deserves examination. Let us consider first the testimony of Zwingli.[84]

The chief burden of Zwingli's testimony was that two years before (in 1523) Stumpf, Grebel, and Manz had proposed to him and Leo Jud certain urgent reforms in the church. In addition he reported a letter from Berne according to which a certain Martin of Berne (who had been in Zurich for a time) is reported to have said, that the Anabaptists in Zurich had three principles: (1) "that there should not be any magistracy," (2) "that all things should be held in common," and (3) "the security of the saints." Another point made by Zwingli was that canon Brennwald had heard third-handed a very bad report about Blaurock, who is supposed to have told an Anabaptist from Zollikon at the beginning of his imprisonment in the previous February, 1525, "As soon as there are enough of you, you should prepare to resist my lords in case they send a company of soldiers against you." Zwingli also reported an ambiguous statement by Grebel which he was supposed to have made at the time of the previous disputation; "just as if the Messiah were already at hand." At the close Zwingli summarized his testimony and accused the Brethren of revolution, saying that "from all this he could infer nothing else but that they had as their final goal to so increase their number that they would be able to free themselves from the control of the authorities." Zwingli's purpose in making the charge of sedition and revolution is perfectly clear; he wanted to curse the Anabaptists with charges which they could not escape; he was turning the trial from one of doctrinal and ecclesiastical questions into one of social revolution. Zwingli's grievous inconsistency in this is clear from the fact that later he himself stated more than once that the conflict between himself and the Brethren concerned only nonessential external things.[85] For his charge of revolution, Zwingli could produce as evidence only two rumors which had come from a third and fourth hand.

Hofmeister's testimony consisted chiefly of a support of Zwingli's charges. Against Grebel he had nothing to present, but he gave the trial further impetus by testifying that Manz "had discussed the magistracy with him and had argued that there was no need for it."

Canon Brennwald, the next witness, gave details about the report which Zwingli had related concerning George Blaurock. Jörg Syz, another witness, confirmed Brennwald's statements. Antoni Walder, the final witness, brought the matter to a very dangerous point for Blaurock. He asserted that he had heard from a secondary source, that Blaurock had inquired of a certain Hottinger from Zollikon who was visiting him in prison, "How do things stand outside, and which party is the stronger?" When Hottinger answered, "Their side is the stronger, that is, the ones against us," Blaurock is said to have replied, "When my lords send their soldiers against you do not be afraid, and don't give way before their force, but be brave and steadfast." After these witnesses had completed their testimony Zwingli made a few additional minor statements about the Brethren.

A critical examination of the trial record by a modern reader will make it quite clear that the testimony against the Brethren was woefully weak. The only part of it which was really serious, consisted of reports of second and third hand, and was directed primarily against Blaurock.

The answers of the accused to the charges were clear and unequivocal. They vigorously denied the charge of revolutionary agitation and of promoting communism, as well as the accusation that they had boasted of having received marvelous signs and visions. They gave a clear statement of their position on various points. The testimony of Felix Manz is typical: "In regard to the charge by Dr. Hofmeister concerning his advocacy of a separate church and the denial of the magistracy, he wanted it known that what he had said was that those who desired to accept Christ and to be obedient to His Word and to follow His example should seek to unite themselves by the sign of baptism and should leave the others with their own faith." As far as community of goods was concerned, he wanted it understood that what he meant was that a good Christian should share with his neighbor when he was in need. He admitted that his opinion was "that no Christian could be a magistrate, nor could he use the sword to punish or to kill anyone, for he had no Scripture for such a thing."

Conrad Grebel's testimony is also important for an understanding of his views. "Conrad Grebel persisted in his conviction that infant baptism was of the devil and that rebaptism was right, and that Zwingli was guilty of false and incorrect teaching. He would not admit that he had ever taught that one should take something from anyone else for nothing. As for the church, he said that whosoever was a gambler, a usurer or any such thing, such a one should not be found among Christians, but should be expelled by the ban, as the Scripture teaches us. He had never taught that men should not obey the authorities."

If Zwingli had no stronger evidence to bring against the Brethren than what he produced at this trial it is easy to see why he found the struggle with the Brethren so difficult, and why he at one time found it necessary to say that the conflict with the old church (Catholicism) was child's play compared to the struggle with the Anabaptists.[86]

Grebel, Manz, and Blaurock were imprisoned in the tower in Zurich in accordance with the mandate of November 18, 1525.[87] Throughout the winter, additional Brethren were captured and added to the number in the tower.[88] Hubmaier does not seem to have been placed in the same prison when he was imprisoned later in the winter. Grebel, according to reports, took advantage of the opportunity to strengthen the Brethren in prison by reading the Scripture and admonishing.[89]

On March 5 and 6, 1526, the whole company of prisoners was given a second trial. The record of the trial reports very little about Grebel and Manz, and only a brief "confession" or letter from Blaurock.[90] It is worthy of note however that Grebel requested permission to have a "writing" printed. On March 7 all the prisoners were again sentenced, this time to life imprisonment.[91] Apparently the second trial was held for the purpose of preparing for the new and severe mandate which was issued against the Anabaptists on March 7, 1526. In this new mandate rebaptizing was sternly forbidden, and death by drowning was set as the punishment for all those who performed it.[92]

But the life-long imprisonment lasted only fourteen days, for on March 21, 1526, all the prisoners escaped by means of a rope through an unlocked window.[93] Grebel, Manz, and Blaurock at first were unwilling to take advantage of the opportunity but finally let themselves be persuaded. The drawbridge happened to be down so they all got over the moat without any trouble. Two of the prisoners, William Exel of Wallis and Fridli Abyberg of Schwyz, elected to remain in the city and were caught again; through them the whole story of the escape became known and was entered upon the records.[94] It is interesting to note their report that when the fleeing prisoners discussed whither they might go, some of them humorously suggested, "Let us go to the red Indians across the sea."[95]

Whither the prisoners actually fled is not known in detail. Fourteen days after the escape Manz baptized a woman at Embrach, which lies north of Zurich in the county of Kyburg.[96] In June, 1526, Blaurock and Manz appeared in Grüningen according to an official report from that district.[97] Grebel however was not with them. On October 12, 1526, Felix Manz, together with Jakob Schupfelberg of Grüningen, was captured in St. Gall,[98] but apparently released again, for on December 3, 1526, Manz and Blaurock were arrested together in Grüningen.[99] After a month's imprisonment, Manz, as is well known, was executed by drowning on January 25, 1527, as the first martyr of the Anabaptists in Zurich.[100]

Not much is known about Grebel's movements after the escape from the tower, in March, 1526. He apparently did not go with Manz and Blaurock. His name appears only once more in the official records and then only in an indirect report. On April 11, 1526, Ulrich Teck of Waldshut testified in his trial before the court in Zurich that he had traveled together with Grebel and others on a journey to Glattfelden, which lies north of Zurich on the road to the Rhine. He says "he knew of no meetings, and all he had done was to accompany Grebel to Glattfelden. When he had asked Grebel whither he was going Grebel had replied that he did not want to say. So he (Teck) likewise could not say and he appeals to my lords in a friendly manner to do their best by him. . . ."[101] Nor do we today know any better than Uli Teck whither Grebel turned his steps. Glattfelden is near to Eglisau on the Rhine, not far from Schaffhausen. Was Grebel pointing toward Hallau, or perhaps Waldshut, or perhaps even more remote places?

It seems that about this time Grebel finally succeeded in having a pamphlet on baptism printed[102] in spite of his failure to secure the permission from the Zurich city council which he had requested on March 6, 1525. As early as the summer of 1524 he had had in mind such a plan, which he often mentioned after that time; but the authorities of Zurich constantly made it impossible for him to get anything printed. Perhaps the pamphlet was finally printed in Basel. At any rate it was widely circulated among the Brethren, and at last reached Zwingli's hand (after a long search by the latter) in the form of a copy which was sent to him in the summer of 1527 by Oecolampad from Basel.

Unfortunately no copy of the pamphlet has been preserved. However, the first part of Zwingli's book against the Anabaptists, called *Elenchus,* consists of a refutation of this pamphlet, in the course of which numerous quotations are made from it. [I have attempted to restore the pamphlet as far as possible by assembling these quotations in a continuous document which will be published in the volume containing Grebel's writings.]

The last news of Grebel is given by Johannes Kessler in his *Sabbata.* There he reports that Grebel and Manz had preached in Appenzell and Graubünden, and that Grebel thereafter went to Maienfeld in the Oberland where he fell a victim to the plague and died.[103] This report by Kessler about Grebel's final activity is probably reliable. Vadian, who was Kessler's good friend, would scarcely have permitted the publication of an incorrect report concerning the death of his brother-in-law. It is possible that Grebel and Manz worked together in Appenzell for a time in the summer of 1526 and that they separated there, Grebel to go to Maienfeld and Manz to return to his home in Zurich.

What drew Grebel to Maienfeld can no longer be determined with certainty. As early as the spring of 1525 the Anabaptist movement had reached as far as this region. Perhaps Grebel wanted to visit the Brethren there, as Manz and Blaurock had done already in the spring of 1525.[104] On the other hand it is possible that he wanted to visit his sister Barbara, the wife of Beat Beli of Maienfeld, hoping to find there a place of rest,[105] although it is not absolutely certain that she was living here as early as the summer of 1526. The long imprisonment in Zurich during the previous winter had no doubt undermined his already weak health, and the constant traveling about had exhausted his strength.

The date of Grebel's death cannot be fixed with certainty. Kessler's phrase "not long thereafter," in referring to Grebel's death, furnishes no time value, since the point of reference is not clear. According to a letter of Zwingli dated November 29, 1526, Grebel had died "several months" before that date.[106] This would point to about August, 1526, or possibly earlier. In the trial of Jacob Grebel, father of Conrad, which took place October 11-30, 1526, the son Conrad is referred to as one who had died earlier, and his children are called orphans.[107] The plague raged in Chur in August, 1526, according to a letter from Comander to Vadian dated August 13,[108] but it was still raging as late as October 2, for on that date Comander wrote to Zwingli about the high mortality.[109]

Thus Grebel escaped the martyr's death which was the lot of his brother-in-the-faith and co-worker Felix Manz, and which would certainly have been his portion if he had come back to Zurich from Maienfeld.[110] His death was a severe blow to the young Anabaptist movement in Switzerland, which could ill afford to lose his strong and moderate leadership.

IX

THINGS MOST SURELY BELIEVED: CONRAD GREBEL'S THEOLOGY

A. Its Development

It is impossible to give a systematic presentation of the theology of Conrad Grebel; an exposition of the fundamental principles which he advocated is all that can be expected. The explanation for this fact is obvious. In the spring of 1522 Grebel was converted at about twenty-four years of age; four short years later, in the summer of 1526, he died as a fugitive far from home. Of these four years, the year and a half after January, 1525, were spent as a legal outlaw according to the decree of the canton of Zurich, which meant that he was in constant danger of arrest and imprisonment. Of these eighteen months Grebel spent scarcely a month at home with his family and his books, while six months, from October, 1525, to March, 1526, were spent as a prisoner in the tower prison in Zurich. And in May, 1525 he sold his books. Under such circumstances theology is not likely to prosper. In the first years of Grebel's life as an evangelical Christian one could scarcely expect extensive theological activity, for he had not devoted himself to theological interests before his conversion and it was months if not more before he was mature enough to think reflectively and systematically about his experience. Furthermore, in those first months and years the Gospel itself was but gradually winning its way into the hearts of the people of Zurich under Zwingli's preaching.

But there is another reason why Grebel's theological thinking was not systematic; it was the fruit of struggle with the living issues of the church of his time. He struggled with the acute and concrete problems of tithes and usury, of baptism and the other sacraments, and finally and above all with the shaping of the life of the church and the fashioning of the daily life of the individual Christian after the example of Christ. Grebel's theological thinking was thus not systematic because it was forged in the fire of urgent current needs, and not in the retreat of a monastery or the relative advantage of a professorship or a pastorate. One point, the authority of the Bible, was taken for granted by him, hence he never felt the need for a theological examination of the problem of how to use the Scripture.

Fortunately the period when Grebel first began to struggle with the issues of the day was for him a time of comparative peace and quiet at home in Zurich. For several months during the spring and summer of 1524 he had time to think, and time to give expression to his inner urge to deal with the problems of the time in writing. His first and most important theological composition, his epistle to Thomas Müntzer, was written at the beginning of September, 1524. In a letter to Vadian at that time he says that he was "full of words," and felt himself driven by the Spirit to testify to others of the truth which had taken possession of his own soul.[1] At that time he mentioned a plan to write two booklets, but he had scarcely undertaken them when the onrushing affairs of life broke off abruptly and forever the peaceful labors which might have led to a more systematic construction of his theology. The short petition which he wrote to the Zurich council in December, 1524, and in which he dealt with the question of baptism, was a document written in the heat of the beginning conflict. With the disputation of January 17, 1525, and the strict mandate of the following day, the crowded and bitter months of labor and suffering were upon him. There were other and more pressing duties than writing theology. He became an evangelist, an itinerant preacher, a personal worker, everything but a theologian. Even his correspondence with his friends seems to have stopped. Only with difficulty was he able to prepare a small pamphlet against Zwingli's defense of infant baptism when death overtook him at the early age of twenty-eight. What we have of Grebel's theological expression is only a number of fragments, all, with the exception of the epistle to Müntzer, apologetic or polemic in character, dealing chiefly with the question of baptism.

Finally it should not be forgotten that Grebel had no theological training of any sort. Hubmaier, Reublin, Menno Simons, Sattler and others had studied theology, but Grebel was a humanist. He had read Homer, Vergil, and Horace; he had studied poetry and geography; but of the Bible and the great theologians of the church he had learned little. Neither did Grebel have practical experience in ecclesiastical matters. Other Anabaptist leaders had been active in practical life as preachers, as priests, as teachers, or as monks, before they joined the movement; but Grebel had been only a student. The rudimentary character of Conrad Grebel's theology is therefore the result of the practical circumstances of his life and of his earlier development.

Furthermore, the available testimony does not permit the portrayal of development in Grebel's theology from his conversion to his death, for the period of time involved is too short and the extent of the content is too meagre. Except for a few incidental remarks in earlier letters, the chief witnesses, which are the epistle to Müntzer, the "Protest," and the letter from Hegenwalt, all come from the same time, a period of about three months from September to the beginning of December, 1524. The later material is too meagre to permit the idea of a later stage of development, and even so it agrees completely with the spirit of the chief writings mentioned above. His "Taufbüchlein" of 1526 treats only the question of baptism and does not manifest any progress in thought over the earlier writings. It is plain then that the three chief writings named above must constitute the primary basis for the delineation of Grebel's theology.

B. The Documentary Sources for the Theology of Grebel

I. Evaluation of the Sources

The first question that faces one who seeks to gather the sources for Conrad Grebel's theology is a problem of methodology. It is the question as to what sources shall be recognized as valid. Grebel's own letters and writings belong without question in the list; the autographs have all been preserved, with the exception of the booklet of 1526. The statements made by Grebel in court are probably also reliable, although it should not be forgotten that the minutes of the trials are not altogether above criticism. Too often the clerk of the court repeats the words of the witnesses in condensed form, and one can never be sure whether he reproduces the exact words or allows his prejudices to color the final form. When the testimony before the court is the testimony of others than Grebel himself, the problem becomes still more difficult. Statements made by friends may well be accepted, but accusations by enemies need to be critically examined, particularly if the statements are mere hearsay evidence and rumors of second and third hand. A document such as the letter of Erhard Hegenwalt to Grebel, who makes assertions on the basis of statements in Grebel's letter to him, may be accepted as reliable.

A second question is whether testimony concerning the teaching of friends and co-workers of Grebel is to be accepted as evidence of Grebel's own views. This would involve testimony about the teaching of Manz, Blaurock, Castelberger, and the Brethren in Grüningen and Zollikon. While such material has value, yet it does not merit full acceptance in the strictest sense of the term. The reason for this is that, although the Brethren worshiped together and considered themselves to be the church of Christ, they did not before Grebel's death set up binding statements of faith in the form of confessions or creeds or even a church discipline. In the early days of the movement, under the pressure of circumstances, each man had to stand more or less on his own theological feet. Gradually the intimate co-operation and fellowship of months and years brought a more complete unity in faith and teaching. Furthermore, many of the early Brethren were simple peasants and artisans, some of whom could neither read nor write,[2] and who at any rate gave little thought to precision of doctrine. Again, the leaders were not wholly agreed in ideas, attitudes, and emphasis. Some of the trials brought forth evident differences in point of view. The most substantial difference was that between Blaurock and Grebel. Blaurock had not worked with the Brethren before the first disputation in Zurich, and after that he and Grebel were really seldom together, except for a few days in January, 1525, and then for a short time at the end of the summer of that year in Grüningen. It was only in prison from October, 1525, to March, 1526, that they first really had intimate fellowship. Blaurock was different in temperament from Grebel. He was a strongly developed, vigorous, independent personality, a man of action, inclined to enthusiasm in contrast to the more moderate and balanced Grebel. He was variously called "the strong George," and "a second Paul." Even Manz was more radical than Grebel, and seems to have been attracted more to Blaurock, for the two of them were frequently together, while Grebel often went his own way. It is doubtful whether one should really think of a permanent working cooperation between the three leaders. For this reason, it would probably be better to use testimony about the views of Blaurock and Manz only in the negative sense. That would mean that views which they deny, should likewise not be attributed to Grebel, but that views which they held are not necessarily therefore to be counted as Grebel's. In general it is correct to say that the program of Blaurock and Manz, at the outset at least, was more radical and not so soberly tempered as Grebel's program. The only testimony regarding Castelberger's views falls in the early period (January, 1523),[3] but it may be allowed some weight, since he and Grebel were later good friends.

Testimony regarding the views of such Anabaptists as the Brethren at Zollikon and Grüningen should also be used chiefly on the negative principle.[4] While it is evident that Grebel's influence must have worked among them, nevertheless outside Brethren from St. Gall, Chur, and Waldshut, also influenced them, and they were Anabaptist leaders with whom Grebel had little or no contact. It is therefore difficult to say to what extent Grebel's views coincided with the views of these groups.

Documents containing the testimony of opponents and enemies of the Anabaptists of Zurich should naturally be treated as polemic material and of little value. The contemporary chroniclers seldom report more than a few general observations, and reflect usually the current opinions of the group to which they belong, whether evangelical or Catholic. Only Kessler reports more extensively and with a certain objectivity; some of his material is usable. Zwingli's own testimony as to the teaching of the Zurich Anabaptists (as found in *Wer Ursach gebe zu Aufruhr, Taufbüchlein, Elenchus*) is not of much value as a source for Grebel's theology, for three reasons. In the first place he never mentions the views of any specific leader, not even Grebel. Second, his attitude is strongly polemical and lacking in objectivity,[5] for he writes primarily with the purpose of presenting the Anabaptists to the people of Zurich and to the world at large in the worst possible light, and to show that he himself had nothing to do with the new heresy. In the third place Zwingli's testimony is not always contemporary for Grebel, particularly in parts of the *Elenchus;* that is, it consists of a recall of statements made by Grebel one to three years earlier, and exact recall is practically impossible. In general therefore Zwingli's testimony concerning the teaching of the Anabaptists is also subject in use to the negative principle, namely, that his statements are to be accepted only when they are favorable to the Anabaptists or affirm an agreement between him and them. For instance, Zwingli's assertion that the differences between him and the Brethren concerned only outward things and did not touch the inner life is to be accepted as plausible.[6] Later polemic writings against the Brethren, such as Bullinger's works, naturally have little or no value for the determination of Grebel's theology, although they have some value for the understanding of the movement in general.

II. List of the Sources

The list of sources given below has been prepared on the basis of the methodological principles established in the preceding section, and is here presented in order to give a brief and systematic survey of the available material.

List of the Sources for the Theology of Conrad Grebel Arranged in Chronological Order and According to Value

1. Self-Testimony by Conrad Grebel

I. *Letters.* All letters are addressed to Vadian, except the last which is addressed to Andreas Castelberger. (*) designates the more important letters, only two of which however rank as outstanding,—the one of Dec. 15, 1524 and the one of May 30, 1525.

1522: Nov. 2, Dec. 1, *Dec. 29.
1523: *July 13, July 14, July 28, Aug. 11, *Nov. 12, Dec. 18.
1524: Feb. 25, *Sept. 3, *Oct. 14, *Dec. 15.
1525: Jan. 14, *May 30, *End of May.

II. *Statements before the Zurich Court.* All are found in Egli's *Aktensammlung zur Geschichte der Zürcher Reformation.*

1525: Nov. 8-18, Egli, No. 692.
1526: March 5-7, Egli, Nos. 933, 934.

III. *Writings.*

1522, Aug. 23: *In Gratiam Reducis Evangelii* (published as an appendix to Zwingli's *Apologeticus Archeteles*).
1524, Sept. 5: *Epistle* to Thomas Müntzer, not published at the time.
1524, December: *Protestation und Schutzschrift* to the council at Zurich, not published at the time.
1526, Spring: *Taufbüchlein.*

2. Testimony by Others About Grebel

I. *Letters.*

1525, Jan. 1: Erhart Hegenwalt to Grebel.

II. *Statements before the Zurich Court* (The dates given below represent the time of Grebel's supposed statements, not the date of the documentation or the report. "Egli" means *Aktensammlung zur Geschichte der Zürcher Reformation.*)

1. By Friends:
1525, Feb. to July: Egli, Nos. 636, 674, 792, 797, 938.

2. By Opponents:
(a) Zwingli
1524, Spring: Egli, No. 692.
(b) Hofmeister
1525, February: Egli, No. 692.

(The list given includes only those deemed significant.)

3. Testimonies Concerning the Doctrine of the Zurich Anabaptists

I. *Self-testimony of the Anabaptists.*

1. Andreas Castelberger, January, 1523 (Egli, No. 623).
2. Felix Manz, November, 1525 (Egli, No. 692).
3. Georg Blaurock, February 18, 1525 (Egli, No. 646); November, 1525 (Egli, No. 692); March, 1526 (Egli, No. 933).
4. The Zollikon Brethren, Feb. 6, 1525 (Egli, No. 636); March, 1525 (Egli, No. 674); June, 1525 (Egli, No. 762).
5. The Grüningen *Eingabe,* June, 1527 (Egli, No. 1201).

II. *Zwingli's polemic writings against the Brethren.*

1. December, 1524: *Wer Ursach Gebe zu Aufruhr* (*Zwingli Werke* III, pp. 355-469).
2. May, 1525: *Von der Taufe, von der Wiedertaufe, und von der Kindertaufe* (*Zwingli Werke* IV, pp. 188-337).
3. July, 1527: *In catabaptistarum strophas elenchus* (*Zwingli Werke* VI, 1-196).

III. *Contemporary Chronicles*

1. 1524-1533, *Johannes Kessler's Sabbata,* pp. 141-2.

III. The Content of Grebel's Theological Writings

1. In Gratiam Reducis Evangelii
August 23, 1522

Grebel's first theological writing was a short Latin poem of sixteen lines composed in the rare "Phalaecean" meter,[7] which appeared as an appendix to Zwingli's booklet *Apologeticus Archeteles,* published August 23, 1522.

Zwingli's booklet was in reality a reckoning with the supporters of the old faith, a "first and last" (*Archeteles*) word. In form it is a reply to the admonition which the bishop of Constance had directed to the canons of Zurich on May 24, 1522, in regard to the transgression of the Lenten fast. But in content it is nothing less than an exposition of the fundamental principle by which Zwingli intended to carry through his reform. It is a defense of the Scripture as the sole authority in matters of faith, and is characterized by strong invective against the papacy as well as joyful testimony for the Gospel.

The importance of the theme is emphasized by the vigor of the language.

Grebel's poem is cast in the same spirit as that of the book itself and easily competes with it in vigor of language. In happy exultation Grebel celebrates the overthrow of the hierarchy and the victory of the Gospel. The bishops had enslaved the people with their bulls and decrees and by the promotion of a despicable superstition, but now God has set up again in all its former glory His divine Word. The Gospel has victoriously broken the chains of its servitude, and victorious it will remain. The spirit of the poem gives abundant evidence that Grebel like Zwingli had adopted with his whole heart the sole authority of Scripture as the foundation for faith and as the guiding principle of life. In the light of history, it is symbolical that this poem, with its emphasis upon the authority of Scripture, stands as the first witness to Grebel's theology. Grebel adopted as his own the so-called "formal principle" of the Reformation, the *sola scriptura,* and to this principle he remained true throughout his life. Zwingli on the contrary, according to Grebel's sincere conviction, abandoned this principle at a decisive point and in a critical moment, so that a year and a half later Grebel felt justified in condemning Zwingli's change of position in the following sharp words: "Zwingli, the herald of the Word, has cast down the Word, has trodden it under feet, and has brought it into captivity."[8]

2. Epistle to Thomas Müntzer
September 5, 1524

The epistle which Grebel wrote to Thomas Müntzer[9] on September 5, 1524, in the name of his brethren and with their signatures, is the most extensive and important document for Grebel's theology. In extent it is longer than all the other theological writings put together (four thousand words in contrast to three thousand three hundred). It is also the only writing which deals with other questions than baptism. It is significant also because it is the *first* witness for the theology of the Swiss brethren, whose leader Conrad Grebel had already become, as this letter clearly shows. Although it bears the form of a letter it is clearly much more than that, and certainly belongs with the theological writings. Since the origin and general character of the epistle has already been thoroughly discussed (in Chapter VII) it will be possible to proceed at once to the anaylsis of its content.

The epistle has a peculiar double character. On the one hand it pays homage to Müntzer "together with Carolostadio" as "the purest heralds and preachers of the purest, divine Word." On the other hand—and this is its primary purpose—it constitutes a strong criticism of Müntzer. In fact the whole epistle, except for the short introduction and the similarly short conclusion, is cast in the form of an admonition and instruction to Müntzer. However, in spite of this superficial form, it is in reality just as much an exposition of Grebel's teaching on the points on which he disagreed with Müntzer. From this point of view it should be treated as a presentation of the program of Conrad Grebel and his followers. Unfortunately the discussion is not rounded out in systematic form and really consists only of a succession of individual points.

The epistle was occasioned by the fact that the Reformation in Zurich at this time found itself in a situation similar to that at Wittenberg, and it is only on the basis of this background that the epistle is to be understood. Grebel devotes the opening section, therefore, to a brief sketch of this situation, including an interpretation of the history of the Reformation up to this time, and furnishing a justification for the rejection by Grebel of the program of the reformers. Grebel acknowledges the valuable service which the evangelical preachers, that is, the reformers at Wittenberg and Zurich, have rendered to the evangelical cause, and which they were in part still performing. They had uncovered the apostasy of the old church. But up to the present they had not restored true Christianity, either as far as the organization and ordinances of the church were concerned or in regard to the behavior of the individual believer. Faith, concerning which there was so much talk, had remained an external and deceptive faith which had failed to produce fruit in life, for sin still reigned everywhere and the church had failed to exercise discipline. Even the ancient papal and anti-Christian forms of baptism and the Lord's Supper were still maintained. It was clear that instead of actually putting into practice the principle of the complete and sole authority of the Scripture, the reformers were still paying altogether too much attention to the authority of men, even though those men were the reformers themselves. The chief cause for this failure of the reformers had been "the false forbearance" (*das falsche Schonen*) practiced by them. With this expression Grebel condemns the tactics of slow and cautious advance which Luther and Zwingli were using. What these men no doubt sincerely considered to be wisdom and prudence, Grebel saw as a spiritless slipping along, as a compromising yielding which was bound to result in serious danger to the cause of the Gospel.

In contrast to these tactics Grebel advocates an heroic and unconditional obedience to divine truth. He would have no half and half; he would proceed at once to the erection of the true church of Christ according to the standard of the Gospel. The Word of God alone should be the guide, without admixture of human wisdom. Of the strategy of "false forbearance" and of human calculation Grebel has had enough. In fact he has had so much of it in Zurich that he has lost confidence in the shepherds there. Zwingli, for his part, had lost confidence in the impetuous young radicals of Zurich, so much that he openly and from the pulpit condemned them as "satans." The breach on both sides was complete. This was the situation in Zurich.

What pleased Grebel and his brethren in Müntzer was simply the fact that he openly and decisively advocated the principle of absolute and unconditional obedience to the Scripture. Müntzer, it seemed, was also one of those who had had enough of "false forbearance." He was not afraid of either the reformers or the princes. Here was a man after their own hearts, thought the Brethren in Zurich. In this sense they also wanted to be, in fact they already were, "seven new young Müntzers."[10]

But it was only in a formal sense on the basis of the principle of unconditional obedience to the Scriptures that the Brethren agreed with Müntzer, for as soon as they examined his program in detail they saw that they would have to disagree with it. Four points they at once rejected completely: (1) the introduction of singing in worship; (2) the adoption of a German liturgy as a substitute for the Latin Mass; (3) the erection of stone tablets of the ten commandments in the church; (4) the endorsement of violent resistance against oppression and persecution. On three additional points in which they were not sure of Müntzer's position, they also took a negative stand. These were: (1) Müntzer still accepts as salary the income from a benefice, whereas the preacher of the Gospel should be supported by voluntary donations of the church and not through money derived from rent and tithes; (2) the Brethren doubt whether Müntzer has actually erected a true Christian church with discipline according to Matthew 18; (3) they doubt also whether Müntzer's actual practice in baptism agrees with the views expressed in his writings, and for this reason they admonish him to cease baptizing children. In the last point their doubts were fully justified, for Müntzer apparently never abandoned the practice of infant baptism as long as he continued as the responsible pastor of a parish.

Finally it should be said that the spirit throughout is thoroughly religious. The social interest which is prominent in Müntzer appears only indirectly in Grebel. Grebel is concerned not with leading a social revolution but with establishing the church of Christ on earth according to the Gospel. This does not mean that Grebel has no interest in social problems, but only that with him the dominant interest is the church, its essence and its evangelical function, which does not include political concerns.

Grebel continues to describe the situation in which the Brethren found themselves in Zurich, by relating how they were strengthened in their attitude by the reading of Müntzer's tract because they saw that he, like them, had the courage to attack the weaknesses of the reformers. They desired to strengthen him in his attitude so that he should not fall away from the divine principle which he had adopted. The admonition of Grebel to Müntzer in this respect is not only the high point in the epistle, it is a classic theological locus for all of Conrad Grebel's writing. "Therefore we entreat and admonish you as a brother by the name, power, word, spirit, and salvation, which has come to all Christians through Jesus Christ our Master and Saviour, that you would earnestly endeavor to preach unafraid only the divine Word, erect and defend only divine institutions, cherish alone what is good and right, namely what may be found in pure and clear Scripture, and reject, hate, and curse all proposals, words, opinions, and institutions of all men, including your own."[11]

This general endorsement and admonition to Müntzer having been given, the criticism begins. "We understand and have observed that you have translated the Mass into German and that you have ordained a new German liturgy. This cannot be good, for we find in the New Testament no teaching about singing [and liturgy]." This sentence announces Grebel's method; everything must be tested by the New Testament, and what is not found therein as the teaching of Christ and the apostles or as an apostolic practice must be abandoned. To this first principle a second standard is added; everything must edify, must produce a true faith leading to right living, and dare not lead to an "external hypocritical faith." It is clear that Grebel is not concerned primarily about an outward form, nor about having an outward legalistic biblicism, but about life and performance. He seeks reality. To Grebel the reformers are the men who are creating and promoting an externalistic type of Christianity. It is remarkable in this connection to note that the reformers likewise accused the Anabaptists of the external legalism of a "hypocritical faith," an accusation which is still made today and still believed. Whatever justification there might be for such an accusation in relation to other Anabaptist leaders and groups, it certainly is not justified in reference to Grebel and the first Swiss Brethren.

The construction of the epistle to Müntzer is fairly clear. Following the introduction and the general account of the Reformation as reported above, Grebel undertakes the criticism of various points in Müntzer's practice. He deals with seven points, as noticed above: liturgy, Mass (Lord's Supper), benefices, tablets, church discipline, force (sword), and baptism. Let us briefly consider his discussion of these points.

(1) *Liturgy or singing.* Grebel proves with nine numbered arguments that singing does not belong in worship: (1) there is no example or teaching about it in the New Testament; (2) it does not edify; (3) Paul forbids singing (Eph. 5, Col. 3); (4) what the Scripture does not positively teach and command is forbidden; (5) Christ requires only the preaching of the Word; (6) human beings may not add to the Word; (7) singing is not justified as a means to eliminate the Mass; (8 and 9) it was not ordained of God and must therefore be rooted out by the word and command of Christ.

It must be admitted that Grebel's arguments do not carry weight today; they are for the most part artificial arguments, for he felt it necessary to find scriptural proofs for a position which cannot be supported from Scripture. The only deeper argument is that contained in a remark under point (5), where Grebel says, "He who sings poorly is annoyed, and he who can sing well becomes proud." But even this observation is not always true. However, although the arguments which Grebel uses are weak, his general position is not so far wrong for his time. Grebel was striking at liturgical singing by the clergy. No less a one than Zwingli himself shared Grebel's views on this point, and it is altogether possible that Grebel derived his views from Zwingli. In the year 1525 such singing actually was suppressed in Zurich and the organ was stilled. In the year 1527 Zwingli went still further and abolished all singing by the congregation because he feared that the external form would interfere with the inner life. Zwingli was not an enemy of culture and music, for he himself was a poet and musician. Grebel likewise can not on this account be considered an enemy of culture and of music, for what he desired was to keep the worship of the church as purely spiritual as possible.

(2) *The Mass or Lord's Supper.* In sixteen numbered arguments Grebel points out the dangers associated with outward ceremonies in worship and opposes a ritualistic conception of the Lord's Supper. (a) The Mass is not to be reformed but abolished (points 7 to 10. In points 7 to 9 there is a certain double reference to liturgy and Mass). (b) Only the words of Jesus are to be used, and they are not to be thought of as a "consecration" (point 12). (c) In order to avoid a "hypocritical devotion" and the worship of bread and a "falling away from the spiritual," everything unusual in connection with the celebration must be avoided, consequently no special bread, no special cup, "no priestly customs and clothing" for the Mass, no singing, no additions (points 13, 14, and 24). (d) The Lord's Supper, if it be received in faith and love, signifies "a union with Christ and the brethren" (points 16 and 17). (e) Therefore the Lord's Supper cannot be taken without "condemnation" if a sincere brotherly life is lacking (points 18 and 19). (f) It is a meal of fellowship, not a sacrament, and for this reason it shall not be celebrated by any one person alone, neither by the preacher nor by the dying person (point 20). (g) It shall not be celebrated in the church house, for that leads to a "false devotion" (point 21). (h) "It shall be practiced often and used much" (point 22). (i) Discipline according to the rule of Christ (in Matthew 18) must precede, for love is destroyed if one has fellowship with "false brethren" (point 23). (j) The time of the celebration could be in the evening after the example of Christ and the Corinthian church, but no fixed time is to be required (point 25.) [The numbering is continuous, 1 to 25, for the discussion of singing and the Mass.]

It is clear from the above analysis that what Grebel is seeking to accomplish by his "rules" is a strengthening of the inner devotion, and that he desires to make the Lord's Supper a true expression of faith and of the fellowship of brotherly love. All the details are to be so ordered that the participant "shall be reminded of the body and blood of Christ, of the testament on the cross, so that he shall be willing to live and to suffer for the sake of Christ and the brethren, the head and members of the body," as Grebel says plainly in point 19.

After Grebel has concluded his arguments in the matter of Mass and liturgy he takes up the practical question as to whether it is possible for Müntzer to carry through all these reforms at once in the light of the practical situation facing him. In his counsel to Müntzer on the point Grebel shows clearly that he is in no sense a fanatic who is ready to hew away impetuously regardless of consequences. He reveals himself as a sober and considerate leader. If Müntzer cannot set up scriptural practices at once, says Grebel, he should rather wait and let things stay as they are and continue the Latin liturgy, although omitting the Mass. He should proceed to instruct the people as to what the ideal should be and should wait until he can carry that ideal through, for it is much better "that a little should be done right according to the Word of God and in a right faith and practice rather than that much should be attempted which would lead to a mixing of true and false faith."

(3) *Source of support.* As a further proof that Grebel demands a thoroughgoing abandonment of the old priestcraft without compromise, we note that he advises Müntzer to surrender entirely the income from his benefice. "If your benefice is supported by tithes and rent as with us, and if you are not supported by the whole church, will you not give up your benefice? You well know how a shepherd should be supported." With this demand Grebel follows the teaching of Paul in the New Testament, but he also probably expresses the general feeling of the common people in Zurich.

(4) *Tablets.* The stone tablets containing the ten commandments which Müntzer had set up a short time before in his church should be removed at once as without foundation in Scripture and as simply a human notion.

(5) *Church Discipline.* The mention of this point brings Grebel back again to his fundamental principle, that the Christian church must be organized exclusively according to "the rule of Christ." Grebel wonders whether Müntzer has actually done this in the full sense of the term. For instance, he must establish Christian discipline according to Matthew 18,

and the brother who does not improve his life according to the Gospel after instruction and admonition must be excluded from the church according to the rule of Christ.

(6) *The Sword.* Another requirement of the Gospel which Grebel fears that Müntzer does not recognize is that of nonresistance under oppression and persecution. For Grebel the church is a suffering church with no right to use the sword or to engage in war. "True believing Christians are sheep among wolves, sheep for the slaughter, who must be baptized in anxiety and need, tribulation, persecution, suffering and death, who must be tested in the fire, and who must find the homeland of eternal rest not by the means of killing but by spiritual means. They use neither worldly sword nor war, for among them killing is done away with altogether." With these clear and strong words Grebel advocates not only the negative nonresistance of suffering, but the positive requirement of refusal to kill. It is noteworthy that Grebel bases his rejection of the sword and war and of killing as a whole, not upon the specific teaching of the Sermon on the Mount but upon the thought of the suffering church. Much has been said and written about "a Sermon on the Mount ethic" among the Anabaptists. Certainly the Brethren believed in the Sermon on the Mount and were inspired by it, but there is no evidence that Conrad Grebel either here in the matter of nonresistance nor anywhere else derived his ethical principles exclusively or even primarily from the Sermon on the Mount. Not one citation from it is to be found in the entire scope of his writings, including his letters.

(7) *Baptism.* The last major part of the epistle to Müntzer deals with the question of baptism. Here Grebel concerns himself with an exposition of the significance of baptism rather than with a refutation of infant baptism by Scripture passages. According to Grebel, baptism signifies for him who has come to Christ through repentance and a change of heart, "that his sins have been washed away through his faith and the blood of Christ, that he has died to sin, and that he must now live in newness of life and spirit, and that he will surely be saved if he has the inner baptism of faith and lives according to its meaning." Here Grebel could scarcely have expressed more

clearly the significance of baptism as a symbol (with backward reference to regeneration and forward reference to sanctification) and as a pledge for a constant renewal of life. Hence Grebel says it does not depend so much upon the age, whether the candidate for baptism is a child or an adult, as upon the attitude. In addition Grebel rejects the conception held at Wittenberg that baptism "strengthens and increases faith." He also rejects the teaching of the church fathers "such as Augustine, Tertullian, Theophylact, and Cyprian," that "baptism saves." This teaching of the fathers "discredits faith and the suffering of Christ for the adult, and the suffering of Christ for unbaptized children." As proof that children are saved without baptism Grebel refers to twenty passages in the Old and New Testament without quoting them in detail. The passages are: Genesis 8; Deuteronomy 1, 30, 31; I Corinthians 14; Wisdom 12; II Peter 2; Romans 1, 2, 7, 10; Matthew 18, 19; Mark 9, 10; Luke 18. The new baptismal forms devised by Luther, Leo Jud, Osiander and those at Strasburg, as well as several "still more shameful" forms, are to be rejected as "treasonable and as exceptional blasphemies,"[12] because they retain infant baptism. The fact that the scholars still hold fast to infant baptism is clear evidence for Grebel that all those who are opposing infant baptism, as for example the Brethren in Zurich, are certain to meet persecution.

Although Grebel does not specifically advocate adult baptism, the implications of his argument are clear. Only responsible personalities can have the experience of belief and change of life which baptism signifies.

At the conclusion of his epistle Grebel again testifies to the fellowship which the Brethren in Zurich hope to maintain with Müntzer, requests mutual intercession, and expresses the hope that Müntzer will soon reply.

The Postscript to the Epistle

The postscript to the epistle to Müntzer, which Grebel wrote a few days after September 5, 1524, is not so extensive as the epistle itself but is perhaps even more important, for it contains the reaction of the brethren to the latest news about Müntzer which had reached them after the writing of the epistle itself. They had heard three things: (1) Luther has attacked Müntzer severely in a "shameful booklet"; (2) Müntzer is in danger of persecution; and (3) Müntzer has advocated a program of violence against the princes, that is, he has endorsed war. The new Müntzer with whom the brethren have now become acquainted is different from the old, and the brethren vigorously express themselves on all three points.

(1) Grebel considers the attack by Luther against Müntzer to be unjust, at least on the basis of Müntzer's writing which Grebel has carefully re-read. However, although Grebel does not believe that Müntzer rejects baptism as Luther charges, he is no longer sure about Müntzer's attitude on the question, although he hopes that Müntzer is against infant baptism and a false use of the ordinance. (2) Müntzer is admonished not to let threatened persecution frighten him, although Luther is apparently ready "to hand him over to the princes and the headsman." Grebel admonishes him to cling closer to the Bible which will be his protection, and not to fall away and follow the "false forbearance" of the Luther group, but rather to continue immovably to preach and to practice the clear Word of God. The Brethren in Zurich also expect persecution, for they have already been grievously slandered by their shepherds. But it must be so. "Christ must suffer still more in his members," but He will strengthen them and hold them fast until the end. They should pray for one another. (3) The fact that Müntzer now advocates the use of violence seriously diminishes the good opinion which the Brethren had of him, for hitherto he has pleased them "better than any other in Germany or elsewhere." Hence Grebel admonishes Müntzer very earnestly to drop this point, together with the other points of the tablets and of singing. Particularly he should not seek to justify and maintain these points in case he falls into the hands of Luther and the Duke of Saxony.

The suspicion and fear that Müntzer is after all not quite sound and reliable, and that he has mixed human wisdom with the Word of God, apparently disturbs Grebel so much that he cannot get rid of the thought. He returns a second time to discuss the point. By no means dare Müntzer act "according to human opinions," whether of his own or of other men. If he has already made a step in this false direction, he must retrace his steps, and in the future must follow only the clear Word of God and the rule of Christ, and "establish and teach only an unadulterated baptism and an unadulterated Lord's Supper." If it is impossible to depend in the future on Müntzer and others like him such as Strauss, Carlstadt, and Stiefel, then matters have come to a serious pass in the world as far as the Gospel is concerned. Then the Wittenberg and Zurich shepherds will continue in their "Scripture perversion" from one blindness to another; of this Grebel is certain. And because he fears this very thing, it begins to appear to Grebel that the reformers will gradually become as bad as the "papists." As for Grebel and his group, they will for their part continue immovably on their course; they will continue to point out the shortcomings of the leaders as they have already done, personally in Zurich, and by letter in Wittenberg.

In conclusion Grebel assures Müntzer once more that the Brethren in Zurich have written to him only out of love, because they and Müntzer stand on the same platform in the matter of teaching, and face the same opposition and persecution.

This appendix is of great importance because it demonstrates unmistakably that Grebel and his brethren maintained an independent position over against Müntzer. They do not spare their new-found hero in any respect. If he deviates from their fundamental principle of the sole authority of Scripture he is lost and the great cause of the Gospel can no longer use him. On three points Grebel is certain that Müntzer has already stepped aside: violence, singing, and tablets; and in the chief ordinances, baptism and the Lord's Supper, he is in grave danger of polluting the divine Word by the addition of human wisdom.

If Grebel had been able to foresee Müntzer's later development and his future program, it is certain that he would have dropped Müntzer without hesitation; that is the primary significance of this document. The principle of loyalty to the Scripture must reign, regardless of who must be cast aside.

3. The Protest and Defense
Early December, 1524

The above title was assigned for the first time in 1910 by Emil Egli to a document submitted by Conrad Grebel to the city council of Zurich. The autograph itself is without a title, and likewise without a date and signature, but there is no question as to its authorship or as to the approximate time of its composition. It is rather brief, having less than two thousand words, and being without paragraphing.

In spite of this brevity, the writing is rich in content. It is essentially an appeal to the Zurich authorities to adopt a scriptural policy in the matter of baptism, which would mean the establishment in Zurich of the practice of adult baptism. As a foundation for his appeal Grebel proves that the only baptism which the Scripture teaches and which the apostles practiced was baptism upon the confession of faith.

The petition is clearly and harmoniously constructed, except for a few minor deviations and insertions, and falls into four unequal parts.

(1) *Introduction.* Grebel first specifies the question at issue. A number have recently advocated that infant baptism is scriptural while others have asserted on the contrary that infant baptism is an error and was invented by the pope. The defenders of infant baptism have endeavored to becloud the issue by confusing the question of baptism with the question of revolution, and have accused him, Conrad Grebel, of seditious agitation. This charge is patently false, but since it has been raised Grebel will refute it by an exposition of his position on baptism. He believes that it will be easy to settle the question of baptism if only everyone will stand fast on the principle which Zurich professes to follow, namely, the sole authority of the Scripture in matters of faith. However, this principle was not observed

in the recent discussion, for although the shepherds (Zwingli, Jud, and Grossmann) knew that infant baptism could not be found in Christ and the apostles, they nevertheless demanded from their opponents that which is impossible, namely, that they show a passage containing a positive prohibition of infant baptism. If one should proceed on such a basis, one would soon get far from Scripture. It is not unimportant that there are those in Zurich who desire to practice the only two sacraments differently than Christ taught them. This introduction constitutes about one fourth of the document.

(2) *Proof that baptism on confession of faith is the only scriptural baptism.* Approximately one half of the petition is devoted to a positive argument for believers' baptism. Beginning with John the Baptist and continuing with Christ and Pentecost to Paul, Grebel shows that both in theory and practice baptism was valid only for such as had experienced a renewal of life and as desired to continue in the new life of righteousness. He summarizes his position in a very clear and effective statement: "From these words it is clearly seen what baptism is and to whom baptism should be applied, namely, to one who has been converted by the Word of God, has changed his heart, and henceforth desires to walk in newness of life. . . . From this I have clearly learned and know assuredly, that baptism means nothing else than a dying of the old man, and a putting on of the new, and that Christ commanded to baptize those who had been taught, and that the apostles baptized no one except those who had been taught. . . . And whoever speaks or teaches anything different does that which he cannot prove by any Scripture, and I should like to hear anyone who can show to me by clear and plain Scripture, that John, Christ, or the apostles baptized children or taught that they should be baptized." At the conclusion of this examination of Scripture Grebel assures the council that he has taken his stand solely because of his love and devotion to the eternal truth of God; and he believes "that the eternal true Word of God will likewise sing into the heart of everyone . . . that this is the truth."

(3) *Practical Action.* In the third part Grebel discusses briefly the practical question of infant baptism. He admonishes the council to have the courage to abolish this "abomination" as they have abolished the other traditional abominations. Why Zwingli is not willing to do so Grebel does not understand, because he is sure that Zwingli in his heart does not believe in infant baptism. The council should proceed nevertheless because God's Word will overcome all opponents since nothing human can resist it. The objection that the form of baptism has no significance is rejected by Grebel with the argument that it is dangerous not to obey the commandments of God. As proof of this he points to the miserable end of the sons of Aaron. The council should not do as it did in the matter of images, namely, first accept the truth and then reject it, which cost the death of Klaus Hottinger. Grebel refutes as an argument against the abolition of infant baptism and the introduction of believers' baptism the strange assertion that a change in the custom would lead to a disturbance in civil affairs. He assures the council that the question of baptism has nothing at all to do with the state and civil affairs. Baptism could have no influence, either for good or evil, on the public welfare. For this reason the council should refrain from using the police authority to support a particular form of baptism and to persecute the opponents of infant baptism.

(4) *Request for a written exchange of views.* In the fourth and final part of the petition Grebel requests a further written exchange of views with Zwingli on the question of baptism. Zwingli should be asked to defend his position in writing as he has done for other opponents on other questions. He, Grebel, will then reply in writing, for he is unable to accomplish anything in an oral disputation with Zwingli. He himself is no speaker and the previous discussions have led only to strife and contention. And if any one else in addition to Zwingli, whoever he might be, should undertake to demonstrate that infant baptism is scriptural (he believes that no one on earth can prove such a thing), Grebel offers to answer such an one.

4. The Booklet on Baptism
Spring of 1526

Zwingli's last writing against the Anabaptists, *In Catabaptistarum Strophas Elenchus,* which was published at the end of July, 1527, was a refutation of two Anabaptist writings. One of them was the so-called *Schleitheim Articles,* while the other had no title. One, if not both, of the writings were sent to Zwingli from Basel by Oecolampad on April 24, 1527. The small untitled writing had been sought by Zwingli for a long time in vain, for the Anabaptists in Zurich had circulated it secretly and had boasted that with it they were able to overthrow Zwingli's principle.[13] No copy of the booklet has been preserved, but fortunately in his refutation of it, which constitutes the first part of the *Elenchus,* Zwingli followed a procedure which permits the reconstruction of the greater portion of the writing. What he did was to quote literally portions of the Anabaptist booklet in the form of a careful Latin translation from the Swiss German in which it was written,[14] and to follow these extracts with his refutation. It appears that Zwingli omitted nothing of the original as far as he went, so that the portions translated represent a continuous document. When the translated passages are put together they constitute a short pamphlet of only thirteen hundred words. Zwingli did not give a complete translation of the last part, although what remained, according to his own statement, was not very much.[15] The original document was therefore a tract of about three fourths the size of Grebel's "petition," and in printed form would scarcely have made more than six pages of a pamphlet in the customary small format of that time.

Zwingli called the writing a "booklet" (*libellum*). He did not call it expressly a printed booklet but since he did not emphasize the fact that it was a manuscript as he did in the case of the second booklet, it is possible that it was printed. Twice he states that the original language was Swiss. The pamphlet was therefore apparently a short tract in the Swiss dialect. Its language indicates that it was designed to reach the common people.

The booklet appeared without an author, and Zwingli did not undertake to name the person, although he had very definite suspicions as to his identity. Beginning with J. C. Füsslin (1753),[16] Conrad Grebel or Felix Manz have usually been suggested as the author, as for example, J. M. Usteri (1882),[17] and W. Koehler (1935).[18] Rudolph Staehelin (1895)[19] decided for Conrad Grebel as does also Blanke apparently (1935) although he is not willing to eliminate Manz altogether. Schuler and Schulthess (1832)[20] thought of Hubmaier, and A. Baur (1888)[21] defended this identification. Usteri (1890) opposed Baur.[22]

In my examination of the problem of authorship I follow for the most part the convincing discussion by Blanke in his commentary on the *Elenchus* (*Zwingli Werke* VI, pp. 70-71, 101).[23]

Zwingli's statements relating to the author give definite points of reference for the solution to the problem. The author is Swiss;[24] he is dead (pp. 65, 80), he is in fact in hell (p. 69), he was a participant in the first two "Tuesday conferences" with the Anabaptists in the autumn of 1524 in Zurich (p. 70), and he had promised Zwingli that all would be well if he would only join the Brethren (p. 103). On the basis of Zwingli's statements Hubmaier is excluded, for in the autumn of 1524 he was not in Zurich at all. Only Conrad Grebel and Felix Manz can be considered as authors and both of them fulfill the above requirements completely.

But such a conclusion does not settle the question of authorship for this only establishes whom Zwingli supposed to be the author. The question still remains whether Zwingli's supposition was correct and also whether it is possible to decide between Grebel and Manz. From the content of the booklet itself no evidence can be adduced against the authorship of either Grebel or Manz. Both had earlier indicated an intention to write. Manz did so on March 6, 1526, in prison, when he said, "You will and must learn that infant baptism is not the baptism of Christ. You have not permitted me to write, because I have been in prison, although I have frequently requested it."[25] Grebel referred at least five times to his intention to write, the last time on March 5, 1526, in prison.[26] In testimony before court on that date this report appears: "Conrad Grebel's answer. . . . He would like to show that Zwingli is in error in such (*sc.* infant baptism) and many other things, and requests my lords to permit him to write like Zwingli, in which case he would be able to prove his position. In case it should not appear then that he was successful in doing so, he would be ready to suffer whatever the Lord should appoint."

Arguments which might be adduced in favor of either Grebel or Manz are not very strong. Both were probably present at the first Zurich disputation in January, 1523, and both heard Zwingli's invective against Faber at that time.[27] Very likely both appealed to Zwingli to join their group. The "sophist" from Wittenberg, whose indefensible arguments for infant baptism are mentioned by the author, was probably Erhard Hegenwalt, who had written "several arguments concerning infant baptism" to Myconius at the end of 1524, as he reported in his letter to Conrad Grebel of January 1, 1525;[28] but both Manz and Grebel could have read the "arguments." The accusation against Zwingli that he did not have the courage to confess the truth because of fear of persecution[29] sounds very much like the accusation which Grebel made against Vadian in similar circumstances;[30] nevertheless such an accusation is nothing specifically Grebelian. I cast my vote for Grebel primarily on the grounds that he was the one among the brethren who did the writing on other occasions. Manz never wrote anything, and Grebel had already planned in 1524 to publish a writing against Zwingli. The content of the pamphlet is too meagre to permit any significant comparison with the other writings of Grebel so that no help can be gained from this source.

The uncertainty as to whether Grebel was the author of the *Taufbüchlein* has been resolved by a discovery by Professor Walter Koehler announced in December, 1938, that Heinrich Bullinger of Zurich identifies Grebel as the author in a letter of June 9, 1536 to Oswald Myconius in Basel. I have retained the discussion above on the problem of authorship in order to support this view, inasmuch as Bullinger wrote his comment ten years after the event, and fails to give the ground for his assertion.[30a]

The date of the booklet may be fixed as the spring of 1526 by two arguments. (1) The *terminus a quo* is November 5, 1525, the date of the publication of Zwingli's *Antwort ůber Balthasar Hubmaiers Taufbüchlein,* for the author refutes an argument found in this book and goes to considerable length to denounce the principle of "synecdoche" which Zwingli used in it.[31] (2) The booklet cannot have been written very late in 1526 for Zwingli says that it had already been circulated for a considerable time (*multo iam tempore*) among the Brethren.[32] On the other hand it cannot have appeared before March 21, 1526, for the author was in prison in Zurich from October 8, 1525 to March 21, 1526. I would therefore suggest a date in the winter months 1525-6 for its composition, with circulation in manuscript and possibly in printed form during the summer following. As title of the booklet I have proposed *Booklet on Baptism* (*Taufbüchlein*), because it deals exclusively with the question of baptism.

The theme of the booklet is very limited. It consists exclusively of a refutation of two arguments in favor of infant baptism which Zwingli used in his writing, *Wer Ursach gebe zu Aufruhr,* written in December, 1524. Grebel begins by giving the first argument of Zwingli in literal citation.[33] Then he follows with a refutation in twelve numbered points. The argument by Zwingli is one of the most common arguments in favor of infant baptism. It runs as follows: the apostles baptized entire families and it is to be presumed that these families were not childless; therefore the apostles baptized children. Zwingli refers to three cases, the household of Stephanas, Lydia and her household, and the household of another unnamed person. Grebel's refutation falls into two parts, of which the first has four subdivisions. (1) Zwingli really dares not use this argument, because he once said that what the apostles did or did not do is not regulative for us, but here he professes to use Paul's conduct as a proof for infant baptism (points 1 and 2). (2) In all the families which are described in the Acts or in the Epistles, not any children are referred to (points 3 and 4). (3) Human "cogitation" and rationalization dare not be determinative here, for one can construe the families with or without children; what is needed is a positive proof from the Scripture for infant baptism, and Zwingli cannot produce that. Zwingli should not depart from the principle which he announced to Faber in the first Zurich disputation of January, 1523, "away with human ceremonies and regulations, we want only the Word of God" (points 5 to 7). (4) The family of Stephanas as well as all the other families which were baptized by the apostles, had all first heard the Word of God, for they served the church afterward. That would have been impossible for children (points 8 to 11).

The second argument which Zwingli used, namely that of "synecdoche,"[34] is to be rejected, as Grebel proves by several examples, as for instance that the church in Jerusalem had all "things" in common, in which "things" Zwingli includes the children in the church. Luke says that John baptized men and women in Samaria, therefore no children were baptized (point 12). The author's argument against "synecdoche" continues further, reports Zwingli, but Zwingli has sufficiently refuted it, and he will therefore not make any further quotations. Zwingli will undertake to refute at length in the third part of his book the argument of the author against the "testament" or "covenant."[35] Apparently in this argument Grebel dealt but briefly with Zwingli's defense of infant baptism as based upon the Old Testament covenant, and did so primarily as an illustration of false and unreliable synecdoche. Zwingli's reply on this point in the third part of his book, is couched in general terms, with few quotations from Grebel's booklet.

On the whole one is justified in saying that Grebel succeeded in refuting Zwingli's argument satisfactorily, although the original argument itself is basically weak in character. Zwingli's refutation, on the contrary, in which he seeks to refute Grebel's arguments step by step, is for the most part futile. He often deviates from the fundamental theme, and takes occasion to make numerous evil accusations against the Anabaptists from various sources, arguments which have no connection at all with the text of Grebel's booklet. The worst spot comes in connection with the discussion of the passage in Acts 2:44. Zwingli had originally interpreted this passage in his first book, which Grebel was attacking, to include the children in the church. Grebel on the contrary places the children among the "things," which the church had in common. Grebel's argument is rather weak, it is true, but both Grebel and Zwingli are wrong in their interpretation, for certainly the author of Acts did not mean to include children at all. But Zwingli seizes upon Grebel's weakness and makes it the occasion for a slanderous attack on the Anabaptists. The product is the worst invective against the Anabaptists which appeared in the contemporary literature of the time. Zwingli condemns the Anabaptists as inhuman because they put children on the level of inanimate "things," which places them below the animals. Then he continues to charge the Brethren with communism, with vice, with brutality, and with similar things. And so Grebel's little booklet on baptism unintentionally gave occasion to a libel which has wrought untold harm to the Anabaptist movement throughout the centuries since that time.

The *Taufbüchlein* was considered by the Brethren as an irrefutable argument and a most powerful support for their position on baptism. It was widely circulated among them and held in such high regard that Zwingli felt it urgent to refute it. As late as 1536 it gave great encouragement to the Brethren in Basel, who, according to Oswald Myconius, had found a copy of it and were using it as an effective weapon of defense for their cause.[36]

C. The Ideological Sources of Grebel's Theology

The problem of the source of Grebel's theological ideas is rather difficult to solve because of the meagerness of the available material. It is perhaps the most difficult problem in connection with his biography, and it will be evident from the ensuing discussion that some work on this problem still remains to be done. On the other hand it is possible that the problem never will be satisfactorily solved, and that all that can be done is to offer some general suggestions which may have only a presumptive and not a final validity. In pursuing the solution two types of sources will need to be investigated, (1) personal sources, and (2) literary sources.

1. *Personal Sources*

In view of the rather thorough discussion of the personal influences brought to bear upon Grebel during his humanistic period and the period immediately following his return from Paris given in Chapters II, III, and IV, it will be sufficient to summarize here what has previously been reported and relate it to the problem under discussion.

In the humanist period from 1514-1522 no contribution was made to Grebel's theological thinking by his friends and teachers such as Vadian, Glarean, and Beraldus. Our previous conclusions also rejected the idea of any personal influence from the more religiously-minded humanists of the type of Erasmus and Faber Stapulensis.

In the period of Grebel's Zwinglianism, 1522-1523, the powerful influence of Zwingli himself upon the young Grebel's theological development is beyond question. It is doubtful whether others, such as Grossman, who had been a chaplain in Zurich since 1518, or Leo Jud, who came to Zurich as a pastor on February 2, 1523, exerted any significant influence. If they did it was all in the direction of Zwingli's own thinking.

In the third, or Anabaptist period of Grebel's life, 1524-1526, he was too far ahead of his brethren and co-workers for them to have made any substantial contribution to his thought. The reverse more likely would have been the case. Simon Stumpf and Wilhelm Reublin may have given some slight stimulus, possibly on the question of infant baptism, but there were really no others who could have made any appreciable contribution. Dr. Gerhard Westerburg was in Zurich only a week in October, 1524, and Andreas Carlstadt but for a few days about the same time. Moreover they came after the fundamental lines of Grebel's thought had been set. If they influenced him, particularly Carlstadt, it must have been through literary channels, and at an earlier period. The most that could be surmised would be some influence in the conception of the Lord's Supper which was an issue at the time of Carlstadt's visit to Zurich, but in which Grebel and Zwingli agreed.

It must be concluded then that through personal contact, Zwingli and Zwingli alone exerted a decisive influence on Grebel's thinking. The personal relations between Zwingli and Grebel did not begin until Grebel's return from Paris in July, 1520, but from that time until October, 1523, they were intimate and constant. Grebel not only fellowshipped with Zwingli in the circle of scholars and friends in Zurich who met with Zwingli to study Greek and Hebrew, and without doubt to discuss issues of the day, but he must have had frequent contacts with Zwingli in personal and intimate discussions as man to man. But above all, Grebel heard Zwingli's preaching regularly for more than three years during the time when Zwingli was developing and expounding his new doctrine and when Grebel was just awakening to the Gospel. Without doubt, as was shown earlier, Zwingli was responsible for Grebel's conversion, and was his spiritual mentor and guide in the formative period of his thinking. Nevertheless it is impossible to specify in detail the contributions which this personal contact made, for the evidence is wanting.

2. *Literary Sources*

The problem of tracing literary influence upon Grebel's thought is considerably more difficult than that of tracing personal influence. The extent of Grebel's writing is so slight, and the themes are so limited, that we must rely chiefly upon the scattered references to the reading which he had done, or to books which had come into his possession. In view of the similarity between some of the ideas which Tertullian held and certain aspects of Grebel's theology, it is tempting to suggest an influence from that great church father, particularly since Grebel procured and forwarded a copy of an edition of Tertullian to Vadian in January, 1522.[36a] Unfortunately Grebel does not say whether he read Tertullian or not. It is possible that Grebel was influenced by the Erasmus edition of Lorenzo Valla's *Annotationes ad Novum Testamentum,* published in Basel in 1518, for he still had a copy of the book in his library in May, 1525.[37] But whatever influence might have come upon Grebel from it would scarcely have been in the direction of evangelical or Anabaptist thought.

We are limited then to publications of the reformers and contemporary religious writers. Let us see what is to be found. In the autumn of 1522 Grebel sent to Vadian a copy of Luther's attack upon the King of England.[38] In November of that year he was awaiting the appearance of Melanchthon's *Scholia on the New Testament,* but he fails to state later whether he actually secured and read a copy.[39] In September, 1523, he sent a copy of Melanchthon's *Annotations on John* to Vadian.[40] He followed with interest the inconsequential controversy between Hutten and Erasmus which took place in the summer of 1523, reporting that he knew of the appearance of Hutten's *Expostulatio,* and of Erasmus' *Spongia.*[41] About the same time he was reading Luther's *Urtayl* about Erasmus.[42] He sent Vadian a copy of Oecolampad's *De non habendo pauperum delectu* which appeared in Basel in July, 1523.[43] All of this shows that Grebel followed with interest the new books and pamphlets that appeared on the Swiss book market, but it shows little else. The books which he mentions are for the most part minor publications of slight importance. They are not the great books of the time. And even the ones mentioned are referred to without comment.[44]

In addition to the writings mentioned above, three more significant titles appear among the books which Grebel read in the summer of 1523, all of which found his explicit approbation. The first one was Zwingli's important writing, *Auslegen und Gründe der Schlussreden,* which he sent to Vadian in the month of July with the approving comment, *"liber perchristianum,"*[45] "a most Christian book." The second was "the most evangelical articles" of Jacob Strauss, a small pamphlet which appeared in 1523 under the title, *Haubtstueck und artickel Christenlicher Leer wider den unchristlichen Wucher,* in which Strauss "painted wealth in its true colors," as Grebel said.[46] About the same time he read *Balaams Eselin,* a slight booklet by Mathis Wurm von Geydertheim, and found it a book "of similar character," that is, a book which pleased him.[47] Strauss evidently made quite an impression on Grebel, for in his letter of September 5, 1524, to Müntzer, about a year later, he praised Strauss and reckoned him among the preachers of the true Gospel. Perhaps he read other books by Strauss, such as: *Von dem innerlichen und ausserlichen Tauff* (May, 1523), *Widder den Simonieschen Tauff unnd erkaufften Chrissum und oel, auch worynn die recht Cristlich tauf begriffen sei* (1523), and *Das Wucher Zu nemen und geben unserm christlichen glauben und bruderliche lieb entgegen ist* (June, 1524), but if he did so, he failed to mention them. *Balaam's Ass* by Wurm deals with a completely different theme and one that could have had but slight significance for Grebel's thinking. The theme is indicated by the sub-title (translated): *Concerning the ban, that it dare not be imposed in the payment of money debts and similar slight matters. And that the clergy are responsible to obey the worldly authorities if they desire to be Christians.*

Of the three men whose writings appear to have won Grebel's approval, at least so far as the evidence goes, it is clear that only Zwingli exerted a significant influence. Wurm contributed nothing at all, and Strauss at the most strengthened Grebel's views on the question of tithes and usury. But Zwingli's writings, together with his personal contacts, exerted a fundamental influence on Grebel. Certainly, in addition to the *Schlussreden* of 1523 which he mentions specifically, Grebel must have read all that Zwingli wrote in those all-important years from 1520 to 1523, and these writings must have furnished him material for his theological structure. Grebel's enthusiastic endorsement of the *Apologeticus Archeteles* has already been mentioned. It may safely be concluded that *Archeteles* and *Schlussreden* made the chief contribution to his thinking. From the former he won his deep conviction concerning the sole authority of Scripture in matters of faith, naturally in combination with other influences from Zwingli, and from the latter he secured more general conceptions as to the character and methods of the much-needed reform of the church. The direct influence of these books should not be overstressed, to be sure, since they represent only the literary precipitate of Zwingli's thought in this period, with which Grebel was certainly well acquainted. There is no direct evidence of connection between these books and Grebel's writings in the form of borrowed phrases or quotations.

In the case of the doctrine of baptism more specific information is available regarding the source of influence. Grebel says expressly that "Zwingli brought him into the matter."[47a] There is no indication that Grebel read any books on the question of baptism during the years 1522-1524 nor that he was personally influenced by anyone other than Zwingli. By the time he came into contact with Carlstadt and Müntzer his convictions on infant baptism were already set. Even so, these men were not outspoken opponents of infant baptism. It is evident that there was widespread doubt among the evangelical preachers of Southwest Germany about this time on the question of infant baptism, and that some reformers, such as those at Strasburg, were no longer insisting upon it,[48] but Zwingli was just as uncertain as many of the others. The hypothesis of outside influence is therefore unnecessary to account for the rise of the new teaching in Zurich, particularly without other supporting evidence.

In the letter to Müntzer of September, 1524, Grebel mentions four preachers from whom he expected much for the future of the Gospel. They are Thomas Müntzer, Andreas Carlstadt, Jacob Strauss, and Michael Stiefel. Does this statement mean that Grebel acknowledged indebtedness to these men in the development of his thought? Not necessarily. What he wanted to say was that so far as he knew these men (he was somewhat incautious), they agreed with his teaching and his conception of the Gospel. He could not have known these men very well. He was certainly in error about Stiefel, for Stiefel was at that time a Lutheran, and remained a true friend and supporter, indeed a worshipper, of Luther to the end of his life.[49] Stiefel was an evangelical preacher, first in the service of

Hartmut von Kronberg (September, 1522 to May, 1523), and then in the service of Count von Mansfeld. Grebel may have learned of Stiefel's studies in Daniel and the Revelation of John, perhaps through a pamphlet by him which is no longer extant. Stiefel was deeply involved in apocalyptic studies in 1524, and it is not impossible that the slight eschatological tinge which manifested itself in two letters of Grebel about that time is due to Stiefel's influence. At any rate the first evidence of this tinge appears in a letter to Vadian dated September 3, 1524, just at the time when Grebel was praising Stiefel in the letter to Müntzer. In this letter he gave a short quotation from Daniel 9:27. Somewhat later the eschatological note reappeared in a letter to Castelberger of May, 1525, in which Grebel prophesied that Zwingli would also go into captivity, according to the book of Revelation. He apparently had reference to Revelation 13:10. Myconius reports in his *Vita Zwinglii,* that the Anabaptists in Zurich delighted in applying the worst prophecies of Daniel to Zwingli,[50] and Zwingli himself states that certain Anabaptists had referred to him as "that old dragon" (Rev. 12:3). Another slight touch of this sort is found in an assertion by Zwingli that in the Zurich disputation of November, 1525, Grebel spoke "just as if the Messiah were already at hand." Just what Grebel may have meant by such a manner of speaking is not clear, nor can we be sure of what Zwingli meant by his assertion.

It is very difficult to come to any clear picture of the relation between Carlstadt and Grebel. How Grebel learned of Carlstadt, whether through his writings or through other connections, can not be determined at this date. Perhaps he had read the earlier booklet by Carlstadt which appeared in Wittenberg in January, 1522, under the title *Von Abtuhung der Bilder und das keyn bedtler unther den Christen seyn soll,* but this is pure supposition. The little booklet of 1523 entitled *Ein Sermon vom Stand der Christgleubigen seelen von Abrahams Schoss und fegfeuer der abgeschydnen Seelen* scarcely deserves consideration. Carlstadt wrote nothing else before his seven tracts on the Lord's Supper which were printed in Basel at the end of

October, 1524.[51] These seven tracts were read by Grebel in manuscript shortly before their publication.[52] The brethren in Zurich, particularly Manz, were quite zealous in distributing the pamphlets after they were printed,[52a] but the teaching which they contained was only slightly different from that which Zwingli and the brethren already held, for in the matter of the Lord's Supper all three stood on much the same platform, and both Zwingli and Grebel give evidence of having held their views before Carlstadt came to Zurich. Grebel, for instance, in his letter to Müntzer of September 5, 1524, manifests a well developed view of the Lord's Supper, which he may have derived from Zwingli. It is true that Grebel read one tract by Carlstadt on infant baptism, which was not published, but he fails to report anything about its content. In any case Grebel's position on this question was already fixed before he saw Carlstadt's pamphlet, as is evident in his letter to Müntzer. It is fair to conclude, then, since Carlstadt did not stay in Zurich and had no further contact of any sort with the Anabaptists, that after all he and Grebel did not have much in common. Although an exhaustive study of this point is not possible here, there can be little doubt that Carlstadt's influence on Grebel was slight.[52b]

Finally a concluding word must be said on the relation between Grebel and Müntzer. [The general problem is thoroughly discussed in Chapter VII but a few pointed observations may serve here to settle the question of the literary influence of Müntzer on Grebel.] It has been shown that the brethren learned of Müntzer *after* they had come to their own position in regard to the church and reform in Zurich, and that they were glad to find in Müntzer one who supported their program. This means in essence that Grebel's theology was fixed in its main lines before Müntzer entered the picture. The epistle to Müntzer is abundant evidence that Grebel was not a disciple of Müntzer but rather a critic. On the other hand a careful examination of the two pamphlets of Müntzer which pleased Grebel and the Zurich brethren so well, and a comparison of the epistle to Müntzer with them, should reveal evidence of the influence of Müntzer's pamphlets (the reading of which gave the occasion for the correspondence) if any such influence exists. Although such an examination reveals little in the way of echoes of Müntzer's ideas or phrases, two items deserve mention in this respect. The phrase, "false hypocritical faith" (*falscher, glichsender glauben*), which appears several times in various forms in Grebel's letter, may be an echo of similar expressions in Müntzer's *Protestation*. Again, the phrase, "a sweet Christ" (*Süsser Christus*), which Grebel uses once in connection with an expression indicating his disparagement of the "learned shepherds" (which is also one of Müntzer's phrases) is directly taken from Müntzer's booklet *Vom getichten Glauben,* and Grebel states this clearly. There is no evidence in the letter that the idea of a "bitter Christ" as over against a "sweet Christ," had become a vital part of Grebel's thinking. One has a distinct impression after a careful study of Grebel's letter, that the few phraseological echoes of Müntzer which come from Grebel's pen were the direct result of the strong impression which Müntzer's style and spirit made upon the Brethren and that they constitute merely an immediate and superficial reflection, rather than evidence of a deep and permanent contribution. In other words, the reaction is imitative and not assimilative. In view of Grebel's sharp criticism of Müntzer's fundamental teachings and attitudes, it is correct to say that there was no direct influence of Müntzer's thought upon the content of Grebel's thinking, but that the influence lay rather in the direction of a strengthening of spirit among the small struggling group in Zurich of which Grebel was the leader.

One more interesting and important question is that of the origin of the nonresistance of the Zurich Brethren which is expressed so definitely in the letter to Müntzer. This idea, namely the absolute refusal to participate in the use of violence and killing, including warfare, in any way at all, which has been so characteristic of the Anabaptists and Mennonites throughout their long history, is among the earliest of the convictions which possessed Conrad Grebel and his associates in Zurich. It appeared as early as 1522 in the teaching that Andreas Castelberger gave in his "Bible school." The "investigation as to what Andreas Castelberg had preached," produced a highly interesting report by Lorenz Hochrütiner, in which among other things Castelberger's teaching against war is reported. Hochrütiner says: "Andreas said much about war; how the divine teaching is so strong against it and how it is sin; and he expressed the idea that the soldier who had plenty at home in his fatherly inheritance and goods and yet went to war, and received money and pay to kill innocent persons and to take their possessions from people who had never done him any harm, such a soldier was before Almighty God, and according to the content of Gospel teaching, a murderer and not better than one who would murder and steal on account of his poverty, regardless of the fact that this might not be so according to human laws, and might not be counted so bad."[53] Castelberger had two reasons for his opposition against war: (1) The divine teaching is strongly against it, and (2) it is sin. Felix Manz in 1525 likewise testified before the court to his belief "that no Christian could be a magistrate nor could he use the sword to punish or kill anyone, for he had no Scripture for such a thing." There is little reason to doubt that the convictions on the question of war and killing which Grebel and the Zurich brethren held in 1524 when they wrote to Müntzer were of the same character. Their pacifism, if it may be called such, was biblical in character; it was derived from the New Testament.

Nevertheless it is possible that the stimulus to thinking along this line, as well as the substantial content of some of the thinking, may have been derived from external sources. If this was the case it must have come from the humanist circles of which Grebel was a member in his earlier years. We need not go far afield to find such influences. In Zurich itself, in the circle of Grebel's intimate friends, there was considerable interest in the question of war and peace. As early as 1520 his good friend Myconius wrote a tract against war entitled *Philirenus,* which he circulated among his friends for criticism. On August 30, 1520, Grebel had a copy in his possession, which he read with great interest and found so true that he expressed the conviction that it deserved to be printed and thus to be made permanent.[64] Other friends however were influential in persuading Myconius to withhold the pamphlet from publication. It is well known that in the years 1520-1522 and even later, the pacifist viewpoint was present in the Zwingli circle in Zurich. Zwingli had probably taken it over from the great humanist Erasmus, who was an outspoken pacifist, and who led a vigorous campaign against war in his day. However the pacifist convictions of Zwingli and his friends must not have been very deep, at least not deep enough to leave any permanent influence upon their thinking, for before long Zwingli was actively engaged in planning a great military alliance to fight the pope, and as is well known he died at the head of the army of Zurich on the battlefield of Cappel in 1531. If, then, Grebel maintained his pacifism while Zwingli lost his, there must have been some fundamental difference in the thinking of the two men on the question. This difference can probably be discovered by a comparison of the pacifism of Erasmus with the nonresistance of Conrad Grebel.

The opposition of Erasmus to war was derived from a number of diverse philosophical, sociological, moral, and religious arguments, many of which are valid and useful in building up a conviction against war.[65] But even though there is a religious tone and coloring in Erasmus' thought on the question of war and peace, nevertheless the Erasmian pacifism was primarily humanitarian in character and not theological and biblical. The one argument against participation in war which Grebel used in his letter to Müntzer, the argument of "the suffering church," is not only not found in Erasmus, but is at the opposite pole from his position. A still further and significant difference between Erasmus and Grebel lies in the fact that Grebel was an absolutist on the question of war and violence, and consistently rejected *all* killing, including therefore wars in self-defense, whereas Erasmus, although he at times used very sharp words against war, was ready not only to permit a defensive war, but even any just war. Doctor Ines Thürlemann, who has made a thorough study of Erasmus as a pacifist, has shown in her doctoral dissertation that this was a characteristic feature of the position of Erasmus on war. She quotes him at one place as saying: "Citizens may be permitted to fight, but it must be a just war. Whether the war is just or not and in what manner and against whom it is to be fought, that must be left to the decision of the ruler."[56] Between the opportunism of an Erasmus who would be willing to let a ruler decide whether a war was just or not, and the absolutism of a Grebel who would dare to say that "among true believing Christians killing is done away with altogether," there is a world of difference. It is unthinkable that Grebel derived his deep conviction on this point from his humanist background. It is possible that the humanist Conrad Grebel of 1520 to 1522 was in spirit an Erasmian pacifist, and that this opened the door of his mind to the teaching of the New Testament, particularly the Sermon on the Mount, and to the logical deduction from the fundamental concept of the "suffering church" that Christians should suffer and not fight; but the Grebel of 1524 was no longer a humanitarian pacifist but a believer in the principle of biblical nonresistance, which is something quite different. It is even doubtful that the chief source of Grebel's conviction was the direct teaching of the Sermon on the Mount on loving one's enemy. I am inclined to hold that Grebel derived his conviction primarily from the central thought of "the suffering church." As stated at another place, in all the extant writings of Grebel, including his letters, there is not one quotation from the Sermon on the Mount, and there is no evidence that this portion of the teaching of Christ exerted an outstanding influence on his ethical and religious thinking more than any other portion of the New Testament.

One word more remains to be said about the source of Grebel's theology, and this is a very important word. Much time has been spent in examining possible sources of personal and literary influence upon Grebel, and little said about the possibility that after all the chief influence upon his mind was the Holy Scriptures of the Old and New Testaments. Zwingli was Grebel's guide, it is true, especially in the early days of his Christian experience, but Zwingli's chief service to Grebel was to point him to the Scripture, to give him the conviction that the Word of God alone was the source of authority in faith and life. Grebel learned the lesson well. He learned it so well in fact that when the time came that he was forced to choose between what Zwingli taught and what he believed the Bible taught, he was ready to make the decision to abandon Zwingli and follow the Bible. In the two years between his conversion in 1522 and his break with Zwingli in 1524, Conrad Grebel had learned to read the Scripture and believe it so thoroughly that for him it became the chief source of his religious beliefs. After all, is it not abundantly clear that in the great era of the Reformation when men were forging new doctrines and systems of doctrines, or reviving long lost fundamentals, the little handful of Anabaptist brethren in Zurich under the leadership of Conrad Grebel were blazing a new trail that did not follow the great highways built by Luther, Zwingli and Calvin and their lesser associates. It is difficult to believe that the great dominant ideas which controlled the life and thought of Conrad Grebel and his brethren, and which were different from the ideas of the reformers, were drawn from any other source than "the clear Word of God" itself, as Grebel so often calls it. The Bible was the chief source of the theology of Conrad Grebel and the Swiss brethren.[56a]

D. The Teaching of Conrad Grebel

As has already been stated, a systematic presentation of Grebel's theology is impossible.[57] Nevertheless it will be worth while to give a brief summary of the chief teachings of Grebel as they have become evident in the historical discussion of Chapters VI, VII, and VIII, as well as in the description of Grebel's writings as given in section B. 3 above. In accord with the methodological principles laid down in section B. 1, only those sources will be used which are included under class "A", namely the letters and writings of Grebel himself, and his own testimony in court. Other material will be used only incidentally. At the outset it is important to recall again Zwingli's own judgment about the Swiss Brethren (including Conrad Grebel as chief), in which he states that the teaching of the Brethren did not differ from Zwingli's own views on any major point of Christian doctrine.[58] This must be interpreted to mean that the great fundamental principles of the Reformation, *sola fide,* justification by faith, and *sola Scriptura,* the sole authority of the Word of God, were equally accepted by them. From this fundamental statement by Zwingli it is clear that Conrad Grebel was thoroughly evangelical in the same sense that Luther and Zwingli were. The differences between Zwingli and Grebel lay primarily in the sphere of the doctrine of the church, its organization, nature, ordinances and discipline, and its relation to the state and the social order, and in the sphere of Christian ethics. This is not to say however that the differences were insignificant, for they were basic and far-reaching. In the matter of ordinances, only in baptism was there a cleavage, and even there it was not on the general character and function of ordinances, but rather on the specific meaning of baptism and the requirements for baptism. In the following discussion the teachings of Grebel will be grouped around five main heads, with a concluding characterization.[59]

The Nature of the Church

The church comes into existence through the preaching of the Word, through the voluntary acceptance of this Word of Truth, and through the consequent conversion and renewal of life of individual believers.[60] By faith the individual members are united and incorporated into the body of Christ.[61] The church therefore has Christ as its head, and the believers as members.[62] This church is in truth a fellowship of brethren in life and suffering, which is maintained by the outward bond of faith and the inward bond of love.[63] When a member of the body fails to maintain love toward the brethren or does not order his life according to the Gospel, he breaks the bond of fellowship.[64] In its earthly and outward form the church regulates its life through ceremonies and forms[65] and through the two ordinances of baptism and the Lord's Supper,[66] but always in conformity with the instructions of the Word of God. The church as a whole must maintain scriptural discipline through its ministers and in accord with the rule of Christ, Matthew XVIII, which means that such brethren who give offense by their sinful conduct and who will not hear the church must be excluded from fellowship by the ban.[67] New members will be received into the church upon the basis of a confession of faith and a separation from sin, upon evidence of leading a new and holy life.[68] The church is served by ministers who are supported by voluntary contributions of the membership.[69] Brethren must be ready to give of their money and goods to aid those who are in need, to the extent of acknowledging the claim of the church upon their possessions,[70] although community of goods is rejected.

The Relation of the Church to the State and to Society

There is no relation between the constitution and practices of the church, such as the ordinances of baptism and the Lord's Supper, and the life of the state.[71] The institutions of church and state operate on different levels. In spiritual matters, the church alone has the power to act, on the basis of the Word of God. In "worldly" matters, that is, in things which do not concern the faith and life of the church, the state has jurisdiction, its authority is recognized by the church, and its commands are to be obeyed.[72] The state is not rejected.[73] The church has no right to seek to rule the world or society from without, nor to control the civil authorities in its interests.[74] Nor has it any claim to the use of force or forceful means of any sort.[75] On the contrary it separates itself from the world.[76] The church is a suffering church which is to expect persecution in this world,[77] and it is not to expect that the mass of men will come into the church. Believers are to separate themselves from the unbelieving mass and to unite in the fellowship of believers.[77] Individual members of the church have the right to seek to elect a "Christian" magistracy or council,[78] in order that the government may be influenced to follow the principles of divine righteousness.[79] Within the membership of the church no tithes or usury are to be levied.[80] The state likewise has no right to levy tithes, for the church is not to be supported by taxes or monies collected by force, but by the voluntary contributions of members.[81]

The Scripture

The Word of God is eternally true[82] and is a dynamic force which converts sinners[83] and destroys opponents.[84] It will "sing its own truth into the heart."[85] If it is not obeyed, or if it is mixed with human opinions in the church, it is polluted, and the church will not prosper but will perish.[86] The Scripture is inspired of God[87] and is the sole standard for the actions of the church as well as for the life of the individual.[88] What is not taught by plain and clear Scripture or illustrated by the example of Christ or the apostles, is to be reckoned as forbidden, as "anathema."[89] A simple faith is necessary to understand the Scripture aright and to appropriate it; no artificial intellectualism can be of any help, rather it will be a hindrance.[90]

The Experience of Salvation and the Christian Life

The sinner is converted by the preaching of the Word,[91] that is, he is brought thereby to the point where he will turn from his sins, abandon them completely, and take up a new life.[92] This conversion is a new birth[93] by which, through the faith of the believer and by means of the blood of Christ, sins are washed away, and the believer dies to sin and receives a new spirit. If he continues to live in this new life and resolutely separates himself from sin, he may be sure of salvation.[94] The new life is the fruit of faith. Faith must have this fruit of the new and holy life, however, or it is but a "false, hypocritical faith."[95] Although the believer in his new life fights sin and overcomes it, he will still feel the power of sin and will humbly confess that he is imperfect and that the "best of men are hypocrites" in the sight of the eternal God and His truth and righteousness.[96] The burden of sin within should weigh more heavily upon the heart than outward tribulations.[97] At times members of the church will fall into sin.[98] When that happens they have thereby broken the bond of fellowship with God and with the brethren and will be set outside the limits of that fellowship.[99] There are therefore no sinless Christians, and there is no sinless church, but sinlessness must be striven after as a goal, for that is the command of the Scripture. Christians must forgive one another.[100] They must set their trust upon God and not in men,[101] and must learn patience through tribulation.[102] Prayer is the avenue to the power of God.[103] Christians may not use force, not even in self-defense. Warfare is not permitted for the Christian, for among the children of God killing is altogether done away with.[104] And if a man thinks that he can deceive his fellow men in regard to his life, he should remember that at the end he will stand before God who knows the hearts and administers a just judgment, and whom no man can deceive.[105]

The Meaning and Administration of the Ordinances, Baptism and the Lord's Supper

The ordinances are symbols and pledges.

Baptism. Baptism is the sign of a change in the inner man, a new birth, a washing away of sin, and accordingly a pledge of obedience to Christ and of the purpose to "walk according to Christ."[106] Since this experience is produced only by the Word, only those who have come to reason and have believed through the Word can be baptized.[107] Children, who do not know the difference between good and evil and who cannot have faith, are not to be baptized, for they are saved by the suffering of Christ without faith and its sign, baptism.[108] Infant baptism was not practiced by Christ and the apostles, for Christ commanded that which the apostles followed, namely that only those should be baptized who have first been instructed in the Word of God.[109] Later in the history of the Church infant baptism was invented by the pope and was continued as an unscriptural and unchristian Roman custom.[110]

The Lord's Supper. The Lord's Supper is a symbol of the fellowship of the brethren among one another and with Christ. It points to the basis for that fellowship, "which is the testament of the body and blood of Christ on the cross." It is also a pledge of brotherly love[111] and faithful, sanctified Christian living.[112] For this reason no one may participate in it who does not have a forgiving spirit[113] and who does not live the life of holiness.[114] The church must proceed with discipline according to the rule of Christ, Matthew XVIII, before the Lord's Supper can be observed.[115] The ceremonial accompaniments of the ordinance must be simple, in order that true devotion may not be disturbed and thus attention be called to outward things and thereby a false external faith be generated.[116] The Lord's Supper should be observed frequently, though the time is not prescribed, and not in the church-house but in the home, in order that no false devotion may be generated.[117] The worship service in general must be simple in all its details, and liturgical singing should be omitted in order that the spirit of the worshipper may be concentrated in true devotion upon the Word of God.[118]

General Characterization

It is clear from the above exposition that Conrad Grebel sought after reality in the spiritual life. He sought to generate and maintain the inner spiritual life through a living faith in Christ and union with Him. This spiritual life must be effective in daily experience, in trust in God, in love toward the brethren, in obedience to the Word, in separation from sin, and in a holy life patterned after Christ. Alone through "incorporation with Christ and the Brethren" can the individual receive the strength which is necessary to live out the Word of God, to conquer sin, and to maintain love. In this strength the believer and the church as a whole will be able to bear victoriously "the baptism of temptation and testing," persecution, suffering, and death and "pass triumphantly through this testing by fire into the homeland of eternal rest."[119]

X

THE SIGNIFICANCE OF CONRAD GREBEL AND THE SWISS BRETHREN IN THE HISTORY OF THE CHRISTIAN CHURCH[1]

Conrad Grebel's significance for the Christian Church lies wholly in the continuing Swiss Brethren movement[2] (Evangelical Anabaptism) of which he was the founder, and in the vision of Christianity which it gave to an expanding world; for no writings in the formal literary sense perpetuated his ideas and no developed organization directly reflected his person. Dying a few short months after the open break with the Zwinglian Reformation which was in effect the beginning of the Swiss Brethren church, he could have no assurance that the faith for which he fought and which was entrusted to a small group of scattered and harried followers, would survive. Yet the movement did survive, both in and outside of Switzerland, to become a vital factor in Christendom with a major contribution to Western culture. The relatively small groups of followers (total baptized membership today of almost 400,000) who were the direct lineal descendants of the original Swiss, Dutch and German Anabaptists, namely the Doopsgezinden, the Hutterites, and the Mennonites of Switzerland, France, Germany, and North and South America, including the remnants of the once large colonies in Russia, have in their own right in varying degrees been the carriers of this vision and channels of its influence.[3] But the Anabaptists' contribution has been far broader and more far-reaching than these groups alone, having penetrated into the main stream of historic Christianity.

The total contribution of Anabaptism can best be understood by setting forth its essential vision of Christianity and then indicating what aspects of this vision have found a broader acceptance. The central controlling idea of evangelical Anabaptism, that of full Christian discipleship in its transformation of life after the pattern of Christ *(Nachfolge)* is well set forth in a characterization by Max Goebel a century ago: "The essential and distinguishing characteristic of this group is its insistence upon the actual personal conversion and regeneration of every Christian through the Holy Spirit, upon full freedom of conscience and religion, upon separation of spiritual and worldly things, of Church and State, and upon the establishment of a true holy Christian church of the reborn . . . which by means of Christian discipline and the ban would exclude everything worldly and sinful and on the other hand would carry out the Christian principles of true brotherly love by means of a sharing of (spiritual and material) goods and through a weaponless and revengeless life. They aimed with special emphasis at carrying out and realizing the Christian doctrine and faith in the heart and life of every true Christian in the whole Christian church, and therefore at the bringing together of all true regenerated believers out of the great degenerate church into a new holy church . . . . That which the Reformation actually originally intended they aimed to accomplish."[4] Sebastian Franck, a contemporary chronicler, writing in 1531, understood the essence of Anabaptism to be that "they taught nothing but love, faith and the cross."[5]

Now holy discipleship is the genuine intent of the New Testament, lying at the very center of the original Christian genius. Its restoration *(restitutio)* is the ideal which has been recaptured and attempted again and again in history both before and after the Reformation. Before Conrad Grebel there were spirits like Peter Waldo of Lyons, St. Francis of Assisi, and Peter Chelchitzki of Bohemia; and after him there have been many down to the Iona Community of our time in Scotland. Through the centuries a divine discontent has stirred in the hearts of many Christians, who, having once experienced Jesus could never again be satisfied with the church as it was nor with the prevailing "Christian" society. This discontent is again stirring deeply today, in Europe perhaps more than in America, and there are not a few voices rising in the homelands of Anabaptism to call for a rectification of the great mistake of the Reformation and the modern adoption of a discipleship vision and church concept *(Gemeinde-Ideal)* which is essentially that of evangelical Anabaptism.[6]

The broad ideal of absolute love and nonresistance rejecting war and violence in every form, both political and personal, which is implied in full discipleship, is however an outstandingly unique contribution of the evangelical Anabaptist movement as initiated by the Swiss Brethren. It is also the one aspect of the Anabaptist way which has found the least echo in historic Christendom. The Quaker nonresistant movement of a century and a quarter later in England probably indirectly drew its ideal on this point from Anabaptism, but certainly the modern pacifist movement, which has all too often secularized the great Christian ideal of love, has no immediate connection with it.

But the most characteristic feature of the Anabaptist contribution, following inevitably from its concept of discipleship, is its insistence upon a new church of truly committed and practicing believers in contradistinction to the prevailing concept of the "Volkskirche" or inclusive church of the Reformation and subsequent periods, held by Catholics and Protestants (Lutheran and Zwinglian) alike, with a church maintained by the powerful patronage of the State, and to which, by birth and infant baptism, the entire population belonged. Grebel and his associates saw this issue clearly and dared to challenge Zwingli directly on it. It was in the months between October, 1523, and January, 1525, that the battle between the two diametrically opposing views was fought out in the very heart of the Swiss Reformation. Zwingli, as Professor von Muralt has said, deliberately rejected the Swiss Brethren call for a church of true believers only and established "a church in which all professing Christians, the nominal, lukewarm, and indifferent ones as well as the really live and active Christians are kept together, a church to which the entire population belongs and which is not the church of genuine believers but only an imperfect human institution."[7] Luther and Calvin made the same basic decision, as did the leaders of the English Reformation, thereby establishing the "Volkskirche" as the official and general pattern for the whole of Protestantism. Only the Swiss Brethren and Dutch Mennonites at this crossroads of Christian history took the road of the free church of committed Christians, thus becoming the fourth major Reformation type.

That the Anabaptist insistence on such a church was not without its effect upon Protestantism however, particularly in its Reformed wing, has been noted by numerous observers. Both the Zwinglian and the Calvinistic church ideal give evidence of Anabaptist influence, particularly in the realm of church discipline. English Puritanism and German Pietism also almost certainly owe something to Anabaptism. But it was only in English Nonconformism that the free church ideal struck its first deeper roots and found permanent organized expression. Whether modern Congregationalism and the Baptist movement still reflect their earlier anabaptistic ideals in undiluted strength may be open to question, but their historic anchorage is clear. Through this channel Anabaptism has made its broadest contribution to our modern culture, as is set forth by Rufus M. Jones in the following statement: "Judged by the reception it met at the hands of those in power, both in Church and State, equally in Roman Catholic and Protestant countries, the Anabaptist movement was one of the most tragic in the history of Christianity; but judged by the principles which were put into play by the men who bore this reproachful nickname, it must be pronounced one of the most momentous and significant undertakings in man's eventful religious struggle after the truth. It gathered up the gains of earlier movements, it is the spiritual soil out of which all nonconformist sects have sprung, and it is the first plain announcement in modern history of a programme for a new type of Christian society which the modern world, especially in America and England, has been slowly realizing, an absolutely free and independent society, and a State in which every man counts as a man, and has his share in shaping both Church and State."[8]

But what personal significance has Conrad Grebel for the historic movement which he founded? The answer is chiefly that he made possible the initial and basic breakthrough. While it is true that during the troubled third decade of the 16th century others longed for and attempted the restitution of the New Testament *ecclesia,* that attempt became triumphant only under Grebel's leadership in Zurich. Historically the case is clear. The Swiss Brethren movement did begin in Zurich, and it did spread from there throughout North Central Europe. It began in Zurich not only because Conrad Grebel and his associates clearly envisaged a voluntary Christian fellowship, a "gathered" free church of believers only, committed in earnest loyalty and holy discipleship to follow Christ under the cross and by His way of love, but because Grebel had the courage to make an unreserved personal commitment to this ideal regardless of consequences. To this commitment he held unflinchingly in the crucial moment when, in bitter determination to annihilate their ideas forever, all the power of Church and State thundered down upon him and his small band of followers. Once the great and irrevocable step was taken, other faithful and noble spirits, including ultimately thousands of martyrs, followed in Grebel's train; but Conrad Grebel was the first Anabaptist. He performed the first adult baptism in Zurich in January, 1525. He was the first to clearly mark the road away from Luther's and Zwingli's mass church into the free church of voluntary commitment, brotherhood, and full evangelical discipleship, of separation of Church and State, and of freedom of conscience. Where others shrank from adoption of the full New Testament ideal because of fear that it could not be carried through in practice, as for instance Luther, Grebel acted. He chose to follow the vision without calculation of possibilities or practicalities, believing that the truth commands, it does not merely advise. For him the Kingdom of God is to be built here and now in the fellowship of believers, in the beloved community of the disciples of Christ. This conviction was the sole ground for the existence of the Swiss Brethren brotherhood and later related groups. Unlike the other reformers, Grebel's is not a sharply delineated figure because of the brevity of his career, but his basic view of the essence of Christianity and the nature of the Church is clear, and his place in church history is secure.

That Grebel and his Swiss Brethren derived their faith solely and directly from the New Testament without any apparent literary or personal antecedents is one of the most striking things about the new movement. Every attempt to trace connections to earlier sources has failed, whether to the Waldensians or the Hussites as Ludwig Keller believed, or to the Franciscan Tertiaries as Albrecht Ritschl suggested. The Anabaptists were biblicists and it was from the biblical fountains alone that they drank. Having taken altogether seriously the *sola scriptura* of the Reformation, they were able to break more completely with the ecclesiastical and sociological forms of the Middle Ages and thus to return to the original ideas of the New Testament. In this spirit Grebel's followers once cried out *"Habend ir Zwingli's, wir wellend Gotts wort haben."*[9]

In Conrad Grebel then, the young Zurich patrician humanist turned evangelical Protestant under Zwingli's preaching, and become first century Christian as a result of his own devout reading of the New Testament, we honor not only the founder of the Swiss Brethren movement and the later Mennonite Church, but also one of the prophetic spirits of Christendom in its great and insistent tradition of reform and regeneration.

NOTES

CHRONOLOGY OF THE LIFE OF CONRAD GREBEL

1498 (?)	Birth in Zurich
1499-1508	Boyhood in Grüningen Castle
1508 (?)-1514	Latin school in Zurich
1514-1515—October-May	Study in Basel
1515—Summer	At home in Zurich
1515-1518	Study in Vienna
1518—Summer	At home in Zurich
1518-1520	Study in Paris
1520-1524	At home in Zurich
1522—February 6	Marriage
1525—January	In Zurich
1525—January 21	Conrad Grebel performs the first adult baptism in Zurich or Zollikon leading to the formation of the Brotherhood of the "Swiss Brethren."
1525—February-March	In Schaffhausen
1525—April	In St. Gall
1525—May	In Zurich
1525—June-October	Intensive evangelism in Grüningen territory
1525—October 8	Arrest in Grüningen
1525—October to March, 1526	In prison in Zurich
1526—March	Escape from prison
1526—March to August	Itinerant labors as a fugitive
1526—August (?)	Death in Maienfeld near Chur, Canton of the Grisons

KEY TO ABBREVIATIONS

MQR—*Mennonite Quarterly Review,* published by the Mennonite Historical Society, Goshen, Indiana, U.S.A., 1927—

VB—*Die Vadianische Briefsammlung der Stadtbibliothek St. Gallen, (Mitteilungen zur vaterländischen Geschichte,* herausgegeben vom Historischen Verein in St. Gallen) I-VII 1888-1913.

ZW—*Huldreich Zwinglis Sämtliche Werke* (Corpus Reformatorum) Edited by Egli, Finsler, Köhler, Blanke, von Muralt, Berlin, later Leipzig, 1905ff.

NOTES

FOREWORD

CONRAD GREBEL, THE ACKNOWLEDGED LEADER OF THE FIRST SWISS BRETHREN

1. *Geschicht-Buch der Hutterischen Brüder, Hersg. von den Hutterischen Brüdern in Amerika, Canada, durch Prof. Dr. Rudolf Wolkan,* 1923, *Standoff Colony bei Macleod, Alberta, Canada.* Gedruckt und in Kommission bei Carl Fromme, GmbH., Vienna. Subtitle: *Geschicht-Buch und Kurzer Durchgang vom Anfang der Welt, wie Gott sein Werk in seinem Volk auf Erden angericht, gehandelt und getrieben hat; demnach*: *Unserer Gemein-Geschicht-Buch.* [A new letter perfect edition of the *Geschicht-Buch,* edited with introduction, notes, and a glossary by Professor A. J. F. Zieglschmid, was published late in 1943 by the Carl Schurz Memorial Foundation, Philadelphia, Pa., under the title, *The Hutterian Chronicle.*] The account of the beginnings in Zurich is found on pp. 34, 35. It is so fully realistic, so vivid in detail, that it must be an eyewitness report. The prominent part played by George Blaurock in the action justifies the inference that the account goes back to the personal tradition of Blaurock himself. This is further rendered plausible by the fact that after he left Switzerland, Blaurock was a leader among the brethren in the Tyrol until his martyrdom in 1529. Without doubt he related to them the stirring story of the early history of the brotherhood in Switzerland. The brethren in the Tyrol to whom Blaurock ministered later fled to Moravia. There, under the leadership of Jacob Hutter (d. 1535), the brotherhood was organized on the basis of Christian communism, and later came to be called the Hutterian Brethren.

It is remarkable that the Hutterian Brethren themselves, although they came from Austria and the Tyrol as their chronicles testify, placed the origin of their brotherhood in Zurich. This they would certainly not have done if they had not had direct eye-witness accounts from men like Blaurock which were incorporated in their earliest chronicles. The chronicles of the brotherhood were begun as early as 1534, by Caspar Braitmichel, who wrote a history of the brotherhood from 1524 to 1534, and who continued the chronicle to the year 1542.

Braitmichel's own testimony as to his work is found in the "Vorrede" to the *Geschichtbuch,* p. XL: "Nun solches alles hab ich bei glaubhaften Menschen auf allerlei Weis ja bei denen, so mit und bei gewesen sind, mich nicht lassen verdriessen zu erkundigen: auch was ich selbst in guter und gewisser Erfahrung hab, das hab ich auf das allerfleissigest zusammentragen, und das in aller Einfältigkeit ohne alle hochprächtige Wort. Nun aber, weil ich es vonwegen Blödigkeit des Gesichts und des Leibs Schwachheit nicht vermag zum End zu bringen, sondern nur bisher auf das zwei und vierzigst Jahr der mindern Zahl, da dem Bruder Leonhard Lanzenstil die Gemein befohlen ist wurden, geführt hätt, so leb ich doch in der Hoffnung, Gott werde andern Ursach geben, solches noch viel fleissiger zum Vollkommensten auszuführen."

It is not possible to determine precisely when Braitmichel began his chronicle or when he ended it. Nor can it be said with certainty whether he wrote it as a continuous production at some time after 1542, or whether he began to write it at some time before 1542, and continued it from that time forward to 1542 as a periodical chronicle. Braitmichel, who died February 27, 1573 (Cf. *Geschichtbuch,* p. 362) was ordained "Diener der Notdurft" Nov. 1, 1538 (*op. cit.,* p. 143) and "Diener des Worts" in 1548 (*op. cit.,* p. 242). Since he signs the "Vorrede" as "Kaspar Braitmichel, ein Diener Jesu Christi und seiner Gemein," he must have completed his part of the chronicle between 1538 and 1573. The Primatialbibliothek in Gran, Hungary, possesses a manuscript known as *Codex Braitmichel,* which bears the title *Geschichte der Gemeinde* 1524-1534. Dr. Robert Friedmann of Vienna and Goshen, who has examined the manuscript, believes that it is practically identical with the first part of the *Geschichtbuch.* If so, the fact that it was circulated as a separate codex suggests that it was written as an independent chronicle in 1534.

The same account of the beginnings of the Anabaptist movement in Zurich as given by Braitmichel is also found in the Dutch language at three other places, printed in (A) *Successio Anabaptistica,* Coloniae, 1603, fol. 19-22 (reprinted in *Bibliotheca Reformatoria Neerlandica, VII,* pp. 24, 25, s'Gravenhage, 1910) and in (B) Carel von Gent's *Het Beginsel en Voortganck der geschillen, scheuringen en verdeeltheden onder de gene die Doopsgesinden genoemt worden,* Amsterdam, 1658 (written in 1615) fol. 3, 4 (reprinted in *B. R. N. VII,* pp. 515, 516), and in manuscript (C) in a codex which is in possession of the Mennonite Church of Heubuden near Marienburg in West Prussia. In all three sources, the account is found in the form of a letter addressed, ostensibly by the Swiss Brethren, to the Brethren at Cologne (Keulen). A careful examination of the three sources has led to the following conclusions: 1.) (C) is a manuscript copy of the printed (A); 2.) (A) and (B) represent two variant translations of an original German letter. A further careful comparison between the Dutch translations and the German account in the *Geschichtbuch* has led to the following conclusions: 1.) since the two Dutch translations are practically identical in content, but variant in form (choice of words, punctuation, spelling, etc.) they cannot possibly be two copies of one Dutch original, but must be independent translations; 2.) the German form in the *Geschichtbuch* cannot possibly be a translation from the Dutch. (The second conclusion was to be expected, since the letter purports to have been written by the Swiss Brethren, who would scarcely have used the Dutch language); 3.) the comparison between the letter and the account in the *Geschichtbuch* proves further clearly that the original German letter must have been an extract from the *Geschichtbuch,* and not vice versa. It is scarcely possible that the original letter was composed by Swiss Brethren (which by the way is merely asserted by the two Dutch historians who reprinted the letter, and is not indicated in the letter itself), for the writers of the letter refer to the Swiss Brethren in the third person, as they would scarcely have done if they were referring to themselves, unless indeed they simply copied out of a book which they were using, such as the *Geschichtbuch.* But it is very unlikely that the Swiss Brethren had a copy of the Hutterian chronicle for use, since there was strong competition between the two groups. Furthermore the name "Swiss Brethren" was originated and used by the Hutterites, not by the Swiss Anabaptists themselves. We are led to the conclusion therefore that the letter was written by Hutterites and not by Swiss Brethren. This conclusion is fortified by the fact that (B), which is a careful and literal translation of the *Geschichtbuch,* states that the letter was written in response to an original request from the brethren "tot Ceulen." The most likely explanation of the whole affair is the following: some Hutterian itinerant apostles came into contact with the Brethren at Cologne and told them about the congregations in the South and Southeast, whereupon the Cologne brethren requested a brief account of the origins of the brotherhood in the South. The Hutterites complied with this request by extracting the account from the

Geschichtbuch, and sending it in a letter to Cologne. The conclusion of the letter to Cologne is noteworthy, "Also hebt ghy die ghetuygenisse des beginsels, daer unne suht ghy geenen twyffel hebben, want wy dit op het alder gewiste erwaren hebben."

2. On Blaurock, who came in May, 1529, from Switzerland to Tyrol, and was burned at the stake at Klausen, Aug. 30, 1529, see Fritz Jecklin, *Jörg Blaurock vom Hause Jacob, Ein Märtyrer der Wiedertäufer in XXI. Jahresber. der historisch-antiq. Gesellschaft Graubündens, Jahrg.* 1892 *Chur, pp.* 1-20; Joseph Beck, *George Blaurock und die Anfänge des Anabaptismus in Graubünden und Tirol. Aus seinem Nachlass hrsg. von Joh. Loserth* in *Vorträge und Aufsätze aus der Comeniusgesellschaft, 7. Jg.* 1. *u.* 2. *Stück, Berlin* 1898, pp. 295ff; Christian Neff, article *Blaurock* in *Mennonitisches Lexikon, Bd.* I, Frankfurt a. M. u. Weierhof (Pfalz) 1913, pp. 227-334; Oskar Vasella, *Von den anfängen der bündnerischen Täuferbewegung* (*Jörg Blaurock*) *in Z. f. schw. Geschichte* XIX (1939), pp. 165-184.

3. The complete account is reproduced in chapter VIII, p. 136

4. *Acta Des gesprächs zwüschenn predikanten Unnd Touffbruderenn Ergangen, Inn der Statt bernn von xi Mertzenns, bisz uf den xvii Desselben Monats Im M. D. XXXVIIIt. Jar. Unnütze Papiere, Bd.* 80, *Staatsarchiv Bern.* The extract quoted is taken from page 37 of the typewritten copy of the original manuscript prepared by Dr. Adolph Fluri of Bern, now in the Goshen College Library. The name of the brother is not given, but it was very likely Hans Hotz of Grüningen, who appears as the chief speaker of the brethren.

5. *Brüderliche Vereinigung etzlicher Kinder Gottes sieben Artikel betreffend. Item ein Sendbrief Michael Sattlers an eine gemeine Gottes samt seinem Martyrium,* 1527 (1533). The second part, that relating to Sattler, was reprinted by Mennonites in 1702 and 1742 in Europe, and in 1745 in Pennsylvania, in *Güldene Aepfel in silbern Schalen.* Copies of the 1702, 1742 and 1745 editions in the Goshen College Library. J. C. Wenger has edited and published an English translation in MQR, October, 1945, pp. 245-253, "The Schleitheim Confession of Faith." See also MQR April, 1942, 82ff. for a discovery of a hitherto unknown 16th century edition.

6. Samuel Geiser, *Die Taufgesinnten-Gemeinden, Eine kurzgefasste Darstellung der Wichtigsten Ereignisse des Täufertums,* Karlsruhe, 1931, was the first history of the group by one of its own number.

7. *Huldreich Zwinglis Sämtliche Werke*: *Corpus Reformatorum Bd.* 88-98, Berlin (later Leipzig). (Hereafter cited as ZW) Bd. VIII, Leipzig, 1914, p. 296.

8. *ZW VIII,* 313.

9. *Ibid.,* 780.

10. *Ibid.,* 382.

11. *Fridolin Sichers Chronik, Herausgegeben von Ernst Götzinger* (*Mitteilungen zur vaterländischen Geschichte. Herausgegeben vom historischen Verein in St. Gallen, Neue Folge,* 10. *Heft.*), St. Gall, 1885, p. 193.

12. *Johannes Kesslers Sabbata mit kleineren Schriften und Briefen. Unter Mitwirkung von Emil Egli und Rudolph Schoch herausgegeben vom historischen Verein des Kantons St. Gallen.* St. Gall, 1902, pp. 142, 143, 314. At three other places Grebel, Felix Manz, and George Blaurock are called arch-anabaptists, "Erzwidertouffer."

13. Johann Stumpf: *Chronica vom Leben und Wirken des Ulrich Zwingli.* (*Quellen und Studien zur Geschichte der helvetischen Kirche, Band I*), *Herausgegeben von Dr. Leo Weiss*) *Zweite Auflage,* Zurich, 1932, p. 69. "Die furnemisten unter iren lerern warend: Conrad Grebel, Felix Mantz, Georg vom Hus-Jacob von Chur genant Blowrock und andere."

14. *Die Chronik des Bernhard Wyss,* 1519-1530. Herausgegeben von Georg Finsler, Basel, 1901 (*Quellen zur schweizerischen Reformationsgeschichte I. Herausgegeben vom Zwingliverein in Zürich unter Leitung von Emil Egli*) p. 79.

15. Bosshart, Edlibach, Pellican, Herman Miles. *Die Chronik des Hermann Miles (Mitteilungen zur vaterländischen Geschichte. Herausgegeben vom Historischen Verein in St. Gallen, XXVIII.)*, St. Gall, 1902, p. 309, names only Conrad Grebel of the Zurich Anabaptists. One section heading reads, "Von doctor Baltasar [Hubmaier] Pfarer zu Waldshut, der widertoufer erster lerer, und siner geselschaft," but it is not certain whether this heading is by Miles himself or whether it was added in 1571 by Magnus Maurer. The latter is more probable.

Contemporary and later historians do not present a uniform conception of the beginnings of the movement. Sebastian Franck, for instance, in his *Chronica, Zeytbuch und Geschichts-Bibel* mentions none of the Swiss Brethren leaders by name, neither Grebel, Manz, Blaurock, nor others. For him apparently the South German semi-Anabaptists, such as Hubmaier, Denck, Hetzer, Rinck, and Hut, are the leaders. (Sebastian Franck, *Chronika, Zeytbuch und Geschÿchtbibel von anbegyn bisz inn diez gegenwertig M.D. XXI. jar.*, 1531, [later editions 1536, 1543] folio 444 *verso*: "Deren Vorsteher und bischoff waren erstlich Huebmör, Melchior Rinck, Johannes Hut, Johannes Denk, Ludwig Hetzer."; folio 440 *verso*: "Entstünde eine neüwe Sect die widerteuffer genant. Under diesen war Johannes Denck . . . yr vorsteher und bischoff.") Later Franck also mentions Michael Sattler, but Grebel and the Swiss leaders are not mentioned. Franck apparently conceived of the movement primarily as South and Middle German in character and not Swiss, although he gives evidence that he had read Bullinger's (1531) book against the Anabaptists. (Cf. Franck, *op. cit.*, folio 405 *recto*, "von dem unverschampten fräfel" and folio 447 *recto*, "Articuli Uldarii Zwinglii wider den bapst und vil andere Sect.")

It is worthy of note that Heinrich Bullinger does not mention a single Anabaptist leader by name in his two books dealing with the movement. (Heinrich Bullinger: *Von dem unverschampten fräfel, ergerlichem verwyren unnd unwarhafftem leeren der selbsgesandten Widertöuffern*, Zurich, 1531; *Der Widertäuffern Ursprung, fürgang, secten, wäsen, förneme und gemeine irer leer artichel, auch ire grund und warin sy sich absunderind . . .*, Zurich, 1560 [2 ed. 1561]. Only in his *Reformationsgeschichte* does he refer to individuals, and here Grebel stands at the head of the list, "Grebel, Manz, and other restless spirits." (*Heinrich Bullingers Reformationsgeschichte nach dem Autographon herausgegeben von J. J. Hottinger und H. H. Vögeli.* Frauenfeld, 1838. pp. 224, 237, 294.)

Urbanus Rhegius names only Hans Denck. The North German polemic writers against the Anabaptists, such as Melanchthon, Luther, Menius, and Althamer, apparently had never heard anything at all about the Swiss Brethren. (Urbanus Rhegius, *Wider den Newen Taufforden, Nothwendige Warnung an alle Christgläubigen*, Augsburg, 1527. Philip Melanchthon, *Underricht wider die Lere der Widerteuffer aus dem latein verdeutschet durch Just. Jonas*, Wittemberg, 1528. Martin Luther, *Von der wiedertauffe an zwen Pfarherrn, ein Brief*, Nuremberg, 1528. Justus Menius, *Der widderteuffer Lere und geheimnis, Aus heiliger schrifft widderlegt*, Wittenberg, 1534. Andreas Althammer, *Ein kurtze unterricht den Pfarherrn und Predigern . . . verordnet, was sie das volck wider etliche verfürische lere der widertäuffer . . . ausz göttlicher Schrift vernomen, und unterrichten sollen*, 1528.)

Chapter I. THE YOUNG PATRICIAN IN ZURICH 1498-1514

1. Caspar Keller-Escher published in 1886 a history of the Grebel family, with illustrations and genealogical tables, under the title *Die Familie Grebel, Blätter aus ihrer Geschichte, gesammelt zur Erinnerung an die am 27. Oktober 1386 erfolgte Einbürgerung. Für Freunde als Manuskript gedruckt*, Frauenfeld, 1884 (1886). In 1887 he published an appendix containing additions and corrections. *Anzeiger für Schweizergeschichte Bd. II* (1877), p. 339, announces a

Grebel family history by a certain Herr von Grebel von Orelli. The announcement is misleading. Dr. Hans von Grebel, Zurich, kindly informs us that there is no other Grebel family history than that by Keller-Escher, and that the above announcement refers to the commission which Dr. Hans Grebel's father, Herr Gottfried von Grebel von Orelli, had given to Keller-Escher and which led to the publication of the book which appeared in 1886.

In addition to the published volume by Keller-Escher several genealogical manuscripts dealing with the Grebel family have been preserved. Chief among these is the *Greblisches Stammbuch,* now in the possession of Miss Anna Kölliker, Mühlebachstrasse, Zurich, but which Dr. E. Corrodi-Sulzer of Zurich considers unreliable. H. W. Zoller's *Fragmenta Genealogica,* manuscript J. 139 in the Zürich Zentralbibliothek, contains material on the Grebel family. The same is true of *Stemmatologia Tigurina, das ist Zürichs Geschlechterbuch, Durch Erhard Dürsteler, Pfarrer zu Ehrlebach* (1678-1766), a three volume manuscript in the Zurich Zentralbibliothek, numbered E 16, E 17, E 18. These three genealogical manuscripts apparently were produced in the first half of the 18th century. Keller-Escher used all three, particularly Dürsteler. My material on the Grebel family in this section is drawn largely from Keller-Escher, except where other sources are indicated. However a careful check has shown that Keller-Escher is not always reliable nor complete, particularly when dealing with the family of Jacob Grebel and Conrad Grebel.

2. Werner Schnyder, "Der Zürcher Handel mit Eisen und Stahl im Spätmittelalter," (*Zürcher Taschenbuch auf das Jahr* 1937, pp. 81-112) pp. 101, 104, mentions the Grebel family era in the Zurich iron business, particularly under Ulrich Grebel, citing as source *Quellen Zur Zürcher Wirtschaftsgeschichte,* pp. 680, 796, 811.

3. The 1471 coat-of-arms is reproduced in Plate II (opposite page 48) from Jean Egli, *Neues historisches Wappenbuch der Stadt Zurich,* 1860, Table 12.

4. The Jacob Grebel family was directly connected with the Murer and Keller families by marriage. Junker Jacob Murer married Margareta Fries, a sister of Dorothea Fries, Jacob Grebel's wife. (Keller-Escher, *op. cit.*) The *Mureria* mentioned thrice by Conrad in November and December, 1520 and July, 1523, as an intimate friend of the Grebels and Vadian, must have been a daughter of Jacob Murer. (Grebel to Vadian, Nov. 7, 1520, *VB II,* 315; Dec. 8, 1520, *VB III,* 210; July 14, 1523 *VB III,* 51.) Fridolin Murer addresses Vadian on June 19, 1520, as his brother-in-law and calls the wife of Jacob Grebel his cousin [*bas*]. (Fridolin Murer to Vadian, June 19, 1520, *VB II,* 287.) A sister of Jacob Grebel, Martha, was married to a Keller, *VB III,* 40, and a daughter of this sister is remembered by a bequest in the will of Dame Agatha Grebel, another sister of Jacob. ("Frow Agathen Greblin gemächt" Staatsarchiv Zurich, *Gemächtsbuch Bd. VI,* 312, fol. 5. Cf. also *VB VII,* 115f.) A connection also was established with the Escher family through the marriage of Dorothea, the youngest daughter of Jacob Grebel, to Hans Conrad Escher (vom Luchs). The connection with the Stucki family came through the mother of Jacob Grebel who was a Stucki. A sister of Jacob Grebel's father, married to an Engelhard, was the mother of Dr. Heinrich Engelhard of Zurich and Conrad Engelhard, *Vogt* of Kyburg. (Hans Georg Wirz, "Zürcher Familienschicksale im Zeitalter Zwinglis," *Zwingliana* VI, 1936, p. 267, note 71.)

Among the most intimate and significant family connections was that between the Jacob Grebel family and the Wirz family, another of the ancient patrician families of Zurich. Through a second marriage of their father, the three sons of Burkhard Wirz, Heinrich, Hans, and Jacob, became step-brothers of Jacob Grebel, and thus uncles to the latter's children. Heinrich Wirz held the office of *Ammann* (manager) of the monastery property at Einsiedeln which had been in the family since 1383. (A. F. Ammann, *Geschichte der Familie Am-*

mann I, Zurich, 1913 p. 317.) Hans Wirz held the similar office of *Schafner* at Wädeschwil. Hans Wirz was particularly close to the Grebel family. Jacob's daughter Martha, as bride of Vadian, with her husband, spent the first six months of her married life at the home of uncle Hans to escape the plague. Visits between the family were frequent. Conrad and a friend Beatus, on the occasion of one such visit at Wädeschwil, were enamored of the lovely and charming Margareta Wirz. (Grebel to Vadian, Dec. 18, 1520, *VB II,* 318.) Conrad's close friendship with his uncle Hans is attested by the fact that he secured his intervention to soften the wrath of his father at the time of his marriage. (Grebel to Vadian, February 2, 1522, *VB II,* 421.) Both uncles Heinrich and Hans were concerned about Jacob Grebel's foreign pensions and spoke to their nephew about the serious consequences which the pensions entailed. (Grebel to Vadian, February 1, 1521, *VB II,* 337.)

The extended monograph by Hans Georg Wirz, *Zürcher Familienschicksale im Zeitalter Zwinglis,* which has been cited above, is a veritable mine of genealogical information about such leading families as the Wirz and Grebel clans. My manuscript was completed before the Wirz monograph appeared but I have profited from it on several minor points. Unfortunately it is being published in installments and is not yet (Dec. 1949) complete. Six of nine chapters have appeared in *Zwingliana* as follows: VI-4(1935) 194-222, VI-5(1936) 242-271, VI-9(1938) 470-499, VI-10(1938) 537-574. However all material affecting the Grebel family and the Anabaptist movement has evidently appeared. Wirz's work is of high quality in every respect. Among other things he presents excellent work on Conrad Grebel, and succeeds in maintaining a fair and sympathetic picture of the Anabaptist movement throughout.

5. Keller-Escher, *op. cit.,* p. 43, although without documentation. The year of death of Ulrich Grebel, father of Jacob, is variously given (each time without documentation) as 1495 (p. 42 and *Stammtafel*) and 1496 (p. 19).

6. The lower chamber of the Zurich Council with 200 members was called the *Grosser Rath.* The upper chamber of 60 members was called the *Kleiner Rath.* I have translated the latter term by "Inner Council."

7. *Urkunden Bauamt C III* 4, *Nr.* 304 *d,* Staatsarchiv Zurich.

8. *Kauf- und Gemächts-Briefe B III* 308, fol. 302, Staatsarchiv Zürich.

9. Keller-Escher, *op. cit.,* p. 43, without documentation says "bald nach 1489." On the same page is found the statement, given without documentation, that the *Bilgerithurm* was Grebel's residence after 1512.

10. The *Glückshafenrodel* was prepared for publication in 1927 by Dr. Friedrich Hegi and was set up in type, but apparently never published. A printed, unbound copy, possibly proof sheets, is in the Zurich Staatsarchiv, with the title *Dis ist das register zum Hafen, und war gemacht und angefangen uff Mittwoch nach dem sonntag Invocavit Anno domini Mo quingentesimo quarto*" (Feb. 28, 1504). The Jacob Grebel family appears on page 186, followed by the family of Hans Wirz, step-brother of Jacob Grebel. The Wirz family list is as follows:

Anna Hanns Wirtzen zu Wedischwil husfrow
Katrinli Wirtz von Wedischwil
Barbeli Wirtz
Andrew Wirtz
Burckhart
Hanns Wirtz der Jung
Dorothe Wirtz
Margretli
Hanns Wirtz, Schafner

11. The wife of Jacob Grebel was Dorothea Fries, daughter of Hans Fries, sometime *Ammann* of Uri. Zoller, *Fragmenta Genealogicia,* fol. 266, and Dürsteler, *Stemmatologia Tigurina,* I, p. 32. Dürsteler, *Ehebuch* (Staatsarchiv Zurich) Ms. E 4, and *Greblisches Stammbuch,* also agree. Cf. Keller-Escher, *op. cit.,* p. 43.

12. *Ehegerichts Protocolle, Tom. I,* p. 22, Staatsarchiv Zurich.

13. According to Dürsteler and Zoller, the oldest child, Barbara, had been married to Leonhard Karli in 1512. She lived somewhere not far from Zurich, for in a letter of September 26, 1518, Conrad refers to a visit made to his sister in connection with a stay at the baths at Baden. (Letter to Vadian, Sept. 26, 1518, *Vadianische Briefsammlung* (hereafter cited as VB) *II,* 202. [*Mitteilungen zur vaterländischen Geschichte, herausgegeben vom Historischen Verein in St. Gallen, XIV,* 1891.] Cf. also letter of Grebel to Vadian July 23, 1518, *VB IV,* where the visit is announced on page 403. In the summer of 1520 Barbara with her two daughters came to the parental home at Zurich for a visit to escape the plague, leaving her husband behind. (Grebel to Vadian, Aug. 3, 1520. *VB II,* 297.) Apparently the husband died during the plague, for Barbara remained in Zurich. Conrad mentions the birth to his sister in February, 1521, of a third daughter, Cleophe. (Grebel to Vadian, Feb. 19, 1521, *VB II,* 341.) In July, 1521, Barbara seems to have been the go-between in arrangements involving Conrad's love affair. (Grebel to Vadian, July 14, 1521. *VB II,* 368.) By 1527 she was married again to Beat Beli of Maienfeld near Chur, for in the sale of the house belonging to the heirs of her brother Conrad, the name of "Barbara Grebel, wife of Beat Beli of Mayenfeld," appears under date of March 18, 1527, among those granting the release. (The *Greblisches Stammbuch* reports: "Anno 1512 Barb Grebel verheiratet mit Leonhart Carle. Anno 1527 hat sie auf absterben mit Beat Beli von Belfort von Fidriss im Prättigau verheiratet." Zoller in *Fragmenta Genealogica* also reports the marriage in 1512 with Leonhart Carli, and 1527 with Beat Beli von Belfort. Dürsteler, *Stemmatologia Tigurina,* III, folio 134 *verso* incorrectly places the marriage in 1531. A letter of Beat Beli to Vadian from Fideris dated May 5, 1530, calls Vadian "brother-in-law," and greets Martha, Vadian's wife, as "sister," *VB IV,* 211. Beli's wife, Barbara, was a sister of Martha, Vadian's wife.) This marriage and residence in Maienfeld is of interest, since, if it took place before 1526, it may account for the fact that Conrad went to this region in the summer of 1526 where he died of the plague. (*Johannes Kesslers Sabbata,* St. Gall, 1902, p. 164.)

The second of the children of Jacob Grebel, Euphrosine, entered the convent of Oetenbach, where she was under the instruction or her aunt, Agathe Grebel, and where she died before July, 1520. (Grebel to Vadian, July 13, 1520. *VB II,* 337. In a letter to Vadian between May 28, and July 14, 1520, Grebel calls the departed nun, Euphrosine, an "Alumna" of a certain "Grebelia," scarcely any one else than the nun, Agathe, sister of Jacob Grebel.)

Andreas Grebel, Conrad's only and younger brother, was for a time (after 1517) a courtier of King Ferdinand of Austria in Vienna. On February 19, 1521, Conrad reports that Andreas, together with a certain "Effinger," had returned to Zurich, Ferdinand having dismissed 400 courtiers. (Grebel to Vadian, Feb. 19, 1521, *VB II,* 341.) On December 18, 1521, Conrad refers to the recent decease of Andreas. (Grebel to Vadian, Dec. 18, 1521. *VB II,* 408.) *In Das Grosse Jahrzeitbuch* of the Grossmünster Church in Zurich the last name entered under the date of September 3 is an *Andres Grebel.* (*Jahrzeitbücher des Grossmünsters Zürich, Ms.* C. 6 698, fol. 120 *verso,* Staatsarchiv Zurich.) Since there is no other recorded Andreas Grebel in the Grebel family genealogy, it is quite probable that this was Andreas, the son of Jacob, brother of Conrad Grebel, who accordingly must have died September 3, 1521. The only other reference to Andreas is found in the testimony of the father, Jacob Grebel, at his trial on the 11th and 12th of October, 1526, where the father is said to have told Alexander Stamp (Scampius?) in 1517 that he had two sons, one at home [Andreas] and the other in Vienna [Conrad]. (Emil Egli, *Aktensammlung zur Geschichte der Züricher Reformation in den Jahren* 1519-1533, Zurich, 1879, No. 1050, p. 499.)

The most prominent of the daughters of Jacob Grebel was Martha, who was married on August 19, 1519, in the chapel at Wädenswil to Joachim von Watt [Vadian], the noted humanist, physician, and later burgomaster and reformer of St. Gall. (Keller-Escher, *op. cit.*) The marriage had been brought about through the mediation of Conrad Grebel, the pupil and devoted admirer of Vadian in Vienna. The preliminary ceremony took place on July 5, 1519. According to Zoller the witnesses for Martha were: Heinrich Engelhard, *Pastor;* Felix Grebel, *Ritter;* Hans Ulrich Stuckhi; Cunrath Engelhard, *Vogt* of Kyburg; Hans Wirz, *Schaffner* of Wädenswil; and Jacob Wirz, *Ammann* of Einsiedeln. (H. S. Zoller, *Fragmenta Genealogica*, Ms. J. 139, fol. 266, Staatsarchiv Zurich.) Conrad, who was in Paris at the time of the wedding, sought in vain to secure funds from his father to make the trip home for the occasion. Because of the raging of the plague in St. Gall, Vadian with his bride spent the six months following the wedding August, 1519 to February, 1520, at Wädenswil, enjoying the hospitality of Hans Wirz, uncle of the bride. (Cf. the following letters: Jacob Grebel to Vadian, Aug. 26, 1519, *VB II*, 246; George Binder to Vadian, Sept. 2, 1519, *VB II*, 246; Leonhard von Watt to Vadian Nov. 2, 1519, *VB II*, 251; Ulrich Lener to Vadian, Nov. 16, 1519, *VB II*, 255, all addressed to Vadian in "Wädeschwil." Feb. 19, 1520, Vadian wrote Ulrich Zasius from Zurich, *VB IV*, 242, that he had just returned to Zurich after six months in the country. "Cum Tigurum nuper rediissem a rure, quo cum coniuge mea sex totas menses delitui.")

The youngest child of the Jacob Grebel family was Dorothea, born about 1509, a child especially beloved by her parents. Conrad first mentions her in a letter of January 12, 1522, when he calls her the "pet of her parents, the tyrant of the house." (Grebel to Vadian, Jan. 12, 1522. *VB II*, 415.) He seems to have been particularly exasperated by the little maid of thirteen whom he accuses of having pilfered some of his clothing. She must have been an active and mischievous little girl, for even her father, in spite of the fact that she was the "pet" of the family, could not refrain from referring to her once in a letter to Vadian, as "that naughty little girl, Dorothy," [*"Das bös meitli dorly."*] (Jacob Grebel to Vadian, Oct. 12, 1523. *VB III*, 40.) Her first marriage to the well-known Johann Jacob Ammann of Zurich, which took place on June 26, 1524, when she was only fifteen years of age, was annulled by the Zurich courts on June 15, 1525. (*Ehegerichtsprotokolle Bd. I, 22 verso et seq.*, Staatsarchiv Zurich.) Shortly after the annulment Dorothea was married to Junker Hans Conrad Escher, with whom she had at least two children. It appears that the marriage must have taken place before October, 1526, for in the above-mentioned trial of Jacob Grebel, a son-in-law of Jacob and brother-in--law of Conrad appears several times in the testimony.

Through a confusion which goes all the way back to the earliest genealogies (Zoller and Dürsteler) two further daughters of Jacob Grebel have been identified as Anna, wife of Bernard Peyer, sometime treasurer of the city of Schaffhausen, and Gertrude, wife of Hans von Waldkirch, sometime burgomaster of Schaffhausen. Keller-Escher repeats the statements, and the later biographers of Grebel as well as writers on the Anabaptist movement in Schaffhausen follow the lead. It is impossible, however, that this identification can be correct, since there is not the least mention of these supposed daughters of the family in Grebel's correspondence or in the correspondence of Vadian. If they had been born before 1504 they would have been mentioned in the lottery list of that year. If born after that time they would surely have been mentioned in the correspondence. They would also have been mentioned in the sale of the house of Jacob Grebel, referred to above. The error seems to go back to Zoller, who infers that the wives of Peyer and Waldkirch were children of Jacob Grebel from the fact that each family later owned a sixth of the *Zehnten zu Kloten.* (Zoller, *Fragmenta Genealogica,* Zurich Zentralbibliothek, Ms. J. 139.) C. A. Bächtold, *Die Schaffhauser Wiedertäufer in der Reformationszeit,* p. 5 (*Beiträge zur vaterländischen Geschichte . . . des Kantons Schaffhausen,* 7. Heft.), Schaffhausen, 1900, and Jacob Wipf, *Reformationsgeschichte der Stadt und Landschaft Schaffhausen,* Zurich, 1929, p. 187, repeat the genealogical error. Both women were daughters of Christoph Grebel of Baden in Aargau, who was a brother of Knight Felix Grebel, son of Hans Grebel, a brother of Ulrich, who was father of Jacob Grebel. This would make Conrad Grebel second cousin to Anna Peyer and Gertrude Waldkirch. (*Ratsmanual Zürich,* 1542; Friedrich Hegi, *Glückshafenrodel Zürich,* 1504.)

14. Grebel to Vadian, Feb. 6. 1522, *VB II,* 421.

15. Grebel to Vadian, Nov. 2, *VB II,* 398.

16. *Tauf- u. Ehebuch Grossmünster,* Staatsarchiv Zurich.

Proof of the marriage is also found in Ziegler's own testimony before the Zurich court on January 9, 1528, where he states that he had just married "Conrad Grebel's widow." (*Ehegerichtsprotokolle,* fol. 85, Staatsarchiv Zurich.) Ziegler secured citizenship in Zurich a few days later, Jan. 28, 1528. (*Bürgerbuch,* fol. 403, Staatsarchiv Zurich.)

17. In view of the facts just cited the assertion of all the previous literature on this point, from Zoller and Dürsteler on down to the present day, including Keller-Escher, that the wife of Conrad Grebel was Agathe von Fynland from Alsace, cannot be accepted. How the name "Agathe von Fynland" came into the family tradition is inexplicable. It apparently goes back to Zoller whose data are not always reliable, and it is altogether possible that it was a pure invention of his. In table VII of the Grebel family tree contained in *Die Familie Grebel,* Keller-Escher shows a Hans Conrad Grebel married to Agathe Wild in 1526. This is however not Conrad, the son of Jacob. The assertion that Conrad's wife was Agathe von Fynland, and that she had been his sweetheart as long as two years before the marriage, is found most recently in *ZW VIII,* 782, note 11, without indication of source.

Not much can be said with certainty about the home of Grebel's wife. Apparently she was living in Zurich when he married her, and had been for at least a year before that time. Early in the year 1521 she had attracted Conrad, for in a letter of February 1, 1521, about seven months after he had returned home from Paris, he wrote to Vadian that he had the desire to marry and to live in Basel. (Grebel to Vadian, Feb. 1, 1521, *VB II,* 337.) Grebel does not speak expressly of marriage, but it is quite clear that he is in love and that this has created the desire to go to Basel. That at this time Barbara was in Zurich is proved by two letters dated in July, 1521, in which Grebel stated that he had the intention of going with his beloved to Basel. (Grebel to Vadian, between May 28 and July 14, 1521, *VB III,* 225 and July 14, 1521, *VB II,* 368.) Before the 22nd of July, 1521, the girl actually went alone to Basel, whither Grebel followed her in August. (Grebel to Vadian, July 22, 1521, *VB III,* 227.) It is possible that she was a native of Basel, but her residence was in Zurich when Conrad became acquainted with her.

Certain somewhat obscure passages in Conrad's letters suggest that his wife may have been a nun in the convent at Oetenbach. He tried to keep the affair from his parents as long as possible, and felt that it would be necessary for them to leave Zurich in case they married, which might have been due to the scandal which would have been aroused by the violation of a nun's vow. Furthermore, in his first letter to Vadian telling about the affair (undated, but written between May 28 and July 14, 1521, *VB III,* 225), Grebel relates that a certain "Grebelia" who had earlier been the instructress of his departed sister Euphrosine, had, as a nun, advised him not to keep the matter hidden from the nuns, and had persuaded him to report the affair. He says he had agreed, with her support, to make an attempt to do something, and not merely to let the affair drift as a hopeless tragedy. The nun "Grebelia" cannot well have been anyone but Agathe Grebel, the sister of Jacob Grebel and aunt of Conrad who was at that time a nun at Oetenbach convent. However, the editor of *Vad. BrS.* holds this "Grebelia" to have been Barbara, the sister of Conrad. He does this on the basis of Conrad's letter of July 14, 1521 where Conrad tells Vadian that he could learn everything from Barbara who knew everything. But he overlooks two facts, first, that the "Grebelia" was a nun, which Barbara was not, and second, that Barbara was no longer a "Grebelia," but since 1512 a "Carli." It is also difficult to see how Barbara could have been an instructress of the departed Euphrosine.

18. Egli, *Aktens.*, No. 1050.

19. Grebel to Vadian, Aug. 11, 1523, *VB III*, 32. It is interesting to note that in the autograph Grebel also writes the name Josua in Hebrew letters: "Gratulor mihi, Josue meum; si videtur, inquam, quia patri, Leopoldo, Dorotheae, Te non visum est. Tu dispice, quae causae assignari possint. Mundum ego autorem huius rusticitatis sive simultatis potius existimo esse." [Dorotheae te in Greek letters in MS.]

20. Grebel to Vadian, Jan. 14, 1525, *VB III*, 104: "Min frow ist gnesen gester, das ist fritag, acht tag. Dasz Kind ist ein Tochter, heisst Rachel; ist noch nit in dem Römschen wasserbad getoufft und gschwemmt."

21. *Schirmbücher VI*, p. 333 et seq., Staatsarchiv Zurich.

22. The assertion of Zoller that the Peyer and Waldkirch families of Schaffhausen each possessed a sixth of the income of the Kloten estate is untenable according to the records of the *Schirmbücher*. See note 13 above.

23. *Gemächtsbuch B VI*, 312, fol. 5, "Frow Agathen Greblin gemächt." Hans Conrad Escher also reports this will in a letter to his brother-in-law Vadian, Oct. 31, 1533, *VB IV*, 136. He was a witness to the will as member of the Council and signed his name to it as "Conrad Aescher."

24. Erhard Dürsteler, *Genealogische Tabellen*, MS. E 94, fol. 246, Staatsarchiv Zurich.

25. Grebel to Vadian, Nov. 21, 1522, *VB II*, 451: "Neque tu me pariter eum familia mea alis."

26. Tafel VII, *Stammtafel* in Keller-Escher, *Die Familie Grebel*. The further data about the descendants of Josua Grebel, are taken from the *Stammtafel*, and the book itself.

27. A daughter of Burgomaster Conrad Grebel, by name Ragula, was married to the genealogist Junker Hans Wilpert Zoller who died in 1709. Since Regula Grebel-Zoller's grandfather, Heinrich Grebel, (1586-1658) was a grandson of Conrad Grebel, it is possible that Zoller had access to reliable family traditions in preparing his Grebel genealogy. He is probably the one who prepared the *Greblisches Stammbuch* mentioned earlier. Dürsteler is certainly dependent on Zoller for much of his material.

28. Keller-Escher, *op. cit.*, p. 43. See also the *Glückshafenrodel* of 1504, where Jacob Grebel is called "Vogt zu Grüningen."

29. Gustav Strickler's *Geschichte der Herrschaft Grüningen*, Zurich, 1908, omits altogether the period of Jacob Grebel's term of office as Vogt, in fact the entire period 1489-1525. Jacob Grebel's name is not even mentioned. An extensive chapter is devoted to "Die Widertäufer und der Bauernaufstand 1525," pp. 126-158. The same author's *Das Schloss Grüningen*, Zurich, 1913, (*Mitteilungen der Antiquarischen Gesellschaft in Zurich, Bd. LXXVII, Heft* 3) also fails to mention Jacob Grebel, but contains interesting pictures of the castle and village of Grüningen from the year 1486 (after *Edlibach's Chronik*) and 1548 (after *Stumpf's Chronik*), and a reproduction of the splendid stained glass panel of the

castle by Joseph Murer of 1563, which is now in the Schweizerisches Landesmuseum, in Zurich. It also gives a half page (p. 149) to "Die Zeit der Wiedertäuferunruhen 1525."

30. Ulrich Ernst, *Geschichte des zürcherischen Schulwesens bis gegen das Ende des* 16. *Jahrhunderts,* Winterthur, 1870, gives a good description of the school life of that time in the chapter, "Die letzten Zeiten vor der Reformation," pp. 14-38. *Die Grossmünsterschule in Zürich, Ansprache vom Rektor J. Schurter,* Zurich, 1915, is based on Ernst and adds nothing new. Thomas Platter's autobiography in *Thomas und Felix Platter, Zwei Autobiographien,* Basel 1840, describes in a very interesting fashion conditions in the *Grossmünster* school in 1524 and 1525, when he was a pupil there. Although this description deals with conditions ten years after Grebel left the school, it is quite probable that little change had taken place.

31. Ernst, *op. cit.,* p. 25, with Salomon Voegelin, *Das alte Zürich,* p. 40, and Nuescheler, *Die Gotteshäuser der Schweiz,* III, p. 438, as sources.

32. Ernst, *op. cit.,* p. 30.

33. The following picture is drawn chiefly from Ernst, *op. cit.,* p. 20ff.

31. *Thomas and Felix Platter, Zwei Autobiographien, Basel,* 1840.

CHAPTER II. AMONG THE SCHOLARS OF BASEL AND VIENNA

1. The matriculation record for the winter semester 1514-1515 begins as follows: "Nomina entitularorum sub rectoratu Magistri Henrici Rinck qui fuit electus ipso die sancti Luce anno millesimo quingentisimo decimoquarto; hic sunt . . . ." As sixteenth in the list of matriculants appears "Cunradus Grebel de thurego constan. dioc."; followed by "Johannes de Hunwil ex olten." "Luce," the date of the election of Rector Rinck, was Oct. 18, 1514. The matriculation register of the previous semester (May, 1514) shows the name of "Magister Henricus Loritus Glareanus Poeta laureatus," followed by several familiar names of students who were Grebel's comrades later: Petrus Tschudi, Fridolin Eckley, Conradus Moser, Johannes Leopoldus Grebel. The matriculation records are now kept in the Basel University library.

2. The material relating to the University of Basel is based on: Wilhelm Vischer, *Geschichte der Universität Basel von der Gründung* 1460 *bis zur Reformation,* Basel, 1860; Rudolf Wackernagel, *Humanismus und Reformation in Basel,* Basel, 1924; Rudolf Thommen, *Basler Studentenleben im* 16. *Jahrhundert* (*Basler Jahrbuch,* 1887, pp. 94-140); and O. F. Fritzsche, *Glarean, Sein Leben und seine Schriften,* Frauenfeld, 1890. Thommen describes conditions after 1530.

3. Wackernagel, *Humanismus und Reformation in Basel,* p. 128.

4. Vischer, *Geschichte der Universität Basel,* p. 194.

5. *Ibid.,* p. 227.

6. *Ibid.,* p.194.

7. Concerning the *bursa* see Vischer, *ibid.,* p. 152. For want of a better term, the latter word will be used hereafter to refer to Glarean's institution.

8. Conrad Grebel and Johann Leopold Grebel to Zwingli, Vienna, Sept. 8, 1517 (Conrad actually did the writing), *ZW VII,* 62-65.

9. Johannes Hinwiler to Vadian, Basel, Jan. 6, 1515. *VB I,* 134.

10. Valentin Tschudi to Zwingli, Basel, July 31, 1514. *ZW VII,* 28.

11. *Rudolf Collins Schilderung seines Lebens, verdeutscht von Salomon Voegelin* (*Zürcher Taschenbuch auf das Jahr* 1859, Zurich, 1859, pp. 179-220). First published in Latin in J. J. Ulrich, *Miscellanea Tigurina* I, Zurich 1721. Very interesting is the report by Collin of his study in Basel, in Voegelin, *op. cit.,* p. 188: "Zum dritten wurde ich von Herrn Xylotectus selber nach Basel gebracht und in die Schule und Wohnung Herrn Heinrich Glareanus, des allertreuesten

Lehrers, aufgenommen. Bei diesem lebte ich ein Halbjahr lang, und erlernte die Anfangsgründe der Mathematik. Ich hätte auch grossen Fortschritt in den Studien gemacht, wenn ich länger seinen Unterricht und seine Erziehung hätte geniessen können. Aber da Herr Glareanus nach Paris reiste, musste ich auch meinen Studienort vertauschen."

12. Wackernagel, *op. cit.,* p. 152.

13. Wackernagel, *op. cit.,* p. 151. Although Glarean was the best of the few humanists in Basel who were associated with the University, and although he was recognized by Erasmus as an outstanding scholar and had been praised by him on numerous occasions, as for instance in a letter to Zwingli, dated May, 1516, in which Erasmus calls Glarean the chief, *princeps,* of the Swiss humanists (a collection of such passages is to be found in Fritzsche, *op. cit.,* pp. 11, 12, and in *ZW VII,* 37, note 2. Wackernagel, *op. cit.,* 429, 430, also has words of praise for Glarean), he was not able for various reasons to adjust himself happily to the life of Basel. He did not feel at home, and finally came to the conclusion that he could do better elsewhere. In May, 1517, exactly three years after his arrival in Basel, he removed from Basel to Paris. It is important to note here, in view of the later trouble between Grebel and Glarean in Paris, that the chief blame in the matter of Glarean's incompatibility in Basel is to be attributed to his own restless and irascible disposition. More than once Glarean was guilty of foolish practical jokes. For instance at one time he rode on horseback into a hall where a disputation was being held, and refused to leave until the entire assembly had been dismissed. He did this because he felt that he had not received sufficient recognition among the professors. (Vischer, *op. cit.,* p. 197. For a similar practical joke see Fritzsche, *op. cit.,* p. 13.)

14. Conrad Grebel to Zwingli, Sept. 8, 1517, *ZW VII,* 64.

15. Salomon Voegelin, *op. cit.,* pp. 188-190: "Zum vierten begab ich mich nach Wien, vom Studium der Poetik angezogen: daselbst angekommen ward ich von den jungen Schweizern empfangen, besonders von Konrad Grebel, und in die Wohnung aufgenommen. Herr Dr. Joachim Vadianus war da mein Gönner und Lehrer. Aber ich ward in meiner Hoffnung betrogen und fand lauter barbarisches Wesen. Die poetischen Vorlesungen, um deren Willen ich mich dahin begeben, kamen mir ganz kindisch vor, da ich an den Vergilius schon zu Luzern unter Herrn Xylotectus mich gewöhnt hatte. Und nicht nur die Vorlesungen, auch die Sitten der Leute, der Weltlichen wie der Studierenden, missfielen mir, da sie fast alle von unlöblicher Trunksucht verdorben waren . . . Als daher Herr Dr. Vadianus in sein Vaterland verreiste, mochte ich auch nicht länger dort verbleiben, obwohl nicht wegen Mangel in Beutel, sondern kehrte, nachdem zwei Jahre verflossen, ins Vaterland zurück."

16. Valentin Tschudi to Zwingli, July 31, 1514, *ZW VII,* 28.

17. P. S. Allen, *Opus Epistolarum Des. Erasmi Roterodami,* II. Oxford, 1910, p. 342: "Praeterea habeo mecum domi meae triginta optimae indolis iuvenes, qui annue solvunt centum et viginti scuta, quamuis labori meo non satis respondeat hoc praemium." See also *ZW VII,* 48: "Sunt mecum iuvenes triginta et vix ulli maiori angustiam quam Glareani: paucos nummos mittunt, et praesertim ii, qui bene habent." The number of pupils and the charges fluctuated: cf. Fritzsche, *op. cit.,* pp. 13, 14.

18. Vischer, *op. cit.,* 152. A description of Glarean's *bursa* and activity in Vischer, *op. cit.,* p. 195f.

19. Wackernagel, *op. cit.,* pp. 126-255, Chapter VI, "Wissenschaft." The following description was taken largely from this extraordinarily rich and detailed work.

20. May be concluded from his letters found in P. S. Allen, *op. cit.,* II, *Letters of* 1514-1517. Erasmus was in Basel again for a brief period from May to August, 1518.

21. Fritzsche, *op. cit.,* pp. 10-21, where the life and activity of Glarean in Basel, 1514-1517, are described.

22. Wackernagel points out that there is no evidence of exchange of letters between Glarean and Rhenanus.

23. Fritzsche, *loc. cit.,* for proof. The following paragraph found in Wackernagel, *op. cit.,* p. 151, is very significant: "In Erasmus, der kurz nach ihm in Basel einkehrte, kam ihm dann diejenige Macht entgegen, die fortan auch für ihn Basel zu einem Ort ohne Gleichen erhob. Erasmus galt ihm als Vater, als Meister. Er nannte ihn den grösseren Teil seiner Seele, seine Zierde, sein Gestirn. Dessen Güte war ihm das kostbarste Geschenk, weit hinausgehend über Gold und Edelstein. In Briefen, in Elegien, legt er seine stürmische Bewunderung des Einzigen nieder."

24. Glarean to Erasmus, Sept. 3, 1516. Allen, *op. cit.,* II, 341. "Quod me Christum sapere docuisti; neque sapere solum, sed imitari, sed suspicere, sed amare." It is doubtful that the fullness of this religious experience came to Glarean before Grebel left Basel in the spring of 1515. Hence its possible influence on the latter should not be overrated.

25. *ZW,* VII, 52. "Adeo quosdam magis invat esse Catullianos Propertianosque quam vel Paulinos vel Christianos."

26. Allen, *op. cit.,* II, 456. Allen's own estimate of the relation between Glarean and Erasmus is given in the following note (Allen, II, 280): "His theatrical temperament was somewhat distasteful to Erasmus, and their relations though friendly, were not always cordial."

27. Wackernagel, *op. cit.,* pp. 245, 246.

28. Glarean's friends in Paris included Faber Stapulensis who was similar in type to the Basel humanists. See the next chapter.

29. See his letters from August to November, 1521, from Basel, in *VB.* See also the letter of Andreas Cratander to Capito, Sept. 20, 1521. Basel, Kirchenarchiv, *Ms. Ki. Ar.* 25*a No.* 48.

30. Grebel and Felix Manz are characterized as "Erasmian Humanists" by Hermelink in his *Reformation und Gegenreformation,* 2. *Aufl.* 1931, p. 115. There is no ground for this conclusion.

31. Fritzsche, *op. cit.,* pp. 16, 17 with proofs.

32. See note 41 below.

33. Binder's personalia, *ZW VIII,* 372, note 12. Tschudi's personalia, *ZW VII,* 27, footnote 1.

34. Statements to this effect at Jacob Grebel's trial on Oct. 12, 1526. Egli, *Aktensammlung* No. 1050, p. 498: "Im selbigen fuenfzechenden jar gab Jakob Grebel seinem sun das burkrecht uf, schickt in gan Wien uf die schuel, daselbs er von keiserlicher Majestat provision erhalten." Also p. 497: "Zu Wien habe sein Sohn alle Fronfasten (the week following the sixth Sunday before Easter) 7 Gl. empfangen, zusammen 28 Gl. Joerg Binder möge davon wissen, da er aus Auftrag desselben bis zu seiner Rückkunft das Stipendium eingezogen habe." Conrad Grebel himself reports in his letter to Zwingli from Vienna, Sept. 8, 1517, that he had already devoted himself to literary studies for two years, supported by a stipend from Emperor Maximilian. "Stipendio Maximiliani caesarie maxime hac tempestate duobus enim annis adiutus ad praedicta literarum studia Viennae incubui, perinde quoque incuburus." *ZW* VII, 63. In a letter from Paris Oct. 26, 1518, to Vadian, *VB* II, 207, Grebel requests Vadian to give to his friend Clivanus (Collin) any balance which might remain due to him (Conrad) of the Emperor's stipend. It must be said that the amount of the stiuend, 7 guilders a year, seems very small.

35. Letter of Ulrich Zwingli to Vadian, Oct. 4, 1512 *ZW* VII, 16.

36. *Bürgerbuch I,* fol. 45 and fol. 198 *verso* (latter incorrect), and *Ratsmanual* 1515, both in Staatsarchiv Zurich. *ZW VII,* 62, note 1, is in error in reporting the surrender of citizenship by Johann Leopold Grebel alone, and also in giving the date as July 3, 1516. That Grebel later resumed his citizenship is proved by his reference to possessing citizenship in his letter of May 1525, to Andreas Castelberger (*Mennonite Quarterly Review* July, 1927, p. 42).

37. Matriculation data in *ZW* VII, 62, note 1. Dr. Robert Friedmann of Vienna kindly checked the matriculation records of the University of Vienna and reports the following data: (1) *Hauptmatrikel* Band III, fol. 170, *Sommersemester* 1515, *sub "Rheinische Nation"*: "No. 282 Cunradus Grebel ex Tzürich, No. 283 Johannes Leopoldus Grebel ex Tzürich." (2) *Rheinische Matrikel* (Band ?) zu 1515 . . . folio 249: "Conrad Moser ex Torrego, Conrad Grepel ex Thurrego, . . . Johannes Leopold Grebel ex Thurego." L. von Muralt (*Zürcher Taschenbuch auf das Jahr.* 1937, p. 114.) reports that the second registration at the University of Vienna occurred not in the summer semester 1516, as reported in *Zwingli Werke* but in the following winter semester 1516/17; reported by the Archive of the University. I follow von Muralt here. Moser's matriculation in *ZW VII,* 65, note 13.

38. Cf. "Situationsplan von der Wiener Universtät und den dazugehörigen Häusern im 15. Jahrhundert" in Joseph Ritter von Aschbach, *Geschichte der Wiener Universität im ersten Jahrhundert ihres Bestehens, Neue Ausgabe,* Vienna, 1870.

39. Hainz Steltzhammer, procurator of the *Bursa Prugk,* to Vadian, Aug. 31, 1516, *CB I,* 242. However, Vadian had also guaranteed accounts for some students in the *Bursa Lilia* of which the procurator also reminded Vadian in a letter of Aug. 4, 1519. There Vadian's brother, Melchior von Watt, was listed among those not paying.

40. Cf. note 45 below.

41. *Pomponii Melae Hispani libri de situ orbis tres, adiectis J. Vadiani Helvetii in eosdem scholiis, addita gnogne in Geographium Catechesi et epistola Vadiani ad Agricolam digna lectu.* First edition by Lucas Alantsee in Vienna, May 1, 1518; second edition enlarged, by Andreas Cratander, Basel, Jan. 1522; third edition, Paris, 1530. It was Vadian's greatest work. Cf. A. Horawitz, *Zur Geschichte des deutschen Humanismus,* Jena, 1874, p. 19.

The dedication, dated May 1, 1518, contains many laudatory references to Grebel as "a youth of very noble character." The students who were closest to Vadian were allowed to contribute Latin poems in the introductory part. The names of the contributors are Conrad Grebel, Johannes Hinwiler, George Binder, Rudolph Clivanus (Collin), and Christopher Crassus. The total list of students around Vadian in Vienna, together with data as to the length of their stay is as follows:

George Binder, of Zurich, six years in Vienna (1513-1519). He wrote from Vienna to Vadian, July 26, 1519, telling of his hope to teach in Zurich. Jacob Zwingli, brother of Ulrich came to Vienna in the autumn of 1512 with Valentin Tschudi, both with recommendations from Zwingli to Vadian (Zwingli to Vadian, Oct. 4, 1512, *ZW VII,* 16). Tschudi stayed in Vienna only a year (see his personalia in *ZW VII,* 27), but Jacob Zwingli, who became a monk in January, 1513, remained until his death in 1517. (See Jacob Zwingli's personalia in *ZW VII,* 18.) Johannes Hinwiler had first come to Vienna in early 1514 to study with Vadian, only to return to Basel the same autumn for a semester of study in Glarean's *bursa,* but came back with Grebel in the summer of 1515. He was still in Vienna in the summer of 1520, from whence he wrote on July 29 to Vadian. Conrad Moser, who also accompanied Grebel to Vienna in 1515 remained there at least two years, for he is mentioned as in Vienna in Grebel's letter of Sept. 8, 1517 to Zwingli (*ZW VII,* 65). Johannes Leopold Grebel, Conrads cousin, remained until the summer of 1517; in January, 1518, he was already in Paris. As evidence of his presence in Paris in January 1518, cf. the following passage in the letter of student Hans Heinrich Frey of Zurich to his brother Ambrosius Frey, dated Paris, January 13, 1518: "Item witter wus von mim sold ich meint nur set jetz XII kronen sin werden so ist mir nun sechs die wil und min herren von Zürich kein studente hand geschickt so ist der Ritter (sc. Felix, father of Johann Leopold) Grebels sun da gsin und hat in ingnan und ist mir also nut me den vi kronen worden und aber er mus mirs wider gen." Staatsarchiv Zurich, A 26. 134; printed in *Zwingliana II*, pp. 92, 93. Rudolph Collin (Clivanus) of Lucerne came in the summer of 1517 and remained till the summer of 1519. Huldreich Kramer of Zurich was recommended by Zwingli to Vadian in June, 1517. (Zwingli to Vadian, June 13, 1517, *ZW VII*, 54.) Grebel mentions him in the letter to Zwingli from Vienna, Sept. 8, 1517, cited above. He was probably a son of the Andreas Kramer in Zurich, who was also a good friend of Grebel. Cf. Kramer's testimony at Jacob Grebel's trial, Oct. 1526, where he calls himself "a good comrade" of Conrad until the "Wiedertouf" separated them. (Egli, *Aktensammlung,* No. 1050, p. 495.) Ulrich Lener of Appenzell wrote to Vadian in 1516 about his probable speedy return to Vienna. (Ulrich Lener to Vadian, Appenzell, July 12, 1516, *VB I,* 159.) Melchior von Watt of St. Gall, brother of Vadian, was in Vienna in 1518. (Melchior to Vadian, Vienna, July 16, 1518, *VB II,* 193.) Andreas Eck of St. Gall was still in Vienna in 1519. (Eck to Vadian, Vienna, June 14, 1519: "ex aedibus Joannis de Hinnwil," *VB II,* 231.) Christopher Crassus (Dick, Schürpff), also of St. Gall, an older student who served as sort of an assistant to Vadian, had been matriculated in Vienna as early as 1508 but was still there in 1519. (Zwingli to Crassus, March 23, 1519, *ZW VII,* 68, where personalia are to be found.) Johann Jakob Zurgilgen of Lucerne was a pupil of Vadian from 1511 to 1515. (Zurgilgen to Zwingli from Paris, Oct. 26, 1518, *VB III,* 174.) He greets his former comrades, Vadian's pupils, who are still in Vienna, "reliquum omnibus discipulis tuis, meis commilitonibus, salutem"; Zurgilgen went from Vienna to Basel in 1515, and from there to Paris in 1517. It is worthy of note that a number of Swiss students followed the route Basel, Vienna (or Vienna, Basel), Paris. Among them were the two Grebels, Zurgilgen, and Valentine Tschudi. Benedikt Burgauer, later a parish priest in St. Gall and friend of Grebel, is said to have been a pupil of Vadian in Vienna. (E. Arbenz, "Joachim Vadian beim Ubergang vom Humanismus zum Kirchenstreit" in *Neujahrsblatt des Historischen Vereins St. Gallen,* 1895, p. 11.) Another member of the circle about Vadian, though not a Swiss and no longer a young student, was Kaspar Ursinus Velius of Schweidnitz near Breslau in Silesia, matriculated in the autumn of 1515. He remained only a year, but returned to Vienna in 1518 as a teacher of Greek to remain until 1521. In August, 1521, he appeared in Basel where he remained until February, 1522, during which time he lived in the house of Cratander and renewed his acquaintance with Grebel who was also there from August to October, 1521. (See Chapter IV, p. 86.) Ursinus was in correspondence with Vadian from 1513 to 1521. (See also "Caspar Ursinus Velius" by Gustav Bauch in *Ungarische Revue, VII,* 1887.) It is interesting to note that Johannes Bünderlin of Linz, who became an Anabaptist in 1526 at Augsburg, also came to Vienna in 1515 in the same semester with Grebel. He was enrolled as an auditor Sept. 19, 1515, and remained in Vienna until 1519. (Christian Neff, article "Bünderlin," *Menn. Lexikon I,* p. 299.) There were probably others in the group of Swiss students around Vadian, but these are all whose names are definitely known.

42. Grebel to Vadian, Paris, Jan. 29, 1519, *VB II,* 215.

43. Ulrich Lener to Vadian, Appenzell, Feb. 14, 1516, *VB I,* 147.

44. Ulrich Lener to Vadian, Appenzell, Feb. 27, 1517, *VB I,* 180.

45. Cf. note 41 above: "Daselbst (Wien) angekommen ward ich von den jungen Schweizern empfangen, besonders von Conrad Grebel."

46. Grebel to Zwingli, Sept. 8, 1517, *ZW VII,* 63.

47. All letters are printed in the *Vadianische Briefsammlung.* Only Johannes Zwick with 72 letters and Heinrich Bullinger with 85, are represented by a larger number of letters, and both wrote their letters over a much longer period of time than Grebel, all of whose letters fall within 8 years. Only one letter from Vadian to Grebel (Dec. 28, 1524) has been preserved.

48. Grebel to Vadian, July 23, 1518, *VB* II, 462.

49. Grebel to Vadian, Paris, Jan. 29, 1529, *VB* II, 211. Grebel's endeavor in this letter to promote a match between his sister Martha and Vadian may have affected his language.

50. Cf. the letters of Grebel to Vadian, Feb. 1, 1521, July 22, 1521, and many others of the years 1519 to 1522, finally the letter of Feb. 6, 1522, in which he reports his marriage.

51. Cf., e. g., his address to Grebel in the *Mela-Kommentar.* Vienna, 1518.

52. *D. Joachimi Vadiani Cos. Sangallensis ad D. Joan. Zuiccium Constantiensis ecclesiae Pastorem Epistola. Tiguri apud Frosch.* The *Epistola* is dated at the end, Aug. 1, 1540. The copy in the Stadtbibliothek Frankfurt a.M. was used.

53. *For biographies of Vadian see the following*: *Joachim Pressel, Vadian in Leben und Ausgewählte Schriften der Väter und Begründer der reformierten Kirche,* Elberfeld, 1860; Ernst Götzinger in *Allgemeine Deutsche Biographie;* Aschbach, *Geschichte der Wiener Universität* Band II, *Die Wiener Universität und ihre Humanisten im Zeitalter Kaiser Maximilians* I. Vienna, 1877, pp. 392-409; Johannes Ninck, *Arzt und Reformator Vadian,* St. Gallen, 1936. The last book came to hand after my manuscript was complete. It is good on Vadian but the section on Conrad Grebel is almost beneath criticism. Werner Näf, *Vadian und sein Stadt St. Gallen.* 1. *Band: Bis* 1518. *Humanist in Wien* (St. Gallen 1944) is excellent.

54. Conrad Grebel observes in his letter to Zwingli from Vienna, Sept. 8, 1517, that Vadian's medical studies just at this time were probably a reason why he was not so successful in his teaching: "Hos ego, ne aliquid obiicas, in Vadiano, non sua negligentia, non maligni natura ingenii praepedito, sed medicinae candidato scilicet tanquam inter Orci cancros derentem desydero." Grebel to Zwingli, *ZW* VII, 63.

55. Cf. Aschbach, *op. cit.,* pp. 403-406.

56. Ernst Götzinger in *Allgemeine Deutsche Biographie.*

57. Aschbach, *op. cit.,* p. 397.

58. Cf. the correspondence from *VB* pertaining to this trip. See also below, Chap. III, footnote 2, for the exact date of the journey. Grebel was Vadian's traveling companion.

59. Grebel to Zwingli, Sept. 8, 1517, *ZW* VII, 64.

60. *ZW* VII, 63. The course for the baccalaureate normally took two years, and was required of all students.

61. Grebel to Vadian, Jan. 29, 1519. *VB* II, 213.

62. Grebel to Vadian, July 13, 1520, *VB* II, 327.

63. As mentioned above, Grebel wrote the foreword "to the reader" for the second edition in 1522. Copy in author's possession. At the close of the first edition Vadian also emphasizes the help he received from Grebel.

64. Grebel to Zwingli, Sept. 8, 1517, cited above, note 59.

65. Grebel to Vadian, Paris, Sept. 26, 1518, and Jan. 29, 1519, *VB II,* 203, 215. That Hailigmaier was a close friend of Vadian is gathered from his letter to Vadian of Sept. 23, 1518, from Vienna, where he expresses his longing to have Vadian return to Vienna, *VB* II, 201.

66. Cf. Aschbach, *op. cit.,* pp. 403-406.

67. Concluded from Aschbach, *op. cit.,* p. *397, et passim.* See also Horawitz, *op. cit.,* p. 189. A., Zur Geschichte des deutschen Humanismus (Jena. 1874) p. 189.

68. See above, Chapter II, note 27.

69. The following description is given by Rudolph Kink, *Geschichte der Kaiserlichen Universität zu Wien,* Bd. II, *Zweite Abteilung,* "Die Zeit der Humanisten," Vienna, 1854, and Aschbach, *op. cit.*

70. A. Horawitz, *op. cit.,* p. 189, footnote 41.

71. Figures from Aschbach, *op. cit.,* p. 125.

72. Description of conditions in Vienna found in Horawitz, *op. cit.,* pp. 139-141.

73. Horawitz, *op. cit.,* p. 141.

74. Collin's autobiography, *op. cit.,* p. 189.

75. Aschbach, *op. cit.,* p. 131.

76. Horawitz, *op. cit.,* p. 188.

77. Johannes Hinwiler to Vadian, July 16, 1518, *VB III,* 168.

78. The letter in *ZW VII,* 63, cited above.

79. Grebel to Vadian, Jan. 14, 1520, *VB II,* 261.

80. Grebel repeatedly speaks of his illness. Soon after his return from Vienna in 1518 he was compelled to visit the thermal baths at Baden in the endeavor to heal a virulent abscess on his back, but to no avail. The abscess became so serious that for a time he could not write. (Grebel to Vadian Sept. 26, 1518, *VB II,* 202.) On January 29, 1519, he wrote from Paris that he was suffering in his feet not less than had already been the case in Vienna. (Grebel to Vadian, Jan. 29, 1519, *VB II,* 213.) He remarks in this letter that his feet pained him because they were pinched by the winter's cold, "and deservedly so, since oft have I consorted with females carnally," but counts the disease a curable one, at least if Vadian will help him by good medical advice. On April 25, 1521, his feet were so inflamed that he could not travel. (Grebel to Vadian, April 25, 1521, *VB II,* 364.) In July, 1521, he reported that the illness often attacked the joints of both hands and feet at the same time. (Grebel to Vadian, July 22, 1521, *VB III,* 228.) November 2, 1521, he requested Vadian again for counsel regarding the use of the baths as a curative measure. (Grebel to Vadian, Nov. 2, 1521, *VB II,* 398.) As late as May, 1525, he wrote to Castelberger that he had great difficulty in walking on account of his feet. (Grebel to Castelberger, May, 1525, *MQR* I. 3 (July, 1927), p. 43.) What the illness was can no longer be determined with accuracy. It may have been rheumatism, or something more serious. L. von Muralt (*Zürcher Taschenbuch auf das Jahr* 1937, p. 128) reports that a Zurich physician, Dr. B. Milt, to whom he submitted the evidence, diagnosed the trouble as chilblain. At any rate it was something which started in Vienna and plagued him to the end of his life.

81. In his address to Grebel written as a supplement to the *Mela-Kommentar* published in 1518, Vadian depicts Grebel and the other young Swiss students as men who had a genuine love for their homeland and who later would bring honor and renown to their fatherland. Grebel's patriotism is testified to at least twice. In his letter to Zwingli from Vienna, Sept. 8, 1517, he relates that the Swiss bought out the entire supply of "barbarissima soliloquia Vimphelingii illius scelestissimi crabronis" (there were 300 copies) in order that the name of Switzerland should not suffer: "quo Helvetiorum fama lederatur minus." Indeed an expensive patriotic service. In his *Poem* to the 1518 *Mela-Kommentar* Grebel makes some very patriotic statements. He speaks of "Helvetia's mighty soil," of "love for the fatherland," and states that Vadian wrote his book to make Helvetia as victorious in the realm of learning as she was on the battlefield of war.

82. Very amusing are the statements of Alantsee. Three times he reproaches Vadian; he cannot understand it at all. "Und ains gefelt mier an euch nix, mein Herr Doktor, dass ir von der universitet zu groben pauren gezogen habt; sy wissent nit, wass gelertt leytt send. Wo ewer kunst hie geacht wer worden hie fuer gold und margariten, so ist ess pey den pauren kom kiselston; sy verstand ess nit," Alantsee to Vadian, Vienna, Nov. 1, 1519, *VB II,* 253. "Mich reutt, dass ir under den groben kuemelcher wonen solt und habt verlassen doctam et pul-

chram Viennam," A. to V., Vienna, July 23, 1520, *VB II,* 295. "Ich wolt, dass ir pey uns zu Wien mit hauss wertt und nit pey den groben ungelerten pawren. Ich bin auch ein paur; mocht under in nit wonen mit iren seltzamenn conspirationes und factiones contra principes," A. to V., Feb. 2, 1522, from Nuremberg. *VB II,* 420.

Chapter III. STRAIN AND STRESS IN PARIS, 1518-1520

1. Two other valuable studies on Grebel appeared shortly after my manuscript was first completed in August, 1935, neither then known to me, and neither of which knew of my studies. The first, "Zürcher Familienschicksale im Zeitalter Zwingli's," by Hans Georg Wirz (*Zwingliana* VI, 4, 1935, and continuing in instalments to 1938) devotes only two pages to Grebel's Paris period, but is exceedingly valuable and altogether fair throughout its entire discussion of Grebel. The second "Konrad Grebel als Student in Paris," by Leonhard von Muralt, (*Zürcher Taschenbuch* auf das Jahr 1937, pp. 113-136) is devoted exclusively to Grebel's Paris period, as the title indicates, and is the most exhaustive, penetrating and fair discussion of Grebel's student years which has appeared anywhere. I have profited from both in the first revision, and have indicated my disagreements where necessary.

2. Grebel probably left Vienna about June 2, stopped at St. Gall for a visit with Vadian July 10, and arrived in Zurich about July 15, 1518. Grebel to Zwingli, Zurich, July 31, 1518, *ZW VII,* 91; *VB I,* 252; Melchior von Watt to Vadian, Vienna, July 16, 1518, *VB I,* 193; Andreas Eck reports that a company of travelers had reached Vienna on the thirteenth day after leaving St. Gall, Eck to Vadian, June 14, 1519, *VB II,* 231. Grebel's letter of July 23, 1518 to Vadian from Zurich recalls with pleasure his visit in Vadian's home in St. Gall and states that the Grebel family had been waiting for some time for Vadian's visit.

3. In a letter dated Sept. 26, 1518, Grebel requests Vadian to bring his books from Vienna on his journey thither. *VB II,* 203. He repeats the request from Paris, Oct. 26, 1518, "Meam librarium Viennae relictam," *VB II,* 205. Again in a letter to Myconius from Paris, June 19, 1519, he mentions his books and complains that he has written to Clivanus about them ten times without result, *MQR II,* p. 232. George Binder reports to Vadian that the books which had been left behind by Vadian had fortunately been saved from a fire, July 26, 1518. *VB II,* 196.

4. Grebel gives instructions concerning this to Clivanus through Vadian in a letter to Vadian from Paris, Oct. 26, 1518, *VB II,* 196. George Binder, rather than Clivanus, evidently drew the remainder of Grebel's unpaid allowance in Vienna according to a statement made by Jacob Grebel in his trial, October, 1526. Egli, *Aktensammlung,* No. 1050, p. 497.

5. See various letters in *VB* between November, 1518 and July, 1519. Johannes Ninck, *op. cit.,* pp. 68-72, describes the trip in detail.

6. Kaspar Ursinus to Vadian, Feb. 11, 1518, *VB II,* 462.

7. Grebel to Zwingli, Sept. 8, 1517, *ZW VII,* 64.

8. Note 20 below.

9. For these and the following statements see Egli, *Aktensammlung,* No. 1050, "Nachgang über Jakob Grebel," pp. 496-500.

10. *ZW VII,* 63, note 3, with proofs. For the royal scholarships to Paris see Ms. B. *VI,* 246. folio 330a. Staatsarchiv Zurich.

11. See note 9 above.

12. Grebel to Zwingli, Zurich, July 31, 1518, *ZW VII,* 93.

13. Grebel to Zwingli, July 31, 1518, *ZW VII,* 92.

14. Myconius to Vadian, July 23, 1518, *VB II,* 195.

15. Vadian to Peter Falk, Zurich, Aug. 5, 1518, *VB VII,* 7.

16. Pomponii Melae, *op. cit.,* Basel, 1522, p. 34. "Ego anno superiore cum mense Augusto Lucernam venissem lacus viscendi gratia, a doctissimo, et vere

ingenuis moribus praedito Ioanne Xylotecto Canonico Lucernate, humanissime exceptus, et in ipsum postri die montem eductus sum, comitantibus nos Osualdo Myconio, eruditio, et pleno ingenui candoris homine, et Conrado Grebelio Tigurino Grebeliae meae fratre spectatissimae indolis adolescente." The description fills about half of the page. Bernard Studer repeats the episode from Pomponius Mela in *Geschichte der Physischen Geographie der Schweiz bis* 1815, Bern, 1863, p. 64. It is found also in P. X. Weber, *Der Pilatus und seine Geschichte*, Luzern, 1913, pp. 249-251. Weber refers to two other reports: *Gessner's Descriptio montis fracti*, and *Joh, Eus. Nierembergii Hist. Naturalis.* 1635. It is somewhat difficult to determine the date of the ascent. Vadian's manuscript was certainly ready for publication in 1521, since the book appeared in January, 1522. Unless Vadian was mistaken, the ascent took place a year before the writing. Hence only the years 1518 and 1521 come into consideration, since Grebel was in France in 1519. If the sentence in Grebel's letter to Vadian from Paris, Jan. 14, 1520, "Trabem ad Lucernam equites ituri noscere coepisti," refers to the ride to Lucerne in which Grebel participated, the date must be 1518, *VB II*, 262. In his letter to Vadian from Zurich, Sept. 26, 1518, Grebel mentions his farewell from Vadian, "Cum a me discederes in Elligow," *VB II*, 203. This could not likely have taken place on any other occasion than the return from Lucerne, when Vadian left the party and went to St. Gall. A request to the Staatsarchiv of Lucerne for information regarding the permission from the police for the ascent of Pilatus, which Studer mentions, brought the reply that no record of such permission could be found in the archives. Willy Brändly's *"Wann war Vadian auf dem Pilatus?"* (*Zwingliana* VIII [1947], p. 425f), confirms this dating. He also cites Maur. Ant. Cappelleri's *Pilate Montis Historia* (Basel, 1767).

17. Grebel to Vadian, July 23, 1518, *VB II*, 46,3.

18. The entire letter to Vadian, Sept. 26, *VB II*, 202-203.

19. It follows from George Hedinger's testimony in Jacob Grebel's trial that he was the escort: "Wiederum zu Hause habe er die Anfrage erhalten, ob er den Sohn Grebels gen Paris führen wolle, und derselben entsprochen. Dieser habe sich zu Freiburg zwei oder drei Tage aufgehalten." Egli, *op. cit.*, No. 1050, p. 498.

20. In his letter of Sept. 26, 1518, to Vadian, Grebel says that two other students from Zurich receiving stipends were to be his traveling companions: "comites erunt duo Tigurini, ex decreto senati urbis Tigurinae regii stipendiarii," *VB II*, 203. According to the decision of the council the two students were "Hans Frey und des Holtzhalben sun," Ms B.VI. 246, folio 330a, Staatsarchiv Zurich, not J. J. Ammann and Urs Hab, as Hans Wirz has it, *op. cit.*, 1935, p. 213. Anm. 27.

21. Budé reported to Vadian from Paris, Oct. 25, 1518, that four or five days earlier some newly arrived students had delivered to him the letters from Vadian, *VB VII*, 9. The students were doubtless Grebel and his companions, for Grebel wrote to Vadian that he had visited Budé. Grebel to Vadian, Paris, Oct. 26, 1518, *VB II*, 205-207.

22. Grebel to Zwingli, Sept. 8, 1517, *ZW VII*, 63: "Mallem tamen inter Glareani mei atque tui discipulos scilicet nactus numerari."

23. Grebel to Vadian, Sept. 26, 1518, *VB II*, 203.

24. Grebel to Vadian, October 26, 1518, *VB II*, 206: "Glareano commoror eiusque sum et coepulo et auditor." There is no record of a matriculation at the University. See note 61 below.

25. Grebel to Vadian, Oct. 26, 1518, *ibid.*, 204. The following quotation is found in Grebel to Myconius, July 18, 1519, *MQR II* (1928), 234.

26. Grebel to Vadian, Jan. 29, 1519, *VB II*, 212: "Ego nihil territus Kalendis Januarii praeceptorum meum cum suis salutavi discessique." Grebel to Vadian, Jan. 14, 1520, *VB II*, 261: "Lutetiam redii, a qua pestem hiems pepulit; Glareani lares nihil illi obstrictus, honesto sodalitio usus, incolo." In a letter to Zwingli,

Jan. 2, 1520, Valentin Tschudi says that the group, Grebel, Girod, V. and P. Tschudi, returned to Paris on January 1: "Illic sex actis mensibus tandem ad Calendas Januarias ad urbem rediimus," *ZW VII*, 249.

27. Grebel to Myconius, July 6, 1520, *MQR II*, p. 238.

28. The chief sources for information concerning Glarean and his Swiss boarding school in Paris are 80 letters of the years 1517-1522: 33 written by Glarean himself; 36 written by his students, of which 15 are by Grebel, 6 by Valentin Tschudi, 5 by Peter Tschudi, 5 by Peter Girod, 4 by Johann Jakob Zurgilgen, and one by Heinrich Frey; and 11 letters by friends of Glarean, of which 4 are by Erasmus to Glarean, 4 by Nesenus to Zwingli, 2 by Budé (one to Vadian and one to Nicholas Beraldus) and one by Myconius to Glarean. Some scattered references are found in other letters, but they are of little value. Seventy-one of the letters were written from Paris, more than 40 of them at the time when Grebel was there. All but three have been printed. From the letter of recommendation for Glarean directed to the king, dated March 14, 1519, it is evident that Glarean had received from the Swiss council a commission to educate the young Swiss students in Paris and to keep them in discipline. "Quoniam enim a nobis commissionem habet, nostrates scolares et adolescentes, ut dirigat, doceat, et litterarum abundare faciat, studio." *Anzeiger für Schweizer Geschichte, N. F.*, V., 1887, 56b.

29. "Zwei Empfehlungsbriefe der XIII Orte für Glarean" in *Zwingliana* V, pp. 222-3, where the letters are printed. "Ein Empfehlungsbrief für Glarean" in *Anzeiger für Schweizer Geschichte, N. F.*, V., 1887, 56b.

30. In a letter to Peter Falk, March 8, 1519, Glarean states that his stipend gave him an income of 150 francs annually, *Freiburger Geschichtsblätter*, IX, 1902, 171. Rhenanus makes the same report to Erasmus, April 24, 1517: "Glareanus ante Call. Junias in Galliam se conferet; habebit annue centum et quinquaginta francos," Allen, *op. cit.*, II, 551.

31. Concerning the change of location see various letters of Glarean and his students and friends of this time, especially Glarean to Zwingli, Aug. 29, 1517, *ZW VII*, 59-61, also Fritzsche, *op. cit.*, 20, 21.

32. See Glarean's letters of this time, especially those to Peter Falk, June 22, 1518, July 5, 1518, and March 8, 1518, all published by Joseph Zimmermann, "Sechs unbekannte Briefe Glareans," in *Freiburger Geschichtsblätter* IX, 1902, 157-178.

33. Among other things it was demanded of Glarean that he give up his stipend and his Swiss boarding school. To Falk Glarean wrote July 5, 1518: "Si unum est relinquendum mallem equidem poetican relinquere quam Helvetiorum pueros." He reports to his friends on several occasions that he was not obliged to lecture publicly; e. g. to Myconius, June 7, 1519: "Stipendium meum in Fausti mutatum est: verum ad publice legendum non adigor, nisi mihi placuerit." *Geschichtsfreund* LXXXIII, 1928, 187. In the above cited letter to Peter Falk, March 8, 1519, he mentions that the "stipendium Fausti" was worth 180 francs: "Stipendium Fausti peto, non minora facturus quam ille, illud est 180 francici."

34. Abel Lefranc, *Histoire du College du France*, Paris, 1893, pp. 101-124; Allen, *op. cit., II*, 454-458. See also Louis Delaruelle, *Guillaume Budé, Les Origines, Les Debuts, Les Idees Maitresses*, Paris, 1907, *Bibliotheque de l'Ecole des Hautes Etudes*, No. 162. Paris, 1893, 101-124, chapter entitled "La Fondation du College de France."

35. The letter of recommendation for Glarean from Erasmus to Bishop Poncher, Feb. 14, 1517 (1518) Allen, *op. cit.*, II, 454-458.

36. He was, however, not content with this situation. Three times during the years of his stay in Paris he sought to secure a better field of activity in Switzerland.[35] As early as the end of 1518 he made application for the vacancy which had occurred among the canons of Zurich, and on two journeys to his native land (the springs of 1519 and 1520), he undertook by personal solicitation

to find a position where he could exercise his talents. He centered his solicitation on Basel where he requested the University to grant him the privilege of establishing a philological institute. All of these plans were fruitless, but finally in February, 1522, he abandoned his private school in Paris and returned to Basel to live, where he was ultimately appointed to the faculty of the University. He writes from Basel to Zwingli, March 4, 1522, *ZW VII*, 494.

37. Glarean's letter to Erasmus from Paris, Aug. 5, 1517, is headed "Parrhisiis a vico divi Jacobi," Allen, *op. cit.*, III, 37. The dwelling is described in his letter to Myconius, 22, 1518, "Domus est mihi pulcherrima cum atrio, hortula, cellario, et propriis aulis pulcherrimis," *Geschichtsfreund* LXXXIII, 177.

38. Grebel to Vadian, Jan. 29, 1519, *VB* II, 212: "Qui cum offensus esset, Glareanum e sua domo concedere iubet. Saluto hospite migrat, et ego quoque migrabam."

39. Concerning the royal Swiss stipends at Paris see A. Waldburger, "Die Schweizer Studenten in Paris als Pensionäre des Königs von Frankreich" in A. F. Ammann, *Geschichte der Familie Ammann*, II, 17-24, Zürich, 1913; F. Jecklin, "Bündner Studenten an der Pariser Universität als Pensionäre der französichen Könige," *Bündnerisches Monatsblatt*, March, 1925, 65-85; J. B. Kälin, "Zur Geschichte der Freiplätze der eidg. Orte auf der Universität zu Paris und der Schwyzer Studenten daselbst," *Mitteilungen des Hist. Vereins des Kantons Schwyz*, vol. 4, 1885, 63-69; A. Buechi, "Glareans Schüler in Paris 1517-1522," *Geschichtsfreund* LXXXIII, Stans, 1928. 150-208. Felix Manz, Grebel's later associate, according to *Hist.-Biogr. Lex. der Schweiz* (1929, V, 19a) was "stud. in Paris." If so, he would have been in Glarean's circle, but there is no evidence for this. Perhaps he came after Glarean left.

40. Grebel to Vadian, Oct. 26, 1518; Jan. 29, 1519; Oct. 6, 1519; Jan. 1, 1520; Jan. 14, 1520; *VB II*, 206, 212, 251, 258, 264.

41. Grebel to Myconius, July 18, 1519, *MQR II*, 244.

42. Grebel to Vadian, Oct. 6, 1519; Jan. 1, 1520, *VB II*, 251, 258.

43. See above, note 31.

44. Grebel to Myconius, Jan. 30, 1519, *MQR II*, 232. The location of the new residence is not known but Grebel says that it was at the home of a highly respected citizen of Paris, a printer.

45. Grebel to Myconius, July 18, 1519, *MQR II*, 234.

46. Grebel to Vadian, July 17, 1520, *VB II*, 294.

47. Jakob Wipf, "Sebastian Hofmeister, der Reformator Schaffhausens," in *Beiträge zur Vaterl. Geschichte*, Bd. 9, Schaffhausen, 1918, 10-12. Also Jakob Wipf, *Reformationsgeschichte der Stadt und Landschaft Schaffhausen*, Zürich, 1929, 109.

48. Fritzsche, *op. cit.*, 20, with proofs.

49. Glarean to Erasmus, Aug. 1517, Allen, *op. cit.*, III, 36: "Benigne me excepit Budaeus, humanissime tractavit Copus, familiarissime mihi cognitus Faber Stapulensis: Quem eum inveni quem tu semper una cum Beato amico nostro praecipuo praedicabas, virum certe integerrimum humanissimumque. Episcopum certa de causa nondum adii. Stipendium habeo privatim, nemini quicquem obligatum."

50. Glarean to Zwingli, Aug. 29, 1517, *ZW VII*, 59: "Bene acceptus a doctissimis viris Luteciae, inter quos est Budaeus, Copus, Faustus atque Faber Stapulensis." Glarean to Peter Falk, April 21, 1518: "Amant me omnes docti apud Parisios," *Anzeiger für Schweizer. Geschichte* 1880, 338.

51. Glarean to Zwingli, Jan. 13, 1519, *ZW VII*, 127: "Budaei hominis eruditissimi et mihi familiarissimi."

52. Glarean to Zwingli, March 25, 1519, *ZW VII*, 156: "Adest Joannes Lascaris, Graecus, mire eruditus, ad quem ego saepe commeo una cum Ammano meo Tigurino."

53. Faber Stapulensis to Agrippa, Nov. 14, 1519, Herminjard, *Correspondance des Reformateurs* I, 60: "Sed per hos menses divagatus sum, neque per annum ferme figam pedem Parisiis."

54. Glarean to Zwingli, Aug. 29, 1517, *ZW VII,* 59-60: 'Faber Stapulensis, qui saepe iam domui meae fuit. Is supra modum me amat, totus integer et candidus, mecum cantillat, ludit, disputat, ridet mecum stultum praecipue hunc mundum, vir humanissimus et benignus."

55. Glarean to Zwingli, Jan. 13, 1519, *ZW VII,* 128; Glarean to Zwingli, May 14, 1519, *ZW VII,* 169.

56. Budé to Erasmus, July 17, 1517, Allen, *op. cit.,* III, 22. Budé to Erasmus, Dec. 21, 1517, *ibid.,* 174: "Post prandium venit Glareanus, ut eum salutaret. Cum ego redirem et Episcopus iam in cubiculum interius se recepisset, redii ut eum ipsi notum facerem: cui Glareano quod a me petiit non negavi, tui gratia qui me ita facere iubeo. Parum tamen mihi est molestus, nec nisi raro video hominem." Budé to Erasmus, Oct. 31, 1518, *ibid.* 437. Budé to Erasmus, April 21, 1518, *ibid.,* 280: "Glareanus tuus in locum Fausti demortui suffectus est, et stipendium habebit. . . . Idem Parisiensi iam notus est et gratus." Budé to Erasmus, April 15, 1518, *ibid.,* 288. Budé to Erasmus, June 30, 1519, *ibid.,* 625. Budé to Nicholas Beraldus, Feb. 24, 1520, summary in Louis Delaruelle, *Repertoire de la Correspondance de Guillaume Budé,* Paris, 1907, 102-104. Reference in Fritzsche, *op. cit.,* 21. Glarean to Zwingli, Jan. 13, 1519, *ZW VII,* 127: "Tota haec hyems in 'Asse' Budaei, hominis eruditissimi et mihi familiarissimi, consumpta ferme est, nisi iam quattuor fere hebdomas aulicor inter homines levissimos."

57. E.g., Glarean to Zwingli, July 7, 1520; Nov. 11, 1520; July 4, Sept. 20, Dec. 21, 1521; *ZW VII,* 333, et passim. Also in five letters to Myconius, July 7, Oct. 14, Nov. 11, 1520, and April 7, Nov. 28, 1521, in *Geschichtsfreund* LXXXIII, 1928, 192 ff. Also in a letter to J. J. Ammann, Dec. 13, 1520, where the different positions are given, in Ammann, *Geschichte der Familie Ammann* II, 353. In the letter to Myconius, Sept. 1, 1520, Glarean gives details from the life of the S.P.Q.R. such as method of election, etc., *Geschichtsfreund, op. cit.,* 193. He gives it also in a letter to Jörg uff der Flüe, Dec. 10, 1520, in *Anzeiger für schweizerische Geschichte,* N.F. 12, 1914, 97-100.

58. Letter of Dec. 10, 1520 in *Anzeiger für schweizerische Geschichte* N.F. 12, 1914, pp. 97-100.

59. Glarean to Erasmus, Aug. 5, 1517, Allen, *op. cit.,* III, 37: "Caeterum qui Parrhisios veni ut graecarer, spe mea lusus sum maxime. Nemo enim est qui insignem autorem Graecum publice legat, neque privatim, quo equidem memini."

60. Glarean to Zwingli, March 25, 1519, *ZW VII,* 69, with personalia for Lascaris in note 5. Also Glarean to Zwingli Aug. 29, 1517, *ZW VII,* 60. In this letter Glarean also states that he is reading Caesar's *Commentaries* to his students. Ammann went with him to Lascaris.

61. It is scarcely possible that Grebel was not matriculated at the University of Paris for he says that he attended the lectures of Beraldus who was one of the professors at the University. (Cf. note 121) However, all attempts to discover positive evidence of such matriculation have failed thus far. Repeated inquiries directed to the officer in charge of the archives which contain the records of the university of Paris have remained unanswered. No printed lists of matriculates at the university covering this period have appeared. A hopeful examination of Alexander Budinsky, *Die Universität Paris und die Fremden an derselben im Mittelalter,* Berlin, 1876, revealed nothing. More promising was Emile Chatelain, "Les Etudiants Suisses de Paris aux XVe et XVIe Siecles," an appendix of 24 pages to his *Les Etudiants Suisses à L'Ecole Pratique des Hautes Etudes* 1868-1891, Paris, 1891. This contains the names of many Swiss students at Paris during the years 1447-1574, but excludes explicitly the diocese of Constance because it included non-Swiss territory. But it is just this diocese in

which Zurich is located. However, a careful check showed that none of the students in Glarean's *bursa* appear in Chatelain's lists even though many of them came from dioceses included in his study. Chatelain says that the university records are quite incomplete for this period. Apparently no central matriculation record (*Hauptmatrikel*) was kept.

62. Valentin Tschudi to Zwingli, June 21, 1518. See note 65.

63. Glarean to Erasmus, Aug. 5, 1517, *loc. cit.*

64. *Ibid.*

65. Valentin Tschudi to Zwingli, June 21, 1518, *ZW VII*, 87-90. Concerning Giustiniani, the first professor of Hebrew in Paris, see *ZW VII*, 124, note 4, and Allen, *op. cit., III*, 278, note to line 356. Giustiniani lectured 1517-1522. After he left, the chair of Hebrew remained vacant.

66. Abel Lefranc, *Histoire du College de France*, Paris, 1893, 60-63. Lefranc says, p. 60: "Mais le texte le plus probant qu'on puisse citer touchant la veritable situation de l'universite, c'est assurement la lettre de Valentin Tschudi a Ulrich Zwingli. C'est pour le sujet qui nous occupe, une piece d'une importance capitale, qui fournit un tableau exact et complet de l'etat des etudes philosophiques et theologiques dans le monde universitaire de la capitale."

67. Grebel to Vadian, Oct. 26, 1518, *VB II*, 205.

68. See note 21 above.

69. Grebel to Vadian, Oct. 26, 1518, *op. cit.*, 206. See also L. von Muralt, *Zürcher Taschenbuch* 1937, p. 125. Von Muralt errs in calling Johann Leopold Grebel a brother of Conrad. He was a cousin.

70. Glarean to Myconius, Oct. 25, 1518, *Geschichtsfreund* LXXXIII, 178; Budaeus to Vadian, Oct. 25, 1518, *VB VII*, 9; Zurgilgen to Vadian, Oct. 26, 1518, *VB III*, 174. Myconius writes Nov. 12, 1518, to Vadian that he has received the letter, *VB II*, 208. J. J. Ammann probably also wrote to his father at the same time, for the father wrote to his son, Dec. 24, 1518: "Din Schriben gethan by Jörg Hedinger, dem stat knecht, han ich wol verstonden, und ist ouch min meinung dich zu schicken gen Basy oder gen Bisa in Italia uf den nechsten herbst nach sant michels tag," *Zwingliana*, Bd. 2, 223. Hedinger was probably the messenger for all of them.

71. Grebel to Vadian, Jan. 29, 1518, *VB II*, 211-216.

72. Valentin Tschudi to Zwingli, July 12, 1517, *ZW VII*, 56: "Novisti Glareani praeceptoris nostri in tradendis optimarum disciplinarum praeceptis fidissimi ingenium, ut, cum quem amet, quam impense ei faveat, contra eundem aut quemvis alium si oderit, ut non irae odiique sui (bona eius venia dixerim) metam sistat."

73. Joachim von Watt, *Deutsche Historische Schriften III, herausgegeben von Ernst Goetzinger*, St. Gallen, 1879, p. 187.

74. Grebel to Vadian, Oct. 6, 1519, *VB II*, 250: "Propterea quod ille simultatem semel indutam nescio quo ministrante Nesso non nisi supremo rogo exuet."

75. Grebel to Myconius, Jan. 30, 1519, *MQR II*, 232: "Apud calchographum civem perhonestum moror mecum est Johan es Henricus Elutherius Tigurinus qui a Glareano priusquam ego discessit. Probapolitanus quidam et quartus famulus." Steam heat is mentioned in the letter to Vadian, Jan. 29, 1519, *VB II*, 212.

76. Glarean to Myconius, June 7, 1519, *Geschichtsfreund* IXXXIII, 187: "Quod a me hospitio abiisset, de quo hoc unum dico, me benignissime tractasse hominem multisque beneficiis quasi obruisse, illum non modo gratiam non retulisse."

77. It is of interest to note that Glarean recovered enough from his temper to greet Grebel five times in letters to Zwingli in the years 1520 to 1522. The letters are to be found in *ZW VII*.

78. Grebel to Vadian, Jan. 29, 1519, *VB II*, 213.

79. Grebel to Vadian, Jan. 14, 1520, *VB II*, 261.

80. See *ZW VII*, 198, note 1; *Rudolph Collins Autobiographie, loc. cit.;* above part IV, note 11; *ZW VII*, 339, note 1; note 70 above; Grebel to Vadian, Dec. 8, 1520, *VB II*, 318: "Ego iam tandem accingor ad iter, Pisas ut petam."

81. Grebel to Vadian, Jan. 14, 1520, *VB II*, 261: "Pecunia illa tanta, quam discedens a patria habui, omnem ventri, libris, vestibus dedi."

82. Egli, *Aktensammlung,* No. 1050, p. 498: "Betreffend seine (Georg Hedingers) Rede zu M. Berger, wie er zuerst 600 und später 300 Kronen dem J. Jakob Grebel gebracht habe." From the statements in Egli, *op. cit.*, p. 496 under (3), it is clear that Conrad Grebel was to receive an annual stipend of 300 crowns. One payment he received and took with him to Paris; 600 crowns the father received, of which the son received nothing.

83. Grebel to Myconius, Jan. 14, 1520, *MQR II*, 235.

84. Grebel to Myconius, Jan. 14, 1520, *MQR II*, 234: "Pecuniae minimam partem ut vix unicam seductores devorarunt."

85. Interesting confirmation of the high cost of living in Paris is found in a letter dated January, 1518, written by another Zurich student in Paris, Johann Heinrich Frei, who addressed a touching appeal to his brother at home for financial help.

86. Glarean to Myconius, June 7, 1519, *Geschichtsfreund* LXXXIII, 187; Glarean to Zwingli, May 15, 1519, *ZW VII*, 168, where he speaks only of "perturbationes nostras." The most important letters to be considered are the two to Myconius, June 9, 1519, and July 18, 1519, *MQR II*, pp. 232-233. See also Grebel to Vadian, Oct. 6, 1519, *VB II*, 249.

87. See Glarean to Zwingli, June 7, 1519, *ZW VII*, 179, and Peter Tschudi to Zwingli, June 16, 1519, *ibid.*, 187.

88. The quarrel of 1518 is described in detail in the letter to Peter Falk, Aug. 6, 1518, *Freiburger Geschichtsblätter,* IX, 166-67. In his letter to Myconius, June 22, 1518, Glarean complains about Zophius, and in the letter of Oct. 25 to Myconius he says of Zophius: "Ille perditissimus perditissime perdidit," *Geschichtsfreund* LXXXIII, 177-179. In a letter to Peter Falk, March 8, 1519, he pours out his heart: "Crede mihi, iucundissime Petre, hoc anno propter captos iuvenes (Quorum negotium nunc prorsus absolutum est) me tanta passum, tum hac quoque cruce agitatum, ut si antea scissem, me certe pedem in Franciam nunquam moturum fuisse." *Freiburger Geschichtsblätter* IX, 170. What teacher has not felt the same at least once?

89. See Grebel's letters to Myconius and Vadian, of Jan. 14, 1520, cited above.

90. See note 86 above.

91. Grebel to Vadian, Oct. 6, 1519, *VB II*, 249. Grebel to Vadian, Jan. 14, 1520: "Bellum illud inter nos et latrones," *VB II*, 262.

92. Grebel to Myconius, Jan. 14, 1520, *MQR II*, 235.

93. Mentioned in a letter from Grebel to Vadian, Jan. 14, 1520, *MQR II*, 235.

94. Grebel to Myconius, Jan. 14, 1520, *loc. cit.*

95. See the letters cited above in note 86.

96. Grebel to Vadian, July 13, 1520, *VB II*, 326.

97. The visit is mentioned in the letter to Vadian of Nov. 7, 1520, *VB II*, 315.

98. Valentin Tschudi to Zwingli, Jan. 2, 1520, *ZW VII*, 249.

99. Grebel to Myconius, Jan. 14, 1520, *loc. cit.*

100. Staehelin reports that the plague came to Zurich about the middle of August and raged there until 1520, cutting down about 2,500 persons in the vicinity of the city, Staehelin, *Zwingli* I, p. 158.

101. Staehelin, *Zwingli* I, pp. 158-159.

102. In his letter of July 18, 1519, to Myconius Grebel mentions his plan to leave Paris on account of the plague and to go up the Seine to the tenth milestone, *MQR II*, 23. On Oct. 6, 1519, he writes to Vadian from Melun and states that he is living there on account of the plague, *VB II*, 251. In the letter of Jan. 1, 1520, to

Vadian, Grebel says he has now returned to Paris because winter had driven the plague away. *VB II,* 259. See also Valentin Tschudi to Zwingli, Jan. 2, 1520, where the report is made of the return to Paris on Jan. 1, 1520, after a stay of six months in the country, *ZW VII,* 249.

103. Beatus Rhenanus to Nesen, *Briefwechsel des Beatus Rhenanus,* 185.

104. See the pertinent letters, cited above, especially Grebel to Myconius, March 7, 1520, *MQR II,* 236, 237.

105. Grebel to Myconius, Jan. 14, 1520, *MQR II,* 234; Grebel to Vadian, Jan. 14, 1520, *VB II,* 261.

106. Grebel to Vadian, Jan. 14, 1520, *loc. cit.*

107. Grebel to Myconius, March 7, 1520, *MQR II,* p. 236: "Salvum te esse iubeo amicorum omnium mihi maxime necessarium." Grebel to Myconius, April 13, 1520, *MQR* II, 238: "Conradus Grebelius, tuus amiculus, tui omnium amantissimus."

108. Grebel calls himself a *Naufragus* in the letter of March 7, 1520, to Myconius, *loc. cit.* In the letter of April 13 to Myconius he says "Naufragium me proprius sit quam portus timeo." In the same letter he writes concerning the letter to his father: "Cum Glareanus hinc solveret et vix paternas litteras exarassem." The letter to Grebel's father has been lost.

109. Grebel to Vadian, April 13, 1520, *VB II,* 271: "Cognoscendus eram, non mittendus."

110. Grebel to Vadian, July 13, 1520, *VB II,* 326: "illud unius tuae epistolae verbum."

111. Grebel to Vadian, Jan. 14, 1520, *op. cit.,* 262.

112. Egli, *Aktensammlung,* No. 1050, p. 459: "H. Heinrich Utinger erzählt, wie er, als Konrad Grebel durch seine Heirat den Unwillen des Vaters erregt, zwischen Vater und Sohn einen Vertrag aufgesetzt habe. Nachher habe ihm aber Konrad im Kreuzgang des Münsters geklagt, wie ihm der Vater nichts gebe."

113. Jacob Grebel's statement in the trial: "die (Summe) sye er sinen (Konrads) Kinden noch schuldig." Egli, *Aktensammlung.* No. 1050, p. 496.

114. *E.g.,* Grebel to Myconius, March 7, 1520, in which he makes many complaints concerning his poverty: "Tam pauper ut vix victum inde habeam, corradere potuissem." *MQR II,* 236.

115. Grebel to Myconius, July 6, 1520, *op. cit.,* 238.

116. Peter Tschudi writes to Vadian from Paris, June 20, and apologizes for writing; he says he is doing it only at the urgent request of Conrad Grebel. Grebel's final departure from Paris was probably the occasion for the letter, and it may be assumed that Grebel took the letter with him. *VB II,* 287. Von Muralt's assertion (*Zürcher Taschenbuch,* 1937, p. 132) based on Wirz (*op. cit.,* 213) that Grebel reached Zurich by the end of April is untenable. Letter #230 is dated "three days before the Ides," i.e., the 13th, but on April 13, Grebel was still in Paris. I date #230 July 13, 1520.

117. Grebel to Myconius, July 25, 1520. "Quod me ames non vulgari more iamdudum mihi persuasum est, quippe qui parentem indignantem mihi tam belle placaveris et intercessione sedula propitium reddideris," *MQR II,* 239. The poem mentioned in the sentence following is found in the letter to Myconius of July 6, 1520, *ibid.*

118. In sharp contrast to this was the unsatisfactory relation with Vadian which has already been mentioned. In Grebel's two first letters to Vadian after his return in July 13 and 17, 1520, the tension is quite evident. Grebel hopes that at least an "armistice in their war" will be possible, since he at least was not so aroused in France that peace would be impossible from his point of view. Grebel to Vadian, July 17, 1520, *VB II,* 294. "Nec ego sic commotus in Gallia fui, ut nullae, si futurum fuisset bellum, a bello nostro induciae sperandae furissent, quemadmodum tu sperabas nolim dicere timebas." In this letter he

also mentions Vadian's question, whether Grebel would become his enemy, "an perduellis futurus fuerim Vadiano."

119. There is no evidence that he studied in Basel after his return from Paris, as some have asserted.

120. Grebel to Vadian, Jan. 29, 1519, *VB II,* 213.

121. Louis Delaruelle, *Nicole Berault, Notes biographiques suivies d'un Appendice sur plusiers de ses publications.* (Etudes *sur l' Humanisme Francais*) in *Le Musée Belge, revue de Philologie Classique, Treisième Année,* 1909, pp. 253-312. This monograph is an enlargement of a monograph with the same title, which appeared in *Revue des Bibliotheques,* 1902, 12. *Année,* pp. 420-444. Delaruelle, *op. cit.,* p. 273, shows that Beraldus made an ambassadorial trip to England in the fall of 1518, from which he returned at the end of October. He then taught at the University until the middle of March, 1519. Following that he made another ambassadorial trip to southern France in the service of Bishop Poncher. Hence Grebel could hear Beraldus from the beginning of November, 1518, until the middle of March, 1519. Von Muralt's comments on Grebel's studying under Beraldus (*Zürcher Jahrbuch,* 1937, p. 128) are not quite fair to Grebel. In the first place he misquotes Grebel, who did not say "I am *now* hearing Beraldus." The "now" is not in the original. Grebel may have been hearing Beraldus before he left Glarean. And even if he did begin after leaving, this cannot be held against Grebel, inasmuch as Glarean forbade him to continue his studies under him. That there was no "unfriendliness" in this, contrary to Von Muralt's charges, is evident from the fact that in the very same letter he indicates that he will attend Glarean's lectures if the latter should get a university appointment and therefore not be able to exclude Grebel from his lectures. According to Delaruelle the printer Badius had announced that he would print Beraldus' lectures on Quintillian's *Institutiones.* This however did not take place. Delaruelle's monograph on Beraldus is still the best on the subject. It is interesting to note that he uses Grebel's letter of Jan. 29, 1519, as proof for the teaching activity of Beraldus, and that beyond this he knows almost nothing to report about his lectures. An evaluation of Beraldus is found in *Musée, belge, op. cit.,* (1909) p. 285. According to this account, Beraldus was not on the same height as Budé and Faber Stapulensis, but was nevertheless a good philologian, and distinguished himself as a teacher of Latin and Greek as well as a learned editor of the ancient classics. He was not religiously inclined, but, like Budé, was for a time favorable toward Luther, although he finally remained with the old faith.

122. See above note 52 and note 60.

123. Zwingli to Vadian, *VB I,* 194; see note 65 above regarding Giustiniani.

124. See note 12 p. 195; also Zwingli to Myconius, Aug. 26, 1522, *ZW VII,* 568. Grebel is mentioned here by Zwingli as participating in the class in Greek and Hebrew under the instruction of Ceporin. See also *Geschichtsbuch, op. cit.,* p. 34, "Es begab sich, dass Ulrich Zwingel und Konrad Grebel, einer vom Adel und Felix Mantz, alle drei fast erfahrene und gelehrte Männer in deutscher, lateinischer, griechischer und auch hebraischer sprach."

125. Grebel to Myconius, Jan. 30, 1519, *MQR II,* 232 and Grebel to Vadian, Jan. 29, 1519, *VB II,* 216.

126. Grebel to Myconius, June 9, 1519, *MQR II,* 232.

127. Grebel to Myconius, March 7, 1520, *MQR II,* 237. Myconius had also expressed appreciation for the pamphlets sent him by Grebel.

128. Grebel to Vadian, July 17, 1520, *VB II,* 292, "Ut comite mea Iliade et tuo munere Pediano ad te venirem."

129. Arthur Tilley, *The Dawn of the French Renaissance,* Cambridge, 1918, p. 596. Tilley gives one of the best descriptions of early French humanism, with a summarizing critique in the closing chapter. The best French work on early humanism in France is Au. Renaudet, *Prereforme et Humanisme a Paris Jusqu'a*

1517, Paris, 1916. L. Geiger's "Studien zum französischen Humanismus" in *Zeitschrift für Geschichte and Literatur der Renaissance* 1886-1887, are of minor importance. Imbart de la Tour, *Les Origines de la Reforme* II, Paris, 1909, has a good chapter, "La Renaissance Francaise" and one, "L'Humanisme Chretien." See also Ernst Walser, "Uber das Wesen der französischen Renaissance" in *Gesammelte Studien zur Geistesgeschichte der Renaissance*, Basel, 1932.

130. The best work on Budé is Louis Delaruelle, *Guillaume Budé, Les Origines, Les Debuts, Les Idées Maitresses,* Paris, 1907 (*Bibliotheque de l'Ecole des Hautes Etudes,* Nr. 162); and the same author, *Repertoire Analytique et Chronologique de la Correspondance de Guillaume Budé,* Paris, 1907. Jean Plattard, *Guillaume Budé* (168-1540) *et les Origines de, l Humanisme Francaise,* Paris, 1923, gives a good but very short resume (only 38 pages). On the other hand Eugene de Budé, *"Vie de Guillaume Budé,"* Paris, 1884, is disappointing. The chapters on Budé in Tilley, *op. cit.*, and Renaudet, *op. cit.*, are excellent.

131. There is no satisfactory biography of Faber Stapulensis. The best is still the old one published in 1852, by K. H. Graf, *Jacobus Faber Stapulensis* in *Zeitschrift für die historische Theologie,* 1852, pp. 2-86, and 165-237, but it is weak on Faber as a humanist. The chapters in Tilley and Renaudet are very good. See also Imbart de la Tour, *op. cit.,* III, Livre I, Chapitre III, "Lefevre d'Etaples."

132. For Badius the standard work is Philippe Renouard, *Josse Badius Ascensius,* 3 volumes, Paris, 1908. Badius was one of the greatest figures of French humanism, a scholar, editor and publisher of Latin Classics, with residence in Paris after 1503. See also the chapters in Tilley and Renaudet. Tilley calls him "at Gaguin's death the most distinguished humanist in Paris, with the exception of Lefevre d'Etaples." It is possible that Conrad Grebel lived with him in the first half of 1519. See note 94 above.

133. Faber Stapulensis, *S. Pauli Epistolae XIV. . . cum commentariis,* Paris, 1512.

134. John Viénot, "Y-a-t-il une Reforme Francaise anterieure a Luther?" in *Bulletin de la Société de l' Histoire du Protestantisme Francais,* 1915, 101, where the posed question is answered in the negative. Viénot reports a statement by Farel in his "Epitre a tous Seigneurs" as follows: "il faisait les plus grandes reverences aux images qu'autre personnage que j'ai connu. . . . Il demeurait dans la vieillesse papale." See also Herminjard, *Correspondance des Reformateurs,* I, p. 239, note 38: 'Deux ans apres avoir publié son commentaire aux saint Paul, Lefebre etait encore plongé en idolatrie et en grosse ignorance. Il n'en sortit que peu a peu et lentement, sous l'influence du mouvement inauguré par Luther et qui, penetrante en France, y fit eclore et fructifier les germes d' emancipation religieuse qui étaient demeurés jusque—la chez Lefevre, vivants sans doutes, mais cachés. . . . On le voit encore en 1519, admettre et defendre le culte des saints et l'efficace des priéres pour les morts." On this question see also L. v. Muralt: "Ueber den Ursprung der Reformation in Frankreich" in *Festschrift für Hans Nabholz,* 1934.

135. Peter Tschudi to Beatus Rhenanus, May 17, 1519, *Briefwechsel des Beatus Rhenanus,* Leipzig, 1886, p. 157.

136. Frobenius to Luther, February 14, 1519, Ludwig Enders, *Martin Luthers Briefwechsel,* I, Frankfurt a.m., 1884, p. 420.

137. Glarean to Myconius, Oct. 15, 1520, *Geschichtsfreund* LXXXIII, p. 195. This letter indicates a neutral attitude with a critical tendency. Glarean to Zwingli, Nov. 1, 1520, *ZW VII*, 362: "Nulli libri avidius emuntur." The third mention of Luther occurs in a letter of April 7, 1521, where the attitude is still more friendly, Glarean to Myconius, April 7, 1521, *Geschichtsfreund* LXXXIII, p. 200. Finally in a letter of July 4, 1521, to Zwingli, Glarean says "Luther is magnificent," and mentions that he had read Luther's pamphlet, *The Babylonian*

Captivity, three times with enthusiasm. Glarean to Zwingli, July 4, 1521, *Zwingli Werke,* VII, 461, "Magnus ille est . . . Ego sane Lutheri pene nulla habeo opera, excepta unica 'Captivitate Babylonica,' qua nihi tam impense placuit, ut illam ab initio ad finem suque ter magna admiratione legerim." Later Glarean took a position against Luther and fell back into a thorough-going support of the old faith, like Erasmus. No doubt the latter's influence was decisive for him.

138. Leonhard von Muralt, "Konrad Grebel als Student in Paris" (*Zürcher Taschenbuch* 1937) pp. 133, 136. Von Muralt is successful in his psychological analysis of Grebel in Paris, though my own analysis differs in some points as is clear from the preceding discussion, but his attempt to create the impression of a vital religious concern and expression in the Glarean circle in Paris seems to me to be unjustified from the sources. Glarean's religious interest was after all superficial and not deep. There is no proof for von Muralt's assertion that "the pupils of Glarean were full of religious questions," which he bases solely on the attitude of one student, Valentine Tschudi, who was preparing for the service of the church and at that time already had an appointment as pastor in his home city of Glarus. Nor is there proof for von Muralt's assertion that Faber discussed the whole round of religious questions with Glarean "and his pupils." The most that we know is that Faber visited Glarean often in his home and passed the time with him "in song and jest, in debating and making sport of this foolish world." "Making sport of this foolish world" is still a long way from the serious discussion of the great religious and theological themes listed by von Muralt in his preceding paragraph as the "Ideenwelt" of Faber.

139. It may be true, as von Muralt says in his summing up of Grebel's Paris spiritual situation, that "in the Paris period Grebel at least got acquainted with humanistic religious ideas concerning a reform of Christendom," though this is seriously to be doubted; but that these "spectated" ideas constituted roots "which were later strengthened through further studies in Zurich and Basel and contributed in a positive sense to the construction of the Anabaptist doctrine and Anabaptist Christianity," is probably wishful thinking. Better sensed is the negative meaning of Grebel's Paris spiritual experience, which the writer correctly assesses in terms of a spiritual breakdown which could be solved only by a radical conversion experience and in this sense constituted a preparation for his work in founding the Anabaptist movement in Switzerland.

CHAPTER IV. CRISIS 1520-22

1. See Chapter III, p. 46, for the time of the return. Ammann heard with pleasure on July 23 in Milan, that Conrad had returned to Zurich, Ammann to Zwingli, *ZW, VII,* 337. Sources for this period of Grebel's life are the thirty-one letters which he wrote at this time. Of these, twenty-eight were addressed to Vadian, all in the *Vadianische Briefsammlung,* and three to Myconius, in *MQR,* Vol. II. Two letters were written to Vadian from Basel, the others from Zurich.

2. Myconius to Vadian, (?), 1520, *VB II,* 325. "Tigurum veni, non postrema causa ut convenirem Conradum nostrum. . . . Verum quia abfuit is, patri eius dedi, qui id faceret."

3. Grebel to Myconius, July 25, 1520, *MQR, II,* 239.

4. See chapter III, p. 46, with proofs.

5. See chapter II, footnote 80, for a description of the illness.

6. Grebel to Vadian, Nov. 19-Dec. 8, 1520, *VB III,* 210.

7. Grebel to Vadian, Apr. 25, 1521, *VB II,* 364, and July 22, 1521, *VB III,* 228, "Manuum simul et pedum frequens et ille ad articularem accedens morbus."

8. Grebel to Vadian, end of October, 1521, *VB III,* 231.

9. Grebel to Vadian, Jan. 4, 1521, *VB II,* 329.

10. Grebel to Myconius, July 6, 1520, *MQR II,* 239, and Grebel to Vadian, Sept. 11, 1520, *VB VII,* 15, "sed quid facies homini, qui hic pedibus paternis trahar, ne dicam, proprio in hac re arbitrio caream?"

11. Grebel to Vadian, Sept. 11, 1520, *loc. cit.*

12. Grebel to Vadian, Sept. 11, 1520, *loc. cit.*

13. Grebel to Myconius, July 25, 1520, *MQR II,* 240.

14. Grebel to Vadian, Nov. 7, 1520, *VB II,* 315.

15. Jacob Grebel to Vadian, Oct. 17, 1520, *VB II,* 313. Grebel describes his dealings with Pucci and then adds, "und darum, so ist min früntlich bit und beger, mir und im zu ratten was zu dun sy; dann so ver es üch und im gefallen wet, das er noch zwey jar fliss het gehan mit gottlicher hilff, würt es im wol erschiessen." Pucci's activities in Durrer. *Schweizergarde in Rom.* I, 219ff.

16. Grebel to Vadian, Sept. 11, 1520, *loc. cit.*

17. Grebel to Vadian, Nov. 7, 1520, *loc cit.*

18. See chapter VI, note 8.

19. Grebel to Vadian, Nov. 19-Dec. 8, 1520, *VB III,* 210.

20. Grebel to Vadian, Jan. 4, 1521, *VB II,* 330.

21. Grebel to Vadian, Feb. 1, 1521, *VB II,* 337. The reason for Grebel's unwillingness was his opposition to the foreign scholarship. "Stipendii causa quam male audiamus parens et filius."

22. Grebel to Vadian, Feb. 1, 1521, *loc. cit.* "Basileam ni peto, prudens sciens vivus vidensque pereo pereoque fato miserrimo . . . et olim prater spem cum meam tum parentum quippiam moliri."

23. Grebel to Vadian, March 19, 1521, *VB II,* 350.

24. Grebel to Vadian, April 8, 1521, *VB II,* 355. His mother's illness is described in a letter to Vadian, April 25, 1521, *VB II,* 364. His father's illness is described in a letter to Vadian, May 28 to July 14, 1521, *VB III,* 225.

25. Grebel to Vadian, Nov. 2, 1521, *VB II,* 398.

26. Grebel to Vadian, Dec. 2, 1520, *VB II,* 318.

27. Grebel to Vadian, Feb. 1, 1521, *VB II,* 336. "Dum hic haereo, nulli rei idoneus, tempus ignaviter perdens et studium literarum sic dissimulans." He cites the Greek proverb, "askopa toxeuein." [Greek letters in original text.]

28. Grebel to Vadian, Feb. 1, 1521, *loc cit.* Also Dec. 18, 1521, *VB II,* 408: "Verum si meae vitae modum cognoscas tam inertem, tam a studiis declinantem." Also to Vadian, Nov. 2, 1521, *VB II,* 398: "Studiis ingenuis operam navavi infelicissiman, intolerabilibus calamitatibus affectus; et haec est causa, quod infaustum totiesque impeditum studiorum cursum mox prorsus abrupturus sim."

29. Grebel to Vadian, Dec. 18, 1521, *VB II,* 408, "Dedisco olim apprehensas literas (si tamen apprehendi) dediscoque in dies magis magisque."

30. Glarean had no doubt learned of the literary ***sodalitium*** at the time of his visit in Zurich early in May, 1520, for on July 7, 1520, immediately after his return to Paris from Switzerland, he greets Zwingli together with his brother Andreas, Binder, Luchsinger, Spross, Utinger, "et omnes tecum graecissantes," Glarean to Zwingli, July 7, 1520, *ZW VII,* 333. Myconius also greets the ***sodalitium.*** Myconius to Zwingli June 10, 1520, *ZW VII,* 322. A description of the circle is found in ***Staehelin, Huldreich Zwingli,*** I, p. 149. It is possible that the group read Hebrew and Greek with Ceporin in the autumn of 1522. See Zwingli to Myconius, Aug. 21, 1522, *ZW VII,* 568. See also "Zwingli als Hebräer," ***Zwingliana*** I, 154.

31. Grebel to Myconius, Nov. 4, 1521, *MQR II,* 240, "Platonisamus Zinlius, Scudus, Ammanus et ego."

32. Albert Burer to Beatus Rhenanus, summer of 1520, ***Briefwechsel des Beatus Rhenanus,*** p. 240. Also cited in *ZW VII,* 322, note 4.

33. Grebel to Vadian, Nov. 7, 1520, *VB II,* 316, where Grebel calls them "Attica mea epigrammata." In the next letter (Nov. 19, 1520, ***op. cit.*** III, 209) he

sends two corrected epigrams, "nondum a Zinlio examinata." In the following letter (Dec. 8, 1520, *op. cit.,* II, 317) a collection "Graecarum dictionum illa Zinliana lima" [limatarum] are mentioned. On Nov. 2, 1521 (II, 398) he is planning to write some epigrams patterned after Lucian as a final "exercitium." He also mentions to Myconius, Nov. 4, 1521, that when he has time he turns Greek epigrams into verse, "Graecum epigramma aliquot expono, in carmen verto," *MQR II,* 240.

34. See chapter III, note 122.

35. Grebel to Vadian, Sept. 11, 1520, *VB VII,* 15, "vellem ne careres Lucianis Homericisque operibus atque utinam Iliados aliunde tibi copia fieret saltem, ob id, quod eam ex nostris collectaneis, in hunc maxime usum scriptis, huius poetarum Graecorum principis oracula nosciturus."

36. Grebel to Vadian, July 17, 1520, *VB II,* 293, "ut comite mea Iliade . . . ad te venirem."

37. Grebel to Zwingli, September 8, 1517, *ZW VII,* 62, "Literas tuas, observandissime Zwingli, minus expectavimus."

38. Grebel to Vadian, Nov. 7, 1520, *VB II,* 316. Sebastian Hofmeister was in Zurich a short time in the summer of 1520, but left early in September. Hofmeister to Zwingli, Sept. 17, 1520. *ZW VII,* 350, with note 1.

38a. Durrer, *Schweizergarde in Rom,* Vol. I, p. 209 and 369, reports that Manz, Febr., 1518, accompanied Kaspar Röist, Commandant of the Swiss Guard, to Rome, planning to join the guard "to satify his desire for further study." His father was Johannes Manz, who presided over the Grossmünster canons 1495-1518. The claim that he studied in Paris has not been proved. According to Bullinger, *Reformationsgeschichte* I, 30, Manz was a zealous student of Hebrew in Zurich (1522) "welcher zich vil in diser sprach mitt Zwingli üpt." Zwingli began his heavy study of Hebrew in early 1522. (Egli, "Zwingli als Hebräer," *Zwingliana* I, 154.)

39. The following data are taken from Zwingli's letters, *ZW VII.*

40. Grebel to Vadian, Jan. 12, 1522, *VB II,* 415.

41. Grebel to Vadian, Aug. 3, 1520, *VB II,* 299.

42. Grebel to Vadian, July 14, 1521, *VB II,* 368.

43. Allen, *op. cit., IV,* p. 598. Also Grebel to Vadian, Dec. 18, 1521, *VB II,* 408.

44. Grebel to Vadian, Feb. 6, 1522, *VB II,* 421: "ibimus ad Erasmum.."

45. Erasmus to Zwingli, September 3, 1522, Allen, *op. cit.,* V. p. 130. "Vadianus non minus placet conspectus quam ante lectus." Also found in *ZW VII,* 581.

46. *Pomponii Melae. . . .* Basel 1522, p. 160. Reference in Allen, *op. cit.* V, p. 130

47. See *ZW VII,* 580, note 1.

48. Myconius to Zwingli, Sept. 23, 1522, *ZW VII,* 584. See Allen, *op. cit* V., p. 131.

49. Grebel to Vadian, Feb. 1, 1521, *VB II,* 337, "Auditurus esses vitae meae non minus miserabilem quam mirabilem historiam." In Greek "ten ton emon kakon apeiresien thalassan." [Greek letters used in the MS.]

50. Grebel to Myconius, Nov. 4, 1521, *MQR II,* p. 240.

51. Grebel to Vadian, Feb. 19, 1521, *VB II,* 341. Various letters after May 28, 1521, witness to the inseparableness of the lovers, and use the name *Holokosme,* Greek for "whole world."

52. Grebel to Vadian, July 22, 1521, *VB III,* 227. "Sollicitus es, qua ratione sicsuncter abire." Also Aug. 4, 1521, *VB II,* 228. "Cunctationis paternae causas rogas."

53. Grebel to Vadian, May 28-July 14, 1521, *VB III,* 226.

54. Grebel to Vadian, July 14, 1521, *VB II,* 368. "Barbara . . . quae quod omnis rei et conscia et internuncia est."

55. Grebel to Vadian, July 22, 1521, *loc. cit.*

56. Grebel to Vadian, May 28-July 14, *loc. cit.* "Iecit aleam arrepta libertate Huttenus. Ego captus ac amore arrepto universam ludam iaciamque aleam."

57. Grebel to Vadian, Sept. 2, 1521, *VB II,* 404. The *Vadianische Briefsammlung* repeats the date, Dec. 2, as Grebel wrote it. Grebel however made a mistake. This error gave rise to the theory that Grebel was in Basel twice, as for instance presented by Neff in *Gedenkschrift zum 400-Jährigen Jubiläum der Mennoniten oder Taufgesinnten,* p. 73.

58. Grebel to Vadian, Aug. 21, 1521, *VB II,* 387. Grebel evidently wrote very soon after his arrival in Basel. Nevertheless several days may have passed after the arrival before the dispatch of the letter.

59. Andreas Cratander to Capito, Sept. 20, 1521, from Frankfurt a. M., in the University Library at Basel, *Ms. Ki. Ar. 25a. Letter no.* 48, fol. 71, "Ursinum Velium celeberrimum poetam et graece doctissimum domi meae alo, item Conradum Grebelium egregiae indolis iuvenem, cuius soror Joachimo Vadiano nupsit; quo officina mea de huius modi doctorum virorum conversatione celebrior instructiorque futura sit." Ursinus writes on Oct. 1, 1521, from Basel to Vadian to praise Grebel: "Dedi hoc negotii Grebellio, adulescenti modis omnibus egregio atque in omnes mire officioso, qui de aliis quoque, quae scribere supersedeo, tecum communicabit. Uxorem tuam, honestissimam feminam, et, quantum ex fratris indole coniectare licet, adulescentem suavem vel ignoti nomine salutem dices." *VB II,* 392.

60. Grebel to Vadian, Sept. 2, 1521, *VB II,* 405. Neff, *op. cit.,* p. 74, misreads the letter. The 24 Gulden were not salary, but rent.

61. When Kaspar Ursinus wrote to Vadian from Basel Oct. 1, 1521, Grebel was still with him at Cratander's shop. See note 59 above.

62. Grebel to Vadian, end of October, 1521, *VB III,* 231.

63. See note 61 above, also other letters of Ursinus about this time.

64. *Caspari Ursini Velii Poematarum Libri V,* Basel (Frobenius) March, 1522.

65. The only evidence for this is the statement of George Binder, *Egli,* no. 1050, p. 949: "Konrad sei damit nach Basel zur Schule gegangen." Since the winter semester did not open until the latter part of October when Grebel had already returned to Zurich he could not have attended whatever his plan might originally have been.

66. Gustav Bauch, "Caspar Ursinus Velius," *Ungarische Revue,* VII, Budapest, 1887, p. 38.

67. Grebel to Vadian, end of October, 1521, *loc. cit.*

68. Grebel to Myconius, Nov. 4, 1521, *MQR II,* 240.

69. Grebel to Vadian, Nov. 2, 1521, *VB II,* 398.

70. Grebel to Vadian, end of October, 1521, *loc. cit.* "Civitate Tiguri donatum me tandem credo." There is no trace in the state archives of Zurich of the reinstatement of Conrad Grebel to citizenship. Concerning the surrender of his citizenship see Chapter II, footnote 36.

71. See note 50 above.

72. For the following dates see Wackernagel, *op. cit.,* pp. 326-333.

73. Fritzsche, *op. cit.,* p. 31. See also Glarean to Zwingli, March 4, 1522, *ZW VII,* 494.

74. Wackernagel, *op. cit.,* p. 330, with proof in Loserth, *Balthasar Hubmaier und die Anfänge der Wiedertaufe in Mähren,* p. 27.

75. Christian Neff, "Hans Denk," in *Menn. Lexikon,* I, 401ff.

76. *Aktensammlung zur Geschichte der Basler Reformation II Band,* No. 46, p. 33. See also Christian Neff, "Hugwald," in *Mennonitische Lexikon,* I, p. 363 f.

77. *ZW VII*, 401, note 3, and Wackernagel, *loc. cit.*
78. Egli, *Aktensammlung*, No. 566, 567, p. 246.
79. Wackernagel, *op. cit.*, 326.
80. Grebel to Vadian, Nov. 2, 1521, *VB II*, 398.
81. Grebel to Vadian, January 30, 1522, *VB II*, 416. "A delitiis meis, a mea vita, ab mea Holocosme non divellar."
82. The following description is taken from Grebel's letter to Vadian, Feb. 6, 1522, *VB II*, 421.

CHAPTER V. GREBEL'S HUMANISM

1. See the valuable article. "Conrad Grebel as a Humanist," by Edward Yoder in *MQR III*, 132-146 (April, 1929).
2. Grebel to Vadian, July 17, 1520. *VB II*, 293.
3. Werner Kaegi, "Hutten und Erasmus" in *Historische Vierteljahrsschrift* XXII, 1929, p. 256, translated.
4. Paul Wernle, *Renaissance des Christentums*, Tuebingen, 1904, p. 151, translated.
5. Ernst Walser, "Ueber das Wesen der französischen Renaissance" in *Gesammelte Studien zur Geistesgeschichte der Renaissance*, Basel, 1932, p. 87.
6. Grebel to Vadian, Dec. 29, 1521, *VB II*, 410.

CHAPTER VI. ZWINGLI'S CONVERT, 1522-1523

1. Sources for this period are chiefly ten letters of Grebel to Vadian, all in the *Vadianische Briefsammlung*. The absence of letters in the periods of February to November, 1522, and January to June, 1523, is conspicuous. Four letters were written in the short period between November 21 and December 29, 1522, and six letters between June 17 and September 6, 1523. The letter dated Dec. 25, 1524, I have placed in 1522; the month and day, Dec. 25, also seem questionable to me, but cannot be more definitely determined.
2. Grebel to Vadian, Nov. 21, 1522, *VB II*, 451.
3. Grebel to Vadian, Dec. 29, 1522, *VB II*, 458. "Mater mea satis impia in me, in coniugem plus nimio rabida est."
4. For sources for the birth dates of the children see *MQR X*, 21-22.
5. Grebel to Vadian, Nov. 21, 1522, *loc. cit.*
6. Grebel to Vadian, Dec. 29, 1522, *VB II*, 410.
7. Grebel to Vadian, Aug. 11, 1523, *VB III*, 33. "Interim tamen habe, mihi spei adeo nihil esse reliqui in parente, ut ab alienissimis potius quam ab ipso pendeam . . . Propter discipulos meos paucis his tecum ago."
8. Statement made in the trial of Jakob Grebel, Egli, *Aktensammlung*, No. 1050, p. 495.
9. Grebel to Vadian, Dec. 25, 1522, *VB VII*, 18; July 28, 1523, *VB III*, 29; Sept. 6, 1523, *VB II*, 446.
10. At the close of the letters of Nov. 21 and Dec. 1, 1522, he uses the greeting "vale perquam evangelicissime." "Vale in Christo" or "valete in Christo" appears in the letters of July 28 and Aug. 11, 1523. Other letters contain Christian greetings. Grebel to Vadian, July 28, 1523, *VB III*, 30. "Precare apud Christum, ut firmam in eum fiduciam geram. Idem ego quoque, ut tibi accidat, precabor."
11. Grebel to Vadian, Dec. 29, 1522, *VB II*, 458. "Timeo de eius salute, ni Christum induat et nova fiat spiritu divino renata creatura."
12. See note 10 above; also Grebel to Vadian, Aug. 11, 1523, *VB III*, 33. "Atque utinam a deo penderem pendeamque, sed ubi, per ignem aliquem succendente volenteque ipso, patientia animam meam hanc, multis expositam et agitabilem procellis, possidere didicero."
13. Grebel to Vadian, June 17, 1523, *VB III*, 19.

14. Grebel to Vadian, Aug. 11, 1523, *VB III,* 32. "Pater noster coelestis faxit, ut incolumem diu habeatis Iuflium isque ministerium suum (quod facit) Paulina libertate et gratia in diem usque extremum ipsi pertractet."

15. Grebel to Vadian, Nov. 21, 1522, *VB II,* 452, where Grebel uses the Greek words: "en theopneustois tois grammasi." [Greek letters in MS.]

16. Grebel to Vadian, July 13, 1523, *VB III,* 26. The matter involved was the question of tithes.

17. Grebel to Vadian, Nov. 12, 1523, *VB III,* 46.

18. Grebel to Vadian, Dec. 29, 1522, *VB II,* 459. "Atque istud in limine esse tempus incipit, quo plerique non fraterne remissis aliorum peccatis corpus Christi indigne et ad iudicium manducamus."

19. Grebel's poem at the end of *Apologeticus Archeteles* of Zwingli, *ZW I,* 327, contains the thought of this paragraph.

20. See note 11 above for the expressions.

21. Grebel to Vadian, Nov. 21, 1522, *VB II,* 452. "Salvebis plurimum episcopum cum universa ecclesia quae Christi capitis per evangelium graciae est."

22. Grebel to Vadian, Nov. 21, 1522, *VB II,* 452. "Atque utinam gratia dei omnes pro me orent et ministerium hoc triumphaturus serio accipiam. Nihil addo, quia nulla plaustra etiam verborum cognoscendum animum hunc meum facto olim periculo depingere possent."

23. Grebel to Vadian, July 28, 1523, *VB III,* 30.

24. Staehelin, *Huldreich Zwingli,* I, 154.

25. The event in the council chamber, see notes 48 and 49 below.

26. *ZW I,* 133.

27. *ZW I,* 285. "Ut Christi beneficium clarius agnoscerent ac gloriam."

28. *Die Chronik des Bernhard Wyss* (*Quellen zur Schweiz. Reformationsgeschichte* I) Basel 1901 p. 9. Also *ZW I,* p. 67.

29. A particularly beautiful passage concerning the service of the minister is found in Grebel's letter to Vadian, July 14, 1523, *VB III,* 52. "Parochum vestrum in Christo incolumem esse et doctum scribam regni coelorum, qui nova cum veteribus, divina cum divinis, testamentum utrunque eruere laboret, IUBEMUS, hoc est, ut is sit, qualis et est deo volente, non solum corpore, verum etiam concionibus et evangelii ministerio valens."

30. *Zwingliana* II, pp. 198 ff. (Not the Basel Erasmus.)

31. Zwingli to Myconius, Aug. 26, 1522, *ZW VII,* 568.

32. Macrinus to Zwingli, Oct. 15, 1522, *ZW VII,* 596.—"Salutem . . . Conrado Grebelio, quem audio singularem evangelii patronum factum, quod mehercle, non mediocriter gaudeo, ut etiam iuvenes, qui ingenio et eruditione praestant, ad ea se studia converterint, ubi sibi ac toti mundo vere prodesse possunt. Item caeteros omnes pure Christianos saluta, quorum apud vos longe plures, tuo beneficio, quam uspiam alibi in Helvetia esse scio."

33. Macrinus to Zwingli, Jan. 25, and Mar. 6, 1523, *ZW VIII,* 15 and 48.

34. Johannes Zwick to Zwingli, Nov. 27, 1522, *ZW VII,* 621.

35. Berchtold Haller to Zwingli, May 9, 1523, *ZW VII,* 77.

36. Grebel to Vadian, Dec. 25, 1522, *VB VII,* 17.

37. Grebel to Vadian, July 13, 1523, *VB III,* 26.

38. Grebel to Vadian, Nov. 21, 1522, *VB II,* 451.

39. Grebel to Vadian, Dec. 29, 1522, *VB II,* 410.

40. Grebel to Vadian, July 14, 1523, *VB III,* 52.

41. On July 14, 1523, and Dec. 25, 1522, for instance, he mentions sending books.

42. Grebel to Vadian, Nov. 21, 1522, *VB II,* 452.

43. Grebel to Vadian, July 13, 1523, *VB III, 27*; and Benedikt Burgauer to Grebel, July 21, 1523, *VB III,* 29.

44. Grebel to Vadian, July 13, 1523, *op. cit.,* 26.

45. Grebel to Vadian, Nov. 12, 1523, *VB III,* 45; Zwingli to Vadian, *op. cit.* 43 and Nov. 11, 1523, *ZW VIII,* 129.

46. Grebel to Vadian, Dec. 1, 1522, *VB III,* 234 and June 17, 1523, *VB III,* 26.

47. *Chronik des Bernhard Wyss,* 14-15.

48. Egli, *Aktensammlung* No. 269, p. 94.

49. Egli, *Aktensammlung,* No. 246, p. 82. According to Emil Egli, *Schweizerische Reformationsgeschichte,* I, p. 65, note 2, this document should be dated the end of May instead of April. Grebel could have taken part in this dinner of course, even though his name does not appear, particularly since plans were discussed at Jacob Grebel's house.

50. Egli, *Aktensammlung* No. 233 and 234, pp. 72-75.

51. Grebel to Vadian, July 13, 1523, *VB III,* 26. "Gentes mundi dixi tyrannos patriae nostrae, quos patres conscriptos vocant, rectius patres decimantes vocaturi."

52. Egli, *Schw. Ref. Gesch. I,* Zurich 1910, p. 67. For a thorough discussion of this problem see Ernst Ramp, *Das Zinsproblem, eine historische Untersuchung,* Zurich, 1949. (*Quellen und Abh. zur Gesch. des schw. Protestantismus,* 4).

53. Egli, *Aktensammlung* No. 252, p. 85, places the first mention of Castelberger's "Schule" in May, 1522. Document no. 623, pp. 276 ff. (to be dated 1523, not 1522, according to Egli, *Schweizerische Reformationsgeschichte*) has an extremely interesting report of Castelberger's "Predigt" in his "Schule." A short biography of Castelberger is found in *ZW VIII,* 342, note 8.

54. A brief biography of Simon Stumpf in *ZW VII,* 195, note 1. In November, 1523, he was deposed from his office, and six weeks later he was banished from the canton of Zurich. To what extent the charge was justified is not clear, but it is certain that his parish was a center of unrest.

55. A brief biography of Reublin in *ZW VII,* 509, Note 6.

56. A brief biography of Haetzer in *ZW VIII,* 361, Note 1.

57. A brief biography of Manz in ZW IX, 26, Note 6.

CHAPTER VII—THE SEARCH FOR THE TRUE CHURCH, 1523-24

1. Sources for this period are chiefly eleven of Grebel's letters to Vadian between Nov. 12, 1523, and Jan. 14, 1525; a letter of Vadian to Grebel, December 20, 1524; a letter of Erhard Hegenwalt to Grebel, Jan. 1, 1525; and Grebel's *Protestation und Schutzschrift* to the Council of Zurich, early in December, 1524. In addition there is the testimony of Zwingli's witnesses at the trial of the Anabaptists in April, 1525, and Zwingli's three accounts of the beginnings of the Anabaptist movement, which are found in his writings against the Anabaptists: *Von dem Touf, vom Widertouf und vom Kindertouff,* May 1525 (*ZW II,* 206-209 257, 286); Answer to Balthasar Hubmaier's *Taufbüchlein* (*ZW IV,* 590-592) unimportant; *In Catabaptistarum Strophas Elenchus* (*ZW VI,* 32-42). The above-mentioned *Protestation* by Grebel is printed at the beginning of the writing *Wer Ursach gebe zu Aufruhr* (*ZW III,* 368-372). Zwingli's letter to the reformers at Strassburg, Dec. 16, 1524, also contains several notes.

2. Egli, *Schweizerische Reformationsgeschichte,* I, p. 52. "Schon am Ende des ersten Jahres [hence at the end of 1519] wusste der Reformator die Mehrheit der Stadt auf seiner Seite."

3. *Taufbuechlein, ZW IV,* 207: "Als wir aber das täglich bessren und zunemen des wortts gesehen, habend wir zu gheiner sündrung nit wollen willigen."

4. Staehelin, *Huldreich Zwingli* I, p. 349: "Die noch immer fortdauernde öffentliche Schaustellung der Bilder in den Kirchen erschien nach der darüber ausgesprochenen Verurteilung als ein Ärgernis, welches nicht früh genug abgestellt werden könne, und auch das Abhalten der Messe wurde als unerträgliche Gewissensbelastung gefunden, nachdem sie mit klaren Worten als Schmähung Gottes bezeichnet worden war."

5. Was not the awareness of this fact probably the reason why Grebel got in contact with Carlstadt in the summer of 1524?

6. See the clear and on the whole sound analysis by Walter Köhler in his introduction to "Zeugenaussagen Zwinglis im Täuferprozess," *ZW IV*, 161. It is questionable however, whether the antithesis "Christianity and Culture" is wholly applicable. It is probably not correct to regard the Anabaptists as completely hostile to culture. In my discussion above of Zwingli's attitude in the problem of "State and Church," I take an essentially different position than Alfred Farner in his valuable monograph, *Die Lehre von Kirche und Staat bei Zwingli,* e.g., in the chapter, "Die Entwicklung des Kirchenbegriffs" and in other passages. In the presentation of the second disputation, p. 93, Farner has in my opinion not analyzed correctly the difference of opinion between Stumpf and Zwingli. See also Koehler's admission that Zwingli actually made a "compromise" on this basic issue, in "Das Täufertum in der neueren historischen Forschung" in *Archiv für Reformationsgeschichte* 37 (1940), 102.

7. Zwingli to Myconius, July 24, 1520, *ZW VII,* 341 ff.

8. "Handlung der Versammlung in Zürich, Jan. 29, 1523," *ZW I,* 557-558.

9. Egli, *Aktensammlung* No. 368, p. 132.

10. Zwingli to Vadian, Nov. 11, 1523, *ZW VIII,* 129 f.

11. *ZW II,* 458-468.

12. Conrad Grebel's "Protestation und Schutzschrift," *ZW III,* 368. "Under welchen auch ich alss ein auffrurer und unman von etlichen gehalten und angezeigt wird, in welchem doch mir ze kurz und ungütlich gschicht, mag ouch mit keiner warheit erfunden und angezeigt werden; iendert geuffruret haben noch iendert in keinen weg ienen ützit gelert noch geredt, das auffrur gebracht noch bringen mög (werden alle die, mitt denen ich ie zu schaffen gehaben, von mir gichtig sein)."

12a. The claim has been made by some writers, that Grebel turned away from Zwingli and took up Anabaptism out of pique partly because of Zwingli's failure to secure his appointment as a teacher in the newly established theological school in Zurich. George Finsler, joint editor of the critical edition of *Zwingli's Werke* in commenting on Zwingli's statement that "Several of them [Anabaptists] came to me and sought my support in securing appointments [benefices]." *ZW IV, p. 387, Von dem Predig Amt* [published June 30, 1525] quotes a passage from Bullinger's *Reformationsgeschichte* (I, pp. 237-238) which is evidently the ultimate source from which this strange charge has been derived. The Bullinger account reads as follows (translated):

"And at first they ["Grebel, Manz and other restless spirits"] were often instructed in special conversations with Master Ulrich; but they would not accept instruction and manifested a bitter hard attitude against Zwingli, whom they accused of not favoring them and being unwilling to promote them. For their opinion was that the old canons should be displaced from their benefices, and lectureships should be established. Manz hoped to secure the Hebrew lectureship and Grebel the one in Greek, supposing that because they were children of citizens and came from good families they should be favored above everyone else. But Master Ulrich was not able at that time to accomplish what they desired but promised to promote them in the future as much as he could. One could not offhand depose old and honorable men, who were also of old families and worthy of respect, and to whom much had been promised by the authorities, which promises should be kept. However, something would come about soon to make possible setting up the lectureships in the languages according to the plan drawn up for this. But these fellows could not wait. In addition they had become so wild in the Anabaptist spirit, that they no longer paid any attention to anything but to spread their Anabaptism." Finsler comments at this point: "To the instructorship in Hebrew then not Felix Mantz, who hoped for it, but Jacob Ceporin, was appointed."

Finsler fails to quote Bullinger's second reference to this matter (*Ref. Gesch. I,* p. 289) where he writes as follows under the heading (topic 160), *How and when Zurich began the Biblical Lectureship in Three Languages*: "Meanwhile they began to look around for learned and practiced men in the languages. And since Mantz and Grebel, who would have been competent enough for the job, had cast themselves out (*sich abgeworffen*) and followed Anabaptism, H. Conradt Pellican from Basel was called to the Hebrew lectureship. Before him and as the first, Jacob Ceporin was appointed as reader." A comparison of the two Bullinger accounts makes it plain that Bullinger does not assert that Grebel and Mantz became Anabaptists after [and because] Zwingli refused them the lectureships. Rather he intimates that Zwingli promised them consideration and that they would have received the appointments had they not unfortunately left the Zwinglian Movement and become Anabaptists. Bullinger, in fact, attributes their Anabaptism to Thomas Müntzer's influence. Emil Egli (*Züricher Wiedertäufer,* Zurich, 1878, p. 19) writes the following on this point, using Bullinger as source, "Their [Grebel and Manz] bitterness against Zwingli arose in part out of personal grounds; Zwingli could not secure for them the desired appointments as instructors in Hebrew and Greek, indeed finally chose a peasant's son, Jacob Ceporin, in preference to them as citizens of the city."

It is impossible that the motive of pique at loss of a desired appointment could have played even a minor part in the attitude of Grebel and Manz toward Zwingli and the basic religious issues of the years 1523-25 which led to the founding of the Anabaptist movement, even apart from the fact that Bullinger was probably fabricating a legend in the matter inasmuch as he fails to mention the case in his earlier writings, and Zwingli likewise fails to make the charge at any time against either Grebel or Manz. Emil Egli himself, in reporting the establishment of the language lectureships (*Schweizerische Reformationsgeschichte,* I, p. 241 f) states that Zwingli had secured Ceporin as "reader" for Hebrew and Greek as early as the fall of 1522, although he was unable to establish the lectureships until June, 1525, after the death of the conservative "Schulherr," Dr. Niessli. But in 1522 Grebel was the warmest of friends of Zwingli and hence could not have been bitter toward Zwingli because of the appointment of Ceporin over his head at that time; while in June, 1525, the time was long past that either Grebel or Manz could have been interested in a lectureship under Zwingli. Furthermore, the action of the Zurich Council setting up a program of reform of the canons was not adopted until September 29, 1523, and Grebel's break with Zwingli began about this time. But, in any case, Zwingli himself makes it abundantly plain that the break with Grebel and Manz came over a much greater issue, namely, that of the nature of the church. There is not the least trace of the "lectureship" episode in any of the existing sources.

13. Conrad Grebel to Vadian, Dec. 18, 1523, *VB III,* 50.

14. Christian Neff ("Conrad Grebel, Sein Leben und Wirken" in *Gedenkschrift zum 400 jährigen Jubiläum der Mennoniten oder Taufgesinnten,* 1925, p. 79.) misreads the letter of Grebel to Vadian, Aug. 11, 1523. The "enemy of the gospel" whom Grebel condemns in the letter was a resident of St. Gall, and could therefore not have been Zwingli. There is no evidence in the available sources before the letter of December 18, 1523, to Vadian, that Grebel was an opponent of Zwingli.

15. *ZW II,* 775.

16. *ZW II,* 682.

17. *ZW II,* 783-4. The testimony of Zwingli and Stumpf is found on p. 784.

18. Stumpf did this very thing. As the consequence of his public agitation against the mass he was finally banished from Zurich on Dec. 23, 1523 (Egli, *Aktensammlung,* No. 463, p. 190). He had voluntarily surrendered his benefice earlier (Egli, *Akts.,* Nov. 3, 1523, No. 441, p. 178).

19. Although Zwingli continued to uphold in theory the sole authority of the Scripture in the life of the church, in practice he made the authority of the Council the final ultimate authority. Farner (*op. cit.*, pp. 102-3) explains that Zwingli did this only when the church was in an extremity ("Notlage") and that he justified his conduct in the matter of the mass primarily on this ground. This means in plain English that Zwingli justified by circumstances his departure from his own principle of the sole authority of Scripture, and that he was ready to make such departures or exceptions when it seemed necessary. All that needs to be pointed out here is that Grebel and the Anabaptists are thus justified out of Zwingli's own mouth. They would permit no such exceptions but demanded consistency. The charge against Zwingli was therefore valid. Ironically from the point of view of the brethren, the "extremities" in which Zwingli felt free to depart from the principle of Scripture authority were chiefly those which arose out of the struggle between them and Zwingli.

20. As is well known, Zwingli finally turned to forceful measures to maintain his position in Zurich as well as to promote and defend the Reformation in Switzerland. Indeed, he finally developed great plans to promote the success of the Reformation in general by a military alliance. Farner himself describes Zwingli's gradual transition to the use of force in religious matters. Cf., for instance, *op. cit.*, p. 109: "Er selbst wird von den Ereignissen gedrängt. Beginnt er doch dem Rat stets grössere Machtfülle in die Hände zu legen, um sein Werk zu halten." After reading Farner's statement concerning Zwingli's use of forceful means "to maintain his own position," one scarcely can avoid a smile when Farner reports, "In seiner Schrift *Von der Taufe* verurteilt Zwingli das gewaltsame Vorgehen der Täufer," particularly when one knows that the "Täufer" were never guilty of any "gewaltsames Vorgehen."

21. The accusation has often been repeated, most recently by Karl Holl in "Luther und die Schwärmer" in *Gesammelte Aufsätze,* and "C.S." in *Reformierte Schweizer Zeitung,* Bd. IV, No. 45 to Bd. V, No. 2, in the article entitled, "Vor vier hundert Jahren," also by Heinrich Boehmer in "Thomas Müntzer und das jüngste Deutschland," in *Gesammelte Aufsätze,* 1927. The accusation is of course founded on a broader basis than Stumpf's statement alone.

22. *ZW II,* 799. See also *ZW I,* 558; "Der geist gottes uss der geschryfft urteilt selbst"; and p. 559; "ich verston die gschryfft nit anders, dann wie sy sich selbst durch den geist gottes usslegt; bdarff keins menschlichen urteils." Many other passages could be cited.

23. *ZW II,* 789 ff.

24. Grebel to Vadian, Sept. 3, 1524, *VB III,* 86: "Persolvissem ego, si non usque adeo tenuis essem." Also Grebel to Vadian, Oct. 14, 1524, *VB III,* 89: "Non tam erga me quam mendicissimos, sed et erga creditores meos, quibus ego plus sexaginta aureorum debito addictus sum et mancipatus . . . quod creditores mihi molesti sunt." Also Grebel to Vadian Jan. 14, 1525, *VB III,* 105: "Ich bin träffenlich nöttig." Grebel was finally compelled to sell his books to secure funds. His letter to Andreas Castelberger of May, 1525, (*MQR I,* July, 1927, pp. 41 ff.), contains a request for aid in finding a buyer.

25. Grebel to Vadian, Sept. 3, 1524, *VB III,* 85: "Vis causam audentiae meae universae: expectavi et non sunt locuti; steterunt nec ultra responderunt." The following quotations are also taken from this letter, p. 85.

26. The letter to Müntzer has often been printed, most recently in Boehmer-Kirn, *Thomas Muentzers Briefwechsel, Leipzig,* 1931, pp. 92-101. An English translation by Walter Rauschenbusch appeared in *American Journal of Theology* (1905) pp. 91-106.

27. "Drei Zeugenaussagen Zwinglis im Täuferprozess," *ZW IV,* 168-175. Also in Egli, *Aktensammlung,* No. 692, pp. 308 ff. Egli (and after him *Zwingli Werke*) dates in April, 1525, the documents in which Zwingli's "Zeugenaussagen"

appear, but a careful examination reveals that this dating is impossible. Grebel, who appears as a witness, was not arrested before Oct. 8, 1525. Blaurock states (Egli, *Aktensammlung,* p. 311) that "er hette die abgefallnen Bruederen im Appenzeller -und Oberland widerumb ufgericht . . . ouch darbi gseit, wie nach vil gefänknussen zuo Zurich und Chur er durch beschlossen tür hinus Kommen und geledigt." But this would have been impossible in the brief time in March and April in which Blaurock's presence in Zurich is not attested by the documents. Further Manz admits that he himself had baptized a candidate at Embrach 14 days after the escape from the tower. His escape however, according to the words of the sentence of death against him on Jan. 4, 1527 (Egli, *Akts.* No. 1109, p. 529) had taken place after he had sworn "Urfehde," and this he had done for the first time on Oct. 7, 1525 (Egli, *Akts.* 835, p. 394). Finally, attention should be called to Zwingli's reference to a statement by Grebel which was said to have been made "in der disputatz am Mentag." Egli holds this "Monday disputation" to have been that of Monday, March 20, 1525, but overlooks the fact that according to the record of this meeting as given in Egli, No. 668, only Manz and Blaurock took part in this disputation, not Grebel, and that the records of the ensuing trial, March 16-25, 1525 (Egli, No. 674) fail to mention Grebel altogether. The disputation of November 6, 1525, was also a "Monday disputation." Further proof of the later date is found in the appearance of Hofmeister as a witness at the trial. Hofmeister was in Schaffhausen in April, 1525, and remained there until he was banished in August of that year. He went at once to Zurich where he still was on April 24, 1526, on which day he addressed a letter from Zurich to the council of Schaffhausen (Wipf, *Ref. Gesch. Schaffhausens,* pp. 206 ff.). Hofmeister was one of the presidents of the November disputation. The mention, in the documents, of the escape from the tower, suggests a date in the spring of 1526. The problem can be solved by breaking apart the documents which Egli has joined together, and assigning some to November, 1525, and others to the spring of 1526.

28. See note 1 above for the references.

29. The meaning of the demand that "alle ding muesstind gemein sin" is not to be taken too far. As a corrective one should refer to similar demands by the leaders of the time. Erasmus, for instance, was the author of a very drastic attack against private property in his *Enchiridion Militis Christiani.* I quote from Paul Wernle, *Renaissance und Reformation,* Tübingen, 1912, pp. 54-55: "Erasmus, der kühn versichert hatte, 'Vom Eigentum weiss christliche Liebe nichts,' und zwar mit dem Zusatz: 'das gelte nicht etwa bloss für die Mönche, sondern für alle Christen' . . . derselbe Erasmus bemerkt, als die Täufer nun wirklich es wagten, den Kommunismus praktisch zu verwirklichen, lakonisch: 'Gütergemeinschaft mag der Liebe anheimgestellt sein, aber der Besitz und das Verfügungsrecht sollen beim Eigentümer bleiben.'" Wernle also quotes Melanchthon: "Und Melanchthon, der als humanistischer Naturrechtler in der ersten Ausgabe seiner *loci* den Satz aufgestellt hatte: 'es fordert die menschliche Societät, dass wir alle Dinge gemeinsam gebrauchen,' freilich nicht ohne ihn durch Einschränkungen ungefährlich zu machen, tilgt den Passus gänzlich, nachdem der Bauernkrieg und das Täufertum einen Anlauf in kommunistischer Richtung gemacht hatte, und nennt den Plato, den er früher lobend zitiert hatte, einen Konfusionär."

It is possible that all that the brethren meant to say was that the church had a right to ask its members to share their possessions with the needy on occasion. An example of this is the case of Anthoni Roggenacher of St. Gall, who placed 100 crowns at the disposal of the church in St. Gall, although there is no evidence that the money was used by the church. See the story in J. J. Simler's *Sammlung alter und neuer Urkunden zur Beleuchtung der Kirchengeschichte vornehmlich des Schweizerlandes I,* Zurich, 1757, pp. 445-449. It is possible of course that the example of the apostolic church in Jerusalem as recorded in Acts did lead the early brethren to project a communism of consumption, but there is not the least evidence that the brethren ever set up a practical program to carry out such a theoretical ideal. This is in contrast to the later Hutterian Brethren community in Moravia.

30. On the point compare also Grebel's admonition to Müntzer in his letter of September 5, 1524: "Sind üwer pfründ gestifft uff zins und zehenden, bede warem wucher, wie by unss, und so nit ein gantze gmein üch ertzücht, wellind ir üch der pfründen entzüchen. Ir wüssend wol, wie ein hirt ernert werden sol." Böhmer-Kirn, *Thomas Müntzers Briefwechsel,* Leipzig 1931, p. 96. Zwingli also reports that the brethren had urged him to give up his benefice with the promise that they would support him. He even claims that they had promised him 100 guilders yearly. (*Von dem Predigtamt, Zwingli Werke* IV, pp. 404-405.)

31. Elenchus, *op. cit.*, p. 33: "Iam ecclesiam piorum suis, iisque piis, senatum suum lecturam esse votis." This passage has been variously interpreted. Did Zwingli mean to say that the brethren proposed to substitute a new pious council for the existing mixed (partly worldly) council, or that they proposed two parallel councils, one for the saints and one for the world, or that they were not thinking of a political council at all but rather a church synod. The last interpretation has been adopted by John Horsch, who gives a corresponding translation of the passage in *MQR VI,* 1923, p. 239: "It was needful that the church elect its own leaders from among the number of the devout." However a careful examination shows that Horsch's translation is not true to the meaning of the original. Furthermore the context does not admit the limitation of the sense to an ecclesiastical synod, for the criticism of the brethren was directed against the existing political council (as in part "worldly"). Their hope was to displace this council *after* the pious had secured a majority in the city. The idea of a displacement of the existing council proves definitely that the brethren had originally (1523-1524) proposed to establish a "Christian" government. Later to be sure there is no evidence of a maintenance of this idea.

32. Elenchus, *op. cit.,* p. 33: "Polliceri quoque copias nostras perfidorum exercitum multo superaturas."

33. Zwingli's *Zeugenaussagen, ZW IV,* 169.

34. Egli, *Aktensammlung* No. 463, p. 190.

35. Zwingli's *Zeugenaussagen, op. cit.,* 171: "So habind Grebel und Simon mer dann einist mit im gerett." *Taufbüchlein, op. cit.,* p. 206: "Die habend uns vorhin offt vermanet." In *Elenchus, op. cit.,* p. 33, note 2, Blanke points out that "constanter" and "conveniebant" used by Zwingli in describing the visits of the Brethren with their proposals are evidence that there were several visits. Zwingli's statements, cited above, mention the visits of Stumpf, Grebel, and Manz, following each other and alone. One sentence mentions Stumpf and Grebel together, but only because they made the same proposals about "alle ding gmein." The sentence is not necessarily to be construed to mean that they made these proposals together on several visits. It is possible that the repeated visits of Grebel and Stumpf are mentioned in contrast with Felix Manz's single visit, "witer so sige Felix Manz uff *ein* zit zu im kommen vor Huyuffs gadenn" (italics mine).

36. The names are found as signatures to the letter to Thomas Müntzer, Sept. 5, 1524, Böhmer-Kirn, *op. cit.,* pp. 99 and 101. On p. 100 Grebel says: "By unss sind nit zwentzig, die dem wort Gottes gloubind."

37. Grebel to Müntzer Sept. 5, 1524, *loc. cit.*: "Wan unsere hirten sind ouch also grimm und wutend wider unss, scheltend uns buben an offenlicher cantzel und Satanas in angelos lucis conversos." Grebel reports the same thing in his letter to Vadian, Oct. 14, 1524, *VB III,* 89: "Nihil moratus etiam summum ducem verbi, qui me invidentiae tabernam et ex Satana angelum lucis et upokriseos calumniatur." [Greek letters in MS. for upokriseos.]

38. Zwingli's *Zeugenaussagen, op. cit.,* 169. According to note 16, "die nüwe Statt" was not a city quarter, but a street near the cathedral. Felix Manz says in his hearing (date uncertain, Egli, *Aktensammlung* No. 692, p. 311), "und wie im ouch fuergehalten, wie sie nächtlich versammlungen ghept habind, da zit er si antwurt: wie er hebraisch gelesen in sinem hus, da sygind etlich zuo im kommen und in allda ghört. Und nach dem lesen gienge dann jedermann widerumb heim. Es sygind sunst etwan wol guot gsellen zuo im kommen, habind aber nie dhein versammlung ghept, die jemants zuo nachteil gereicht habe." Grebel reports in his letter to Vadian, Sept. 3, 1524, *VB III,* 85: "Deinde lego aliquot auditoribus evangelium Matthaei Graecum."

39. The occupations are mentioned in various documents in Egli, *Aktensammlung.*

40. This is proved by the fact that he wrote the letter to Müntzer personally in the name of all.

41. Grebel to Vadian, Sept. 3, 1524, *op. cit.,* p. 85: "Rescribo Andreae Carolostadio."

42. Grebel to Müntzer, Sept. 5, 1524, *op. cit.,* p. 99: "Der Andress Castelberg hat Carolostadio geschriben." This passage is found in the appendix to the letter, not in the first part. Did Castelberger write the letter to Carlstadt in the name of all, as Grebel did to Müntzer, or did he write the letter that Grebel himself had wanted to write on Sept. 3? (See note 41 above.)

43. Grebel to Müntzer, Sept. 5, 1524, *op. cit.,* p. 101: "Wir hand ouch sunst kein copy behalten, denn allein dess briefs, so wir zu Martino, dinem widersächer geschriben habend."

44. Grebel to Müntzer, Sept. 4, 1524, *op cit.,* p. 100: "Des Huiufen Bruder schribt," together with p. 99, "so kumpt (zu) Hansen Huiufen von Hall hie unserem mitburger und mittbruder, der by dir gewäsen ist inn kurtzen, ein Brief."

45. Grebel to Vadian, Sept. 3, 1524, *VB III,* 85: "Quod conscribam et colligam locos . . . nempe duos communes, nisi alius quispiam praeveniat, in publicum deturbaturus."

46. *Ibid.,* p. 86 "Quam ad te demigrare et abstrahi quasi a carne et costa mea, curis, studiis, vigiliis coeptisque meis."

47. Grebel to Vadian, Oct. 14, 1524. *VB III,* 88: "Tum libelli plus minus octo legendi gratia nobis cum nuncio exhibiti."

48. *Ibid.,* p. 89: "Neminem habeo fere propitium ex omni hominum congnatorum et affinium genere."

49. See note 37, above, at the end.

50. *Ibid.,* p. 89: "In patientia doceat me Christus magister noster frenare et possidere animam."

51. Hermann Barge, *Andreas Bodenstein von Carlstadt,* II, Leipzig 1905, pp. 216, 217 with proof. Here Barge repeats the assertion based on Egli, of the personal visit to Grebel and Manz to Müntzer, which I reject, pp. 35 ff. Zwingli was vexed that Carlstadt did not visit him during his stay in Zurich.

51a. *ZW IV,* 464: "Quem tamen melancholicus quorundam spiritus sic a congressu nostro deterruit, ut ne salutaverit quidem."

52. "Von dem getichten glauben," was written before December, 1523, and the "Protestation" in December, 1523. Both writings were published in 1524. See Wolfgang Metzger, "Muentzeriania," in *Thüringisch-Sächsische Zeitschrift für Geschichte und Kunst,* XVI, 1927, pp. 62-64. Both writings were finally published *in extenso* in O. H. Brandt, *Thomas Müntzer, Leben und Schriften,* pp. 126-144, Jena, 1933 but with modern spelling.

53. Grebel to Müntzer, *op. cit.,* p. 93: "Wir verstand und hand gesehen, dass du die mess vertütschet hast und nüwe gsang uffgericht. Mag nit gut sin, wann wir findet in dem nüwen Testament kein ler von singen, kein bispil."

A large part of this letter is devoted to a debate with Müntzer on this very subject. The three "Messordnungen" are reprinted by Emil Sehling in *Die evangelischen Kirchenordnungen des* 16 *Jahrhunderts,* I, Leipzig 1902, with the titles: (1) *Deutsch Kirchenampt, Alstedt* 1523; (2) *Deutsch Evangelische Messe, Alstedt* 1524; (3) *Ordnung und Verechnunge des teutschen Amptes zu Alstadt, Eylenburg,* 1524. Müntzer also published a German baptismal liturgy, the earliest of the Reformation, entitled, *Von der Taufe, wie man die heldet,* 1524. This liturgy was in use in 1523 before Luther's, but was not printed until after Luther's in 1524. It is of course, a ritual for the baptism of infants.

54. Grebel to Müntzer, *op. cit.*, p. 93. "In dem so wir semlichs merkend und beklagend, wirt zu unss heruss gebracht din schriben wider den falschen glouben und touff, sind wir nach bass bericht worden und befestet und unss wunderbarlich erfreuwt."

55. Grebel to Müntzer, *op. cit.*, p. 92: "Liber bruder Toman, lass dich umb gotz willen nit wunderen, dass wir dich ansprechend on Titel . . . und dass wir ungeforderet und dir unbekant habend gedörfen ein gmeinkünftig gsprech ufrichten."

56. Grebel to Müntzer, *op. cit.*, p. 99: "In dem so kumpt Hansen Huiufen von Hall, hie unserem mitburger und mittbruder, der by dir gewäsen ist inn kurtzen, ein brief und schantlich büchlin (an) . . . ." Grebel's statement as quoted above in note 55, that the brethren wrote to Müntzer "unrequested" and "unknown to him," suggests the inference that no one of the little group in Zurich, not even Hans Huiuf, had had personal contact with Müntzer. On the other hand two other passages might seem at first to suggest personal contact. They are as follows,—p. 95: "Dass du unserem bruder also fründtlich geloset und bekent hast dich ouch etwas ze fil nachgelassen haben;" and p. 97: "Man soll ouch dass evangelium und sine annemer nit schirmen mit dem schwert oder sy sich selbs, alss wir durch unseren brüder vernommen hand dich also meinen und halten." The second passage does not require personal contact, for it may refer merely to a report which Huiuf had heard in Saxony. The first passage suggests a personal conversation between Huiuf and Müntzer. However, a closer examination of the passage raises grave doubts as to the authenticity of the supposed conversation, for it seems scarcely possible that Müntzer would have accepted an "admonition" from Hans Huiuf and confessed to him a shortcoming; Müntzer was not likely a man to confess shortcomings; furthermore, there is no evidence that Müntzer modified his program in the direction of the ideas of Hans Huiuf and his brethren in Zurich.

Otto Schiff in "Thomas Müntzer als Prediger in Halle," (*Archiv für Ref. Gesch. XXIII* H. 3/4 pp. 287 f) and following him Karl Simon in "Die Züricher Taufer und der Hofgoldschmied Kardinal Albrechts" (*Zwingliana* (1934) VI, H.1, pp. 50-54) conclude that Huiuf conferred personally with Müntzer. Simon (*op. cit.*, p. 52) suggests a meeting "perhaps during Müntzer's journey to South Germany." This is out of the question, for Grebel's letter is addressed to "Thomas Müntzer zu Alstett am Hartz," which indicates that the Zurich brethren thought Müntzer still at his old residence and that they knew nothing of his precipitate flight from Alstett on August 7, 1524 and his activity in Mühlhausen to Sept. 27, which was not at all secret. If Huiuf met Müntzer it was before August 7. Simon is also wrong in his remark (*op. cit.*, p. 53, note 5): "Freilich klingt die Huiuffsche Unterschrift des erwähnten Briefes fast so, als ob sich die persönlichen Beziehungen nicht erst neuerdings angeknüpft, sondern bereits seit langer Zeit bestanden hätten." The signature reads, "Hans Huiuf din lantzman von Hall." There is nothing in this signature that would suggest personal contact with Müntzer at all. "Landsmann" signifies only a fellow-resident, either of Halle or of Saxony. Must all "countrymen" be personal acquaintances? Simon produces convincing evidence to support the assumption that the Huiuf of the Grebel group in Zurich was Hans Huiuf, son of the court goldsmith of Cardinal Albrecht of Mainz. O. Schiff, "Thomas Müntzer and die Bauernbewegung am Oberrhein" (*Historische Zeitschrift,* 1912, 110. Bd., pp. 67-90) contributes little to the problem of "Müntzer and the Anabaptists."

57. Grebel to Müntzer, *op. cit.,* p. 100: "Dess Huiufen bruder schribt, du habest wider die fürsten geprediget, dass man sy mit der faust angriffen solte."

58. Grebel to Müntzer, *op. cit.,* p. 101.

59. Grebel to Müntzer, *op. cit.,* p. 99.

60. *Heinrich Bullingers Reformationsgeschichte nach dem Autographen herausgg. v. J. J. Hottinger und H. H. Vögeli, Band I,* Frauenfeld, 1838, p. 237.

61. *Ibid.,* p 224.

62. Emil Egli, *Die Züricher Wiedertäufer zur Reformationszeit, Nach den Quellen des Staatsarchivs dargestellt.* Zürich, 1878, p. 19. Walter Koehler assumes the historicity of the visit to Müntzer in "Das Täufertum in der neueren kirchen-historischen Forschung" (*Archiv für Ref.-Gesch.* 37 (1940) p. 100): "Der Besuch von Grebel und Manz bei Müntzer im Herbst 1524 in der Nähe von Schaffhausen."

63. Heinrich Bullinger, *Der Widertoufferen ursprung, fürgang, Secten, wäsen, fornemme und gemeine irer leer Artickel . . . Getruckt zu Zürych bei Christoffel Froschower imm Mertzen Anno M.D.* LX. Folio 2 *recto* and *verso.*

64. Bullinger, *op. cit., Ausgabe* 1561, fol. 8 v.

65. Boehmer-Kirn, *Thomas Müntzers Briefwechsel,* p. 161.

66. Merx, *Thomas Münzer und Heinrich Pfeiffer* (1523-25). Göttinger, 1889. p. 100, note 4, summarizes Müntzers journeys in this period.

67. Otto H. Brandt, *Thomas Müntzer, Sein Leben und seine Schriften,* Jena 1933, p. 16. Merx, however, as well as others, does not bring Müntzer back to Mühlhausen till the middle of February, 1525.

68. See below in this chapter, pp. 130 ff.

69. See below, p 123. He was there with Westerburg and Carlstadt, to bring back to Zurich the newly printed booklets by Carlstadt.

70. Heinrich Bullinger, *Von dem Unverschampten fräfel der selbstgesandten Widertöufferen* Zurich, 1531, folio vii *recto.* Bullinger also says that the "Touffer" are "montanistisch," fol. xiii *verso.* Finally, folio LXXIII, "die widertoufferische Rott" is "ein Kessler gesellschaft."

71. Bullinger, *Der Widertoufferen Ursprung,* fol. 2 v.

72. Jacob Berchtold, *Das Zwinglibild und die Züricherischen Reformationschroniken.* Leipzig 1929 (*Zurich Dissertation, Band V, Quellen und Abhandlungen zur Schweizerischen Reformationsgeschichte*). This excellent work gives an exhaustive discussion of "Heinrich Bullinger als Historiker" with a section devoted to "Tendenzen in Bullinger's Geschichtschreibung." The quotation is taken from this section, p. 135.

73. *Von der Taufe wie man die heldet,* 1524. See note 53 above.

74. Grebel to Müntzer, *op. cit.,* pp. 92, 95.

75. Grebel to Müntzer, *op. cit.,* p. 93.

76. Grebel to Müntzer, *op. cit.,* pp. 98, 99.

77. Annemarie Lohmann, *Zur geistigen Entwicklung Thomas Müntzers* (*Beiträge zur Kulturgeschichte des Mittelalters und der Renaissance,* Bd. 47), Leipzig, 1931. Karl Holl, "Luther und die Schwärmer" in *Gesammelte Aufsätze zur Kirchengeschichte* I, pp. 420-467, 4 u.5.Aufl., Tübingen 1927. Heinrich Böhmer, "Thomas Müntzer und das jüngste Deutschland," in *Gesammelte Aufsätze,* pp. 187-222, Gotha, 1927.

78. Ernst Correll, *Das Schweizerische Täufermennonitentum,* Tübingen, 1925, p. 4, note 1. W. Köhler's objection, "das geht zu weit" in his article, "Die Zürcher Täufer," in *Gedenkschrift zum 400 jährigen Jubiläum der Mennoniten,* p. 49, note 1, is not valid in so far as it applies to the Zurich Anabaptists. It is not in the province of this discussion to deal with the question of Müntzer's relation to the Anabaptist movement in general. However, it might be pointed out that hitherto the chief, if not the only, connection between Müntzer and the Anabaptists, has been the supposed but legendary connection through Zurich.

79. It is not known what writings of Carlstadt Grebel read. It is possible, also, that Grebel was led to write by reading some of Luther's writings, although any attempt to name such writings must be purely speculative.

80. Grebel to Vadian, Sept. 3, 1524, *VBIII*, 85. "Thomae Münzero . . . scribo primum; forsitan et Lutherum compellabo, fiducia verbi divini percitus."

81. Erhard Hegenwalt "An cunradt Grebel und ander sin mitbrudern in Christo zu Zürich," Jan. 1, 1525, Stadtbibliothek St. Gallen, Ms. 31, 222: "Und damit ich beschlüss, hat mir Martinus empfollen (da ich yn fraget, ob er üch allen mit ein schryben wolt), ich solt üch sagen sinen grüss damit yr nit meinet er wer üch ungünstig; sprach aber, er wöst üch nit ze schriben uff sölch üwer brieff. Wass ir geschriben habt, dass wis ich nit."

82. Grebel to Müntzer, Sept. 5, 1524, *op. cit.*, pp. 99, 101.

83. *Ibid.*, p. 96.

84. *Ibid.*, p. 93.

85. *Ibid.*, p. 96.

86. Perhaps he had read Stiefel's booklet, *Das Evangelium von dem verlornen Sohn*, which was published in 1524. Two copies of this booklet are in the Zentralbibliothek in Zurich. Strauss writings are mentioned in the letter of Grebel to Vadian, July 13, 1523, *VB III*, 26. "Advehitur huc ad nos Iacobi Strussii libellus sive articuli evangelicissimi, quibus colore suo pingitur census." A copy of the booklet, which has only three pages, is to be found in the Ratschulbibliothek in Zwickau. The other two writings of Strauss mentioned above are also found in Zwickau. See Bossert's biographies of Strauss in *Allgemeine Deutsche Biographie* and *Herzog's Real-Enzyklopaedie;* Also Herman Barge's *Jakob Strauss* (*Schriften des Vereins für Reformationsgeschichte*, No. 162, 1937).

87. *ZW VIII*, p. 53, Note 5. See also the biography by Bertheau in *Allgemeine Deutsche Biographie.*

88. *ZW I*, 446, 479.

89. Hegenwalt to Grebel, Jan. 1, 1525: "Ich weiss wol, das ir ein mal (do ich noch by üch zu Zürich was) ouch schriben woltend wyder den doctoren und predicanten zu Sanct Gallen; da bat ich üch dorfür. Hant ir mir dan zemal gefolget, mein ich nit, das es üch sol gerüet han. Ich red dass des doctors halb, dem ir villicht scharff gnug geschriben hant allsament, etc."

90. Hegenwalt to Grebel, Jan. 1, 1525: "Ir werdent aber villicht antwurt finden in dem büchli, so ussgon wirt wider Karolostadium in einer gemein."

91. On Westerburg see the monograph by G. E. Steitz, *Dr. Gerhard Westerburg, der Leiter des Bürgeraufstands zu Frankfurt a.M. im Jahre* 1525 in *Archiv für Frankfurts Geschichte und Kunst*, N.F. 5(1872), pp. 1-215, also the biography by Brecher in *ADB*. An excellent account of Westerburg and his relation to the Anabaptist movement is also to be found in Karl Rembert's *Die Wiedertäufer im Herzogtum Jülich*, Berlin, 1899, pp. 33-49.

92. Grebel to Vadian, Oct. 14, 1524, *VB III*, 88; "Nuncii nomen est Gerardus Westerburg, si forte legisti eius de Sopore Animarum libellum." According to Barge, *Andreas Carlstadt*, II, 18, Westerburg's booklet is nothing but a condensation and popularization of Carlstadt's sermon *Von Stand christgläubiger Seelen*. It bears the title, *Vom Fegfewer unnd standt verscheyden selen eyn Chrystliche Meynung*, 1523.

93. *ZW VI*, 188; Jackson, op. *cit.*, 252-255.

93a. A. Hulshof, *Geschiedenis van de Doopsgezinden te Straatsburg*, Amsterdam, 1905, p. 188. The writing by Calvin is found in *Corpus Reformatorum Vol. XXXIV*, *Joannis Calvini Opera* Vol. VII, Brunsvigae, 1868, columns 45-142, under the title: *Brieve Instruction Pour Armer Tous Bons Fideles Contre Les Erreurs De La Secte Commune Des Anabaptistes.* Par M. Jehan Calvin. A Geneve, Par Jehan Gerard, 1544. The statement of contents reads: "Icy premierement sont reproves cinq articles, contenuz en une resolution composee par les patriarches de la secte, qu' ilz ont commune entre eux. Assavoir: Du Baptesme des petiz enfans. De l' excommunication. Du droit de porter armes. De la puissance des Princes. Du iurement. Item deux autres, De l' incarnation de Jesus Christ, De La vie et condition des ames entre la mort et le iour de la resurrection derniere." This last topic is the one referred to, and is treated in columns 114-137. Hulshof states in a sheet of *Stellingen* laid into his book, that the attack by Calvin against the doctrine of the sleep of souls was not in its first form (?) directed against Anabaptists but against a Reformed sect.

94. W. Köhler, in his article in the *Gendenkschrift . . . der Mennoniten*, pp. 49 f., gives a detailed account of this episode, using the documents in *Aktensammlung zur Geschichte der Basler Reformation*, I, pp. 174 f. and the Karlstadt-Bibliographie in *Zentralblatt für Bibliothekswesen*, 1904, Bd. 21, pp. 323-331. See also *Zwingli Werke* IV, p. 464, with notes. The Brötli letter is found in Egli, *Aktensammlung*, p. 302.

95. Egli, *Aktensammlung*, No. 566, p. 246, Aug. 11, 1524.

96. *Ibid.*, p. 246.

97. Egli, *Aktensammlung*, No. 618, p. 270, Jan. 12, 1525, gives the mandate for the disputation. The mandate of Jan. 18, 1525, Egli, No. 622, p. 276, says that "etlich daruf ire kind ungetoufft gelassen."

98. Benedikt Burgauer to Grebel, July 21, 1523, *VB III*, 28: "Egi quibusdam qui . . . proclamarunt . . . infantes, qui fidem propriam non habent, non baptizandos."

99. *Taufbüchlein* (1525) *ZW IV*, 228: "Do man aber das so blümplig hatt angenomen, die Zeichen vestend den glouben, do hatt man je müssen dem kindertouff widerreden; denn der kond in den kinden den glouben nit vesten, so sy nit gluben könnend."

100. See the collection of evidence in John Horsch, *Infant Baptism, Its origin among Protestants and the Arguments advanced for and against it*, Scottdale, Pennsylvania, 1917, pp. 13-28.

101. So feared *Chorherr* Konrad Hofmann in his complaint against Zwingli in December, 1521, published in Egli, *Aktensammlung* No. 213, p. 64: "Für neue Lehren über Dinge des Glaubens oder der Sitten, so bezüglich der Kindlein, sollte Zwingli Nachweis bei einem merklichen und guten Lehrer finden."

102. Hubmaier's testimony concerning it is found in *Ein gesprech Balthasar Hübmörs von Fridberg Doctors, Auf Mayster Ulrichs Zwinglens zu Zürch Tauffbüchlen von dem Kindertauff*, Nicolspurg 1526, fol. Diii b: ". . . 1523. Und darnach im selben jar umb Philippi unnd Jacobi (May 1) hab ich mit dir persönlich conferiert die schrifften von den touff auf dem Zürchgraben. Da hastu mir recht geben, dass man die kinder nit touffen solle, ee sy im glauben underricht seyent." Cited from *ZW IV*, 228-9. But already in December of the previous year, 1525, Hubmaier had made the same statement regarding Zwingli's position, in the discussion with Zwingli and others. George Binder reports in his letter to Vadian, Dec. 20, 1525, *VB III*, 128: "Balthazar narrationem longam orsus dixit . . . Zvinglium enim (cum quo argumentum hoc primum contulerit) olim Tiguri dixisse: pueros, antequam fidem essente docti, non esse baptizandos, idque in articulis suis scripsisse." Binder angrily rejected the accusation with these words: "Quod, quam falsum sit et minime verum tute ipse in proximo concilio audivisti. Ecce quam invidia atque odium 'pseudobaptistous' illos excaecaverit."

103. Hubmaier did not relinquish infant baptism in Waldshut until January, 1525. See his letter to Oekolampad, Jan. 16, 1525, *Briefe und Akten zum Leben Oekolampad*, I, pp. 341-344.

104. *Taufbüchlein, Zwingli Werke* IV, 228: "Denn der irrtumb hat ouch mich vor etwas jaren verfürt, das ich meint, es wäre vil wäger man touffte die kindle erst, so sy zu gutem alter komen wärend."

105. Grebel's *Protestation und Schutzschrift, ZW III,* 371: "Bin gewüss, meister Ulrich disse tauffs meinung alsso verstan und vil bas dan wir, aber weiss nicht, auss was ursach nicht öffnen." Grebel makes the same statement about Jud und Grossmann. Egli, *Aktensammlung,* No. 622, p. 314: "So zwifle er ouch nit dann dass Löw, Kaspar, und allsammen wol Wüssins, dass man die Kinder nit also toufen söllte, wenn si öchter die warheit sägen wöllind."

106. Balthasar Hubmaier's testimony in his *Gesprech, op. cit.,* fol. D 3 b: "Ja, du hast es also gehalten, geschriben und predigt an offenlicher cantzel; das haben vil hundert menschen gehört auss deinem mund gen." Cited from *ZW II,* pp. 228-229. Hans Hottinger's testimony is found in Egli, *Aktensammlung,* No. 655, p. 291, Feb. 25, 1525: "Ich weiss nit, wess ich mich fröwen soll. Hüt prediget er eins, morn widerrüefet er's. Und namlich hat er prediget vor jaren, dass man die kindlin nit taufen sölle, jetz aber sagt er, man sölle sie taufen." The third testimony is found in a letter from the time soon after Zwingli's death, published by Fiala in *Anzeiger für Schweizer Geschichte,* N.F.II, 1874-1877, pp. 334-339. "Und derselbig Jakob Grebel hatt ein Sunn, der fast wol gelert unnd geschickt was. Der hört ein predig von Zwinglin, das man die kinnd nit solt douffen. Das lart er unnd sine gsellen in den dörffern, unnd fieng an die altten lütt zu touffen." This however seems to have been written by a Catholic opponent of Zwingli.

107. "Grebel sagte: er wellti gern mit dem Zwingli disputieren: dann der Zwingli habe in in die sach bracht und im mängs gseit, darin er im jetz kein bestand welle gen, und jetz im hindersich gang." Egli, *Aktensammlung* No. 797, p. 378, Aug. 9, 1525 (incorrectly dated, really July according to von Muralt). In a very interesting and valuable letter of Georg Binder to Vadian, Dec. 20, 1525 (*VB III,* 128) the following passage is found: "Balthazar narrationem longam orsus dixit, se Zvinglii verbis et scriptis et aliorum in hanc sententiam commotum inisse."

108. J. M. Usteri, "Darstellung der Tauflehre Ulrich Zwinglis," in *Theol. Studien und Kritiken* 1882, p. 208.

109. See Oekolampad's letter to Zwingli Nov. 21, 1524, *ZW VIII,* 252, and Oekolampad's letter to Hubmaier, Jan. 18, 1525, *Briefe und Akten zum Leben Oekolampads* I, 344.

110. Gerhard Roussel to Oekolampad, Aug. 24, 1524, *Briefe und Akten zum Leben Oekolampads* I, 312: "Itemque de parvulis citra baptismi gratiam degentibus, quod audiam quendam apud vos esse, qui baptismum ad annos discretionis differendum scribat." Erasmus had also heard of the argument about infant baptism for he wrote in the summer of 1524 from Basel, "Schon sind viele Gegner der Kindertaufe" (reported in Keller, *Die Reformation und die älteren Reformparteien,* Leipzig, 1885, with reference to *Erasmi opera* 1703, III, p. 804). In a letter to Tunstall, which Allen dates June, 1523, Erasmus writes as follows: "Nam anarchiam iam pridem mussant ii, quos Anabaptistas vocant: aluntur et alia dogmatum monstra, quae, si proruperint, efficient ut Lutherus propemodum orthodoxus videri possit. Mussatur et illud, baptismum nec in adultis nec in parvulis esse necessarium." (Allen, *op. cit.,* V, 295.) But the dating is certainly incorrect, and must be June, 1525, which date the letter itself bears.

Ulrich Hugwald had already in 1522 defended infant baptism against those who attacked it. See *Propositiones Ulrichi Hugualdi,* printed as an appendix to *Der Wiedertäufer Ulrich Hugwald* by Otto Clemens (*Beiträge zur Reformationsgeschichte, zweites Heft,* Berlin, 1902, 45-85). Propositio No. 42 (p. 80) reads as follows: "Quare vehementer errant hoc loco, qui velint nullos baptisari nisi qui credunt et iam parati sunt Christum assumere, qui mos olim fuit philosophorum sectis." Horsch, *Infant Baptism,* p. 27 misreads Keller, *op. cit.,* p. 374, for Hugwald had not demanded believers' baptism as Horsch says, but rather had defended infant baptism against those who would have believers' baptism only.

111. Proof in John Horsch, *Infant Baptism,* pp. 24, 25 with footnotes 36-38; See also J. M. Usteri: "Die Stellung der Strassburger Reformatorem Capito

und Butzer zur Tauffrage" in *Theol. Stud. und Krit,* 1884, pp. 456-525. Urbanus Rhegius reports criticism of infant baptism and agitation for believers' baptism in Constance early in 1524, as Horsch points out, *op. cit.,* p. 27, on the basis of *Briefwechsel der Brüder Ambrosius und Thomas Blaurer* I, Freiburg, 1908, p. 94.

112. Vadian an Grebel, Dec. 28, 1524, *VB III,* 99. Grebel could not understand why Vadian did not act according to his knowledge. His letter to Vadian, May 30, 1525, *VB III,* 116 he writes: "Tu probas doctrinam, Zinlius improbat; quid expectas ergo, cum scias prius . . . . Si sana est doctrina, ut sana est, ut tu quocunque animo fateris."

113. Grebel to Vadian, Dec. 15, 1524, *VB III,* 96: "Andere, die göttliche warheit verstanden habend von dem touff, wellend ire kind nit touffen lassen; sind von minen herren gemant, doch bestanden. Do hand (sy) recht begert und angeruft und appelliert uff die geschrift. Do hand bed rett beschlossen, dass alle die den kindertouff widerkristlich sagend und ire kindli nit touffen wellend, gegen den dry hirten ire gründ bewisind und die hirten ire widerumm, in bywäsen vierer uss den retten."

114. Blanke gives a thorough critical discussion of the problem of the Tuesday meetings in his commentary on the *Elenchus,* in *ZW VI,* pp. 37-40. I differ from him only in rejecting the identification of the discussion which Grebel reported in his letter to Vadian of December 15, 1524, as one of the Tuesday meetings. Three reasons speak against the identification: (1) Grebel reports the Zwinglian representatives to be the three pastors and four councillors, whereas Zwingli reports once that they were Zwingli, Jud, Grossman, and Myconius (Blanke, *op. cit.,* p. 37, note 3), and at another place (Blanke, *op. cit.,* p. 38, note 5) that the group consisted of all the Zurich preachers. (2) According to Grebel only one opponent of infant baptism spoke, but according to Zwingli several took part in the discussion. (3) Grebel reports that the council had decided to hold one more meeting, whereas Zwingli states that the council had decided to hold no more meetings (letter of Zwingli to Franz Lambert, Dec. 16, 1525). The three sources for Zwingli's statements are: "Brief an Franz Lambert und die anderen Brüder in Strassburg," *ZW VIII,* pp. 261 ff.; *Taufbüchlein, ZW* IV, p. 207, 286, 257; *Elenchus, ZW VIII,* p. 37 et passim. For details see Blanke's discussion.

115. Elenchus, *op. cit.,* p. 37, note 4, where Blanke gives the translation.

116. Grebel's comments on this point are to be found in his *Protestation und Schutzschrift* which he probably wrote at the beginning of December or late November (Egli dates it at the beginning of 1525 in *Reformationsgeschichte* I, p. 297). Köhler published the first critical edition in *Zwingli Werke* III, 1914, pp. 368-372, with historical introduction. Neff published a reprint of Köhler's edition in *Gedenkschrift,* pp. 128-133. Bender and Correll published an English translation with introduction and notes in *Goshen College Record Review Supplement,* Jan. 1926, pp. 23-31. Schuler and Schulthess had published extracts in *Zwingli Opera,* 1834, pp. 231 ff. Staub printed a complete but uncritical edition in *Die Beziehungen des Täufers Konrad Grebel zu seinem Schwager Vadian,* Zurich, 1895, pp. 71-76. The quotations given below are taken from Köhler in *ZW III.*

117. The first proof that the Brethren were considered a faction is found in Grebel's letter to Vadian, Dec. 15, 1524, *VB III,* 97. "Ouch uff unser genenten party hie fröw ich mich, dass gott richter ist."

118. "Protestation und Schutzschrift," *op. cit.,* p. 368.

119. Already in his letter to Müntzer, Sept. 5, 1524, *op. cit.,* p. 100, Grebel had foreseen the coming persecution: "Wir werdend ouch mit der zitt sächen die verfolgung durch sy uber uns gan."

120. Vadian to Grebel, Dec. 28, 1524, *VB III,* 99.

121. *Taufbüchlein, ZW IV,* 207, cited in Blanke, *op. cit.,* p. 37, note 1.

122. Cited in Blanke, *op. cit.*, p. 41, note 1, from Heberle, "Die Anfänge des Anabaptismus in der Schweiz" in *"Jahrbücher für deutsche Theologie"* III, 1858, p. 275, who has the citation from Hetzer's introduction to his translation of Oekolampad's booklet, *De Eucharistia,* 1526.

123. Vadian to Grebel, Dec. 28, 1524, *loc. cit.*

124. Grebel to Vadian, Jan. 14, 1525, *VB III,* 104.

125. It is noteworthy that Grebel refers to infant baptism as a "Roman" institution, and thereby gives expression to the characteristic "evangelical" spirit of the Reformation. The expression is significant in evaluating the Anabaptists as the fourth Reformation type. Grebel is not thinking of sectarianism or revolution, but feels himself a thorough "evangelical" demanding only a thoroughly consistent application of the two basic principles of the Reformation, the "Materialprinzip" (*sola fide*) and the "Schriftprinzip" (*sola scriptura*).

126. *Ibid.*: "Etlich sagend, man werd den doctor von Walltzhut auch beschriben. Ich gloubs aber nit; denn er ist wider den Zwingli dess toufs halb und wirt wider in schriben, so er nit abstatt."

127. Hubmaier to Oekolampad, January 16, 1525. *Briefe und Akten zum Leben Oekolampads* I, Leipzig 1927, pp. 341-343: "Scripsi de baptismate XXII conclusiones cum 64 notulis adiectis; ea omnia propediem videbis." In this letter Hubmaier also mentions the approaching disputation at Zurich on infant baptism: "Hoc die, qui in albo doctorum sunt Tiguri, conveniunt de baptismate parvulorum, scripturae locos collaturi. Ubi Zwinglis cum suo Leone per diapason dissidet a nobis."

128. In the discussion of an undated letter of Hubmaier to Zwingli (*ZW VIII,* 254-255, where the date of the letter is set in November, 1524) the editors of Zwingli's letters surmise that Hubmaier passed through Zurich on his journey from Schaffhausen to Waldshut at the end of October, 1524. The letter contains a request for instruction on baptism, and "setzt sichtlich voraus, dass er kürzlich in Zürich war." I accept this dating and the visit in Zurich as a proved fact, and find further evidence for it in Grebel's recent relation to Hubmaier.

129. *Geschichtbuch der Hutterischen Brüder,* 1923, p. 34: "Indem begab es sich, dass einer von Chur zu ihnen kam, nämlich ein Pfaff mit Namen Georg vom Haus Jakob, den man sonst hat genannt Blawrock . . . Der ist auch zum Zwingel erstlich kommen und von Glaubenssachen viel mit ihm gehandlet und geredt, aber nichts ausgerichtet. Da ward ihm gesagt, dass andere Männer da seien, die eifriger sein dann der Zwingel. Welchen Männern er fleissig nachgefragt und ist zu ihnen kommen, nämlich zum Konrad Grebel und Felix Mantzen und hat mit ihnen geredt und sich ersprächt Glaubenssachen halb. Seind auch der Sachen eins wurden mit einander."

CHAPTER VIII. TRIUMPH UNDER PERSECUTION, 1525-25

1. Sources for this period are scant. Two of Grebel's letters belong here, one to Vadian, May 30, 1525, and one to Castelberger at the end of May, 1525. The chief sources are the various pertinent documents in Egli's *Aktensammlung,* 1525 and 1526. Kessler's *Sabbata* also contains valuable material.

2. Only Bullinger records this disputation, having attended it as a young man of 20 years (*Heinrich Bullinger's Diarium, Quellen zur Schweizerischen Reformationsgeschichte* II, Basel, 1904). He wrote minutes for an Anabaptist disputation (*Diarium,* p. 16). Was it the one of January, 1525, as Egli thinks? (See *Diarium,* p. 9, note 4.) The description, as given in his *Reformationsgeschichte* I, p. 238, is very brief. According to his account only Reublin was active in the disputation besides Grebel and Manz. The two mandates are found in Egli, *Aktensammlung,* No. 622, p. 276, Jan. 18, 1525, and No. 624, p. 278, Jan. 21, 1525. It is possible that Georg Cajacob received his name "Blaurock" on this occasion.

The Hutterian *Geschichtbuch,* p. 34, reports the following concerning it: "Denn als sie eines mals ein Gespräch gehabt von Glaubenshändeln in einer Versammlung, da redet dieser Georg vom Haus Jakob auch darzu sein Erkanntnis. Da fraget man, welcher jetzt geredt hätte. Darauf einer sprach: Der im Blaben Rock hätte geredt. Also bekam er den Namen darnach, vonwegen, dass er ein blaben Rock getragen hat." If this account is reliable, it has reference to the first disputation in Zurich, where Blaurock, as a stranger, appeared in public the first time.

3. The above dating is derived from the documents. Egli *Aktensammlung* No. 636, document 4, pp. 284-286, should probably be dated February 5, rather than January 29 as Egli thinks without evident cause. It would be difficult to believe that a week elapsed between the hearing on January 29 and the sentence on February 7. Document 1, p. 283, contains a statement by Hans Oggenfuss, according to which Grebel had held communion services in Jakob Hottinger's house in Zollikon about two weeks earlier. That must have taken place January 23, at the latest. It is hardly possible it could have been seven days earlier, for that would have been one day before the disputation of January 17. At this communion service however evidently no one was baptized, *Terminus ad quem* for the first adult baptism would therefore be about January 23 or 24. *Terminus a quo* is determined by Zwingli's assertion in the *Elenchus* (*Zwingli Werke* VI, 40), that the news of the first adult baptisms reached him three or at most four days after the last discussion, that is after January 17. The meetings were first forbidden in the mandate of January 21. I do not believe that adult baptism was introduced before this interdiction, before the seriousness of the situation became fully evident to the brethren. In this conclusion I differ somewhat from Blanke, who has thoroughly examined the question in his commentary to the *Elenchus.* In my judgment Blanke's acceptance of January 30 for the date of Egli's document No. 636 is not sound.

I cannot agree with the view that the first adult baptism must without question have taken place in Zollikon, as is commonly held. The statements of the witnesses in No. 636 do not agree, but so much is certain, that Jakob Hottinger was baptized in his own home in Zollikon by Felix Manz in the presence of Georg Blaurock with Grebel not present. If however the first baptism had taken place in Zollikon, Hottinger would surely have been present. It would probably be better to place the first adult baptism on the evening of January 21 in a small group in Zurich, probably at the home of Felix Manz. On the following days further baptisms were performed in various places in Zollikon, chiefly by Manz and Blaurock. The baptism of a group of 15 persons, of which Zwingli heard, and concerning which Marx Bosshart testifies in No. 636, document 1, did take place in Jacob Hottinger's house. It is noteworthy that among the names of those baptized in Zollikon none appears of those who had joined Grebel in writing the letter to Müntzer, except Johannes Brötli. Hans Oggenfuss was not yet baptized as late as February 6. Hans Huiuf and Heinrich Aberli were also baptized later. Wilhelm Reublin is not among those baptized at Zollikon. It is therefore clear that there was no unified and organized plan of procedure among the brethren. Prof. Blanke of Zurich identifies the house of the first baptism as the "Obristen Haus" in Zollikon.

Margarete Hottinger of Zollikon asserted as a witness at a trial: "Dann wie Grebel und Manz zuo inen gen Zollikon kommen sygind und inen da glesen und von den dingen gredt habind, da habe sich noch niemas lassen toufen (i.e. before January 17), bis dass Blawrock kommen syge; der habe zum ersten angefangen ze toufen." Egli, *Aktensammlung,* No. 692, p. 311.

4. Blaurock's testimony on this point, given February 18, 1525, is found in Egli, *Aktensammlung,* No. 646, p. 289: "Jörg vom hus Jakob von Chur seit: er wüsse nit anders, dann dass er der erst gsin syge, so sich habe lassen toufen und vom tisch des Herrn gegessen." In his "Bekenntniss" of March, 1526, Blaurock

had written: "Ein anfenger des toufs Cristi und des Herren brots bin ich's mit sampt mine userwelte briederen in Christo Konraden Grebel und Felix Manz." Egli, *Aktensammlung* No. 933, p. 443.

5. *Geschichtbuch der Hutterischen Brüder,* 1923, p. 35.

6. Egli gives a good summary of the early activity in his *Schweizerische Reformationsgeschichte* I, 1916, pp. 326-327. Jakob Hottinger's description given in testimony before court is vivid and most interesting. Egli, *Aktens.*, p. 284.

6a. The phrase "rose-red blood of Christ," used by Blaurock and found in testimony given by Jakob Hottinger in February, 1525 concerning Blaurock's preaching (Egli,*Aktensammlung,* p. 284) may be an echo of the title of a Strauss booklet of 1524 bearing the title, *Ain schone liepliche Unnderricht, zu bedencken unnd empfahenn den kostbarlichen hayligesten leib Christi und sein rossenfar-besplut zu nyessenn,* Augsburg, 1524.

7. Egli, *Aktensammlung,* February 6, 1525, No. 636, p. 283, document IIe: Hans Ockenfuoss Antwurt.—"Es syg ouch bi 14 tagen, da wäre er zuo Zollikon in Jakob Hottingers hus. Da seite Kuonrat Grebel und andere, die redtind vom touf und nachtmal. Darnach zerschnitte der Grebel ein brot, und teilte es under si; darvon esse er ouch, der gstalt, dass si nun fürhin ein christenlich leben füeren und halten wölltind."

8. Egli, *Aktensammlung,* p. 285. The witness was Kläwi Kienast.

9. Egli, *Aktensammlung,* February 18, 1525, No. 645, p. 288.

10. Johannes Kessler, *Sabbata,* 1902, p. 144.

11. Egli, *Aktensammlung,* March 7, 1526, No. 934, p. 444, does not give Anna Manz's statement in his abstract.

12. Kessler, *loc. cit.*: "In dem hat sich begeben, das der eegenannt Cunrat Grebel (wie obstat) uss der statt und landschaft Zürich abgewichen, ob er anderen enden möchte sinen widertouf bereden, anzepfen und fürnemlich in den evangelischen stetten und länder die gelerten predicanten überloffen und angewendt, ob er die mochte sinens widertoufs bereden, damit der handel mer für schub und ansechens gewünne."

13. Egli, *Aktensammlung,* March 16-25, 1525, No. 674, pp. 301-302, the letter of Johannes Brötli of Hallau to Fridli Schumacher and other fellow believers in Zollikon: "Sind wir gen Schaffhausen gangen, Ja, wir hand unseren lieben bruoder Kuonrad Grebel da funden. Wir sind bi den Doctoren beiden gesin und hand mit inen ze nacht gessen." Two weeks later Brötli reports: "Kuonrat Grebel ist betrüebt, aber in Christo."

14. Joh. Strickler, *Aktensammlung zur Schweizerischen Reformationsgeschichte in den Jahren* 1521-1532, Zurich, 1878, under date of February 1, 1525, No. 985, p. 336.

15. Egli, *Aktensammlung,* No. 674. See note 13 above.

16. From Hubmaier's book, *Der uralten und gar neuen Leerern Urtail, Das man die jungen Kindlen nit tauffen solle, biss sy im glauben underricht sind.* (Nikolsburg, 1526), cited from C. A. Baechtold, *Die Schaffhauser Wiedertäufer in der Reformationszeit in Beiträge zur vaterländischen Geschichte,* Vol. 7, Schaffhausen, 1900, p. 87. Baechtold quotes from Kirchhofer, *Hofmeister,* p. 430, note 70.

17. Egli, *Aktensammlung,* February 10, 1525, No. 638, p. 286.

18. Baechtold, *op. cit.,* p. 92.

19. Egli, *Aktensammlung,* No. 692, p. 313, incorrectly dated April, 1525, by Egli; it should be either November, 1525, or March-April, 1526, preferably November, 1525.

20. According to a statement by Hofmeister (Egli, *Aktensammlung,* No. 692, pp. 309-310), Grebel was still in Schaffhausen after De Coct's second ride to Zurich. De Coct died soon after, about March 20. See note 33 below.

21. (Conrad Grebel) to (Andreas Castelberger), undated and without address or superscription but certainly written at the end of May, printed for the

first time in original Latin and in English and German translations, in *MQR I*, No. 3 (July, 1927), pp. 41-53 where the introduction gives detailed proof for date, author and addressee.

22. Egli, *Aktensammlung,* Nov. 18, 1525, No. 863, p. 406.

23. The wife of Hans von Waldkirch was a Grebel but not a sister of Conrad, as Bächthold and after him Wipf have asserted. Baechtold, *op. cit.,* p. 103. Jakob Wipf, *Reformationsgeschichte der Stadt und Landschaft Schaffhausen.* Zurich, 1929, p. 187. See Chapter I, footnote 30 for proof.

24. See note 37 below.

25. *ZW VIII,* 143, note 4, on the basis of various letters in A. L. Herminjard, *Correspondence des Reformateurs dans les pays de Langue Francaise,* I, Paris, 1896.

26. Herminjard, *op. cit.,* p. 313.

27. *Ibid.,* p. 308.

28. *Ibid.,* p. 312.

29. *Ibid.,* p. 339, Myconius to Anemund de Coct, before Feb. 20, 1525.

30. *Ibid.,* p. 137.

31. See note 29 above.

32. Egli, *Aktensammlung,* No. 692, p. 309.

33. *Ibid.,* pp. 301-310.

34. *Ibid.,* p. 310. See Egli, *Aktensammlung,* Nos. 646, 668.

35. Zwingli to Vadian, March 31, 1525, *ZW VIII,* 313-314. I agree with the view of the editor (note 3, p. 313), that Zwingli was mistaken in reporting that Grebel was still in Zurich on March 31. He evidently did not know that Grebel was in St. Gall as early as March 25.

36. Kessler, *Sabbata,* p. 143. See Benedict Burgauer to Grebel, July 21, 1523, *VB III,* 28.

37. Kessler, *op. cit.,* p. 144. "Uliman, wie er vormals durch den Laurenzen Hochrütiner wider den kindertouf underricht, ist er uf der fart zu Schaffhausen an den Cunrat Grebel gestossen und by im in so hoche erkantnus des widertoufens kommen, das er nit wolt mit ainer schüssel mit wasser allein begossen, sunder ganz nackend und bloss hinus in dem Rhin von dem Grebel undergetruckt und bedeckt werden."

38. Concerning the Anabaptist movement in St. Gall, see Emil Egli, *Die St. Galler Täufer,* Zürich, 1887, and John Horsch, "The Swiss Brethren in St. Gall and Appenzell" in *MQR VII* (1933), pp. 205-226. Both rely materially on Kessler's account of the Anabaptists of St. Gall, *op. cit.,* pp. 143-149. Ninck's account, *Arzt und Reformator Vadian,* 109-119 is not original and is derisive only.

39. Kessler, *op. cit.,* p. 145.

40. *Ibid.,* p. 145.

41. *Fridolin Sichers Chronik, herausgegeben von Ernst Götzinger,* St. Gallen, 1885, p. 190. "Do hub ain hie zu Sant Gallen die sect des widertofs, das eben ganz überhand hat. Lufend aim sontag in das wasser henab, hiess die Sitteren, glich als obs ain process were."

42. Bullinger, *Reformationsgeschichte* I, p. 289.

43. Gabriel Giger to brethren and sisters at Zollikon, Egli, *Aktensammlung,* Aug. 5, 1525, No. 795, p. 377: "Es sind wol fünf hundert menschen getouft in dem cristelichen touf uf dem land und in der stadt."

44. Egli, *St. Galler Täufer,* p. 32, based on *Ratsbuch St. Gallen,* 1525, *May* 12.

45. Kessler, *op. cit.,* p. 149. According to Kessler, p. 144, Grebel had earlier sent a letter of four sheets to the Brethren at St. Gall, apparently at the time when Kessler was still conducting Bible classes, and, according to Hochrütiner, after the question of the baptism of infants had already been raised. "Nit lang darnach schickt der oftgemelt C. Grebel ainen vierboginen Brief an die brüder, denen ich sölte vorlassen, wie alle die red, so ich des toufs halben geredt, werend uss dem tüfel; vermanet sy ernstlich sy vor mir ze hüten. Wie mir nun die brüder

den brief überantwurtend und verlesen, vermanet ich sy entgegen." See the Sabbata *Kommentar,* p. 561, also Egli's *St. Galler Täufer* (Zurich, 1887) pp. 36-38, also the "Beilage," pp. 55-56, which reprints the minutes of the council on this matter. See also note 26 of Chapter IX below.

46. See note 35 above.

47. Zwingli to Vadian, May 28, 1525, *ZW VIII,* 330-334.

48. Grebel to Vadian, May 30, 1525, *VB III,* 116-118.

49. Egli, *Aktensammlung,* Aug. 2, 1525, No. 792, p. 372. The dating, "am vergangenen Osterfeiertage," is missing in the transcript of the testimony given by Egli, but is in the original according to L. von Muralt. Egli (*Züricher Täufer*) tried to exploit this visit of Grebel against him.

50. The time cannot be definitely determined and is set only by the time of the departure from St. Gall and the sojourn in Oberwinterthur.

51. See note 21 above.

52. Grebel to Vadian, *op. cit.,* p. 117. "Credisne, insanos esse nos aut toto inferno, nedum daemonibus plenos, qui parati simus usque in mortem testari, in aem autem, quam Zinlius et alli parant, dum veritatem in mendacio detinent?"

53. Egli, *Aktensammlung,* No. 763, p. 360.

54. *Staatsarchiv Zürich* EII 433, p. 80. Not in Egli's *Aktensammlung.*

55. See L. v. Muralt, article "Grüningen," in *Mennonitisches Lexikon* II, pp. 193-195.

56. In his article, "Die Revolution 1525 und das Täufertum" in the *Gedenkschrift zum 400 jährigen Jubiläum der Mennoniten oder Taufgsinnten,* Ludwigshafen 1925, B. H. Unruh has discussed the social demands of that time in greater detail. "Göttliches Recht" was of course one of the principal ideas in the pamphlets of the period. It is worthy of note that Grebel took up this slogan (see text), which proves, no doubt, that the Zurich Brethren also desired a social reform; but if so, it was a reform of such a nature that the essential character of the church would remain untouched. For a basic discussion of major differences between Anabaptism, peasant movements, and related socio-economic movements and theories see Ernst Correll, *Schweiz. Täufer-Mennonitentum,* pp. 13, 29f., 39f., 42-51.

56a. The activities of Manz in Chur are graphically reported in a letter of the Council of Chur to the Council of Zurich, July 18, 1525, in Egli, *Aktensammlung,* No. 776, p. 367. Manz probably had returned to Chur soon after he was released from prison in Zurich (on March 25, 1525, he was still in prison, Egli *Aktensammlung,* No. 675, p. 304). Blaurock reports concerning his activity in Chur and Appenzell and his imprisonment in Chur, Egli, *Aktensammlung* No. 692, pp. 310-311. As early as August, 1525, some "sisters" from Chur had met in "Sister" Manz's house, Egli, *Aktensammlung,* August, 1525, No. 795, p. 377. Also on May 25, 1525, Salandronius wrote to Zwingli from Chur, "Grebelliani et Mantzii spiritus in nostris montibus spirant." *ZW VIII,* p. 329.

57. Egli, *Aktensammlung,* July 12, 1526, No. 770, p. 364.

58. Egli, *Aktensammlung,* March 12, 1526, No. 938, p. 446.

59. Egli, *Die Züricher Wiedertäufer,* p. 42.

60. Egli, *Aktensammlung,* July 11, 1525, No. 768, p. 363. A certain Ulrich Ryhener says: "So nun Marx Bosshart jetz verschiner tagen entwichen was, hat in sin volk zuo Marxen Bossharten gschickt gen Bäretschwil, damit er nüt mit dem Grebeli hin und her umbhin gienge, sonder daselbs blibe." The joint letter of petition to the council of Zurich also testifies to the cooperation. See note 62 below.

61. Egli, *Aktensammlung,* July 11, 1525, No. 767, p. 362.

62. Egli, *Aktensammlung,* July 6, 1525, No. 766, p. 362. The letter is incomplete in *Egli.* It was published in full in English translation by Correll and Bender in the *Goshen College Record Review Supplement,* January, 1926, pp. 31-32.

63. Egli, *Aktensammlung,* July 11, 1525, No. 767, p. 362.
64. Egli, *Aktensammlung,* Aug. 2, 1525, No. 791, p. 372.
65. Egli, *Aktensammlung,* Aug., 1525, No. 795, p. 376.
66. Egli, *Aktensammlung,* August 9, 1525 (to be dated in July according to L. von Muralt, see No. 770), No. 797, pp. 378-379, incomplete in *Egli.* The citations offered here are from a copy of the document in the Staatsarchiv in Zurich made by Ernst Correll.
67. L. v. Muralt, "Jörg Berger" in *Zwingliana* V, 107 (1930).
68. Egli, *Aktensammlung,* Aug. 9, 1525, No. 796, p. 378.
69. Egli, *Aktensammlung,* March 12, 1525, No. 938, pp. 446-447.
70. See L. v. Muralt, "Jörg Berger," *op. cit.,* and Egli, *Aktensammlung,* passim.
71. Egli, *Aktensammlung,* Sept. 20, 1525, No. 824, pp. 391-392.
72. Egli, *Aktensammlung,* Oct. 8, 1525, No. 837, p. 395; Oct. 12, 1525, No. 841, p. 397. See also Von Muralt, "Jörg Berger," *op. cit.,* p. 108.
73. Egli, *Aktensammlung,* October 8, 1525, No. 837, p. 395; Oct. 31, No. 850, p. 400.
74. Zwingli to Vadian, Oct. 11, 1525, *ZW VIII,* 382-383. "Cunhardus Grebelius cum Georgio isto, mota mente homine, Grüeningae captus est ac in nervum coniectus; quaesivit semper malis avibus bene ingeniatus aliquam tragoediam; nunc nactus est." Zwingli is afraid that the father, Jacob Grebel, an influential member of the council, will defend his son. "Faxit deus optimus, ut nihil eius verbum offendatur; nam quidam soceri tales sunt, ut non modo parum spei, sed etiam parum fidei illis tribuam." It was the first and only time Grebel was arrested.
75. Egli, *Züricher Wiedertäufer,* p. 41. The following quotations are taken from the same source, pages 41 and 42.
76. Von Muralt, "Jörg Berger," *op. cit.,* p. 107.
77. Von Muralt, article "Grüningen," *Mennonitisches Lexikon* II, p. 193.
78. Egli, *Aktensammlung,* Nov. 1525, No. 853, p. 401. Berger's recommendation, Egli, No. 845, p. 399.
79. Egli, *Aktensammlung,* November 1525, No. 873, pp. 409-410.
80. Bullinger, *Reformationsgeschichte* I, pp. 294-298.
81. Egli, *Aktensammlung,* November 1525, No. 864, p. 406.
82. Von Muralt, "Jörg Berger," *op. cit.,* pp. 115-116.
83. Von Muralt's qualifying statement, "die keine organisierte Kirche und keinen Staat braucht," which is found in the sentence cited, is not supported by the evidence given. All Anabaptist history shows that the Brethren wanted a well-organized church, and that they established one as soon as possible. It was of course not a state Church nor a pastors' and theologians' Church, but a brotherhood. Perhaps von Muralt also makes this distinction, but if so it is not clearly expressed.
84. The record of the trial in Egli, *Aktensammlung,* No. 692, pp. 308-314.
85. Horsch has a collection of citations on this subject in his article, "An Inquiry into the Truth of Accusations of Fanaticism and Crime against the Early Swiss Brethren, II," *Mennonite Quarterly Review* VIII, 76, April, 1934. See, e.g., *ZW IV,* 206, 316, and III, 406, 872.
86. Zwingli to Vadian, May 28, 1525, *ZW VIII,* 332: "omnes pugnae priores lusus fuerunt prae ista."
87. The mandate of March 7, 1526 (*Egli* No. 934) imprisons the Anabaptists in the New Tower (Hexenturm). According to Zwingli's letter of March 7 to Vadian (*ZW VIII,* 542) the condemned Brethren were put into the same tower where they had been before ("in eam turrim, in qua prius delituerunt").
88. See the statements of the various prisoners concerning their activity, in Egli, *Aktensammlung* No. 933, p. 443.
89. Egli, *Aktensammlung,* No. 691, p. 308, to be dated March or April, 1526. See note 84 above.

90. Egli, *Aktensammlung,* March 5 and 6, 1526, No. 933, pp. 442-444. The hearing is incompletely reported in Egli. For instance, Grebel's important answer is lacking: "Er wölle auch darbringen, das Zwingli in denen und vil anderen Dingen irre, und pitt ouch mine herren, das im ouch gunind zu schriben wie dem Zwinglin, so wölle er bewyssen. Er find es sich darin dass ers nit darthuy, wöllt er darumb liden was Gott wöll." (Cited from the transcript by Ernst Correll.) This quotation is very important for the dating of Grebel's booklet which Zwingli discusses in the *Elenchus*. See note 102 below.

91. Egli, *Aktensammlung,* March 7, 1526, No. 934, p. 444. The sentence was very severe and was evidently decided upon in this form only after a debate in the Council. Zwingli evidently defended the severe sentence and wrote somewhat mockingly and with malicious joy about it to Vadian on the day of the sentence, *ZW VIII,* 542: "Est . . . hoc ipso die per senatum diakosion decretum, ut catabaptistarum coryphaei in eam turrim in qua prius delituerunt coniicantur, pane et aqua delicientur, donec aut spiritum reddant aut manus. Additum quoque, ut, qui posthac tingatur, prorsus mergatur: lata iam sententia. Socer senatus misericordiam nequicquam imploravit." Conrad's father, Jacob Grebel, it is clear, favored the milder punishment. (Staehelin, *Huldreich Zwingli* II, p. 44, translates the last sentence incorrectly.) Already at the first imprisonment of his son, Oct. 8, 1525, the father seems to have used his influence toward mildness, for at that time Zwingli expressed to Vadian his dissatisfaction and distrust toward the elder Grebel: Zwingli to Vadian, Oct. 11, 1525, *ZW VIII,* 383. See note 74 above. The animosity of Zwingli toward the elder Grebel increased from that time on until it finally brought death to the old man. See note 107 below. The bitterness of tone against the Anabaptists in Zwingli's letter of March 7 to Vadian, as well as his mention of the father-in-law as intercessor, justifies the conclusion that his hostility toward Jacob Grebel was at least partly conditioned and increased by the latter's attitude of toleration toward the Anabaptists. That of course does not mean that Jacob Grebel was an Anabaptist. It does however signify more than a natural paternal interest in the son.

George Binder was very sorry for the position in which his old friend Conrad Grebel found himself. He wrote to Vadian about it March 11, 1526: "Conradus noster miserrimus cum 12 aliis perpetuis carceribus adiudicatus est, nisi resipiscat." *VB IV,* 9.

92. Egli, *Aktensammlung,* March 7, No. 936 and 937, p. 445.

93. Egli, *Aktensammlung,* No. 691, pp. 307-308, to be dated March 21 or April 4, 1526, according to L. Von Muralt, contains details about the flight. Following L. v. Muralt (Jörg Berger, *Zwingliana* V, p. 112, note 65) I date the flight from the New Tower on March 21, 1526, instead of on April 5, 1525, with Egli, *Aktensammlung* No. 691, 692. The chief reason against the latter date is the fact that Conrad Grebel, who was among the fugitives, was in St. Gall on Palm Sunday, 1525 which fell on April 9 that year. Also he was not among the prisoners of March, 1525, in Zürich. It can be proved that he was imprisoned on Oct. 8, 1525, for the first time.

[*Note*: The unpublished manuscript for the volume on Switzerland of the so-called *Täuferakten* (*Quellen zur Geschichte der Wiedertäufer*) which was to be published by the *Verein für Reformationsgeschichte*, was kindly made available to me by the Professor Leonhard von Muralt of Zurich. Von Muralt's collations have made some corrections of Egli's *Aktensammlung* necessary. Wherever these corrections have been used the source has been indicated.]

94. Egli, *Aktensammlung,* April 11, 1526, No. 953, p. 457, reports concerning further hearings of those re-imprisoned.

95. According to v. Muralt's collation of the original manuscript in the Zurich Staatsarchiv this passage in No. 691 is to be read "Inden," not "Juden" as in Egli's *Aktensammlung*.

96. Egli, *Aktensammlung,* No. 692, p. 312.

97. Egli, *Aktensammlung,* No. 1106. The names are missing in Egli. Citations according to v. Muralt's collation. The dating, according to v. Muralt, should be June, 1526.

98. St. Gallen, *Ratsbuch* folio 151, 1525, Staatsarchiv St. Gall. Citation according to the copy of v. Muralt.

99. Egli, *Aktensammlung,* Dec. 3, 1526, No. 1080, p. 517.

100. Egli, *Aktensammlung,* Jan. 5, 1527, No. 1109, pp. 529-530.

101. Egli, *Aktensammlung,* April 11, 1525, No. 953, pp. 458-459. This passage is missing in *Egli.* Cited from the copy by Correll.

102. Credit for the discovery of the documentary of proof of Grebel's authorship of this pamphlet belongs to Walter Köhler. See Walter Köhler, "Der verfasser des Libellus Confutationis in Zwingli's *In Catabaptistarum strophas elenchus,* in *Mennonitische Geschichtsblätter,* 3 Jahrgang, Nr. 1/2 Dezember, 1938, pp. 11-12. The proof is a direct statement by Bullinger in an unpublished letter of June 9, 1936, to Oswald Myconius. Fritz Blanke had offered detailed evidence supporting his belief in Grebel's authorship, in his commentary to the *Elenchus, Zwingli Werke,* VI, pp. 65-71 passim. I shall discuss this writing as well as the authorship in Chapter IX, pp. 186 ff.

103. Johannes Kessler's *Sabbata,* p. 164.

104. See note 56a above. According to the letter of Jacob Salandronius of Chur to Vadian, March 13, 1526, there was at that time a great Anabaptist movement in Maienfeld, which was soon shattered by persecution *VB IV,* 12.

105. See Chapter I, footnote 13.

106. Zwingli to Oekolampad and the Strassburg Brethren, Nov. 29, 1526, *ZW VIII,* p. 782: "quod Cunhardi, filii eius, uxor marito ante menses aliquot mortuo. . . ."

107. Egli, *Aktensammlung,* October, 1526, No. 1050, pp. 496, 500. This is probably not the place to discuss the case of Jacob Grebel, whose execution on October 30, 1526, caused so much criticism against Zwingli. But there is something very strange about this trial. Bullinger, *Reformationsgeschichte* I, pp. 373-4, says in an often quoted sentence: "Darvon ward vil geredt, und vermeint man, so er nitt in yl dahin gericht, were imm hernach amm läben nüt beschähen . . . vil achtetend das sin liblicher Sun Conradt Grebel, der ein widertouffer was nitt die minste ursach an sines vatters seligen todt gewesen." The connection between Jacob Grebel's death and his son's "re-baptizing," a connection which many in Zurich saw at that time, really exists, according to my opinion. See the discussion above (note 91) with the account of the severe penalty of March 7, 1526. John Horsch sees in Jacob Grebel, probably correctly, a representative of toleration in Zurich. ("The Struggle between Zwingli and the Swiss Brethren in Zurich," *MQR VII,* pp. 152-155, July, 1933.) Walter Koehler (*ZW VIII,* 780-782) gives a detailed discussion of the case with an essentially different conclusion. Both refer to the pertinent literature.

It must not be forgotten, of course, that Jacob Grebel was a leader of the aristocratic and conservative junker party in Zurich, whereas Zwingli depended for his support mainly on the more democratic craft guilds, so that Zwingli's animosity against Jacob Grebel was conditioned in part by this political situation.

108. Comander to Vadian, Aug. 13, 1526, *VB IV,* 468: "Pestis irruit, quae potissime in Christi familiam grassatur." Also on March 13, 1526, Salandronius reports the plague at Maienfeld, *VB IV,* 12. Wolfgang Ulimann left the community on that account.

109. Comander to Zwingli, Oct. 2, 1526, *ZW VIII, 729*: "Und jetz muss ich aber einest schriben; ursach, das der sterbent by uns inbricht."

110. The assumption that Grebel died in prison, which Keller-Escher (who even has him lying on the prison straw), Neff, and others have made, is wholly without foundation. It probably arises from earlier guesses which were uncritically repeated.

CHAPTER IX. THINGS MOST SURELY BELIEVED

1. Grebel to Vadian, Sept. 3, 1524, *VB III*, 85: "Plenus sum enim sermonibus, et coartat me spiritus uteri mei." It is a quotation from Job 32:18. He mentions here the two writings he is planning; "postremo omnium est, quod conscribam et colligam locos . . ., nempe duos communes, nisi alius quispiam praeveniat, in publicum deturbaturus."

2. William Exel of Wallis for instance, was one who "could neither write nor read." Egli, *Aktensammlung*, April 4, 1526, No. 691, p. 307. Citation according to Correll's transcript, since Egli is incomplete.

3. Egli, *Aktensammlung*, Jan. 20, 1523, No. 623, pp. 276-278. The date was corrected by Egli himself from 1525 to 1523.

4. Two letters from the Zollikon brethren to the council, Egli, *Aktensammlung*, March, 1525, No. 674, p. 300, and the *Grüninger Eingabe*, Egli, *Aktensammlung*, No. 1201, pp. 547-548, are incompletely reproduced. The *Grüninger Eingabe* is described by L. von Muralt in "Jörg Berger," Zwingliana V, pp. 115-6. It should be stated that the possibly excessive caution which I am here advocating does not mean that I believe that any major difference in doctrine existed between Grebel and his brethren. On the contrary I believe that they were substantially in accord. I merely wish to insist on a thoroughly sound method in deriving material on which to make positive statements about Grebel's theology.

5. See Blanke's opinion, *ZW VI*, 32, note 2: "Zwingli's drei Entstehungsberichte sind also keine tendenzlose Geschichtsquellen, sondern sie verfolgen jedesmal die gleiche bestimmte Absicht," i. e., "dass das Täufertum eine sektiererische Richtung sei und dass er das an Hand der Entstehungsgeschichte beweisen wolle."

6. Cf. *ZW IV*, 206, 316, and III 406, 872. I do not mean to suggest of course that there were not substantial and far-reaching differences. Zwingli did not sense the epochal character of the Anabaptist principles.

7. The Phalaecean meter is based on a line of eleven syllables divided into five feet. It was named from Phalaecus, an Alexandrian poet who used it, and was used in Latin by Catullus, Petronius, and especially by Martial. It was employed chiefly for epigrams.

8. Grebel to Vadian, Dec. 18, 1523, *VB III*, 50.

9. Following the usage in Boehmer-Kirn, *Thomas Müntzer's Briefwechsel*, Leipzig, 1931, the spelling "Müntzer" is used instead of "Münzer."

10. The signature of the appendix to the letter.

11. Grebel to Müntzer, Sept. 5, 1524, in Boehmer-Kirn, *op. cit.* p. 93.

12. Luther's Taufbüchlein, *Das taufbuchlin verdeutscht*, was published soon after Easter 1523. Leo Jud's *Taufliturgie* was an imitation: *Ein kurze und gemeine Form fuer die schwach gleubigen kinder zu Thouffen* . . . Zurich, summer of 1523. Andreas Osiander's *Ordnung wie man Tauffet, bissher im Latein gehalten, verteutscht* . . . appeared in Nürnberg, 1524. The Strassburg booklet was published with the title: *Ordnung des Herrn Nachtmal; so man die mess nennet, sampt der Tauff un Insegnung der Ee, wie jetzt die diener des wort Gottes zu Strassburg, erneuert, und nach göttlicher geschrift gebessert haben uss ursach in nachgehender epistel gemeldet.* See Gustav Kawerau, "Liturgische Studien zu Luthers Taufbüchlein," in *Zeitschrift für kirchliche Wissenschaft und Kirchliches Leben*, Leipzig, 1889.

13. *Elenchus*, p. 31. The citations from *Elenchus* are all taken from the critical edition, *Zwingli Werke* VI, pp. 1-196. A complete translation of the *Elenchus* into English is found in Samuel Macaulay Jackson, *Selected Works of Huldreich Zwingli*, Philadelphia, 1901, pp. 123-258 under the title, *Refutation of the Tricks of the Anabaptists.* Christian Hege discusses the new critical edition in *Mennonitische Geschichtsblätter*, 2. Jahrgang (1937) pp. 18-25, under the title, "Zwingli's Elenchus, Ein 5. Neudruck der Streitschrift gegen die Täufer."

14. *Elenchus,* p. 30: "in duabus primis partibus priore semper loco ipsorum verba ponam fideliter ex Germanica in Latinam linguam traducta."

15. *Zwingli Werke, Schuler und Schulthess* III, p. 387.

16. Füsslin, J. C., *Beyträge zur Erläuterung der Kirchen Reformations-Geschichten des Schweizerlandes* V, Zürich 1753, p. 468.

17. Usteri, J. M. "Darstellung der Tauflehre Zwinglis" in *Theologische Studien und Kritiken,* Gotha 1882, p. 222.

18. *Zwingli Werke,* IV, p. 6.

19. Staehelin, *Huldreich Zwingli,* I, p. 528.

20. Schuler und Schulthess, *op. cit.* III, p. 362.

21. Baur, August, *Zwinglis Theologie* II, Halle 1888, p. 181; also "Zu Zwinglis Elenchus" in *Zeitschrift für Kirchengeschichte* X, 1889, pp. 336 et passim.

22. Usteri, J. M., "Zu Zwinglis Elenchus," *Zeitschr. für Kirchengeschichte* XI, 1890, pp. 161 ff.

23. The analysis beyond note 28 on page 188 is my own, not Blanke's.

24. *Elenchus,* p. 69: "Quamvis maximo argumento est lingua Helvetica, qua sic est scripta, ut externum aut peregrinum verbum nullum habeat." Further citations are indicated in the body of the text by page numbers of the *Elenchus,* original given in parentheses.

25. Egli, *Aktensammlung,* March 5, 1526, No. 933, pp. 442 f. Egli is incomplete. Cited from Correll's copy. Manz spoke two other times of writing. Egli, No. 692, pp. 308ff: "Felix Mantz gitt sin antwurt also, von wegen des kindertouffs, er habe vormals dick begert, das Zwingli sine grund inn geschrifft stalte. Das sige nun beschehenn. Nun wenn man inn darumb erforder, darüber zu antwurtenn, wölle er sine grund ouch inn geschrifft stellenn und dann eine gantze gmeind darumb lassen urteilenn und das jederman by sinen worten und gschrifften belibe." Cited after Correll's copy, since Egli is incomplete. See also Egli, No. 675, p. 304.

26. Egli, *Aktensammlung,* March 5, 1526, No. 933, pp. 442ff. Egli incomplete, cited after Correll's copy. Grebel mentions his intention to write about baptism for the first time expressly in the letter to Müntzer, Sept. 5, 1524: "Ob du oder Carolostadius nit gnugsam wider den kindertouff schriben werdend . . . so wirde ich min heil versuchen (Cunrat Grebel) und dass ich angehebt han follen uss schriben wider alle, so biss har (on dich) von dem touff verführlich und wüssenlich schribend" (Boehmer-Kirn, *op. cit.,* p. 98). He mentions writing in his letter of May, 1525 to Castelberger (*MQR* I. 3, p. 42), "Contra quem, si non rescribo civitatem hanc lusurus, nunquam rescribam." In his letter to Vadian of May 30, 1525, he says: "testimonium dabo . . . scripto libello, nisi Deus vetet." On the following August 9, 1525, (Egli, *Aktensammlung,* No. 797, p. 379) it is still clearer: "Witer hab och Kurat Grebel gret, wenn man sin schriben liesy in truck usgan so wette er dann mit Meister Ulrich Zwingly disputieren." The other passages quoted, Grebel to Vadian, Sept. 3, 1525 and Jan. 14, 1525, are not quite so clear, but point to his intention to write.

Johannes Krüsi, a St. Gall Anabaptist who was sentenced to death in Lucerne on July 27, 1525 states in the course of his trial that Grebel had shown him an unprinted booklet, apparently of his own writing:" Item der jung Grebel habe zum ersten anzöggt und im ein Büchli bracht und anzöggtt, das selb büchli sye geschryben gsin und nit truckt." Willy Brändly, "Tauferprozesse in Luzern im XVI Jahrhundert," *Zwingliana* VIII (1944), p. 69 quoted from the Lucerne Ratsbuch).

27. *Elenchus,* p. 55. In the translation of the accusation of the Anabaptists referring to Zwingli's attitude toward the Vicar Faber, Zwingli uses the word "exclamavit." According to this the author heard Zwingli's statement at the first disputation in January, 1523. The minutes of the disputation, *Zwingli Werke,* I, 296, where Zwingli's expression is found, do not say that Zwingli "exclamavit."

28. Erhard Hegenwalt to Grebel, Jan. 1, 1525. Ms. 31, 222, Stadtbibliothek St. Gallen, Vadiana.

29. *Zwingli Werke* VI, p. 102.
30. Grebel to Vadian, March 30, 1525, *VB III*, pp. 116-117.
30a. Heinrich Bullinger to Oswald Myconius, June 9, 1536: "Conscript tamen opusculum Grebelius una cum fece suorum, cui respondit Zuinglius in Elencho." Quoted by Koehler in "Der Verfasser des Libellus confutationis" (*Menn. Geschichtsblätter*, 2. Jahrg. 1937, p. 12) from the ms. in the *Simmlersche Sammlung*, Zurich Zentralbibliothek.
31. *Elenchus*, pp. 80, 81. The original quotation is to be found in *Zwingli Werke* IV, p. 361.
32. *Elenchus*, p. 31.
33. Grebel's quotation is to be found in *Zwingli Werke* III, pp. 410, 411.
34. *Synecdoche* a figure of speech by which the part is put for the whole, the whole for a part, the species for the genus, or the material for the thing itself.
35. *ZW VI*, 99, 100. In the third part Zwingli attempts to prove from the idea of the covenant that the apostles baptized the children of believers. This discussion is found in the *Elenchus*, *ZW VI*, 155-172.
36. "Surgunt catabaptismi defensores novi. Repererunt libellum Tigurinorum, in quo putant fortissimis argumentis pugnatum, quae tamen illis iudicantur frivole, ut nullo negotio valeant expugnari fundamenta, vero nova poni, quae nemo nisi mendacio movere loco possit." Oswald Myconius to Heinrich Bullinger, June 2, 1536, ms. in the *Simmlersche Sammlung*, Zurich Zentralbibliothek, reported by Koehler in "Der Verfasser des Libellus confutationis," *op. cit.*, p. 12.
36a. It was probably the edition of Beatus Rhenanus, *Opera Tertulliani*, Basel, July, 1521. See *Beatus Rhenanus Briefwechsel*, p. 288. It is interesting to note that Menno Simons read Tertullian. Cf. Cornelius Krahn, *Menno Simons*, Karlsruhe, 1936, p. 42.
37. Grebel to Castelberger, May, 1525, *MQR II*, July, 1927, p. 43; *Annotationes Erasmi in Novum Testamentum*. A second edition was published.
38. Grebel to Vadian, November 21, 1522, *VB II*, 451.
39. Grebel to Vadian, November 21, 1522, *op. cit.*, 452.
40. Grebel to Vadian, Sept. 7, 1523, *VB II*, 445.
41. Grebel to Vadian, July 13, 1523, *VB III*, 26: "Adfertur Hutteni item invectiva in Erasmus." Hutten's pamphlet *Cum Erasmo Roterodamo . . . Expostulatio*, appeared in Augsburg, July, 1523. (*Böcking, Opp. Hutteni*). Grebel to Vadian Sept. 6, 1523, *op. cit.* p. 446. Erasmus' booklet appeared in September, 1523 in Basel with the title *Spongia Erasmia adv. aspergines Hutteni.*
42. Grebel to Vadian, July 13, 1523, *VB III*, p. 26. The title of the booklet was *Urtayl Doctor Martin Luters und Philippi Melanchthonis von Erasmo Roterdami.*
43. Grebel to Vadian, Sept. 6, 1523, *op. cit.* II, p. 445.
44. In his letter of Oct. 14, 1524, to Vadian, Grebel mentions Westerburg's booklet, *De Sopore Animarum*, (*VB III*, 89). It is probably the Latin edition of the pamphlet published in 1523, *Vom Fegfeuer und Stand verscheiden Seelen.* According to Steitz (*Dr. Gerhard Westerburg*, in *Archiv für Frankfurts Geschichte und Kunst, N. F. Bd.* V, *Frankfort* a.M., 1872), who discusses the booklet in detail (pp. 14-21) it was a piece of propaganda for the ideas of Karlstadt. It was probably of no significance for Grebel's theological development. The same is true of the booklets which Grebel mentions in his letter of Jan. 14, 1525 to Vadian (*VB III*, p. 105): "Ess sind nüwe büchli vorhanden: einss wider den zinss und zehenden, ein Archeteles, einss wider den nüwen abgott dass schonen, ein waghals; einss wider den kindertouff (trisarcheteles), einss von der hurery, einss von der widergeburt, eins von gwalt, krieg, einss." I was unable to identify the booklets; the following possibilities might be noted: 1.) Caspar Hedio, *Von den Zehnten*, Strassburg 1524; 2.) Andreas Karlstadt, *Ob man gmach faren und des ergernüssen der schwachen verschonen soll*, Basel, 1524; 3.) Clemens Ziegler, *Von der waren nyessung beyd leibs und bluts Christi . . . und von dem Tauff wie*

man den sonder allen zusatz öl, saltz oder beschwerung handeln soll, 1524; 4.) Jakob Strauss, *Das Wucher zu nemen und zu geben, unserm Christlichen Glauben und brüderlicher lieb . . . entgegen ist,* Strassburg, June, 1524.

45. Grebel to Vadian, July 13, 1523, *op. cit.* p. 26.

46. *Ibid.*, p. 26.

47. *Ibid.*, p. 26. The full title of the booklet is given later in the text.

47a. Egli, Akts., No. 797, p. 378, July 9, 1525.

48. "Am 23. Nov. 1524 hatten die Strassburger Geistlichen an Luther geschrieben und sich dabei auch über ihre Stellung zur Kindertaufe und der Taufliturgie ausgesprochen. Sie hielten, so führen sie hier aus, an der Praxis der Kindertaufe fest, obleich sie wüssten, dass dieselbe weder dem Brauch der ältesten Christenheit noch dem Taufbefehl der H. Schrift genau entspreche: scripturo doctos Christum iubet baptizari." Kawerau, *Liturgische Studien zu Luther's Taufbüchlein, op. cit.*, p. 636. See also the discussion of this point in Chapter VI, p. 44ff.

49. See the article on Stiefel in the *Allgemeine Deutsche Biographie.*

50. Pointed out by Blanke, *Elenchus,* p. 43, note 4. At this place in the *Elenchus* Zwingli reports that certain Anabaptists had called him "the dragon" (cf. Revelation 12, 3f.): "De antiquo dracone, quem me volebant, deque eius capitibus, quibus reliquos verbi symmystas, omnia implebant."

51. The two writings are listed in the *Verzeichniss der gedruckten Schriften des Andreas Bodenstein von Karlstadt* (*Zentralblatt f. Bibliothekswesen* XXI, 1904) as numbers 87 and 95.

52. Grebel to Vadian, Oct. 14, 1524, *VB III,* p. 88.

52a. See the discussion by W. Köhler in "Die Zürcher Täufer" in *Gedenkschrift zum 400 jährigen Jubiläum der Mennoniten,* Ludwigshafen, 1925, pp. 49-51.

52b. Walter Koehler, *op. cit.*, pp. 49-53, is unwilling to surrender the theory of external influence on the Zurich group, particularly Carlstadt and Müntzer, but he, like others who insist on such outside influence, do not and cannot trace a single major idea in Anabaptism to outside sources. Until such contributions have been traced, it must be insisted that the Zurich Anabaptist group was autochthonous, in opposition to Koehler's statement, "Die Autochthonie im Sinne einer reinen Bodenständigkeit existiert nicht" (p. 49, *op. cit.*).

53. Egli, *Akts,* Jan. 20, 1523, No. 623 p. 276f. Egli later corrected the date of the document from 1525 to 1523, 1525 being the former date in his *Aktensammlung.*

54. Grebel to Vadian, Aug. 3, 1520, *VB II,* p. 299: "Legi, dum nihil aliud agere scirem, Myconii de non bellando dialogum Philirenum, vel ob veritatem perpetuitate dignum." See the discussion of the *Philirenus* in *ZW VII,* pp. 232-3, note 2. According to the note, Zwingli was the leader of the friends of peace in Switzerland. But as early as 1524 he had given up his peace principles, for at that time he had preached a stirring war sermon. Cf. Grebel to Vadian, Jan. 14, 1525, *VB III,* p. 105: "et populus applausit manibus." Grebel names "soldiering" ("Kriegen") as one of the sins of the Zurich pastors, placing it together with "schonen, toufen, und herren nachtmal," Grebel to Vadian, Dec. 15, 1524, *VB III,* p. 96.

55. *Ines Thürlemann, Erasmus von Rotterdam und Joannes Ludovicus Vives als Pazifisten.* Freiburg (Schweiz) 1932, p. 20ff. Doctoral dissertation at the University of Freiburg.

56. *Ibid.*, p. 44.

56a. In using the Scripture Grebel endeavored to be true to the objective Word and avoid subjective modification of Scripture truth. In September, 1524, he was studying the Gospel of Matthew with some pupils, but he emphasizes the fact that he was "interpreting not prophesying." Grebel to Vadian, Sept. 3, 1524, *VB III,* 85: "pro mea virili interpretans, non prophetans."

57. The best exposition of the teaching of the Swiss Brethren (not syste-

matic) is that by John Horsch in a series of four articles in the *Menn. Quar. Review,* entitled, "The Faith of the Swiss Brethren," *MQR IV,* (1930) 241-266, V, (1931) 7-27, 128-147, 245-259. Horsch's *Mennonites in Europe* (Scottdale, 1942) contains a section on "Life and Faith of the Early Mennonites," pp. 293-380. Cf. the lengthy discussion of Horsch from the Zwinglian point of view by Leonhard von Muralt, *Zwingliana* VI, Heft 2 (1934), 65-82 under the title, "Zum Problem: Reformation und Taeufertum." In 1938 von Muralt published a valuable monograph on this subject entitled, *Glaube und Lehre der Schweizerischen Wiedertäufer in der Reformationszeit* (101. *Neujahrsblatt zum Besten des Waisenhauses in Zürich für* 1938, Zürich, 1938).

58. *Zwingli Werke* III, 872.

59. The delineation follows Grebel's terminology rather closely. Extensive quotations are given in the footnotes in Grebel's own words. The quotations from the letter to Müntzer are taken from Boehmer-Kirn, *Thomas Müntzers Briefwechsel,* and cited as *Epistel,* p. —. Grebel's *Petition of Protest and Defence,* is quoted from Zwingli Werke III and cited as *Protestation,* p. —. The *Taufbuechlein* is quoted from *Zwingli Werke* VI and cited as *Elenchus,* p. —.

60. *Protestation,* p. 370: "So einer bekert durchs wort Gottes sin gemuet geendert." The proposal of the leaders of the Brethren (Grebel, Manz, and Stumpf) at the beginning, that Zwingli should gather by an appeal all those who would be willing to join a free church, is based upon this conception of the church. *Elenchus,* p. 33.

61. *Epistel,* p. 94: ". . . in glouben der lib Christi und ein inlibung mit Christo und den brüderen. . . ."

62. *Epistel,* p. 95: ". . . dass er umb Christi und der brüderen, des houptes und glidern willen, läben und liden will." Grebel an Vadian, Nov. 21, 1522, *VB II,* 542: "Salvebis plurimum episcopum cum universa ecclesia, quae Christi capitis per evangelium graciae est."

63. See notes 61, 62 above. See also *Epistel,* p. 94: ". . . dass wir warlich ein brott und lib und ware brüder mitteinander werind und sin weltind . . ."; "die liebe, dass inner band."

64. *Epistel,* p. 94: "So einer aber sich funde nit brüderlichen mögen läben . . . schendt die liebe, dass inner band."

65. *Epistel,* p. 96: "Züch mit dem wort und mach ein christenliche gmein mit hilf Christi und siner regel," p. 101: ". . . wellist allein götliches claress wort und brüch mitsamp der regel Christ, unvermischtem touff und unvermischtem nachtmal uffrichten und leren"; p. 93: "Wellist dich ernstlich flisen, allein göttliche brüch uffrichten und schirmen, allein gutt und recht schetzen, dass in heiterer clarer gschrift erfunden mag werden." Grebel said to Pastor Hans Brennwald of Hinwil (Egli, *Akts.* Aug. 9, 1525, No. 797, p. 379): "du sollt weder mine Herren, noch niemant ansechen und sollt allein tuon, was dich Gott geheissen hat; und was der mund Gottes geredt, demselbigen sollt nachgan." *Epistel,* p. 97: "Es ist wissheit und rates me dann gnug in der gschrift, wie man all stend, alle menschen, leren, regieren, wisen und fromm machen sol."

66. *Protestation,* p. 369: ". . . sidmal nicht ein kleins ist, wiewol es anders fürgeben wird, die zwo einigen Zeremonien von Christo uns verlassen anders brouchen, dann sy Christus befolhen hat."

67. See note 65, first quotation. *Epistel,* p. 97: "Welcher sich nit besseren, nit glouben wil und dem wort und hendlen Gottes widerstrebt und also verhart, den sol man, nach dem im Christus und sin wort sine regel geprediget . . . sol man nit tötten, sunder ein heiden und zoller achten und sin lassen." Egli, *Akts.,* No. 692, p. 313: "Der kilchen halb seit er (Grebel) wölcher ein gitler, wuocherer, spiler und anders syge, wie dann die gschrift das uswist, der solle niendert under den Christen sein, sondern mit den bann usgeschlossen werden."

68. Egli, *Akts.* August 2, 1525, No. 792, p. 373. Grebel antwortet auf die Frage von Finsterbach, "was man thun müsste, um sich taufen zu lassen," "einer

müsste zuovor von ebrechen, spilen, sufen und von wuocherzins stan." *Protestation*, p. 369: ". . . sondern alein, wie dann der Touff bedeut die, die sich besseren ein new leben an sich nemend, den lasteren absterbend, mitt Christo begraben werden und mitt im newrung des lebens auss dem touff ufferstand." Almost the same words are found on p. 370.

69. Epistel, p. 96: ". . . und so nit ein gantze gmein üch ertzücht, wellind ir üch der pfründen entzüchen. Ir wüssend wol, wie ein hirt ernert werden sol. Cf. a similar proposal of the brethren to Zwingli, *Zwingli Werke*, IV, p. 405.

70. It is thus that I interpret Zwingli's assertion in the trial of November, 1525, *ZW IV*, p. 171: "Item so habind Grebel und Simon mer dann einist mit im geredt und all weg daruff trügen, dass alle ding gmein müsstind sin." In the same trial (Egli, *Akts.*, No. 692, p. 313) Grebel denied having said anything about "having things in common." Manz and Blaurock likewise in the same trial denied having preached communism of goods. Manz claimed to have taught only that a good Christian should share with his neighbor who might be in need. See the discussion on this point in Chapter VII, note 29, where the example of Anthoni Roggenacher's charity is reported. In another trial (Egli, *Akts.* No. 933) Grebel testified that he had never taught, "dass man jemands nüts umb das sin geben söllte."

71. *Protestation*, p. 371: "Wil euwer weissheit ouch des vermandt haben, burgerliche und stattliche recht auss dem tauff nicht geschweget werden noch gebessert."

72. Egli, *Akts.*, No. 933 pp. 442ff . . . Egli is incomplete. Quotation from Correll's transcript: "Wolle sunst minen herren ghorsam sin inn allen anderen weltlichen dingenn."

73. Grebel expressly denied (Egli, No. 933), that he had ever taught "die oberkeit söllte dannen getan werden," or "dass man der oberkeit nit ghorsam sin söllte." Blaurock and Manz also denied the charge. The proposal of the Brethren to Zwingli, that the new free church should elect a Christian council as soon as they had a majority, certainly contradicts the assertion that the Brethren rejected the magistracy. See *Elenchus*, p. 33.

74. *Epistel*, p. 97. See note 76 below.

75. *Epistel* p. 97: "Man soll ouch das evangelium und sine annemer nit schirmen mit dem schwert oder sy sich selbs . . . Sy gebruchend weder weltlichs schwert nach krieg, wann by inen ist dass töten gar abgetan." Grebel points out four errors of the Zurich pastors in his letter to Vadian, Dec. 15, 1524. (*VB III*, p. 96) with "kriegen" at the head of the list: "vom ietzigen kriegen, schonen, touff und herren nachtmal."

76. *Elenchus*, p. 33. Zwingli's report of the program of the Brethren: "Non ergo unquam esse sperandum sic coalituros in unum esse omnium animos, ut Christianis liceat vivere. In Actis enim apostolicis eos, qui credidissent, ab aliis secessionem fecisse ac deinde factum esse, ut, qui crederent, ad eos, qui iam nova ecclesia erant, concederent. Perinde ergo nobis esse faciendum."

77. *Epistel*, p. 97: "Rechte glaubige Christen sind schaff mitten under den wölffen, schaff der schlachtung, müssend in angst und nott, trübsal, verfolgung, liden und sterben getoufft warden." *Epistel* p. 100. "Und ob du darumb liden müsstest, weist wol, dass es nit anderss mag sein. Christus muss noch mer liden in sinen glideren."

78. See note 73 above.

79. Based on the general tenor of Grebel's statements at various times.

80. Zwingli's testimony, *ZW IV*, p. 169, where he reports that Simon Stumpf had proposed: "das sy ein besonnder volck und kilchenn söttind uffrichtenn, und ein christenlich volck darin han, . . . das ouch weder mit zinssen als mit annderem wucher beladenn were." See also Grebel's requirement of Finsterbach, that whoever desired to be baptized "müsste zuovor von wuocherzins stan." Egli, *Akts.*, No. 792. Grebel restricted his demand regarding the abandonment of

interest, to refusal to collect interest, not to pay interest, as is evident from his assertion: "er habe nie gelert, das man jemands nüts umb das sin geben söllte." Egli, *Akts.*, No. 692, p. 313.

81. See note 69 above.

82. *Protestation* p. 371: "das ewig war wort Gottes."

83. *Protestation,* p. 370: ". . . so einer bekert durchs wort Gottes."

84. *Protestation,* p. 371: "Weiss aber gewüsslich, so man das einige wort frey, einfaltiklich fürgeby, niemand darwider möge, Gott ouch die redt der Gottlosen zerströwen würde" . . . . "Das es die ewig warheit Gottes ist, die da niemand überwinden mag. Cf. the speech of Grebel to the "Ratsherren auf der Ratsstube" in Zurich, 1522: "und sofer mine Herren nit lassint das Evangelium fürgan, so werdint si zerstört werden" in Egli, No. 269, p. 94. Also the poem, "In gratiam reducis Evangelii," *ZW I,* p. 327: "verbum evangelicum arduis triumphis ducit perpetuoque victa ducet."

85. *Protestation,* p. 371: "Das ewig war wort Gottes wird ouch einen jeglichen in seinem Herzen singen, er thue dann darwider oder nit, diss die warheit sein wil."

86. *Epistel,* p. 93: For Grebel this was the real cause for the failure of the Reformation to that time. "In semlichem allem bringt dass faltsch schonen, die verschwigung und vermischung dess götlichen wortes mit dem menschlichen. Ja, sprechend wir, ess bringt allen schaden und macht alle götliche ding hinderstellig, bedarf nit underscheidens und ertzellens."

87. Grebel to Vadian, Nov. 21, 1522, *VB II,* 452: "Si quantum vellem, tantum etiam posses in theopneustois grammasi."

88. See note 65 above, also *Protestation,* p. 369: "Dass man die gechrift sölt lassen reden, wir nichts dartzuo noch darvon söltend thun."

89. *Epistel,* p. 94: "Wass wir nit gelert werdend mit claren sprüchen und bispilen, sol unss alss wol verbotten sin, also stünd es geschriben, dass tu nit." *Elenchus,* p. 55: "Nemo debet aut baptizare aut aliud quid agere, sed propter disertam scripturam aut facta, quemadmodum multa testimonia divinarum literarum comprobant. . . . Paulus docet, anathema esse, quicquid non in evangelio atque sermonibus apostolorum contineatur:" Several times in the *Epistel to Müntzer* Grebel uses the expression "gschrift und bispil" or something similar. *Epistel,* p. 96: "So wir kein gschrift noch bispil in den nüwen Testament finden . . . Nach aller gschrift bispil und gebott."

90. Grebel to Vadian, Dec. 15, 1524, *VB III,* p. 96: "Ich gloub dem wort gottes einfaltiklich uss gnad nit uss kunst; kunst halb wüstind irs ouch wol, ja tusend malen bass."

91. See note 60 above.

92. *Protestation,* p. 370: ". . . das gleich wie sy inwendig durch die zukunftt des heiligen geistes gereinigt ouch eusserlich mit wasser begossen wurdend zu bedeutung des innerlichen abweschens und absterbens den sünden."

93. Grebel to Vadian, Dec. 29, 1522, *VB II,* pp. 458-9; "Mater mea satis impia in me, in coniugem plus nimio rabida est. Timeo de eius salute, ni Christum induat et nova fiat spiritu divino renata creatura."

94. *Epistel,* p. 97: "Den touff beschribt unss die gschrifft, bedütte, dass er durch den glouben und dass blut Christi (dem getoufften dass gmüt enderendem und dem gloubenden vor und nach) die sünd abgewäsche sin; dass er bedütte, dass man abgstorben sie und sölle der sünd und wandlen in nüwe des läbens und geist, und dass man gwüss selig werd, so man durch den inneren touff den glouben nach der bedütnuss läbe."

95. *Epistel,* p. 92: "Also ouch jetzund wil iederman in glichsendem glauben selig werden, on frücht dess gloubens, on touff der versuchung und probierung, on liebe und hoffnung, on rechte christenliche brüch, und beliben in allem alten wäsen eigner lasteren."

96. Grebel to Vadian, Dec. 15, 1524, *VB III,* p. 96: "Got fürdere sin warheit

und grechtikeit und gschende alle personen. Sy sind (dass ist wir alle) lugenhaftig; die besten sind glichsnere, amen."

97. Grebel to Vadian, Oct. 14, 1524, *VB III,* p. 89: "peccatorum onus merito non me solum, sed omnes christianos magis gravare debet intus, quam quae foris impetunt procellae afflictionum."

98. Only on the assumption of the possibility of sinning among Christians is the requirement of excommunication from the church, which Grebel expressly demands (see footnote 67 above for proofs), logical.

99. *Epistel,* p. 95: "So einer aber sich funde nit brüderlichen mögen läben . . . schendt die liebe, dass inner band." See also the evidence in note 67.

100. Grebel to Vadian, Dec. 20, 1522, *VB II,* 459: "Atque istud in limine esse tempus incipit, quo plerique — utinam non ipsa quoque — non fraterne remissis aliorum peccatis corpus Christi indigne et ad iudicium manducamus."

101. Grebel to Vadian, Aug. 11, 1523, *VB III,* p. 33: "Atque utinam a deo penderem pendeamque."

102. Grebel to Vadian, Oct. 14, 1524, *VB III,* 89: "Si istuc non fit, in patientia doceat me Christus magister noster frenare et possidere animam . . . Sed sic quoque ducetur callus Christi beneficio." Grebel to Vadian, Aug. 11, 1523, *VB III,* p. 33: ". . . sed ubi, per ignem aliquem succendente volenteque ipso, patientia animam meam hanc, multis expositam et agitabilem procellis, possidere didicero."

103. Grebel to Vadian, July 28, 1523, *VB III,* p. 30: "Precare apud Christum, ut firmam in eum fiduciam geram. Idem ego quoque, ut tibi accidat, precabor." Grebel to Castelberger, May, 1525. *MQR I,* (July, 1927) p. 42: "Dum redeo, precor Dominum ut significaret quid factu potius esset."

104. See notes 74, 75 above.

105. Grebel to Vadian, May 30, 1525, *VB III,* p. 116: "Patientia et vitae eorum exitus et dies domini magnus probabunt . . . Noli te, quaeso, perdere. Si hic fallis homines, non lates coram domino deo, cognitore cordium et iusto iudice."

106. See notes 68, 92, 94 above for the evidence. Felix Manz held baptism to be a sign of the union of believers, "sin meinung, namlich dass er die, (die) sich Christi welltind annemen und dem wort gehorsam (sin), ouch nach Cristo wandlen, zuosammen wellte suochen und sich mit denselben durch den touf vereinbaren und die anderen irs gloubens lassen pliben." Egli, *Akts.,* No. 692, p. 312.

107. Egli, *Akts.* Aug. 8, 1525, No. 797, p. 389. Grebel said to Pastor Hans Brennwald of Hinwil he "sollte die kinder erst toufen, wann si zuo ir vernunft kämind." *Protestation,* p. 371: Christum die gelerten geheissen täuffen, die apostel niemands geteufft haben dann allein die gelerten."

108. *Epistel,* p. 98. "Dass alle kinder die noch nit zu underscheid dess wüssens gutts und böss kummen sind und von dem baum desz wüssens noch nit gessen habend, dass sy gwüss selig werdind durch das liden Christi."

109. See note 107, second quotation.

110. This idea was common among the first Anabaptists. Gabriel Giger, whom Grebel had baptized as early as January, 1525, testified before court: "Der vorder touf (das ist der kindertouf) der sye von dem Bapst ufgesetzt; das habe in darzuo geursacht, dass er sich jetz mit dem göttlichem touf habe lassen toufen." Egli, *Akts.* March, 1525, No. 674, pp. 297-8. Grebel and the Brethren apparently found this argument an effective one among the evangelically minded population who desired only to be rid of everything "papistical." Grebel expressed the same idea concerning the origin of infant baptism in his *Protestation,* p. 368: "Die andern (sc. vermeinend) das der kindertouff schlecht, falsch und aus dem endchrist dem bapst und seinen anhengeren erwachsen und erdacht sey (als dan war ist)."

111. *Epistel,* p. 94: "Die wil dass brott nüt anders ist dann brot, im glouben der lib Christi und ein inlibung mit Christo und den Brüderen . . . wann (p. 94) ess ermant in ouch nit an den lib und blut Christi, dess testamentes an dem

crütz, dass er umb Christi und der brüderen, dess houptes und glideren willen, läben und liden well."

112. When Grebel conducted the Lord's Supper for the first time among the brethren in Zollikon, ". . . die redtind vom touf und nachtmal. Darnach zerschnitte der Grebel ein brot und teilte es under si; darvon esse er ouch, der gstalt, dass si nun fürhin ein christenlich leben füeren und halten wölltind." It is the testimony of Hans Ockenfuss, Feb. 6, 1525, Egli, *Akts.* No. 636, p. 283.

113. See note 100 above.

114. *Epistel,* p. 94: "So einer aber sich funde nit brüderlichen mögen läben, isst er zu der verdammnuss." ". . . Wann so manss bruchte in der gmein, sollt ess unss antzeigen, dass wir warlich ein brott und lib und ware brüder mitteinander werdind und sin weltind."

115. *Epistel,* p. 95: "Sol nit on die regel Christi Mathei xviii gebrucht werden."

116. *Epistel,* p. 94: "Wann ess bringt ein glichsenden andacht und anbettung dess brotes und ein abtzug von dem innerlichen, . . . (p. 95), wann es bringt ein falschen andacht . . . wan on die selb so loufft jederman nach dem usseren, dass inner die liebe lasst man faren."

117. *Epistel,* p. 95.

118. Grebel advances nine arguments in support of his demand that singing be abolished, *Epistel,* pp. 93-94. See the discussion of this point above.

119. *Epistel,* p. 97.

X

THE SIGNIFICANCE OF CONRAD GREBEL AND THE SWISS BRETHREN IN THE HISTORY OF THE CHRISTIAN CHURCH

1. The best recent American bibliographical reports in church history give full recognition to the Anabaptist wing of the Reformation. See for instance: Roland H. Bainton, *Bibliography of the Continental Reformation, Materials Available in English,* Chicago, 1935; also Wilhelm Pauck, "The Historiography of the German Reformation During the Past Twenty Years; IV. Research in the History of the Anabaptists," *Church History* IX (December, 1940) 335-364; E. Teufel, "Täufertum und Quakertum im Lichte der Neueren Forschung," *Theologische Rundschau,* 1941, 24-57, 103-127, 183-197; 1942, 27-32, 124-154; 1943, 56-80; 1948, 161-181 (not yet complete); Walter Köhler, "Das Täufertum in der neueren kirchenhistorischen Forschung," *Archiv für Reformationsgeschichte,* 1940, 93-107; 1941, 349-364; 1943, 246-270; 1948, 164-186.

2. For a fuller presentation of the faith of the Swiss Brethren see my discussion of "The Anabaptist Vision" in *Church History* XII (March, 1944), pp. 3-24, reprinted with slight revisions in MQR XVIII (April, 1944), pp. 67-88. See also: John Horsch, "The Faith of the Swiss Brethren" in MQR IV (October, 1930), pp. 241-266, and V (Jan., April, October, 1931), pp. 7-27, 128-147, 245-259; John Horsch, *Mennonites in Europe* (Scottdale, 1942), the section, "Life and Faith of the Early Mennonites," pp. 293-380; Robert Friedmann, "Conception of the Anabaptists," *Church History* IX (December, 1940), pp. 341-364; L. von Muralt, *Glaube und Lehre der Schweizerischen Wiedertäufer in der Reformationszeit* (Zurich, 1938); Johannes Kühn, "Das Motiv der täuferischen Nachfolge," pp. 223-238 in his *Toleranz und Offenbarung* (Berlin, 1923); and Don Smucker, "The Theological Triumph of the Early Anabaptist-Mennonites: The Re-Discovery of Biblical Theology in Paradox," MQR XIX (January, 1945), pp. 5-25. For the social, economic and general cultural implications see Ernst Correll, *Das schweizerische Täufermennonitentum, Ein soziologischer Bericht* (Tübingen, 1925) and Ernst Troeltsch, *The Social Teaching of the Christian Churches,* II (London, 1931), the section "The Sect-Type and Mysticism within Protestantism," pp. 691-820 with footnotes pp. 946-990. Max Goebel gave a good general characterization as early as 1849 in his *Geschichte*

des christlichen Lebens in der Rheinisch-Westphälischen evangelischen Kirche, I (Coblentz, 1849), the section "Die wiedertäuferische Richtung," particularly pp. 134-139, but based primarily on the northwest German Anabaptists. Menno Simons' theology is treated in John Horsch, *Menno Simons, His Life, Labors and Teachings* (Scottdale, 1916) and Cornelius Krahn, *Menno Simons 1496-1561, Ein Beitrag zur Geschichte und Theologie der Taufgesinnten* (Karlsruhe, 1936). J. C. Wenger made a special study of "The Theology of Pilgram Marpeck" in MQR XII, (October, 1938) pp. 205-256. Roland H. Bainton's "Changing Ideas and Ideals in the 16th Century" in *Journal of Modern History* VIII (Dec., 1936), pp. 417-443, should not be overlooked. Robert Friedmann's *Mennonite Piety Through the Centuries* (Goshen, 1949) contains a special study on "Anabaptism and Pietism," pp. 3-88. Franklin H. Littell's Brewer Prize volume, *The Anabaptist View of the Church,* soon to appear as a publication of the American Society of Church History, brings fresh insights. See also his "Anabaptist Theology of Missions," MQR XXI (Jan., 1947), pp. 5-17. The special "Anabaptist Theology" number of the MQR for April, 1950, will contain the following papers: "The Anabaptist Theology of Discipleship" (Harold S. Bender); "Anabaptism and Protestantism" (Robert Friedmann); "Prolegomena to an Anabaptist Theology" (Cornelius Krahn); "The Restitution of the True Church" (Franklin H. Littell); "Anabaptist Theology in the Light of Modern Developments" (Don E. Smucker); "Menno Simons' Theology Reviewed" (Leonard Verduin); "Some Aspects of the Doctrinal Position of the Swiss Brethren as Revealed in their Polemical Writings" (John C. Wenger). The second volume of the late Professor Walter Köhler's *Dogmengeschichte,* probably to be published in Zurich, the manuscript of which I have seen, will be the first history of Christian thought to give full recognition to Anabaptism in the total movement of Christian doctrine.

3. Specific historic Anabaptist-Mennonite ideals, subsidiary to the major vision to be described later, not always carried out in practice nor equally shared by all groups in all times and places but still vigorously alive, include the following: Religion must be consistently taken into and expressed in daily life, and in all areas of life; Christian love must be expressed in mutualism and solidarity in economic life; the life of nonconformity to the world must include both a separation unto God and a separation from the worldly manner of life in society and includes simplicity, sincerity and humility; the Christian conscience anchored in the Word of God must operate in personal responsibility (not priestly nor exclusively pastoral authority) but within the framework of brotherhood discipline; the commitment to holy living is the responsibility of the democratic Christian community as well as of the individual; all participation in war and violence must be refused.

4. Max Goebel, *op. cit.,* 135f.

5. Sebastian Franck, *Chronica, Zeitbuch und Geschichtsbibel* (1531) fol. 444 verso.

6. See for instance Dietrich Bonhoeffer, *The Cost of Discipleship,* N.Y. 1949, with its severe criticism of the historic position of the State church of Germany on this central issue. In some respects, though not in all, Bonhoeffer would be a good Anabaptist. See also D. Elton Trueblood, *Alternative to Futility,* N.Y. 1948, which has a considerable Anabaptist ring to its penetrating analysis and challenge to modern Christendom.

7. L. von Muralt, "Zwingli als Sozialpolitiker," *Zwingliana* V (1931) p. 280.

8. Rufus M. Jones, *Studies in Mystical Religion* (London, 1909) p. 369. A similar statement is given by E. Troeltsch, *Die Bedeutung des Protestantismus für die Entstehung der modernen Welt* (Munich and Berlin, 1911), pp. 59-63.

9. *Johannes Kessler's Sabbata* (St. Gall, 1902) p. 149.

APPENDIX

A. SELECTIONS FROM GREBEL'S WRITINGS

I

A Poem Appended to Ulrich Zwingli's Apologeticus Archeteles
Published August 23, 1522

[Translated from the Latin by Edward Yoder]

Their fierce spleen let together vent the bishops,
Such in name, but full truly wolves rapacious,
For that now olden light of Truth again is
Shining bright in the world with Gospel splendour;
And this too by Divine direction, since the
Lucifers triple-tongued and bold are conquered.
Nay more (for I shall speak, a truthful prophet),
Because now their dominion and oppression,
Because now keys and canons, tome of Simon,
Murders base of the conscientious people,
For that this grim array of wares so holy,
Their dear bulls, thunderbolts, base superstition,
All these things does the Gospel Word lead conquered
And will lead in a glorious triumph alway.
Such in name, but full truly wolves rapacious,
Their fierce spleen let together vent the bishops.

Conrad Grebel in gratitude for the Gospel recovered.

II

From a letter of August 11, 1523, *to Vadian*

[Translated from the Latin by Edward Yoder]

Meanwhile, however, learn that there is so far no hope left to myself in father that I am dependent on absolute strangers rather than on himself. And would that I had depended upon God and may depend on Him! But when shall I through some fire that is kindled by His will learn to possess in patience this soul of mine, exposed to many storms and tossed about! Because of my pupils I am speaking with yourself in these few words. Take you in good part these petty trifles of mine, and you will give greeting from myself to your dear souls, so many as there are. Fare well in Christ.

[Original Latin in *Vadianische Briefsammlung*]

III

From a letter of September 3, 1524, *to Vadian*

[Translated from the Latin by Edward Yoder]

You desire the cause for my complete boldness: Waited have I and they [Zwingli and his supporters] have not spoken; they stood still nor have they answered further. I shall both answer my part and shall show the knowledge of God. For I am full of words and the spirit of my belly constrains me. Behold, my belly is as new wine without a vent, which bursts the new wineskins. I shall speak and I shall breathe a little more freely; I shall open my lips and make answer. I shall not accept the person of man and I shall not make God equal to man. For I do not know how long I shall remain alive, if also after a moment my Maker may take me away. (Hear, ye shepherds!)

And as Daniel prophesies, there will also be in the temple the abomination of desolation, and the desolation will continue even unto the consummation and the end, because even according to Ezekiel, certain, when they drink the most pure water, befoul the remainder with their feet and the sheep feed on what has been trampled by the feet of these, and they drink what these make foul with the feet. Webs do they spin not by the Spirit of God; they make a plan and not from God, so that sin is added to sin, so that they descend into Egypt without consulting the mouth of the Lord, so that hope is put in the help and strength of Pharaoh and trust is placed in the shadow of Egypt, so that the strength of Pharaoh becomes for a confusion and the trust in the shadow of Egypt becomes a disgrace. Etc.

[Original Latin in *Vadianische Briefsammlung*]

IV

From a letter of September 5, 1524, *to Thomas Müntzer*

[Taken from the translation from the German
by Walter Rauschenbusch]

Just as our forebears fell away from the true God and the knowledge of Jesus Christ and of the right faith in Him, and from the one true, common, divine Word, from the divine institutions, from Christian love and life, and lived without God's law and gospel in human, useless unchristian customs and ceremonies, and expected to attain salvation therein, yet fell far short of it, as the evangelical preachers have declared, and to some extent are still declaring; so today, too, every man wants to be saved by superficial faith, without fruits of faith, without baptism of test and probation, without love and hope, without right Christian practices, and wants to persist in all the old fashion of personal vices, and in the common ritualistic and antichristian customs of baptism and of the Lord's Supper, in disrespect for the divine Word and in respect for the word of the pope and of the anti-papal preachers, which yet is not equal to the divine Word nor in harmony with it; in respecting persons and in manifold seduction there is grosser and more pernicious error now than ever has been since the beginning of the world. In the same error we, too, lingered as long as we heard and read only the evangelical preachers who are to blame for all this, in punishment for our sins. But after we took the Scriptures in hand, too, and consulted it on many points, we have been instructed somewhat and have discovered the great and hurtful error of the shepherds, of ours too, namely, that we do not daily beseech God earnestly with constant groaning to be brought out of this destruction of all godly life and out of human abominations, and to attain to true faith and divine institutions. The cause of all this is the [policy of] false caution, the hiding of the divine Word, and the mixing of it with the human. Aye, we say it harms all and frustrates all things divine. There is no need of specifying and reciting.

While we were marking and deploring these facts, thy book against false faith and baptism was brought to us, and we were more fully informed and confirmed, and it rejoiced us wonderfully that we found one who was of the same Christian mind with us and dared to show the evangelical preachers their lack, how that in all the chief points they are acting with a false caution and set their own opinions, and even those of Antichrist above God and against God, as befits not the ambassadors of God to act and preach. Therefore we beg and admonish thee as a brother by the name, the power, the word, the spirit, and the salvation, which has come to all Christians through Jesus Christ our Master and Saviour, that thou wilt take earnest heed to preach only the divine Word without fear, to set up and guard only divine institutions, to esteem as good and right only what may be found in pure and clear Scripture, to reject, hate, and curse all devices, words, customs, and opinions of men, including thine own.

. . . .

[Let this suffice], since thou art much better instructed about the Lord's Supper, and we only state things as we understand them. If we are not in the right, teach us better, and do thou drop singing and the mass, and act in all things only according to the Word, and bring forth and establish by the Word the usages of the apostles. If that cannot be done, it would be better if all things remained in Latin and without changing and accommodating. If the right cannot be established, then neither do thou minister according to a usage of thine own or the priestly usage of the Antichrist, and at least teach how it ought to be, as Christ does in John 6, and teaches how we are to eat and drink His flesh and blood, and has no regard for the apostasy and the antichristian caution, of which the most learned and foremost evangelical preachers have made a regular idol and have propagated it in all the world. It is much more desirable that a few be rightly taught through the Word of God, believing and walking aright in virtues and customs, than that many believe falsely and hypocritically through adulterated doctrine. Though we admonish and beseech thee, we are in hopes that thou wilt do it of thine own accord; and we admonish the more willingly, because thou hast so kindly listened to our brother and confessed that thou too hast given too much, and because thou and Carlstadt are esteemed by us the purest proclaimers and preachers of the purest Word of God; and if you two rebuke, and justly, those who mingle the words and customs of men with those of God, you must by rights cut yourselves loose and be completely purged of the benefices of the priesthood and all new and ancient customs, and of your own and ancient notions. If your benefices, as with us, are supported by interest and tithes, which are both true usury, and if you do not get your support from an entire church, we beg that you will give up your benefices. Ye know well how a shepherd should be supported.

. . . .

Go forward with the Word and establish a Christian church with the help of Christ and His rule, as we find it instituted Matthew 18 and applied in the epistles. Use determination and common prayer and decision according to faith and love, without command or compulsion, then God will help thee and thy little flock to all sincerity, and the singing and the tablets will cease. There is more than enough of wisdom and counsel in the Scripture, how all classes and all men may be taught, governed, instructed, and turned to piety. Whoever will not amend and believe, but resists the Word and doings of God and thus persists, such a man, after Christ and His Word and rule have been declared to him and he has been admonished in the presence of the three witnesses and the church, such a man we say, taught by God's Word, shall not be killed, but regarded as a heathen and publican and let alone.

Moreover, the gospel and its adherents are not to be protected by the sword, nor are they thus to protect themselves, which, as we learn from our brother, is thy opinion and practice. True Christian believers are sheep among wolves, sheep for the slaughter; they must be baptized in anguish and affliction, tribulation, persecution, suffering, and death; they must be tried with fire, and must reach the fatherland of eternal rest, not by killing their bodily, but by mortifying their spiritual enemies. Neither do they use worldly sword or war, since all killing has ceased with them; unless, indeed, we are still of the old law; and even there (much as we consider it) war was a plague after they had once conquered the Promised Land. No more of this.

On the matter of baptism thy book pleases us well, and we desire to be further instructed by thee. We understand that even an adult person is not to be baptized without Christ's rule of binding and loosing. The Scripture describes baptism thus, that it signifies the washing away of sins by faith and the blood of Christ (to him that is baptized, changes his mind and believes before and after it); that it signifies that a man is dead and ought to be dead to sin and walks in newness of life and spirit, and that he shall certainly be saved if by the inner baptism he lives his faith according to this significance; so that the water does not confirm or increase faith, as the scholars at Wittenberg say, and how it gives very great comfort and is the final refuge on the deathbed. Also that it does not save, as Augustine, Tertullian, Theophylact, and Cyprian have taught, dishonoring faith and the suffering of Christ in the case of the old and adult, and dishonoring the suffering of Christ in the case of the unbaptized infants. We hold according to the following passages, Gen. 8, Deut. 1, 30, 31, and I Cor. 14, Wisdom 12, 2 Peter 2, Rom. 1, 2, 7, 10, Matt. 18, 19, Mark 9, 10, Luke 18, etc., that all children who have not yet come to discernment of the knowledge of good and evil, and have not yet eaten of the tree of knowledge, that they are surely saved by the suffering of Christ the new Adam, who has restored their vitiated life, because they would have been subject to death and condemnation only if Christ had not suffered, but have not yet grown up to the infirmity of our broken nature, unless, indeed, it can be proved that Christ did not suffer for the children. But as to the objection that faith is demanded of all who are to be saved, we exclude children from this and hold that they are saved without faith, and we do not believe from the above passages (that children must be baptized), and we conclude from the description of baptism and from the accounts of it (according to which no child was baptized), also from the above passages (which alone apply to the question of children, and all other Scriptures do not refer to children) that infant baptism is a senseless, blasphemous abomination, contrary to all Scripture, contrary even to the papacy; since we find that for many years after the apostolic times believers and unbelievers were baptized together by Cyprian and Augustine, for six hundred years, etc. Since thou knowest this ten times better and hast published thy protests against infant baptism, we hope that thou art not acting against the eternal word, wisdom, and commandment of God, according to which only believers are to be baptized, and art not baptizing children. If thou or Carlstadt will not write sufficiently against infant baptism with all that applies, as to how and why we should baptize, etc., I (Cunrat Grebel) will try my hand, and I have already begun to reply to all who have hitherto (excepting thyself) misleadingly, and knowingly, written on baptism and have deceived about the senseless, blasphemous form of baptism, as for instance Luther, Löw [Leo Judae], Osiander, and the men at Strasburg, and some have done even more shamefully. Unless God avert it, I and we all are and shall be surer of persecution on the part of the scholars, etc., than of other folks. We pray thee not to use nor to receive the old customs of anti-Christianism, such as sacrament, mass, signs, etc., but to hold to the Word alone, as beseems all ambassadors, and especially thee and Carlstadt, and as ye do, more than all the preachers of all nations.

Regard us as thy brethren and take this letter as an expression of great joy and hope toward you through God, and admonish, comfort, and strengthen us as thou art well able. Pray to God the Lord for us that He may come to the aid of our faith, since we desire to believe. And if God will grant us also to pray, we too will pray for thee and all, that we all may walk according to our calling and estate. May God grant it through Jesus Christ our Saviour. Amen. Greet all the brethren, the shepherds and the sheep, who receive the word of faith and salvation with desire and hunger, etc.

. . . .

Cunrat Grebel, Anderesz Kastelberg, Felix Mantz, Hansz Oggenfüss, Bartlime Pur, Heinrich Aberli, and other brethren of thine in Christ, if God will, who have written this to thee, wish for thee and us all and all thy flock till further message the true Word of God, true faith, love, and hope with all peace and grace from God through Jesus Christ. Amen.

I, Conrad Grebel, meant to write to Luther in the name of us all, and to exhort him to cease from his [policy of] caution, which he uses without [authority of] Scripture and which he has established in the world, and others after him. But my affliction and time would not permit. Do you do it according to your duty, etc.

. . . .

[From the Postscript to the Epistle]

The brother of Huiuf writes that thou hast preached against the princes, that they are to be attacked with the fist. Is it true? If thou art willing to defend war, the tablets, singing, or other things which thou dost not find in express words of Scripture, as thou dost not find the points mentioned, then I admonish thee by the common salvation of us all that thou wilt cease therefrom and from all notions of thine own now and hereafter, then wilt thou be completely pure, who in other points pleasest us better than anyone in this German and other countries. If thou fallest into the hands of Luther or the duke [George of Saxony], drop the points mentioned, and stand by the others like a hero and champion of God. Be strong. Thou hast the Bible (of which Luther has made Bible, Bubel, Babel) for defense against the idolatrous caution of Luther, which he and the learned shepherds in our parts have propagated in all the world; against the deceitful, weak-kneed faith, against their preaching, in which they do not teach Christ as they should, although they have just opened the gospel for all the world that people may or should read for themselves; but not many do it, for everybody follows their authority. With us there are not twenty who believe the Word of God; they trust the persons, Zwingli, Löw [Leo Judae], and others, who elsewhere are esteemed learned. And if thou must suffer for it, thou knowest well that it cannot be otherwise. Christ must suffer still more in His members. But He will strengthen and keep them steadfast to the end. May God give grace to thee and us. For our shepherds also are so wroth and furious against us, rail at us as knaves from the pulpit in public, and call us *Satanas in angelos lucis conversos.** We, too, shall in time see persecution come upon us through them. Therefore pray to God for us.

[From the *American Journal of Theology,* January, 1905.]

V

From the "Protest and Defense" to the Zurich Council, December, 1524

[Translated from the German by Ernst Correll and Harold S. Bender]

From which words one can clearly see how the apostles understood the command of Christ as above related from Matthew [Matt. 28:19], namely, that as they went forth they should teach all nations that to Christ is given all power in heaven and in earth, and that forgiveness of sins in His name should be given to everyone who believing on His name should do righteous works from a changed heart. After the receiving of this teaching and the descent of the Holy Spirit which, by speaking in tongues, was evidenced to those who had heard the word of Peter [Acts 10:40f], they were thereafter poured over with water [baptized] meaning that just as they were cleansed within by the coming of the Holy Spirit so they also were poured over with water externally to signify for the inner cleansing and dying to sin.

And as evidence that this is the meaning of baptism we read in the XXIInd chapter of the Acts of the Apostles [22:14-16] where Paul tells how it went with him on the road to Damascus, and how that after he had come Ananias comes and speaks these words—"And he said,

* Satans changed into angels of light.

the God of our fathers hath appointed thee to know his will, and to see the Righteous One, and to hear a voice from his mouth. For thou shalt be a witness for him unto all men of what thou hast seen and heard. And now why tarriest thou? arise, and be baptized, and wash away thy sins, calling on his name." From these words we clearly see what baptism is and when it shall be practiced, namely upon one who having been converted through God's Word and having changed his heart now henceforth desires to live in newness of life, as Paul clearly shows in the Epistle to the Romans, in the sixth [chapter], dead to the old life, circumcised in his heart, having died to sins with Christ, having been buried with Him in baptism and arisen with Him again in newness of life, etc. To apply such things as have just been related to children is without any and against all Scripture.

Of such passages and their like the entire New Testament Scripture is full: from which I have now clearly learned and know of a surety that baptism is nothing else than a dying to the old man and the putting on of a new; also that Christ commanded to baptize those who had been taught and that the apostles baptized none except those who had been taught, for Christ indeed baptized no one without external evidence of readiness, and certain testimony [of faith] or desire. Whosoever says or teaches other than this does something which he can prove with no Scripture and I should like to listen to anyone who, out of the Scriptures, can prove to me clearly and in truth that John, Christ, or the apostles baptized children or taught that they should be baptized.

[Taken from the *Goshen College Record Review Supplement,* January, 1526]

VI

A Letter of December 15, 1524, *to Vadian*

[Translated from the Latin by Edward Yoder]

My dear doctor and brother-in-law. The matter that you did command me I could not perform. The truth will not be bound to the occasion, therefore do you understand this in good part. Such is my request; may it be done. Others who have comprehended the divine truth about baptism do not wish to have their children baptized. They have been warned by my lords, but still stand firm. So have they prayed for justice and have petitioned and appealed to the Scripture. Then both Councils enacted that all they that declare the baptism of children to be unchristian and are unwilling to baptize their children, must present their reasons before the three pastors and the pastors theirs in turn, in the presence of four men from the Councils. Zwingli and the men appointed thereto have transgressed the said decision; the simplest one, but the one nearest to God, they have taken in hand and dealt with, God and the world know in what way. This one, however, has confuted all their wisdom with the help of God and His truth. Upon this both Councils have come to a new decision, that they should come together, as was done before.

Enough for this. You request something new that is at hand but not yet printed. The lion is "kretzing" with the famous Kretzen, the sophist of Augsburg. Zwingli is writing on "force." Whether he will struggle with the same one, I know not, but it is quite possible. This Zwingli is also writing of "the disturbers" or "on making disturbance"; it may well strike ourselves. Mark you, it will bring about something. May God advance His truth and righteousness and confute all persons. They are (that is, we all) deceitful; the noblest are like them, amen. May God grant us His mercy, so that you may shrink from dealing with spiritual matters by human wisdom, and that we may with yourself also stand by and defend the truth and may pray that God send strong laborers into the great harvest. Also may peace and faith and salvation continue and be attained.

One matter must I speak of. Usury and interest bring to ourselves in this world a passing and fading comfort and joy, or usury silences the stranger so that it does not indicate the coming sword. If it is believed and beloved and defended as Christian, then the truth of God is the most unreliable untruth. In the present struggle they defend baptism and the Lord's Supper, and they also believe the same. I believe the Word of God simply and out of grace, not out of skill; by skill you know it well also, yea, a thousand times clearly. For this cause have I spoken and still speak. For this cause may God grant us His perfect mercy that we may obey, that you may submit to the Word without condition and also obey the same. Otherwise it is quite to be feared that matters stand not so well as we falsely comfort ourselves. Narrow is the way; many things hinder the entrance thereon.

Your letter with the booklet sent to me gives us a wicked blow, but God has His judgment seat, etc. Were I more angry, I would have sinned; there is need that you be better persons openly. In the confession of the truth I know how this is due to the pastors and others. I rejoice also that of our so-called faction here, God is the judge. They talk of writing about "the disturbers." By their fruits we shall know them, by their expelling and consigning to the sword. I do not mean that persecution will be lacking. May God give grace.

I hope to God that He will apply the remedy of patience to the same, amen, if it then cannot be otherwise.

If the booklets will be printed and I live and can, I shall send them to you. Pray you to God for the advancement of His will and our piety, or rather mine own; especially God through Christ Jesus, amen.

Greet from myself, my sister, and all the pupils and beginners in the Word of God and the godly life, that they (be it their wish) may also pray for us in these perilous times. God knows why, why they are perilous. You have not written; I have not become vexed over it and have answered, have spoken the truth according to the Scripture out of a kindly feeling toward yourself. Do you take it graciously and simply.

Given at Zurich. On Thursday after Saint Mary's, etc., in the year 1524.

Conrad Grebel, your sincere brother-in-law.

I had rather we were unanimously brethren in the truth of Christ, etc.

[Original Latin in *Vadianische Briefsammlung*]

VII

A Letter of January 14, 1525, *to Vadian*

[Translated from the German by Edward Yoder]

My greeting before all. My dear doctor and brother-in-law. Learn you that we are all in health. Kasper Trismegander, the preacher at the Spital, has on the Thursday just past defended the baptism of children in his sermon to the preachers. Jakob Hottinger opposed him on it, but conducted himself in an orderly manner, and naught has as yet happened to him from my lords. A disputation, however, has been set for the coming Tuesday in the presence of both Councils, that all they who be against and in favour of the baptism of children should come together. Tomorrow the proclamation will be made.

My wife was delivered yesterday, that is Friday, a week ago. The child is a daughter and is named Rachel; it has not yet been baptized and watered in the Romish water bath.

Certain are saying that the doctor from Waldshut will also be invited by writing. But I believe it not, for he is opposed to Zwingli on the matter of baptism and will write against him, in case he does not give way. There are others will do the same.

Urbanus Rhegius, merchant preacher at Augsburg, has written against Karlstadt on the Lord's supper. Zwingli and the Zwinglians have 96 articles in defense of the unchristian water bath. The clear light of day must expose and confuse these men. Zwingli today in a public sermon pronounced the Lord's bread and wine a holy body and blood of Christ, etc. Naught more.

I pray that you be willing to give my affair with *Konrad Eppenberg* your serious attention and he also, etc. I am desperately in need.

There are new booklets at hand: One against interest and tithes, an Archeteles, one against the new idol of defense, a rash one; one against the baptism of children (*trisarcheteles*); and one on fornication; one on the new birth; one on force; one on war. Zwingli has in hand a splendid booklet to the king of France, one on the love of God and one's neighbor. On Friday, that is, yesterday, he preached to the Confederates a warlike and complete sermon, and the people did cheer!

Greet you from myself all my wellwishers, my sister and all yours.

Given at Zurich. On Saturday after the twentieth Day, in haste.

Conrad Grebel, your devoted brother-in-law.

[Original German in *Vadianische Briefsammlung*

VIII

A Letter of May 30, 1525, *to Vadian*

[Translated from the Latin by Edward Yoder]

Greeting be to you and peace in the Lord, not in the world so that it can be in the Lord. For the kind benefits you have done me I am very thankful, and I desire and yearn that you may be wondrously rewarded by the Lord God, the God of good gifts. Still when I reflect, when there comes to my mind your combat against those who are truly my Christian brethren (freely and frankly and like a Christian do I speak), I would not wish for more acceptable recompense to be made to another than what has been done to me generously by yourself (that I might be free to say to yourself what must be said); for though you do know this of yourself, still you have not been moved to give a ready ear more to the doctrine of the Spirit than to the doctrine of the flesh. Grant that you have over-loaded myself with benefits, grant that you yourself know, still you do not have regard. Although, I say, you do know it, still I declare: it is wholly or at least very largely your own fault if aught will be decided against these by way of prison, money fine, banishment or death.

Beware, beware of innocent blood; innocent it verily is, alike if you know and if you know not; wish you it, wish you not, innocent it is. Their patience and the end of their life and the great day of the Lord will prove the same. Unto your own destruction in this matter of sacred letters were you born, even as unto this state in this position of dignity, unless you take heed and recover your wits. I invoke heaven and earth as witnesses; I beg you to suffer me as I speak this, which through Christ our Lord and Saviour is true in the truth. The Lord permitting, I shall even unto death give witness to the truth, in which these men surely are and you could be also. I know what is pressing yourself on; it is money instigates yourself, I trow, or your wisdom of the flesh or the evil faction of Zwingli an enemy of the truth in this matter. Do not destroy yourself, I beg you. If you deceive men here, you will not escape notice before the presence of the Lord God, the Knower of hearts and the just Judge. Rather draw you away from the usury of money; trust God, humble yourself, be content with little, draw away from the bloody faction of Zwingli, flee from your own wisdom to divine wisdom, so that you become a fool to the world, but wise to the Lord; become a child, otherwise you cannot enter into the kingdom of God. Why do you not believe Zwingli even for your salvation, who, according to the clear Scripture, Ps. 14, Ezek. 18 has publicly declared that money leads to damnation? And Gregory, the ninth Pope of this name, did exclude from the Lord's Supper anyone that exacted from a debtor aught more than the principal.

If you desire not to stand with the brethren, at least do not resist them, so that you may be the more excusable, and do you not give an example of persecution to other cities. By faith in Christ, by heaven and earth and whatever in them is, I declare to you sincerely and truly that it is alone from love to yourself that I have admonished you on this wise. Therefore I adjure you through Christ, do you not despise me as I speak and warn from Christ; and give you anxious heed, so that it may have been spoken to yourself for recovering your wits and not for a testimony. If you yield, I shall lay down my life for you; if you yield not, I shall lay it down for these our brethren in the face of all men who will resist the truth. For I shall give testimony to the truth with the spoiling of my goods and even of my home, which is all that I have; I shall give testimony with imprisonments, with banishments and with death, and with written booklet, unless God forbid. But if I shall not write in refutation, all others will not sleep.

You do approve the doctrine, Zwingli disapproves it. Why do you wait then, seeing that you know it beforehand? Do you wait so that you may have a pretext for rejecting the doctrine and even persecuting the same? My dear Vadian! Why do you not testify as we do; why do you exercise only the power and arm of the flesh, wresting the Scripture after your will against ourselves? Believe you we are insane or full of hell itself, not to say, of demons, we that are prepared to testify even unto death, to that death, moreover, which Zwingli and the others prepare, while they hold back the truth in falsehood? If the doctrine is sound (as sound it is), as you admit with partial consent, and you are taking away election from these, why do you not elect yourself or another, or why are you not elected or why does not the Council make election and baptize? Why does it not elect? Why do not the priests, who strive against the doctrine and are not elected? See how you do catch yourself and do indicate by your own words that you have somewhat else in mind than what the words present; for if these do not baptize, not a one of you should baptize to whom you assign this duty and who, you say, are the elect. Thus do you show that you desire to have baptism held up to derision and contempt, the precepts of the doctrine approved by yourself and of baptism. For the doctrine of the Lord and the precepts have been given to the end that they be fulfilled and put into practice. I say again, if you deceive the Council, who do not observe this, you will not deceive the Lord.

Pray you to the Lord for myself, so that His just will alone may be willed in us, and I in return shall also pray in a manner brotherly and unceasingly. Bear with me in a patient Christian spirit and guard yourself. Fare you well in the Lord Jesus Christ. Greet from myself my sister and the household with expressions of thanks.

At Zurich. On Tuesday before Pentecost in the year 1525.

To Joachim Vadianus, my brother-in-law and brother in the Lord.

[Original Latin in *Vadianische Briefsammlung*]

IX

From Grebel's Testimony before the Zurich Court, November, 1525 *As Recorded by the Court Reporter*

[Translated from the German by Harold S. Bender]

Conrad Grebel remains firm that infant baptism is from the devil and re-baptism is right, and that Zwingli teaches falsely and wrongly.

He does not admit that he ever taught that one should require anyone to give his own [wealth] away for nothing.

As regards the church he says, whoever is covetous, a usurer, a gambler, or in other ways guilty of vice, should according to the teaching of Scripture in no case be considered among the Christians, but excommunicated with the ban.

He also says he never requested of Zwingli or others that they preach nothing except that which should beforehand have been discussed with him [them] but rather that he had said in the Löwenhaus that he who desires to preach should take the Word of God in his hand and not patch it out with something else.

Also, he never taught that one should not be obedient to the authorities; accordingly he knows nothing of having discussed this matter at any time with H. Martin of Berne, either concerning the authorities or concerning having things in common.

Concerning Dr. Bastian [Hofmeister] he says, that he never told him that the state should be abolished.

[Original German in Egli's *Aktensammlung*]

X

From the *Taufbüchlein* as quoted by Zwingli in his *Elenchus* in 1527, but written by Grebel in the spring of 1526.

[Translated from the Latin by Samuel M. Jackson]

One of Zwingli's grounds for advocating the baptism of infants is the family of Stephanas. For he says: It is more likely than not that the apostles baptized the children of the faithful, for Paul says, I Cor. 1:16, And I baptized also the household of Stephanas; a second is in Acts 16:15, when Lydia was baptized and her house; a third in verse 33, a little after, And he was baptized, he and his house, straightway. In these families it is more likely than not that there were infants. Thus far they.

We reply first that Zwingli says in his book that an act of the apostles can prove nothing, which is not true. Second, grant that it is true; the obscure testimony which he alleges concerning the act of Paul, I Cor. 1:16, and concerning Lydia, can therefore by his own admission prove nothing.

Third. Just before this fundamental argument of Zwingli's Paul says: Some of the family of Chloe tell me that there are strifes and contentions among you, etc. [I Cor. 1:11.] As here infants announced and could announce nothing (for they could know nothing), so the infants of Stephanas' family were not baptized, if indeed there were infants in that family. For Zwingli thrusts them into it, in spite of the testimony of Scripture?

Fourth. All testimony that mentions families excludes children. This is self-evident.

Fifth. No one ought to baptize or do anything else according to the reason, opinion and sentiment of man, but according to express Scripture or fact, as the mass of testimony of divine Scripture proves. Just as Zwingli himself has often exclaimed against the vicar and other enemies of God, and will not admit anything which depends upon human judgment or the custom of the fathers. But now he hastens to do what the enemies of truth have thus far done.

Paul teaches that what is not in the gospel or in the discourses of the apostles is anathema.

John 17:20 gives a good reason through the mouth of Christ as he says: Neither pray I for these (i.e., the apostles,) alone, but for them also which shall believe on me through their word. The apostles have their word from Christ, but Christ has [His] from the Father.

Sixth. By the same rule by which Zwingli thrusts infants into the family I thrust them out, but by Scripture; this Zwingli does without Scripture, for infants cannot be counted among the baptized families.

Seventh. Grant that there were infants in these families, the truth yet does not favor that those infants were baptized. But it follows with insult to truth and divine wisdom.

Eighth. The last chapter of his epistle shows that the apostle neither knew nor baptized children. Zwingli dishonestly keeps this back; it works against his foundation of glass. Paul describes this family to the learned when he says: Ye know the house of Stephanas, that it is the first-fruits in Achaia, and that they have addicted themselves to the service of the saints—that ye submit yourselves to them and to every one that helpeth with us and laboreth. Paedobaptism and paedobaptists do not recognize a family of this sort; they do away with it, for it is against them.

Paul, a man of truth, wished in this first chapter [of First Corinthians] to show that he had baptized but few at Corinth, but Zwingli and his witnesses make Paul a liar, and say that he baptized many when they assert that he baptized infants in the house of Stephanas.

Tenth. How the reality is, this text shows which says: Let no one say he was baptized in my name and thence be puffed up on my account. If infants then should speak and be factious (as those Zwinglians would have it) they were rightly baptized.

Eleventh. It is not true that Paul baptized Corinthian children.

Why? Because he baptized believers alone or saw that they were baptized by others. As we shall establish it from Acts 18 and 19, to the confusion and disproof of the misleading paedobaptist contention.

It is thus in the Acts, 18:8. When Paul was at Corinth, Crispus, the ruler of the synagogue, believed in the Lord with his whole house, and many Corinthians who heard at the same time believed and were baptized. Infants could not hear, they could not then believe much less be baptized. For the hearing faithful were baptized. And here the whole house was rendered faithful, from which infants are excluded, and they were so excluded because there were none there, or if there were they were not counted in it and accordingly not baptized, for the faithful families were baptized.

So also Acts 16:31 has: Believe in the Lord Jesus and thou shalt be saved and thy house. And that his house was saved with him follows on: And they spake unto him the word of the Lord, and to all that were in his house. Then further: And he was baptized, and all his, straightway. He heard the word of the Lord, and so he was baptized, and all who were in his house; they, too, heard and so were baptized. Where again infants are excluded, for they could not hear and believe, as follows on: And he rejoiced with his whole house, because he had believed in God.

Twelfth. Philip preached to the whole city of Samaria, where doubtless there were infants. Yet Luke speaks in these insuperable words:

And they were baptized, men and women. Men and women, says Luke. But if some [commentator scholist] should say, as a certain Wittenberg sophist lately did: Under the word "women" girls are also included, and under "men" males, this is fiction. For preceding these words we find: Philip preached, they believed. They, the men and women, I say, believed and were baptized. So here falls *synecdoche,* Zwingli's other basis. This synecdoche is a comprehensive mode of speech to the effect that where Scripture speaks of believers baptized, infants, too, are included among them, as he strives to prove by perverting the Scripture passages that do not contain this.

[Taken from *Selected Works of Huldreich Zwingli.* Edited by S. M. Jackson]

B. A CHRONOLOGICAL LIST OF THE LETTERS AND WRITINGS OF CONRAD GREBEL

I. *The Letters of Conrad Grebel*

	To	*From*	*Date*	*Printed*
1.	Zwingli	*Vienna	Sept. 8, 1517	ZW VII, 62-65
2.	Vadian	Zurich	July 23, 1518	VB II, 270-271
3.	Zwingli	Zurich	July 31, 1518	ZW VII, 91-92
4.	Vadian	Zurich	Sept. 26, 1518	VB II, 202-203
5.	Vadian	Paris	Oct. 26, 1518	VB II, 204-207
6.	Vadian	Paris	Jan.29, 1519	VB II, 211-216
7.	Myconius	Paris	Jan. 30, 1519	MQR II, 231-232
8.	Myconius	Paris	June 9, 1519	MQR II, 232-233
9.	Myconius	Paris	July 18, 1519	MQR II, 233-234
10.	Vadian	Melun	Oct. 6, 1519	VB II, 249-257
11.	Vadian	Paris	Jan. 1, 1520	VB II, 258-259
12.	Myconius	Paris	Jan. 14, 1520	MQR II, 234-236
13.	Vadian	Paris	Jan. 14, 1520	VB II, 261-264
14.	Myconius	Paris	March 7, 1520	MQR II, 236-238
15.	Myconius	Paris	April 13, 1520	MQR II, 238
16.	Vadian	Paris	April 13, 1520	VB II, 271-272
17.	Myconius	Zurich	July 6, 1520	MQR II, 238-239
18.	Vadian	Zurich	July 13, 1520	VB II, 326-327
19.	Vadian	Zurich	July 17, 1520	VB II, 292-294
20.	Myconius	Zurich	July 25, 1520	MQR II, 239-240
21.	Vadian	Zurich	July 29, 1520	VB II, 297
22.	Vadian	Zurich	Aug. 3, 1520	VB II, 299
23.	Vadian	Zurich	Sept. 11, 1520	VB II, 315-316
24.	Vadian	Zurich	Nov. 7, 1520	VB II, 315-317
25.	Vadian	Zurich	Nov. 19, 1520 to Dec. 8, 1520	VB III, 209-212

* Dispatched in the name of Conrad and Johann Leopold Grebel

26. Vadian	Zurich	Dec. 8, 1520	VB II, 317-319
27. Vadian	Zurich	Jan. 4, 1521	VB II, 328-330
28. Vadian	Zurich	Feb. 1, 1521	VB II, 336-338
29. Vadian	Zurich	Feb. 19, 1521	VB II, 341-342
30. Vadian	Zurich	March 19, 1521	VB II, 350-351
31. Vadian	Zurich	April 8, 1521	VB II, 355-356
32. Vadian	Zurich	April 25, 1521	VB II, 364
33. Vadian	Zurich	May 28, 1521	VB II, 366
34. Vadian	Zurich	May 28, 1521 to July 14, 1521	VB III, 225-227
35. Vadian	Zurich	July 14, 1521	VB II, 368-369
36. Vadian	Zurich	July 22, 1521	VB III, 227-228
37. Vadian	Zurich	Aug. 4, 1521	VB III, 228-229
38. Vadian	Basel	Aug. 21, 1521	VB II, 387-388
39. Vadian	Basel	Sept. 2, 1521	VB II, 404-405
40. Vadian	Zurich	End Oct. 1521	VB III, 231-232
41. Vadian	Zurich	Nov. 2, 1521	VB II, 398-399
42. Myconius	Zurich	Nov. 4, 1521	MQR II, 240-241
43. Vadian	Zurich	Dec. 18, 1521	VB II, 408
44. Vadian	Zurich	Dec. 29, 1521	VB II, 410
45. Vadian	Zurich	Jan. 12, 1522	VB II, 415
46. Vadian	Zurich	Jan. 30, 1522	VB II, 416
47. Vadian	Zurich	Feb. 6, 1522	VB II, 421
48. Vadian	Zurich	Nov. 21, 1522	VB II, 451-452
49. Vadian	Zurich	Dec. 1, 1522	VB III, 234-235
50. Vadian	Zurich	Dec. 25, 1522	VB VII, 17-18
51. Vadian	Zurich	Dec. 29, 1522	VB II, 458-459
52. Vadian	Zurich	June 17, 1523	VB III, 19-20
53. Vadian	Zurich	July 13, 1523	VB III, 26-27
54. Vadian	Zurich	July 14, 1523	VB III, 51-52
55. Vadian	Zurich	July 28, 1523	VB III, 29-30
56. Vadian	Zurich	Aug. 11, 1523	VB III, 32-33
57. Vadian	Zurich	Sept. 6, 1523	VB II, 445-446
58. Vadian	Zurich	Nov. 12, 1523	VB III, 45-46
59. Vadian	Zurich	Dec. 18, 1523	VB III, 49-50
60. Vadian	Zurich	Feb. 26, 1524	VB III, 58-59
61. Vadian	Zurich	July 31, 1524	VB III, 83
62. Vadian	Zurich	Sept. 3, 1524	VB III, 84-86
63. Müntzer	Zurich	Sept. 5, 1524	*Thomas Müntzers Briefwechsel,* Böhmer–Kirn, 92-101
64. Vadian	Zurich	Oct. 14, 1524	VB III, 88-90
65. Vadian	Zurich	Dec. 11, 1524	VB III, 94-95
66. Vadian	Zurich	Dec. 15, 1524	VB III, 95-97

67. Vadian	Zurich	Jan. 14, 1525	VB III, 104-105
68. Castelberger	Zurich	May, 1525	MQR I, July, 1927, 41-53
69. Vadian	Zurich	May 30, 1525	VB III, 116-118
70. Zollikon Council	Grüningen	July 5, 1525	*G. C. Record Review Supplement,* Jan., 1926, pp. 31-32

II. *Letters to Conrad Grebel*

Benedikt Burgauer	St. Gall	July 21, 1523	VB III, 28-29
Joachim Vadian	St. Gall	Dec. 28, 1524	VB III, 98-99
Erhart Hegenwalt (Not printed)	St. Gall	Jan. 1525	Stadtb. St. Gallen, Ms. 31, 222: 8 pp.

III. *Writings by Conrad Grebel*

1. *Conradus Grebelius Tigurinus Helvetius, Melam alloquitur.* May, 1518. In *Pomponii Melae, Hispani libri de situ orbis tres,adiectis I, Vadiani Helvetii in eosdem scholiis addita quoque in Geographium Catechesi et epistola Vadiani ad Agricolam dignam lectu.* Viennae 1518, folio 2 *recto* and *verso.*
2. *Ad Joachimum Vadianum.* Sometime in 1520.
   A handwritten poem in Grebel's autograph on the inside of the front cover of *Joachimi Vadiani Helvetii, de Poetica Carminis ratione, Liber ad Melcheorem Vadianum fratrem,* 1520. The book is in the Zurich Zentralbibliothek, Gal Tz 295.
3. *Conradus Grebelius Tigurinus Helvetius, vere candido lectori.* Zurich, December 24, 1520. A brief composition constituting the introduction to the 1522 Basel edition of Vadian's *Pomponii Melae Hispani libri de situ orbis tres* found on folio 2 *recto* and *verso.* A copy of the 1522 Mela edition is in the author's possession.
4. *Conradus Grebelius in gratiam reducis evangelii.* Zurich, August 23, 1522. A poem printed on the last page of Zwingli's *Apologeticus Archeteles,* Zurich, 1522. Modern Reprint in *Zwingli Werke* I, p. 321. A copy of the original edition is in the author's possession.
5. *Protest and Defense.* December, 1524.
   A statement addressed to the Zurich Council. Autograph in the Zurich Staatsarchiv. Modern reprint in *Zwingli Werke* III, pp. 368-372. English Translation in *Goshen College Record Review Supplement,* January, 1926, pp. 23-31.
6. *Taufbuechlein.* Called by Zwingli *Libellus Confutationis.* Spring of 1526. Translated in part into Latin by Huldreich Zwingli in his *Catabaptistarum Strophas Elenchus,* Zurich, 1527. Modern reprint of this Latin translation in *Zwingli Werke* VI, pp. 1-196, English translation of the *Elenchus* in S. M. Jackson, *Selected Works* of *Huldreich Zwingli,* Philadelphia, 1901, pp. 123-258.

IV. *Other Statements by Conrad Grebel*

1. *Statements at the Zurich Disputation of October* 26-28, 1523. Several brief statements found in the record of the disputation printed in *Zwingli Werke* II, pp. 692, 783, 785, 789, 793.
2. *Testimony before the Zurich Court.* November 8-18, 1525, or March 5-7, 1526. A brief statement printed in Emil Egli, *Aktensammlung zur Geschichte der Züricher Reformation* 1519-1533, Zurich, 1879, as No. 692, p. 313, and in J. C. Füsslin, *Beyträge zur Erläuterung der Kirchen-Reformations-Geschichten des Schweitzerlandes,* I, Zurich, 1741, pp. 243-252. Original in the Zurich Staatsarchiv.

C. A CHRONOLOGICAL LIST OF PUBLISHED GREBEL BIOGRAPHIES AND BIOGRAPHICAL MATERIAL

1782 Leonhard Meister: "Conrad Grebel." In *Berühmte Züricher.* Basel, pp. 199-206.

1858 J. Heberle. The first extensive scholarly treatment of Grebel based on original sources is Heberle's "Die Anfänge des Anabaptismus in der Schweiz" *Jahrbücher für deutsche Theologie* (Stuttgart) 1858, pp. 225-280. This was the basis for the treatment of Grebel by C. A. Cornelius in his *Geschichte des Münsterischen Aufruhrs* (Leipzig) II (1860) *Zweites Buch, die Wiedertaufe,* "Der Ursprung der Wiedertaufe" pp. 1-30, where Grebel is directly treated pp. 19-20. *Beilage* I, pp. 240-249 is the letter of Grebel to Müntzer of 1524, and *Beilage* III, pp. 250-251, is the letter of Grebel to Vadian, May 30, 1525.

1867 J. C. Mörikofer: "Konrad Grebel, Der Wiedertäufer." In *Ulrich Zwingli,* Zweiter Theil, Zurich, Cap. 48, pp. 278-287.

1879 Gerold Meyer von Knonau: "Konrad Grebel." In *Allgemeine Deutsche Biographie,* Bd. 9, Leipzig, pp. 619-622.

1890 "Zur Beurteilung Konrad Grebels" (anon.) in *Mennonitische Blätter* (Hamburg-Altona) 1890, pp. 1-4. See also *MB,* 1889, pp. 111-112, "Aus dem Briefwechsel Konrad Grebels" by Ludwig Keller.

1895 Max Staub: *Die Beziehungen des Täufers Konrad Grebel zu seinem Schwager Vadian, Zurich,* pp. 78

1922 Christian Neff: "Konrad Grebel, Der Täuferführer zu Zurich." In *Mennonitische Jugendwarte III,* Ludwigshafen, pp. 8-24, 56-68.

1925 Christian Neff: "Konrad Grebel, Sein Leben und Wirken." In *Gedenkschrift zum 400 Jährigen Jubiläum der Mennoniten,* Ludwigshafen, pp. 65-128.

1926 Ernst Correll: "Conrad Grebel and the Revival of Geography."

In *Goshen College Record Review Supplement.* 1926 (May-June) pp. 48-52

1926 *Historisch-Biographisches Lexikon der Schweiz,* Vol. III, 726f. Sixty words on Conrad in the article *"Grebel."* Prints a picture of Hans Conrad Grebel 1615-1674, (great-grandson of Conrad) by Seb. Walch, from an etching in the collection of the Bibliotheque National, Berne.

1928 Christian Neff: "Konrad Grebel." In *Mennonitisches Lexikon* II, 163-169.

1928 Walter Koehler: "Konrad Grebel." In *Die Religion in Geschichte und Gegenwart* Bd. 2, Spalte 1435.

1929 Edward Yoder: "Conrad Grebel as a Humanist." In *MQR* April, 1929, Vol. III, pp. 132-146.

1936 Harold S. Bender: "Conrad Grebel, the First Leader of the Swiss Brethren." In *MQR,* January, April, July, 1936. Vol. X, 5-45, 91-137, 151-160. (Covers only the period to 1522.) Youth and Early University Years, January, pp. 5-45; Grebel's Study in Paris, April, pp. 91-137; The Humanism of Conrad Grebel, July, pp. 151-160.

1936 Hans Wirz: "Der Ratsherr Jakob Grebel und seine Stiefbrüder Wirz, sein Sohn Konrad Grebel und sein Schwiegersohn Vadian." In *uwingliana* VI, pp. 207-222. (To 1523.)

1938 Hans Wirz: "Der Zwiespalt im Hause Grebel. Die Anfänge des Kampfes Zwischen Volkskirche und Täufertum." In, *Zwingliana* VI, pp. 470-486 (to 1525). Also: "Die Zuspitzung der Gegensätze, 1525-1527. Der Untergang von Konrad und Jakob Grebel." In *Zwingliana* VI, pp. 486-499, 537-544.
The above materials appeared as sections of the extended study of "Zürcher Familienschicksale im Zeitalter Zwingli." Considerable other material is included with the Grebel material, but the main line of interest most of the time is Conrad Grebel. A monograph was to be published in revised and enlarged form in 1945. A proof copy of that date was made available in 1946. Publication may be expected shortly.

1936 Leonhard von Muralt: "Konrad Grebel als Student in Paris." In *Zuercher Taschenbuch auf das Jahr* 1937, pp. 113-136.

1937 Johannes Ninck: "Konrad Grebel." In his *Arzt und Reformator Vadian,* St. Gallen. pp. 109-119. Treated chiefly in connection with St. Gall.

1938 Harold S. Bender: "The Theology of Conrad Grebel." In *MQR,* January and April, 1938, Vol. XII. pp. 27-54, 114-134.

1938 Harold S. Bender, "Conrad Grebel, The Founder of Swiss Anabaptism." In *Church History* VII, April 1938, pp. 157-178.

1941 Harold S. Bender: "Conrad Grebel as a Zwinglian." In *MQR,* April, 1941, Vol. XV, pp. 67-82.

BIBLIOGRAPHY

A. *Archival Sources*

The following major archives and libraries contain original documents which were used, and which are cited at the appropriate places in the notes: Staatsarchiv Bern; Staatsarchiv Zurich; Zurich Zentralbibliothek; Stadtbibliothek St. Gallen "Vadiana"; Universitätsbibliothek Basel. Other archives used for minor points are not listed individually here. Most of the important documents used have already been made available in published form and are cited from these sources. Attention is called to the following lengthier unprinted documents cited: *Acta des Gesprächs zwischen predikanten unnd Taufbrudernn. Ergängen inn der Stadt Bern, Im M.D. XXXVIIIt. Jar.* MS Staatsarchiv Bern Unnütze Papiere, Bd. 80, pp. 305; letter of *Erhart Hegenwalt to Konrad Grebel,* now in the Stadtbibliothek St. Gallen, MS. 31, 222, an 8-page letter written at Wittenberg in Saxony in January, 1525. Certified typewritten copies of both documents are in the Goshen College Library.

B. *Printed Books and Periodicals*

The following list is not intended to be an exhaustive bibliography of the early history of the Swiss Brethren, but rather a compilation of material used in the preparation of this volume. The numerous titles listed in the notes to Chapter X are not repeated in the bibliography.

Allen, P. S. : *Opus Epistolarum Desiderii Erasmi Roterodami,* Tom. 1-7. Oxonii 1906 ff.

Althammer, Andreas: *Ein kurtze unterricht den Pfarherrn und Predigern . . . verordnet, was sie das volck weder etliche verfürische lere, der widertäuffer . . . ausz göttlicher Schrift vernomen, und unterrichten sollen,* 1528.

Ammann, Aug. F.: *Geschichte der Familie Ammann von Zurich.* Zurich 1913.

Arbenz, E.: "Joachim Vadian beim Uebergang vom Humanismus zum Kirchenstreit." In *Neujahrsblatt des Historischen Vereins St. Gallen 1895.*

Aschbach, Joseph, Ritter v.: *Geschichte der Wiener Universität im ersten Jahrundert ihres Bestehens.* Vienna 1865-77.

Bächtold, C. A.: *Die Schaffhauser Wiedertäufer in der Reformationszeit. Beiträge zur vaterländischen Geschichte . . . des Kantons Schaffhausen,* 7. Heft, Schaffhausen 1900.

Barge, Herman: *Andreas Bodenstein von Carlstadt.* Leipzig 1905.

Barge, Herman: "Die gedruckten Schriften des Predigers Jakob Strauss." In *Archiv für Reformationsgeschichte* XXXII (1935), pp. 100-121, 248-252.

————: *Jakob Strauss. Schriften des Vereins fur Reformationsgeschichte* No. 162, Leipzig 1937.

Bauch, Gustav: "Caspar Ursinus Velius." In *Ungarische Revue* VII, Budapest, Jahrg. 1887.

Baur, August: *Zwinglis Theologie, Ihr Werden und ihr System.* Halle 1885-88.

Beck, Joseph: "Georg Blaurock und die Anfänge des Anabaptismus in Graubünden und Tirol." In *Vorträge und Aufsätze aus der Comeniusgesellschaft* VII. Berlin 1898.

Bender, Harold S.: "Conrad Grebel, The First Leader of the Swiss Brethren (Anabaptists)."
In *MQR* X (1936) pp. 5-45 (Youth and Early University Years); 91-137 (Grebel's Study in Paris); 151-160 (The Humanism of Conrad Grebel).

————: "The Theology of Conrad Grebel." In *MQR* XII (1938) pp. 27-54, and 114-134.

————: "Conrad Grebel, The Founder of Swiss Anabaptism." In *Church History* VII (1938), pp. 157-178.

————: "Conrad Grebel as a Zwinglian." In *MQR* XV (1941) pp. 67-82.

————: "The Anabaptist Vision." In *Church History* XIII (March 1944).

Berchtold, Jacob: *Das Zwinglibild und die Zürcherischen Reformationschroniken.* (Zürcher Dissertation) *Quellen und Abhandlungen zur Schweizerischen Reformationsgeschichte V. Leipzig* 1929.

Blanke, Fritz: (Einleitung und Kommentar zu) *In catabaptistarum strophas elenchus, Huldreich Zwinglis Sämtliche Werke, herausgeg.* von Egli, Finsler, Köhler, Blanke, von Muralt. Bd. VI Leipzig 1939, pp. 1-196.

Blaurer, Ambrosius und Thomas: *Briefwechsel der Brüder Ambrosius und Thomas Blaurer.* ed. T. Schiess. I, Freiburg 1908.

Böhmer, Heinrich: *Thomas Müntzer und das jüngste Deutschland.* In *Gesammelte Aufsätze.* Gotha 1927.

Brandt, Otto.: *Thomas Müntzer, Sein Leben und seine Schriften.* Jena 1933.

Büchi, Albert: "Glareans Schüler in Paris (1517-1522) nebst 15 ungedruckten Briefen." In *Geschichtsfreund LXXXIII,* Stans 1928.

de Budé, Eugene: *Vie de Guillaume Budé.* Paris 1884.

Budinsky, Alexander: *Die Universität Paris und die Fremden an derselben im Mittelalter.* Berlin 1876.

Bullinger, Heinrich: *Von dem unverschampten fräfel, ergerlichen verwyren unnd unwarhafftem leeren der selbsgesandten Widertöuffern.* Zürich 1531.

————: *Der Widertäufferen Ursprung, furgang, secten, wäsen, fürneme und gemeine irer leer artickel, auch ire grund und warin sy sich absunderind.* Zurich 1560. (2. Aufl. 1561).

————: *Reformationsgeschichte nach dem Autographon herausgegeben von J. J. Hottinger und H. H. Vögeli.* Frauenfeld 1838-1840.

————: *Diarium* (1504-1574). ed. Egli, *Quellen zur Schweizerischen Reformationsgeschichte* II. Basel 1904.

Chatelaine, Emile: *Les Etudiants Suisses à l'Ecole Pratique des Hautes Etudes (1868-1901) avec un appendice sur les Etudiants Suisses de Paris aux XVe et XVIe Siecles.* Paris 1891.

Clemen, Otto: "Der Wiedertäufer Ulrich Hugwald." In Clemen, *Beiträge zur Reformationsgeschichte.* II, Berlin, 1908, pp. 45-85. *Propositiones Ulrichi Hugwaldi* as "Beilage."

Collin, Rudolf: *Schilderung seines Lebens, verdeutscht von Salomon Voegelin. Zürcher Taschenbuch auf das Jahr* 1859. Zürich 1859.

Cornelius, C. A.: *Geschichte des Münsterischen Aufruhrs.* Leipzig 1855-1860.

Correll, Ernst: *Das Schweizerische Täufermennonitentum.* Tübingen 1925.

————: "Conrad Grebel and the Revival of Geography." In *Goshen College Record Review Supplement,* 1926 (May-June) pp. 48-52.

Correll, E. H., and Bender, H. S.: "Conrad Grebel's Petition of Protest and Defense to the Zurich Council in 1524. A Translation with notes and introduction by E. H. Correll and H. S. Bender. Appendix: Conrad Grebel and Marx Bosshart's Petition to the 'Great Council' of Zurich for a Letter of Safe Conduct." In *Goshen College Record Review Supplement,* January 1926, pp. 23-32.

Correll, E. H., Bender, H. S., and Yoder, Edward: "A letter of Conrad Grebel to Zwingli Sept. 8, 1517. Edited by E. H. Correll, H. S. Bender and Edward Yoder." In *Goshen College Record Review Supplement,* September 1926, pp. 33-37.

Correll, Ernst, and Bender, H. S.: "A Letter of Conrad Grebel to Andreas Castelberger May 1525. Edited by Ernst Correll and H. S. Bender. Translation by Edward Yoder." In *MQR* I (1927) July, pp. 41-53.

Delaruelle, Louis: "Nicole Berault, Notes biographiques suivies d'un appendice sur plusieurs de pes publications." In *Etudes sur l'Humanisme Francais, Le Musee Belge, Revue de Philologie Classique,* Treizieme Année 1909 pp. 253-312.

———: "Notes Biographiques sur Nicole Berault suivies d'une Bibliographie de ses oeuvres et de ses publications." In *Revue de Bibliotheques,* Douzieme Année 1902. Paris, pp. 420-445.

———: *Repertoire Analytique et Chronologique de la Correspondance de Guillaume Budé.* Paris 1907.

———: *Guillaume Budé, Les Origines, Les Debuts, Les Idées Maitresses.* Paris 1907:

Dürr, Emil and Roth, Paul: *Aktensammlung zur Geschichte der Basler Reformation in den Jahren* 1519-1534. Bd. I, 1519-1525. Basel 1921; Bd. II, 1525-1527. Basel 1933.

Durrer, Robert, *Die Schweizergarde in Rom und die Schweizer in Päpstlichen Diensten* I, Luzern 1927.

Egli, Emil: *Die Züricher Wiedertäufer zur Reformationszeit.* Zürich 1878.

———: *Aktensammlung zur Geschichte der Zürcher Reformation.* 1519-1533. Zürich 1879.

———: *Die St. Galler Täufer.* Zürich 1887.

———: *Schweizerische Reformationsgeschichte* I (1519-1525). Zürich 1910.

Egli, Jean: *Neues historisches Wappenbuch der Stadt Zürich.* Zürich 1860.

Ernst, Ulrich: *Geschichte des zürcherischen Schulwesens bis gegen Ende des sechzehnten Jahrhunderts.* Winterthur 1879.

Farner, Alfred: *Die Lehre von Kirche und Staat bei Zwingli.* Tübinggen 1930.

Farner, Oskar: *Huldrych Zwingli, Seine Entwicklung zum Reformator* 1506-1520. Zurich, 1946.

Franck, Sebastian: *Chronika, Zeytbuch und Geschychtbibel von anbegyn bisz inn diez gegenwertig M.D. XXI. jar.* 1531.

Freys E. u. Barge, H.: "Verzeichnis der gedruckten Schriften des Andreas Bodenstein von Karlstadt." In *Zentralblatt für Bibliothekwesen XXI,* April 1904.

Fritzsche, Otto Fridolin: *Glarean, Sein Leben und seine Schriften.* Frauenfeld 1890.

Füsslin, J. C.: *Beiträge zur Erläuterung der Kirchen-Reformations-Geschichten des Schweizerlandes,* I-V Zürich 1741-1753.

Gedenkschrift zum 400 jährigen Jubiläum der Mennoniten oder Taufgesinnten. Ludwigshafen 1925.

van Ghendt, Carel: *Het beginsel en voortganck der geschillen, scheuringen, en verdeeltheden onder de gene die Doopstgesinden genoemt worden.* Amsterdam 1658. In *Bibliotheca Reformatoria Neerlandica* III. 's Gravenhage 1910, pp. 489-564.

Geschicht-Buch der Hutterischen Brüder. Geschicht-Buch und kurzer Durchgang von Anfang der Welt, wie Gott sein Werk in seinem Volk auf Erden angericht, gehandelt und getrieben hat; demnach: Unserer Gemein-Geschicht-Buch. Herausgegeben durch Rudolf Wolkan, Wien. Macleod, Alberta, Canada 1923.

Geschichtbuch (new edition). *Die älteste Chronik der Hutterischen Brüder.* Herausgeben von A. J. F. Zieglschmid. Philadelphia, 1943.

Götzinger, Ernst: *Joachim Vadian, der Reformator und Geschichtschreiber von St. Gallen.* Halle 1895.

Graf, K. H.: "Jacobus Faber Stapulensis." In *Zeitschrift für die historische Theologie.* 1852.

Heberle, J.: "Die Anfänge des Anabaptismus in der Schweiz." In *Jahrbücher für deutsche Theologie.* III. Stuttgart 1858.

Hege, Christian: "Zwinglis Elenchus." In *Mennonitische Geschichtsblätter,* II, 1937.

Hermelink, Heinrich und Maurer, Wilhelm: *Reformation und Gegenreformation.* 2. Aufl. 1931.

Herminjard, A. L.: *Correspondance des Reformateurs Dans les Pays de Langue Francaise I,* (1512-1526). Paris 1866.

Holl, Karl: "Luther und die Schwärmer." In *Gesammelte Aufsätze zur Kirchengeschichte I,* 2. u. 3. Aufl. Tübingen 1923, pp. 420-467.

Horawitz, Adalbert: *Zur Geschichte des deutschen Humanismus.* Jena 1874.

Horsch, John: *Infant Baptism, Its Origin among Protestants and the Arguments Advanced For and Against It.* Scottdale, Pennsylvania 1917.

Horsch, John: *Mennonites in Europe.* Scottdale, 1942.

———: "The origin and Faith of the Swiss Brethren." In *Goshen College Record Review Supplement,* January 1926, pp. 1-14.

———: "Origin and Principles of the Anabaptists." In *Review and Expositor* VIII (1911) pp. 406-419.

———: "The Swiss Brethren in St. Gall and Appenzell." In *Mennonite Quarterly Review* VII, 1933, pp. 205-226.

———: "The Faith of the Swiss Brethren." In *MQR* IV (1930) pp. 241-266, V (1931) 7-27, 128-147, 245-259.

———: "The Rise and Early History of the Swiss Brethren Church." In *MQR* VI (1932) I. "The Rise of State Church Protestantism," pp. 169-191. II. "The Beginnings in Zurich," pp. 227-249.

———: "The Struggle between Zwingli and the Swiss Brethren in Zurich." *MQR* VII, 1933, pp. 142-161.

———: "An Inquiry into the Truth of the Accusations of Fanaticism and Crime against the Early Swiss Brethren." In *MQR* VIII, 1934, pp. 18-31, 73-89.

———: "Die Stellung der Schweizer Brüder zu Thomas Müntzer." In Der *Hilfsbote,* Kassel, 1911, pp. 83-87.

Hubmaier, Balthasar: *Der alten und neuen Lehrer Urteil, dass man die Kinder nicht taufen solle.* 1525.

Hulshof, Abraham: *Geschiedenis van de Doopsgezinden te Straatsburg van* 1525 *tot* 1557. *Amsterdam* 1905.

Jackson, S. M., Ed.: *Selected works of Huldreich Zwingli.* Philadelphia 1901.

Jecklin, Fritz: "Bündner Studenten an der Pariser Universität als Pensionäre der französischen Könige." In *Bündnerisches Monatsblatt,* März 1925.

Jecklin, Fritz: "Jörg Blaurock vom Hause Jacob. Ein Märtyrer der Wiedertäufer." In *XXI. Jahresbericht der historisch-antiq. Gesellschaft von Graubünden.* Jahrg. 1891.

Kaegi, Friedrich: *Dis ist das register zum Hafen, und war gemacht und angefangen uff Mittwoch nach dem Sonntag Invocavit Anno Domini MD. quingentesimo quarto* (28. Febr. 1504). Printed, but not published. Proof sheets in Staatsarchiv Zürich.

Kaegi, Werner: "Hutten und Erasmus." In *Historische Vierteljahrsschrift XXII.* 1929.

Kälin, J. B.: "Zur Geschichte der Freiplätze der eidg. Orte auf der Universität zu Paris und der Schwyzer Studenten daselbst." In *Mitteilungen des Hist. Vereins des Kantons Schwyz* 4. 1885.

Keller, Ludwig: *Die Reformation und die älteren Reformparteien.* Leipzig 1885.

Keller-Escher, Caspar: *Die Familie Grebel, Blätter aus ihrer Geschicht gesammelt zur Erinnerung an die am 27. Oktober* 1386 *erfolgte Einbürgerung. Für Freunde als Manuscript gedruckt.* Frauenfeld 1886. *Nachtrag* 1887.

Kessler, Johannes: *Sabbata.* ed. E. Egli und R. Schoch. St. Gallen 1902.

Kink, Rudolph: *Geschichte der Kaiserlichen Universität zu Wien.* Vienna 1854.

Köhler, Walter: "Die Zürcher Täufer." In *Gedenkschrift zum* 400 *jährigen Jubiläum der Mennoniten.* Ludwigshafen 1925.

———: "Konrad Grebel." In *Religion in Geschichte und Gegenwart,* II, 1928, Spalte 1435.

———: "Der Verfasser des Libellus Confutationis (Konrad Grebel)." In *Mennonitische Geschichtsblätter,* III, 1938.

———: "Das Taufertum in der neueren kirchen-historischen Forschung." *Archiv für Reformationsgeschichte.* 37 (1940) pp. 93-107.

Lefranc, Abel: *Histoire du College de France depuis ses origines jusqu'à la fin du premier Empire.* Paris 1893.

Lohmann, Annemarie: *Zur geistigen Entwicklung Thomas Müntzers. Beiträge zur Kulturgeschichte des Mittelalters und der Renaissance.* Bd. 47, Leipzig 1931.

Luther, Martin: *Dr. Martin Luthers Briefwechsel,* ed. Ludwig Enders. Leipzig, 1884-1932.

———: *Von der wiedertauffe an zwen Pfarherrn, ein Brief.* Nürnberg 1528.

Meyer von Knonau, Gerold: "Konrad Grebel (Wiedertäufer)." In *Allgemeine Deutsche Biographie* IX (1879), pp. 619-622.

Meister, Leonhard: *Berühmte Züricher.* Zurich 1786.

Melanchthon, Philip: *Underricht wider die Lere der Widerteuffer auss dem latein verdeutschet durch Justus Jonas.* Wittenberg M. D. XXVIII.

Menius, Justus: *Der widderteuffer Lere und geheimnis, Aus heiliger schrifft widderlegt.* Wittenberg 1534.

Mennonitisches Lexikon. Herausgegeben von Christian Hege und Christian Neff. Frankfurt a.M. und Weierhof (Pfalz), 1913 ff.

Merx, Otto: *Thomas Münzer und Heinrich Pfeiffer* (1523-1525). Göttingen 1889.

Metzger, Wolfgang: "Müntzeriana." In *Thüringisch-Sächsische Zeitschrift für Geschichte und Kunst.* XVI. Halle a.d.S. 1927.

Miles, Hermann: *Chronik.* In *Mitteilungen zur vaterländischen Geschichte.* St. Gallen 1902.

Mörikofer, J. C.: *Ulrich Zwingli.* Leipzig 1867-1869.

Müntzer, Thomas: *Thomas Müntzer's Briefwechsel.* ed. H. Boehmer und P. Kirn. Leipzig 1931.

v. Muralt, Leonhard: "Jörg Berger." In *Zwingliana* V (1929-1930), pp. 66-71, and 103-126.

———: "Zum Problem Reformation und Täufertum." *Zwingliana* VI Heft 2 (1934).

———: "Konrad Grebel als Student in Paris." In *Zürcher Taschenbuch auf das Jahr* 1937, 113-136.

———: Article "Grüningen" in *Mennonitisches Lexikon* II (1937). 193-195.

———: *Glaube und Lehre der Schweizerischen Wiedertäufer in der Reformationszeit.* In 101. *Neujahrsblatt zum Besten des Waisenhauses in Zürich für* 1938.

———: "Zwingli als Sozialpolitiker," *Zwingliana* V (1931) pp. 276-296.

Näf, Werner: *Vadian und seine Stadt St. Gallen* 1. *Band: Bis 1518. Humanist in Wien.* St. Gallen, 1944.

Neff, Christian: "Konrad Grebel, der Täuferführer zu Zürich." In *Mennonitische Jugendwarte* III (October, 1922, pp. 8-24; January, 1923, pp. 56-68).

———: "Conrad Grebel, Sein Leben und Wirken." In *Gedenkschrift zum 400-jährigen Jubiläum der Mennoniten oder Taufgesinnten.* Ludwigshafen 1925, pp. 65-133.

———: "Konrad Grebel." In *Mennonitisches Lexikon,* Bd. II, pp. 163-169. (The instalment containing this article appeared in 1928.)

Ninck, Johannes: *Artzt und Reformator Vadian.* St. Gallen, 1936.

Pfister, Rudolf: "Die Entwicklung Zwingliis zum Reformator." In *Zwingliana* VIII (1948) 521-535.

Plattard, Jean: *Guillaume Budé* (1468-1540) *et les Origines de l' Humanisme Francais.* Paris 1923.

Platter, Thomas und Felix: *Zwei Autobiographien.* Basel 1840.

Pomponius Mela: *Pomponii Melae Hispani libri de situ orbis tres.* ed. Joachimi Vadiani. Vienna 1518. Later editions Basel 1522, and Paris 1530.

Pressel, Joachim: *Vadian.* In *Leben und Ausgewählte Schriften der Väter und Begründer der reformierten Kirche.* Elberfeld 1860.

Rauschenbusch, Walter: "The Zurich Anabaptists and Thomas Münzer." In *The American Journal of Theology* IX, (1905, pp. 91-106.)

Rembert, Karl: *Die "Wiedertäufer" im Herzogtum Jülich,* Berlin 1899.

Renaudet, Augustin: Préreforme et Humanisme à Paris jusqu'à 1517. Paris 1916.

Rhegius, Urbanus: *Wider den Newen Taufforden. Nothwendige Warnung an alle Christgläubigen.* Augsburg 1527.

Rhenanus, Beatus: *Briefwechsel des Beatus Rhenanus,* Gesammelt und herausgegeben von Adalbert Horawitz und Karl Hartfelder, Leipzig 1886.

Schiff, Otto: "Thomas Müntzer als Prediger in Halle." In *Archiv für Reformationsgeschichte* XXIII, 1926, pp. 288ff.

Schurter, J.: *Die Grossmünster Schule in Zürich.* Zürich 1915.

Schweizer, Paul: *Geschichte der Schweizerischen Neutralität.* Frauenfeld 1893.

Sehling, Emil: *Die evangelischen Kirchenordnungen des XVI. Jahrhunderts. I.* Leipzig 1902.

Sicher, Fridolin: *Chronik.* Herausgegeben von Ernst Götzinger. *Mitteilungen zur vaterländischen Geschichte.* XX. St. Gallen 1885.

Simmler, J. J.: *Sammlung alter und neuer Urkunden zur Beleuchtung der Kirchengeschichte vornehmlich des Schweizerlandes* I. Zürich 1757.

Simon, Karl: "Die Züricher Täufer und der Hofgoldschmied Kardinal Albrechts." In *Zwingliana* VI, 1934, pp.50-54.

Staehlin, Ernst: *Briefe und Akten zum Leben Oekolams,* Bearbeitet von Ernst Staehelin, Leipzig 1927, 1934.

Staehelin, Rudolf: *Huldreich Zwingli* (2 vols.) Basel 1895-1897.

Staub, Max: *Die Beziehungen des Täufers Conrad Grebel zu seinem Schwager Vadian Auf Grund ihres Briefwechsels.* Zürich 1895.

Steitz, Georg E.: "Dr. Gerhard Westerburg." In *Archiv für Frankfurts Geschichte und Kunst.* N.F.V. Frankfurt a.M. 1872.

Strickler, Gustav: "Das Schloss Grüningen." In *Mitteilungen der Antiquarischen Gesellschaft in Zurich LXXVII Heft* 3. Zurich 1913.

————: *Geschichte der Herrschaft Grüningen.* Zurich 1908.

Strickler, Joh.: *Actensammlung zur Schweizerischen Reformationsgeschichte* (1521-1532) Zurich 1878.

Studer, Bernhard: *Geschichte der Physischen Geographie der Schweiz bis 1815.* Bern 1863.

Stumpf, Johann: *Chronica vom Leben und Wirken des Ulrich Zwingli. Quellen und Studien zur Geschichte der helvetischen Kirche.* I. Ed. Leo Weisz. Zweite Aufl. Zürich 1932.

Successio Anabaptistica, Coloniae, 1603. In *Bibliotheca Reformatoria Neerlandica,* VII. 's Gravenhage 1910, pp. 1-87.

Thommen, Rudolf: "Basel Studentenleben im 16. Jahrundert." In *Basler Jahrbuch* 1887.

Thürlemann, Ines: *Erasmus von Rotterdam und Joannes Ludovicus Vives als Pazifisten.* (Dissertation.) Freiburg (Schweiz 1932.)

Tilley, Arthur: *The Dawn of the French Renaissance.* Cambridge 1918.

de la Tour, Imbart: *Les Origines de la Reforme,* II. Paris 1909.

Ulrich, J. J.: *Miscellanea Tigurina.* I. Zurich 1721.

Usteri, J. M.: "Darstellung der Tauflehre Zwinglis. Mit besonderer Berücksichtigung der wiedertäuferischen Streitigkeiten." In *Theologische Studien und Kritiken.* Gotha 1882.

————: "Die Stellung der Strassburger Reformatoren Capito und Butzer zur Tauffrage." In *Theologische Studien und Kritiken.* Gotha 1884.

Vadianische Briefsammlung der Stadtbibliothek St. Gallen, I-VII. Herausgegeben von Emil Arbenz und Hermann Wartmann. St. Gallen 1888-1913.

Vasella, Oskar: "Von den Anfängen der Bündnerischen Täuferbewegung." In *Zeitschrift für Schweizerische Geschichte* 19 (1939), pp. 165-184.

Vienot, John: "Y-a-t-il une Reforme francaise anterieure a Luther?" In *Bulletin de la Societe de L'Histoire du Protestantisme Francais.* 1915.

Vischer, Wilhelm: *Geschichte der Universität Basel von der Gründung* 1460 *bis zur Reformation.* Basel 1860.

Wackernagel, Rudolf: *Humanismus und Reformation in Basel.* Basel 1924.

Waldenburger, A.: "Die Schweizer Studenten in Paris als Pensionäre des Königs von Frankreich." In *Geschichte der Familie Ammann, von A. F. Ammann,* Zurich 1913.

Walser, Ernst: "Über das Wesen der französischen Renaissance." In *Gesammelte Studien zur Geistesgeschichte der Renaissance.* Basel 1932.

von Watt, Joachim: *Deutsche Historische Schriften.* Herausg. von Ernst Götzinger. St. Gall 1879.

Weber, P. X.: *Der Pilatus und seine Geschichte.* Luzern 1913.

Wernle, Paul: *Die Renaissance des Christentums im* 16. Jahrhundert. Tübingen 1904.

————: *Renaissance und Reformation.* Tübingen 1912.

Wipf, Jakob: *Reformationsgeschichte der Stadt und Landschaft Schaffhausen.* Zürich 1929.

————: *Sebastian Hofmeister, der Reformator Schaffhausens.* In *Beiträge zur vaterländischen Geschichte* 9. *Heft.* Schaffhausen 1918.

Wirz, Ludwig. *Helvetische Kirchengeschichte.* Zurich 1807 ff.

Wirz, Hans: "Zürcher Familienschicksale im Zeitalter Zwinglis." In *Zwingliana,* VI, Hefte 4 (1935), 5 (1936), 9 (1938), 10 (1938).

Wyss, Bernhard: *Chronik des Bernhard Wyss* 1519-1930. *Herausgegeben von Georg Finsler. Quellen zur schweizerischen Reformationsgeschichte I,* Basel 1901.

Yoder, Edward: "Nine Letters of Conrad Grebel. Edited with a translation and notes by Edward Yoder." In *MQR* II (1928) pp. 229-259.

Yoder, Edward: "Conrad Grebel as a Humanist," *MQR III* (1929), pp. 132-146.

Zimmermann, Joseph: "Sechs unbekannte Briefe Glareans." In *Freiburger Geschichtsblätter.* IX, 1902.

Zürcher Stadtbücher des XIV. und XV. Jahrhunderts, herausgegeben von Hans Nabholz, Bd. I. Leipzig 1906.

Zwingli Huldrych: *Huldrych Zwinglis Briefe* (1512-1526). Übersetzt von *Oskar Farner.* Zurich 1918-1920.

Zwingli, Ulrich: *Eine Auswahl aus seinen Schriften. ed. Finsler, Köhler, Rüegg.* Zürich 1918.

Zwingli, Huldreich: *Huldreich Zwinglis Sämtliche Werke, I-X. Corpus Reformatorum Band 88-98. ed. Emil Egli, Georg Finsler, Walther Köhler, Fritz Blanke, Leonhard von Muralt,* Berlin, later Leipzig, 1905 ff.

Zwingli, Huldreich: *Huldreich Zwinglis Werke. ed. Schuler und Schulthess.* Zürich 1828 ff.

NOTE ON JACOB STRAUSS AND "WUCHER"

To be read in connection with the discussion on Strauss and Grebel on pages 194-196.

[The picture of Strauss presented in the following note is drawn from two books by Herman Barge: *Jakob Strauss, Ein Kämpfer für das Evangelium In Tirol, Thüringen und Süddeutschland,* Leipzig, 1937 *(Schriften de Vereins für Reformationsgeschichte,* Jahrgang 54, Heft 2, (Nr. 162), 174 pp., and *Die gedruckten Schriften des evangelischen Predigers Jakob Strauss,* in *Archiv für Reformationsgeschichte* XXXII (1935), pp. 100-121, 248, 252. The struggle in Eisenach is treated in R. Jauering, *D. Jakob Strauss, Eisenachs erster evangelischer Geistlicher, und der Zinswucherstreit in Eisenach,* in *Mitt. des Eisenacher Geschichtsvereins,* 4. Heft (1928).]

In the summer of 1523 Conrad Grebel read with approval a booklet by Jacob Strauss, Lutheran preacher in Eisenach, which he characterized as "most evangelical" and as "painting wealth in its true colors." In his letter of September 5, 1524, he praised Strauss as one of the preachers of the true Gospel. (See above, Chapter VII, pp. 111, 120, and Chapter IX, p. 194 ff.) The warmth of Grebel's commendation for Strauss, both in 1523 and 1524, suggests that he must have been deeply interested in what Strauss had written, and possibly in what Strauss had done. This interest, however, was not in the latter's theology but in his social ethics, for this was the only weighty theme treated in the five small booklets known to have come from his pen (all in the years 1523 and 1524), and action in this area constituted also his chief claim to fame in public life. Strauss became widely known in the years 1523-24 as the champion of the common man against the oppression of the wealthy through his fight against the *"Wucher"* or interest which was widely considered to be usury. The South German Peasants, who drew up a constitution *(Bundesordnung)* at Memmingen in February, 1524, listed Strauss as third (next to Luther and Melanchthon) in the list of evangelical leaders in whom they had confidence, "Doctors who are distinguished as advocates of divine righteousness." In fact, Strauss' espousal of the underdog in the economic struggle led the conservatives to class him with the revolutionary leaders of the time such as Thomas Müntzer.

But Strauss was not a "radical" in any sense of violence at all. He was only a vigorous exponent and practitioner of ideas held by many evangelicals including Luther himself. In every sense of the term he was a good Lutheran preacher, of whom Luther had "the best opinion," as he writes in a letter of April 15, 1524, to Strauss. Born in Basel sometime between 1480 and 1483, he entered the ranks of the Catholic theologians with the degree of Doctor of Theology sometime after 1516, after having been a Dominican monk since 1500. He early accepted the evangelical faith. The record of his life is lost after 1527, but from 1521 until then he is known to have served as a Lutheran preacher in the following appointments: Hall in Tyrol, January, 1521 to May, 1522; Wertheim, September to November, 1522; Eisenach, January, 1523 to autumn, 1525; Schwäbisch-Hall, most of 1526; Baden-Baden, January to October, 1527. Throughout this time he was a devoted follower of Luther, never following any radical trend, nor associating with any Anabaptist or "spiritualist" groups. He came into public prominence through his conflict with the leaders of the city of Eisenach in 1523 about the matter of "Wucher," in the course of which he put one of the members of the council under the ban (the first exercise of the ban in the history of the German evangelical church), and finally moved the city council to adopt a decree limiting interest to five per cent. (Eisenach was, according to Barge, the first German city to limit interest.)

The evangelical leaders like Luther who retained some phases of Catholic opposition to the financial practices of the time and added to it a passion for social "righteousness" particularly in the early years of the Reformation, vigorously attacked the interest system, calling it usury *(Wucher)*. Luther did so in 1519 in his *Grosser Sermon vom Wucher,* in which he condemned the *Wucherer* as a hardened sinner fallen into gross and ungodly selfishness in contrast to the true Christian who seeks to obey the "love-command" of God. Zwingli took a similar attitude. Strauss and Luther agreed completely in their basic views on interest and related economic questions, according to Barge.

Strauss became active in the matter of interest in 1523 after his appointment as preacher at the St. George church in Eisenach. There he preached a sermon on *Wucher* containing fifty-one theses which was published in early 1523 as a six page booklet under the title *Haubtstück und Artickel Christlicher Leer wider den unchristlichen wucher,* which went through four editions in 1523, two at Erfurt, one at Strassburg, and one at Augsburg. This is the booklet which Grebel praised in his letter of July 13, 1523, to Vadian because it "painted wealth in its true colors." (Barge, *Jakob Strauss,* p. 65, Anm. 184, quotes this passage from Grebel's letter and identifies the book as *Widder den Simonieschen Tauff*. But this must be a confusion by Barge, for the latter tract does not treat of "wealth" at all but is an attack against the retention of certain traditional elements in the baptismal liturgy.) Since the fifty-one theses on "wealth" were merely stated and not proved, Strauss published a second and much larger booklet of forty-seven pages in June, 1524, designed to give the proof. It bears the title, *Das(s) wucher zu nemen und geben, unserm Christlichen glauben, und brüderlicher lieb (als zu ewiger verdamniss rey-*

chent) entgegen ist, unüberwintlich leer und geschrifft, and went through two editions at Erfurt and Strassburg in 1524.

Since Grebel endorsed so heartily the views of Strauss on "wealth," we can best learn Grebel's views by studying the theses of Strauss. The essence of these theses is as follows:

1. Deuteronomy 15 and Luke 6:35 are commandments of God which cannot be evaded. (Deut. 15:7, 8—If there be among you a poor man of one of the brethren within any of thy gates in thy land which the Lord thy God giveth thee, thou shalt not harden thine heart, nor shut thine hand from thy poor brother: but shalt open thine hand wide unto him, and shalt surely lend him sufficient for his need. Deut. 15:11—For the poor shall never cease out of the land: therefore I command thee, saying, Thou shalt open thine hand wide unto thy brother, to thy poor, and to thy needy, in thy land. Luke 6:35—But love ye your enemies, and do good, and lend, hoping for nothing again.)

2. One penny of interest above capital is sin, it is *Wucher.*

3. It would be better for every Christian to suffer hunger, thirst, martyrdom, death, and hell, than to deny Christ and His Word.

4. All taking of interest is a gross rejection of the cross and life of our Lord Christ. The simple man who was hitherto misled and did not understand the Gospel, and paid *Wucher,* and now has learned the truth, should not pay *Wucher* any more. If, however, it is taken from him by force he should not resist force with force.

5. We speak much of the Gospel, but are afraid to attack those main points which are in opposition to it.

6. Neither Dr. Eck (a leading Catholic theologian and enemy of Luther) nor all other scholars of the world will be able to cover up Deuteronomy 15 and Luke 6:35 with their glosses.

7. God has spoken once and He will not change.

A careful study of Strauss' writings gives convincing proof that he was not a revolutionary of the type of Müntzer, even though Grebel in his ignorance mentioned the two in the same breath, but a careful and deep theological thinker and a thorough Christian of high ethical conceptions. His preaching emphasized the ethical effect of the Gospel in life, especially the divine commandment of love from the point of view of mutual aid to others. From this central point of view he attacked *Wucher* as wretched selfishness *(liebeleere Selbstsucht),* and on this fundamental premise of love he attempted to build up an evangelical type of social ethic. He was not able to win the victory in his battle against *Wucher* or in his attempt to Christianize the economic and political order of his day any more than Luther did. Luther complained almost despairingly to the end of his life about the "mammonic attitude" *(mammonische Gesinnung)* of his fellow men. But whereas

Luther, and probably Strauss, surrendered in the battle against human "mammonic selfishness" and sought refuge in the forgiveness of God, thus compromising with the evil world, Grebel and his followers refused to surrender and compromise, insisting rather that the Christian must live the life of love according to the spirit and commands of Christ, even though this meant a complete break with contemporary society and the professing church. Grebel and the Anabaptists wanted to apply the principle of Christian love to actual everyday practice. They refused to deny Christ, and so received as their lot martyrdom and death. But their message and proposal for a Christian society was no more "radical" and revolutionary than was that of Jacob Strauss. Perhaps one should say that both were "radical" in the sense that they sought to get at the root of social and economic evil, and both were "revolutionary" in the sense that the principle they advocated would have brought substantial changes. "Interest" or *Wucher,* which may not seem so important to moderns, was merely the symbol of the evil economic system which Strauss and Grebel were attacking.

Strauss does not mention "tithes" in his writings, but most of those who became critical of the existing economic order in Reformation times also attacked this "evil." Those who sought justice for the poor, and desired to relieve the burdens of the oppressed, demanded that this form of "involuntary servitude" also be abolished. The church, they insisted, should be supported by the voluntary contributions of its members. Grebel joins *Zinsen* and *Zehnten* as one evil, meaning thereby the whole evil system of economic exploitation of the poor in his time, particularly in rural areas.

The wide gulf between the keen social conscience of a man like Grebel and many of the evangelical leaders of his time can well be illustrated by Melanchthon's attitude on *Wucher* as expressed to Strauss in April, 1524, on the occasion of a visit to Strauss in Eisenach at that time, in the course of which he entered into a discussion of *Wucher* and the general question of the application of the "law of Christ." Melanchthon insisted that it was not necessary to judge public affairs by the law of Christ, for the Gospel gives freedom to follow whatever laws are best adapted to maintain law and order. If only preachers would preach the "Gospel" in place of attempting to set up political principles, all would be well.

INDEX

THE AUTHOR

Harold S. Bender was born July 19, 1897, at Elkhart, Indiana. He held degrees from the following institutions: BS, Goshen College, Goshen, Indiana; BD, Garrett Biblical Institute; ThM, Princeton Theological Seminary; MA, Princeton University; and ThD, Heidelberg University.

He became dean of Goshen College in 1933 and from 1944 he served as dean of Goshen College Biblical Seminary until his death, September 21, 1962.

In the Mennonite Church he was active in many organizations and committees most notable as chairman of the Historical and Research Committee and the Peace Problems Committee. He was ordained to the ministry June 18, 1944. He became president of the Mennonite World Conference in 1952 and served until his death.

In 1927 he founded the scholarly quarterly, *The Mennonite Quarterly Review*, and served as its editor until his death. He served as editor of *The Mennonite Encyclopedia*, a four-volume monumental contribution to Christendom. In addition to numerous articles in various scholarly magazines he was also author of *Two Centuries of American Mennonite Literature*, *These Are My People*, *Mennonite Origins in Europe*, *Biblical Revelation and Inspiration* and *The Anabaptist Vision*.